Debating
Development
NGOs and the Future

Essays from
Development in Practice

Co-edited and introduced by
Deborah Eade and Ernst Ligteringen

A Development in Practice Reader

Series Editor: **Deborah Eade**

Published by Oxfam GB
(Oxfam in Great Britain)
for Oxfam International

First published by Oxfam GB in association with Oxfam International in 2001

© Oxfam GB 2001

ISBN 0 85598 444 9

A catalogue record for this publication is available from the British Library.

Available from Bournemouth English Book Centre, PO Box 1496, Parkstone, Dorset, BH12 3YD, UK; tel: +44 (0) 1202 712933; fax: +44 (0) 1202 712930; email: oxfam@bebc.co.uk

and from the following agents:
USA: Stylus Publishing LLC, PO Box 605, Herndon, VA 20172-0605, USA; tel: +1 (0)703 661 1581; fax: + 1(0)703 661 1547; email: styluspub@aol.com

Southern Africa: David Philip Publishers, PO Box 23408, Claremont 7735, South Africa; tel: +27 (0)21 674 4136; fax: +27 (0)21 674 3358; email: orders@dpp.co.za

For details of local agents and representatives in other countries, consult our website: http://www.oxfam.org.uk/publications.html, or contact Oxfam Publishing, 274 Banbury Road, Oxford OX2 7DZ, UK tel. +44 (0)1865 311311; fax +44 (0)1865 312600; email publish@oxfam.org.uk

Printed by Information Press, Eynsham

Oxfam GB is a registered charity, no. 202 918, and is a member of Oxfam International.

Debating Development is based on the tenth-anniversary double issue of *Development in Practice*, Volume 10: 3 & 4, issued in August 2000, published by Carfax Publishing, Taylor & Francis Ltd. The views expressed in this book are those of the individual contributors, and not necessarily those of the editors or publisher.

Contents

Development in Practice, Oxfam International, and Debating Development

Development in Practice is an editorially independent journal, supported by funding from affiliates of Oxfam International. It is published by Carfax/Taylor and Francis.

Oxfam International was founded in 1995 and officially registered in The Netherlands. It is a group of non-government organisations dedicated to fighting poverty and related injustice around the world. There are currently eleven affiliates: CAA/Oxfam in Australia, Intermón (Spain), Novib (Netherlands), Oxfam America, Oxfam in Belgium, Oxfam Canada, Oxfam GB, Oxfam Hong Kong, Oxfam Ireland, Oxfam New Zealand, and Oxfam Quebec.

Debating Development is one aspect of the collaboration facilitated by Oxfam International through *Development in Practice*. Co-edited by Ernst Ligteringen, Executive Director of Oxfam International, and Deborah Eade, Editor of *Development in Practice*, this book contains contributions from current or former staff or trustees of various member organisations.

While the views expressed in the articles in this book are those of the named authors, they are not necessarily those of Oxfam International, *Development in Practice*, or Oxfam GB. All three organisations are committed to publishing material that stimulates and contributes to debates about development and humanitarian action.

The Editor and Management Committee of *Development in Practice* acknowledge the support given to the journal by affiliates of Oxfam International, and by its publisher, Carfax Publishing, Taylor & Francis Ltd.

Contributors

Professor Haleh Afshar teaches politics and women's studies at the University of York (UK) and has written widely on subjects related to feminism, Islam, and development.

José Antonio Alonso is Professor of Applied Economics at the Universidad Complutense in Madrid.

Mary B. Anderson is President of The Collaborative for Development Action Inc. and is also Director of the Local Capacities for Peace Project, and Co-Director of the Reflecting on Peace in Practice Project. Her many published works include the introductory essay to the first in the series of *Development in Practice Readers, Development and Social Diversity* (1996) (also available in Spanish).

Ian Anderson works in international structured finance. He was Chair of Oxfam Hong Kong (1987-97) and continues to serve as Vice Chair. He was also a founding trustee board member of Oxfam International (OI), of which he is now Chair.

Sylvia Borren is Director of the Dutch NGO Novib, one of the member agencies of Oxfam International.

Cândido Grzybowski is a sociologist and is Director of IBASE, the Brazilian social and economic research NGO.

John Hailey is Director of the Management Research Centre at Oxford Brookes University, England. He was a founder of the International NGO Training and Research Centre (INTRAC), and has a particular interest in the strategic and management issues facing NGOs.

Judy Henderson was, until 1999, the Chair of Oxfam International and a member of the international board of Greenpeace. She is a Commissioner on the World Commission on Dams, the Chair of Australian Ethical Investment Limited, and a board member of the Environment Protection Authority of New South Wales (NSW) in Australia.

David Husselbee worked in the NGO sector from 1983 to 1998, most recently as Programme Director for SCF-UK in Pakistan and Afghanistan. He is currently Director for Social and Environmental Affairs at adidas-Salomon AG, where he heads a programme to improve working conditions in the supply chain and to involve international companies in the development issues relevant to countries where they buy products.

Jaime Joseph is a member of Centro Alternativa, an action-research NGO that works in Metropolitan Lima; he is Co-ordinator of the School for Leaders and Research.

Allan Kaplan is Director of the Community Development Resource Association (CDRA), which seeks to build the capacity of organisations engaged in development and social transformation. His books include *The Development Practitioners' Handbook* (Pluto Press, 1996) and *The Development of Capacity* (UN NGLS, 1999).

Dot Keet is a Senior Researcher at the Centre for Southern African Studies in the School of Government, University of the Western Cape, a member of the Alternative Information and Development Centre in Cape Town, and an activist in Jubilee 2000 (SA).

Gerd Leipold advises NGOs on campaigning and organisational development. He has been a consultant to ActionAid, Consumers' International, Greenpeace, the International Committee of the Red Cross (ICRC), Oxfam, and others. He was previously director of Greenpeace Germany and director of the disarmament campaign of Greenpeace International.

Brian Murphy has since 1979 worked for Inter Pares, an independent Canadian international organisation for social justice, both in the field and at its headquarters in Ottawa. His present duties focus on policy development and programme support for the work of Inter Pares in Asia, Africa, Latin America, and Canada.

Paul Nelson is Assistant Professor in the Graduate School of Public and International Affairs, University of Pittsburgh. Before assuming this post, he worked for 15 years as policy analyst for several US-based NGOs.

Vijay Padaki has been a management researcher, trainer, and consultant in various institutional settings for more than 30 years. His specialised interests are in organisation and institutional development, and in partnership management.

Abikök C. Riak is a programme officer with the World Vision Sudan Programme. Before receiving her MA in international development planning, she worked as a researcher with the Institute for Food and Development Policy (Food First) in San Francisco.

Chris Roche has been with Oxfam GB since 1994 and is currently Head of Programme Policy in the International Division. He previously worked for ten years for ACORD, an international NGO consortium.

Hugo Slim is Senior Lecturer in International Humanitarianism at Oxford Brookes University, a Trustee of Oxfam GB, and an International Adviser to the British Red Cross. He previously worked for the British NGO, Save the Children (SCF).

Andy Storey is a lecturer at the Development Studies Centre, Kimmage Manor, Dublin, Ireland. He previously worked as an NGO researcher and campaigner, and as a development worker in Rwanda.

Josefina Stubbs worked for Oxfam GB in various capacities for more than ten years, most recently as head of its programme in Central America, Mexico, and the Caribbean, based in the Dominican Republic. She holds degrees from the University of Santo Domingo and from ISS in The Netherlands.

Rajesh Tandon is Executive Director of the Society for Participatory Research in Asia (PRIA) and Chairperson of the International Forum on Capacity Building. He is a leading thinker and writer on issues concerning NGOs and civil society.

Stan Thekaekara is Director of ACCORD, an NGO that works with tribal communities in south India.

Alison Van Rooy is Senior Researcher at the North–South Institute, where she works on issues of civil society, democratisation, and good governance, particularly in relation to Canada, the USA, Cuba, Malaysia, and Japan. A former Rhodes Scholar and Research Fellow at the Canadian Department of Foreign Affairs, she holds degrees from the universities of Trent, Dublin, and Oxford.

Alan Whaites is Director for Policy and Advocacy at World Vision International; he previously worked at World Vision UK.

NGOs and the future: taking stock, shaping debates, changing practice

Deborah Eade and Ernst Ligteringen

We are all products of our times. Today's world is marked by rapid and significant changes that affect us all as individuals and as societies, as working, thinking, and living beings who must continue to share our planet and its finite resources. Economic growth, which brought unprecedented levels of well-being and prosperity to many millions of people in the latter part of the twentieth century, has nevertheless left – and continues to leave – many thousands of millions of fellow human beings living in poverty, hunger, fear, and oppression. The faith that such growth would somehow trickle down to the poor and dispossessed and lift them out of their misery has proved tragically unfounded. The hope that ordinary people could, by invoking their right to a share in the full benefits of development, shake off the legacies of inequality and injustice has been a vital source of inspiration to the NGO movement worldwide. Victories have been won, oppressive régimes have been overcome, the universality of human rights is a concept that is gaining ground as never before. Yet, as the gulf between rich and poor widens year by year, it becomes harder to maintain the optimism of earlier times. Development has not delivered its promise. Perhaps it never could have done. But the very pace and scale of the changes before us now make it essential to re-orient our missions as international development NGOs.[1] The turn of the century is as good a moment as any to take stock. The turn of the millennium is an even better one.

This Reader, the tenth title in the series, is in turn based on the tenth-anniversary issue (Volume 10:3&4) of the journal, *Development in Practice*. In collaboration with Oxfam International, a number of development practitioners and commentators from many different backgrounds were invited to contribute their individual perspectives on core issues concerning the relevance and effectiveness of international development NGOs. In a modest way, this collection is an expression of our belief that NGOs *can* and indeed *must* become learning organisations, and that the best place to start is by standing back from the daily bustle and reflecting on some of the larger questions behind our very *raison d'être* in a changing international context.

In bringing together these contributions, we did not seek to impose our own opinions or simply to reflect the views of our respective institutions. Nor was it our intention to encourage self-absorbed debates on what constitutes a development NGO, or to suggest that the issues facing Northern (international) NGOs are essentially different in kind from those faced by NGOs in the South – and much less to present Northern and Southern NGOs as homogeneous blocs. Our guiding principle was that of inviting open discussion on the following questions: what forms do social and economic injustice take in today's world? What forms will they take in the future? And how relevant are today's development NGOs to the task of tackling the root causes of injustice? To put it another way: if NGOs exist not merely to administer charity, but also to shape the ways in which the international community understands and responds to poverty and injustice, how do they (we) need to change their (our) own ways of working?

On the relevance of NGOs

Opening this *Reader,* **Alison Van Rooy** (North–South Institute, Canada) demonstrates that, as products of the latter half of the twentieth century, most contemporary development NGOs are deeply rooted in the international aid industry, as development has evolved into what she terms as 'an occupational category'. The NGO movement has achieved an enormous amount, and the increasing capacity of Southern NGOs should also be celebrated as a success. But times are changing, and international NGOs (INGOs) in particular should question whether they are still relevant in this new reality. Van Rooy concludes that many of the ways of working that have been institutionalised by INGOs are now obsolete, and that new capacities and organisational forms – North and South – are urgently needed.

The transition from the international relations of the Cold War period to today's processes of increasing globalisation and economic integration demands different *skills* and different *roles* from NGOs, especially those working in the international arena. An ability to analyse and interpret these changes is essential. Offering two Latin American perspectives, both **Jaime Joseph** (Centro Alternativa, Peru) and **Cândido Grzybowski** (IBASE, Brazil) relate the importance of these faculties to the phenomenon of neo-liberal globalisation; and they point to risks and opportunities for civil-society organisations in general, and for NGOs in particular. Being seduced into a palliative role by wealthy international powers and the institutions that they largely control, basically in order to advance their globalisation agenda, is suggested as a serious risk for NGOs, while the main opportunity lies in the chance to shape the evolving globalisation process so that it makes a contribution to a more equitable global order. **Andy Storey** (Development Studies Centre, Ireland) highlights a specific form of this risk as the international financial institutions adopt the language of NGOs – *participation, empowerment, equity* – to serve as a rhetorical cloak for their own neo-liberal agendas.

Advancing an alternative development paradigm in the interests of the global majority has been the distinctive mission of development NGOs. **Rajesh Tandon** (PRIA, India) asks whether NGOs can offer (or have the necessary skills and are in a position to argue for) a credible alternative to the international rise of the neo-liberal doctrine, which is often equated with globalisation. Historically, NGOs have been stronger on critique and protest than on developing constructive and viable proposals that can genuinely transcend the local level. Critical to their *political* as well as their institutional sustainability is the need for NGOs to anchor themselves firmly in their own societies; for, unless they do so, their legitimacy as the champions of those who are marginalised from the decisions that affect their lives is seriously called into question.

On the mission of NGOs

If globalisation is the process of worldwide movements of goods, money, services, communications, technology, and, to a lesser extent, people, it surely presents profound risks as well as opportunities. The core question when considering the relevance of INGOs therefore concerns their understanding of the impact of all aspects of globalisation on people living in poverty, and their capacity to counter the threats to people's livelihoods and security, and to advance the opportunities to build societies based on equity and justice. Accepting a narrow monetarist perspective of globalisation – often referred to as 'globalisation from above' – will not allow NGOs to pursue their distinctive mission, and it might ultimately alienate them from their roots and purpose. The opportunities must lie in developing a broader understanding of global realities, but one that is critically grounded in what these realities mean for the global majority, and one that is committed to working for a global system which is based on equal rights for all – what some activists refer to as 'globalisation from below'.

Focusing on the mission of INGOs in the globalisation era, **José Antonio Alonso** (Universidad Complutense de Madrid, Spain) concentrates on the need for the greater management of international public assets and effective global governance. While economic activity is globalising rapidly, political structures and even the intellectual underpinning of government for the common international good are lagging behind. Transnational corporations (TNCs) have long developed the expertise and power to exploit the advantages of globalisation, and to work for the dismantling of national and international legal barriers to private enterprise. At the national level, democracy does well where there is a balance between the interests of business, government, and civil society. At the global level at which economic, political, and social development takes place today, that balance has yet to develop.

Jaime Joseph argues that it is time to face up to the link between democracy and development, and this is as relevant at the local and national levels as it is in terms of global processes. This makes it imperative for NGOs to bring their grassroots development work into line with their analytical and lobbying capacity. Too often, there is a split between the kind of service-delivery work that NGOs do or support on the ground and the more critical political perspective that once motivated them. Healing the rift between the two could revitalise the NGO sector. **Hugo Slim** (Oxford Brookes University, UK) reminds us of the value of the international human-rights framework for NGOs' purpose, and implies that a comprehensive defence of all human rights – civil, political, economic, social, and cultural – as underpinning both their development and their humanitarian relief work would serve NGOs better than to continue engaging in mistaken ideological debates about the comparative importance of one set of rights over another.

Haleh Afshar (University of York, UK), discussing the position of Islamist women, makes a plea in this respect for NGOs to work from a better understanding of the different priorities emerging from diverse cultures and realities, and not to act solely within the narrow economic interpretation of what globalisation means. The changing paradigm calls for new forms of international solidarity, says **Brian Murphy** (Inter-Pares, Canada), and is also giving rise to new forms of local struggle and identity. NGOs have too readily succumbed to the notion that globalisation in its present form is inevitable and irreversible, and so have confined their role to alleviating its most deleterious effects. At the same time, NGOs risk trading their core values for forms of technical professionalism that are disconnected from their ethical mission. To be part of a movement that seeks to transform the world, and to build social justice, NGOs need to rediscover the values of citizen participation and develop genuine respect for diversity.

On the roles and relations of NGOs

The central issue is the relevance of INGOs' methods of interaction with people (the marginalised majority) whose interests they ultimately seek to serve, and with civil-society organisations, government, and business.

Vijay Padaki (a management consultant in India) and **Abikök Riak** (World Vision-Sudan) underline the importance of NGOs as value-driven entities, and their need to act in harmony with their organisational values, and to find ways of working as well as institutional forms which are appropriate to them. **John Hailey** (Oxford Brookes University, UK) stresses that this value base is the principal distinctive characteristic of NGOs, as compared with other institutions in international (aid) relations.

However, in applying these values to their actions, **Mary B Anderson** (Collaborative for Development Action, Inc., USA) argues that INGOs need to acknowledge the inequalities in the aid relationship and relate this to their responsibility to determine their proper roles in any given context, roles that must be based on mutual respect between the various parties involved. The word 'partnership' has today become devalued through uncritical over-use, often to mask paternalistic practices on the part of NGOs. **Sylvia Borren** (Novib, The Netherlands) proposes that in order to carry out an empowerment mission, INGOs must be far clearer about their different roles, their wider impact, and their own operational standards. From the Dominican Republic, **Josefina Stubbs** (formerly Oxfam GB) reviews the overall impact of INGOs on Caribbean women's organisations and on local NGOs' work on gender, and stresses the positive as well as the negative effects of the real influence that development funding has on local civil society.

Ever since the debates of the early 1990s on 'scaling up', or the role of what David Korten called 'fourth generation' NGOs, advocacy has been viewed as the NGOs' distinctive role in a changing world, and in changing the world. However, as thinking on the role(s) of civil society is still developing, **Alan Whaites** (World Vision International) and **Dot Keet** (University of the Western Cape, South Africa) emphasise the importance of asking questions about INGOs' legitimacy and accountability as advocates of pro-poor policy change. INGOs should take up the gauntlet, argue both **Ian Anderson** (Oxfam International, Hong Kong) and **Paul Nelson** (University of Pittsburgh, USA), and go out and demonstrate the effectiveness of their advocacy work in furthering their wider mission. This in turn implies the need to develop more sensitive methods to monitor and evaluate their efforts. With reference to three quite different 'successful' public campaigns, **Gerd Leipold** (formerly Greenpeace International, UK) reflects on the growing potential, as well as the real limitations, of NGOs' capacity to exercise influence through such means.

Business is an increasingly powerful sector in the globalising world. A comparison of direct foreign investment with international aid flows underscores its importance in driving global change. NGOs are starting to take note of this reality and direct their advocacy increasingly to the corporate as well as the government sector. However, the corporate sector – like the global government sector – should not be seen as homogeneous, argues **David Husselbee** (adidas-Salomon AG, Germany), as some corporations are now demonstrating an increasing awareness of social, environmental, and human-rights issues. **Judy Henderson** (Australian Ethical Investment Ltd., Australia) suggests that NGOs need to find ways to interact effectively with business in order to harness its potential to contribute to development, both through advocacy strategies and by collaborating with the private sector as appropriate.

On the effectiveness of NGOs

In the end, it all comes down to an assessment of how effective INGOs are in the context of advancing globalisation, and what they might need to learn how to do (or, indeed, habits that they need to 'un-learn') in order to optimise their impact.

Allan Kaplan (CDRA, South Africa) argues that a shift is needed in capacity-building activities from a focus simply on tangible results to an appreciation of what is often intangible; and from a static appraisal to a dynamic, developmental reading of any changes that take place as a result of NGO action. **Chris Roche** (Oxfam GB, UK) warns of the limitations of the linear cause-and-effect type of analysis that is fostered by a traditional focus on projects, and the associated tendency of INGOs to see their Southern 'partner' organisations in exclusive, project-bound terms. He proposes that impact assessment should be seen as part of the very process of change, and so must take into account a far wider range of factors than has conventionally been the case. **Stan Thekaekara** (ACCORD, India) stresses that the contemporary obsession with quick returns on project funding is inappropriate as a way of understanding impact, and that this can be appreciated only over time and from a range of perspectives.

Pulling the threads together

Though focusing on different issues, and approaching them from such a breadth of experience, the contributors to this book do nevertheless coincide in a number of ways. All of them agree that the rapid and far-reaching processes of change that are taking place today leave no room for complacency among development NGOs. Ethical values are absolutely critical in shaping and guiding NGO action, and to mortgage these for short-term gain will condemn NGOs at best to irrelevance, at worst to becoming self-serving dinosaurs. However, values do not in themselves substitute for a high quality of analysis, or for the sensitivity with which NGOs must 'read' the world around them from the perspective of those whom they seek to serve. There is a real challenge to INGOs to ensure that they do not confuse 'being on the side of the poor' with partial or myopic vision, for this will not in the long term be of any real help in bringing about change. On the other hand, INGOs have a particular duty to avoid projecting their own institutional or sectoral interests as though these necessarily represent the interests of people living in poverty, and to beware of being lured into acting as stooges for powerful international interests, be these financial, governmental, or commercial. It is vital to be vigilant and receptive to new ideas, but without slavishly following the crowd, or throwing treasured beliefs away simply in order to appear modern and forward-looking. Analysis is no good without commitment, but commitment alone is not enough to ensure that NGOs act with both integrity and intelligence in an increasingly complex environment.

Our contributors also insist on the need to balance a belief in the universality of rights with respect for diversity and difference. For INGOs especially, this means learning how best to dovetail their own values and ways of working with the often quite different perspectives of their 'partner' organisations, to say nothing of the ultimate (intended) beneficiaries of any action they take. What is needed is honest dialogue, based on mutual respect, and this cannot be taken for granted, or rushed. Even as the wheels of globalisation seem to be turning ever more rapidly, so NGOs need to (re-)learn the virtues of patience and gentle responsiveness, and not seek to rush people and processes faster than they are ready to go.

Finally, this collection is testimony to the belief – passionately expressed by NGO representatives from Latin America and Asia, academics from Europe and North America, and activists from Africa and Australia alike – that globalisation 'from above' is not the only way in which the world can be organised. Equally, it is an affirmation of the knowledge that change is possible, but that it will be brought about only by inspiring a global movement to work for the common good of humanity – that is, *globalisation for all.* Will the twenty-first century see NGOs still living complacently in the past, or will they genuinely rise to the challenges ahead?.

Note

1 As staff members of international NGOs, we have focused our discussion on their roles and responsibilities, and their enormous potential to encourage alliances across national and cultural borders. Many of the points made here would apply equally to NGOs working to change their own societies for the benefit of those who suffer material hardship or are excluded from full participation in other, less tangible, ways.

Good news! You may be out of a job: reflections on the past and future 50 years for Northern NGOs

Alison Van Rooy

Introduction

Let me begin by telling you what you already know: NGOs are a *very* popular topic of research these days. There are now dozens of courses on development NGOs offered in universities and training centres, compared with none a decade ago.[1] There are thousands of articles and hundreds of books on NGO work currently available, an increase from a couple of dozen in the early 1980s. There are now officials designated as NGO or Civil Society Liaison workers in almost all the bilateral aid agencies and most of the multilateral ones. And, despite incredibly poor methods of counting, the population of Northern agencies devoted to international development and solidarity work (let alone community organisations in developing countries) has grown in leaps and bounds: from negligible numbers before 1966, it rose to almost 40,000 in 1996.[2] There is even a big 'backlash' literature, offering critiques of the phenomenon – truly a sign of having arrived (see Sogge et al. 1996). In short, non-government development programmes, projects, management styles, and ideologies have been part of a spectacular growth industry.

All of this you know, of course. What we don't know is what will happen next. This article traces the likelihood of one option: that Northern development NGOs have worked themselves out of a job (or, rather, out of most of the jobs they are now doing). Having done a good job so far, most are no longer suited to the world in which we now live. In the turmoil of today's new politics, this obsolescence might actually be a *good* thing for the future of social justice on our planet. In the pages that follow, I try to explain why, and what I think ought to come next.

War, compassion, religion, and zeal: an opening in history

First, however, it may be useful to skim over (in an admittedly irresponsible fashion) some of the vast history of mobilisation in Northern countries over issues and peoples in the South.[3] Canada is probably a typical example.

How missionary zeal first created Northern NGOs

Many of Canada's first voluntary organisations were offshoots of nineteenth-century missions overseas; connected by an institutionalised church, members of Canadian congregations were made aware of poverty elsewhere in the world. From a country itself dominated by immigrants, Canada's missionaries were sent—and continue to be sent—to developing countries (in particular, to China, India, and Commonwealth Africa). These missions represented often the first and sometimes the only contact by and with Canadians. Indeed, one of the oldest overseas assistance agencies is from Canada; *Les soeurs de la congrégation de Nôtre Dame*, founded in Quebec in 1653, is still undertaking literacy work in Latin America (Smillie 1995:37).

Today, many of Canada's highly organised and institutionally 'mature' NGOs remain church-affiliated: the Mennonite Central Committee (MCC), Lutheran World Relief (LWR), World Vision Canada, and the Canadian Catholic Organisation for Development and Peace (CCODP) are prominent examples. While most NGOs are now secular, church-based organisations maintain a stronger financial footing through congregational support, and many have become politically prominent— perhaps demonstrating a relationship of cause and effect. While the churches have suffered from historical accusations of 'rice-bowl Christianity' (selling food for conversion), that perception is increasingly unfounded in the mainline church community. The Ecumenical Council for Economic Justice has been a big player in the debate about debt-forgiveness, for example; and the churches were leading elements in solidarity work in Central America in the 1980s.

Although faith-inspired solidarity work has largely replaced missionary zeal, secular organisations have long overtaken the churches in dollars and numbers. While organisations like the Red Cross became active in Canada early in the century, it was not until the post-war period that secular NGOs surged ahead of their church-based counterparts. Why?

Why World War II gave birth to 'development' as an occupational category

The overwhelming moral shock of the two world wars opened up the world to Canadians and others in (what was to become) 'the North'. It is important to underline this point: a Western consciousness about *international* responsibility was born of the wars and, with it, international institutions like the League of Nations, the UN, the Bretton Woods system, and the now more than *4000* inter-governmental bodies created for cross-border action. Foreign aid was clearly one of these new institutions. In 1950, following the success of the Marshall Plan for Europe, the infamous Colombo Plan for the developing world was put into motion.

The Colombo Plan to Assist South and Southeast Asia involved Britain, Canada, and other Northern countries in a response to the region's poverty and the perceived threat of Chinese communism to Korea and Indochina. The Plan was to deliver technical assistance, food aid, and some economic assistance, on the assumption that the creation of a ten-year carry-over period was sufficient to get the region on its feet. Markets were to be built, industry established, and communism deterred; and all of this was to be accomplished as quickly as possible, just as the Marshall Plan had managed to do in Europe.

After ten years, however, disillusionment with the Colombo Plan set in. The UN declared its first (of many) development decades, and countries throughout the North began to expand their aid programmes in other ways. Development, once seen as a short-term quick fix of modest investment, became an established industry.

The activity of Canadian NGOs working overseas during this period was also expanding. In 1964, the precursor to CIDA (Canadian International Development Agency) helped to fund the highly successful voluntary agency, CUSO (Canadian University Services Overseas)—the new training ground for young Canadians interested in the developing world. Other NGOs were also established in response to the growing demands in developing countries, and many set up projects and sent volunteers overseas. The experience of the Suez crisis in 1956, the Cuban revolution, growing concern about apartheid in South Africa, US intervention in Southeast Asia, and the Biafran civil war all contributed to a rise of interest and social activism in Canada (Murphy 1991:170). As the first volunteers from CUSO and SUCO (its Québécois equivalent, *Service Universitaire Canadienne à l'Outremer*) returned in large numbers to Canada, that awareness took on a greater political force at home, and the beginnings of a formal aid lobby in Canada took shape.

With that formal aid lobby came an NGO business in Canada that now, 30 years on, numbers about 250 organisations and about 2000 people, spending at least US$312 million a year. (In 1997, US$137 million came from official development assistance (ODA) and US$175 million from individual donations.[4]) In the rest of the donor community, official agencies are less generous; Figure 1 shows that NGOs raise more than twice what they receive in ODA throughout the Northern donor community; but, as Figure 2 illustrates, with wildly fluctuating degrees of support.

Figure 1: Northern NGOs: patterns of spending and official funding (US$m, 1969 –97)

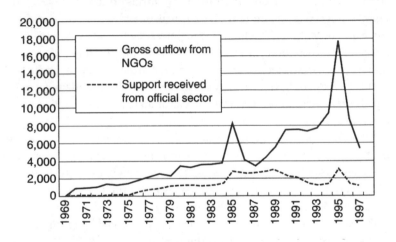

Source: OECD DAC, Development Co-operation, various years.

Many of the leaders of today's NGOs are returned volunteers from CUSO's first forays into West Africa in the 1960s and, now retiring, have spent the whole of their career in NGOs, often hopping among NGOs and in and out of CIDA. This community, and the institutions they have created, now forms an important (though very small) occupational category in Canada. I am one of its members.

The thawing Cold War: a turning point

It is a truism, hardly novel, that the end of the Cold War changed things for NGOs. Some of the changes were immediate and obvious: large

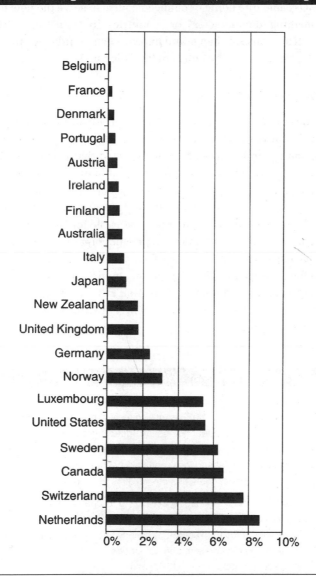

Figure 2: Percentage of ODA to NGOs: OECD DAC, 1993-1997 average

[Source: OECD DAC, Development Co-operation, latest year available.

Note: For a good discussion of the dilemmas of accounting, see Ian Smillie: 'A note on NGO funding statistics', annex 1 to 'Changing partners: Northern NGOs, Northern governments', in Ian Smillie and Henny Helmich (eds.) (1993) Non-governmental Organisations and Governments: Stakeholders for Development, Paris: OECD.]

Good news! You may be out of a job 23

amounts of cash were made available to East and Central Europe, and a host of NGOs came into being or changed course to serve the new needs of the 'emerging democracies' or 'countries in transition'.[5] Those phrases—full of a sense of change and improvement—indicated the same kind of enthusiasm felt at the outset of the Colombo Plan.

Democracy's enthusiasms

When the Berlin Wall came down, perhaps the greatest embarrassment for political pundits was the surprising and unforeseen speed of change in Eastern and Central Europe. No one expected that long Cold War to turn so quickly into hot transition (or, for that matter, such lukewarm social development subsequently). The impact on the aid industry, and on solidarity movements, was immediate. Money was made available through aid agencies (although most of it ineligible for ODA status), and a few Northern NGOs and many domestic organisations without international experience followed the flow of cash. New programmes in judicial reform, stock-market regulation, environmental protection, 'civil-society building', 'democratic transition', all came flooding into the region (see Box A for a typical example). But things had also been changing there.

Box A: The new kind of project

The Civil Society Development Foundation, established by the European Union's aid programme in Slovakia in 1993, is now one of the country's three most important grant-providing foundations. As an independent foundation, it has supported 387 projects in support of human rights and minorities, health, environment, education, social services, and volunteer development. In addition to providing grants, the Foundation's assistance aims to improve the following:

- awareness of the role and functioning of NGOs in an open civil society;
- the level of information-exchange among NGOs;
- the legal framework of the third sector, by helping to enhance the qualification of NGOs to influence policy-makers and authorities;
- networking and cooperation among NGOs; and
- the organisational capacities of NGOs, by strengthening their infrastructure as well as by extending their activities.

(Adapted from text found at
http://europa.eu.int/comm/enlargement/pas/phare/pt/civil.htm)

Certainly, the wars in the former Yugoslavia (along with continuing assistance to Albania) altered the foreign-aid picture, generating vast amounts of humanitarian and post-conflict reconstruction money: an average of some US$4 billion a year throughout the 1990s—a full 7 per cent of the world aid bill. In 1997, the States of the former Yugoslavia received more than any other country in the world other than China, India, and Egypt.

However, while many felt that there was a drain away from ODA-eligible countries to the hot new areas of East Central Europe, the truth is that over the 1990s there was a drop in the amounts to both, which has been overcome by dramatic rises in private investment (see Figure 3 for a comparison of flows to developing countries (total) and flows to the countries of the Former Soviet Union and Central and Eastern Europe). All over the world, declining conventional aid is being swamped by private flows—but not, evidently, to the same countries and for the same purposes.

Figure 3: Comparative flows East and South, US$ millions

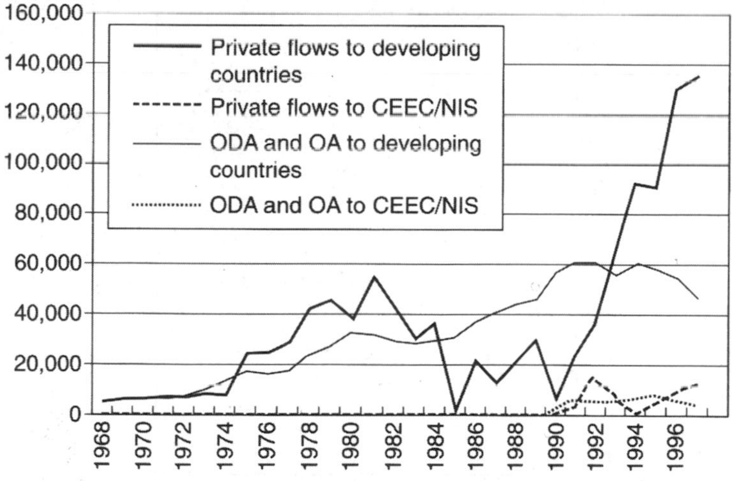

CEEC = Countries of Central and Eastern Europe

NIS = Newly Independent States (ex - USSR)

OA = official assistance; ODA = official development assistance

(Source: OECD, DAC, 1992)

Third-wave democracies and their critics

While Western imaginations were preoccupied with Europe in the early 1990s, they forgot what had been big news in the 1980s: the so-called 'third wave' of democratic change in the developing world (Huntington 1993). The argument there was that Africa and the Americas were celebrating a resurgence—or, sometimes, the novelty—of more-or-less democratic rule by more-or-less popularly elected rulers.

Certainly, 'democratisation' funding began to swell—in 1998, to US$858 million, or 1.5 per cent of ODA (see Figure 4). Big supporters, not surprisingly, were the USA, Canada, Germany, and the Nordic countries, which created new units for democratic development and, from 1989, for 'good governance'. That enthusiasm, of course, led to funding for those NGOs that were involved with voter education, specialist training (parliamentary reform, party formation), or—at the macro level—human-rights advocacy.

Figure 4: DAC funding to democratic development, US$ millions

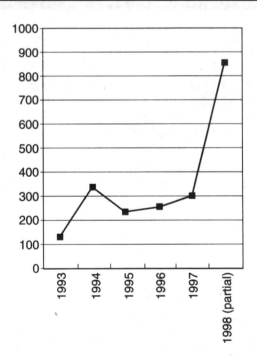

(Source: OECD DAC 1992)

The emphasis on governance and democracy left many of the traditional NGOs out of the loop, but brought in domestic organisations—the bar associations, the auditing umbrella groups, the parliamentary research centres – which had not had an international presence in earlier years, as well as the labour unions, which had long been present. Below, I offer an explanation of why in my view this shift is actually to be welcomed.

The civil-society bandwagon

Another change to affect the NGO star was the rise of enthusiasm for 'civil society'. How did all this transformation—in Europe, Africa, and the Americas—come about, after all? The explanation most commonly offered was the desire to establish civil society (particularly on the part of East and Central Europeans), arising from the shackles of central control (economic and social) and authoritarian régimes. Indeed, while civil society itself may not have emerged in 1989, that date certainly marks the re-emergence of this term into Northern consciousness, where it now dominates liberal political thinking.

The term has an interesting ancestry in political philosophy (Cicero, Locke, Hume, Paine, Hegel, and Gramsci all wrote about it), but it is in everyday politics that the idea of 'civil society' has attracted money, organisations, and programmes to push it along (Van Rooy 1998). The enthusiasm for the term (despite or because of its numerous definitions) arises in part from a populist culture, and an urge to modify the alternate evils of capitalist and communist systems. For East and Central Europeans, at least, the appeal of 'civil society' lay in the possibility of a different moral, social, and political future which would rival the emancipatory vision of socialism, yet also embrace 'this democracy thing'.

The impact on Northern NGOs has been remarkable. For one thing, their role becomes—almost automatically—central to the task of society building, not that of mere helpmates. They become part of the 'third sector', the tidy counterbalance now said to mediate between State and market excesses. Far from being underdogs in the world of runaway capitalists and irresponsible governments, the whole NGO world is brought to the table under the heading 'civil society'. Jessica Mathews of the US Council for Foreign Relations even makes the assessment that, 'increasingly, NGOs are able to push around even the largest governments' (Mathews 1997:53). This rhetorical shift is enormous, even if the reality is not nearly so dramatic.[6] It means that Northern NGOs have new roads open to them, and potential, if not yet real, responsibilities above and beyond project work. I describe some of these new paths at the end of this paper.

Social capital! Social capital!

The shift of attention to NGOs and civil society has been given added weight with the newfound enthusiasm for 'social capital'. The notion, promoted (but not invented) by Putnam et al. (1993), has the important attribute of sounding like economics—a factor in social and economic production. As financial and physical capital was joined by human capital in the 1980s (thereby raising the etymological value of 'soft' stuff like labour standards and education), the idea of social capital has changed the way in which the big players are thinking about NGOs and development.

At its core, social capital is meant to describe the outcomes of trust, the necessary social binding agent. Putnam and his team set out to explain why northern Italy was so prosperous, while southern Italy has been so bedraggled. Their answer was that northern Italians have learned to live together, trust one another, and build up relationships through non-market activities (singing in choirs, playing *bocce*) that *also* strengthen market transactions (you are less likely to sue the tenor in your choir than you are to sue a stranger). This social glue, called social capital, is also described as the strength of family responsibilities, community volunteerism, selflessness, and public or civic spirit.

What does one do to build up social capital, if it is so important for development? A major response has been to invest in Northern NGOs and, more often, directly in Southern organisations working in their own communities or the realms of national policy-making. (Indeed, there is a well-funded World Bank project to study social capital and its implications for Bank planning.[7]) Social capital has meant that the importance of community organisations has been notched up the policy ladder: more than inexpensive service providers, more even than political watchdogs, civil-society organisations (CSOs) are seen to be at the core of society's workings. What a novel thought.

The global NGO jamboree

A further factor in the rise of Northern NGOs has been their dramatic prominence in the UN world-conference circuit in the last decade. These jamborees have not only created new NGO networks and skills, but, more importantly, they have generated a new standard of global governance. Now more than ever, it matters what governments say in international declarations, for there are significant crowds holding them to account at home.[8] The November 1999 demonstrations outside the World Trade Organisation (WTO) meetings in Seattle saw more than 700 organisations and between 40,000 and 60,000 people take part: the biggest rattling of swords in recent history. Certainly, the plethora of events in the preceding 20 years also counted: the Stockholm Environment Conference of 1972 and the first Women's Conference in Mexico in 1975 were catalytic. But, by the time of the 1992 Earth Summit in Rio, the snowball was gathering lots of NGOs, and *new* NGOs, in its roll down the mountain.

Indeed, while the conferences carved out a permanent role for NGOs in UN governance (Foster and Anand 1999), they had the unintended but foreseen impact of exhausting many small, cash-strapped, and overwhelmed organisations. Conference fatigue took its toll; and while the roll-calls grew, many individual organisations dropped out of the circuit. However, the impact on their own identities and 'global consciousness' was important in pulling issues of trade, finance, and global governance into their own work. Again, using a Canadian case, the (domestic) Canadian Council for Social Development (CCSD) was at the time of writing cooperating with the network building up around the World Bank's Structural Adjustment Policy Research Initiative (SAPRI) to consider the implications of economic reform on social development, prior to the Copenhagen Plus Five follow-up meetings in June 2000. CCSD, involved in the 1995 World Summit for Social Development, has now stretched its policy frontiers further.

Solid, unapologetic, fundamental success

Given all this transformation, especially in the past decade, can we say anything meaningful about NGO success? Absolutely.

A vast proportion of the NGO literature that has emerged from academia in the past couple of decades has been concerned with effectiveness (see Najam 1998, among others). Are NGOs' endeavours more or less effective than those of donors, or of national governments? In some ways, of course, the effectiveness debate is an hypothetical exercise, for it is almost impossible to compare what *has* worked against what *might have* worked if there had been a comparable programme/ approach/organisation run by someone else. The methodological problem is that there are very few comparable areas; by and large, donor agencies and national governments work in different areas from NGOs (in the fields of meso or macro policy-making and spending, rather than agency-to-Southern-NGO-to-community support, where NGOs are more common).

Still, there are ways of measuring the effectiveness of given programmes or projects against their stated aims (did the health of the village improve?), or in comparison with programmes run by others (was CUSO's administration of relief supplies more time- or cost-effective than Oxfam's?), or against its own internal processes (did the project change to reflect adequately the changes in the community's perception of the causes of the problem?). Many of the studies of NGO effectiveness (reams of which are summarised in an important report sponsored by the Finnish government, Kruse et al. 1997) can say something about this kind of accounting, planning, and management effectiveness, but very little about effectiveness in the larger sense. Have the millions of micro efforts by Northerners, conducted in an often *ad hoc*, uncoordinated, under-financed, and sometimes amateurish and paternalistic way, made a significant difference to the sustainable improvement of the lives of people living in 'the South'?

I think so. Indeed, I think that there has been a *fantastic* level of success at this larger level. Let me explain a few of the reasons why.

Equity is on the agenda

I'm a big believer in the squeaky-wheel phenomenon: those who make noise – especially strategic, credible, well-supported, constituency-based noise – *can* shift the agenda. When I was researching environmental activism around the time of the Earth Summit in Rio (Van Rooy 1997), I was struck by the 'archeology' of issue change. Why do some topics and policy issues get attention, and others not? My unoriginal answer is that sustained debate, particularly over 'low' policy, low-cost, highly salient, and new policy areas, does makes a difference. The problem for most activists is that the timeframe for agenda change is much longer than the usual project or campaign, and so success is less immediate and tangible. (The campaign against child labour in the rug-making industry and lobbying in favour of the landmines treaty are remarkable exceptions; see Chapman 1999 and Chapman and Fisher 2000 for more examples.)

Today, concerns about the inequities of globalisation (and governance, and investment, and trade, as well as aid) *are* on the agenda. Equity concerns *do* matter (although, obviously, not enough). Witness:

- Corporate Social Responsibility is a demand of sufficient importance to Northern consumers that corporations throughout the world are changing their practices: Nike in Indonesia, Shell in Nigeria, and Placer Dome in the Philippines have had to do business differently (see also Elkington 1997).
- The World Bank, assailed by campaigns against some of its large infrastructure projects, has undertaken a *Voices of the Poor* exercise to ask questions about equity goals and impacts of Bank work.[9]
- The new round of the WTO, if resurrected after the NGO demonstrations in Seattle, is to deal with the inequitable barriers faced by developing countries in trading their goods with the North.
- Long-running demands by coalitions like Jubilee 2000 for attention to the debt of the poorest countries have finally been met with (imperfect but promising) action by the G8 nations.

I argue that a large part of the equity battle is won when the problem is set squarely on the policy table—the place where many mistakenly feel that the battle is begun. Getting the debate to go further is easier, of course, if there is broad consensus on the nature of the problem and its solution. In the case of the landmines treaty, which came into effect in 1999, there was evidence of a widespread agreement on both. As Canadian Minister of Foreign Affairs Lloyd Axworthy said:

> Perhaps the best example to date of this new diplomacy was the international campaign to ban landmines. Why? Because it showed the power behind a new kind of coalition. Like-minded governments and civil society formed a partnership of equals, united around a common set of core principles. (Department of Foreign Affairs 1998)

Where battles continue to rage is where that 'core set of principles' is lacking. For NGOs concerned about the impact of the over-liberalisation of markets, for example, the mountain is decidedly steeper. Yet even here, the issue is at least debated.[10]

Official aid is better

Practices and priorities for all foreign aid, including that from non-government sources, have improved (see Dollar 1999). ODA, though diminished in volume, is better administered, in the following respects.

- *Tied aid is down*: Over the past 20 years at least, we have seen a decline in the amount and type of aid that is tied to procurement in the donating country—a link that increases the cost of development interventions by a conventionally estimated 15 per cent. Figure 5 shows a long and welcome decline in those numbers.

- *Environmental impact is better assessed*: There are now standards throughout the bilateral and multilateral donor community to assess the potential impact of projects on the physical environment. While intention does not replace action (O'Brien et al. 2000), procedures are a necessary prerequisite (see, for example, OECD, DAC 1992).

- *Gendered analyses make a difference*: Similarly, in both official and non-government circles, there has been a serious, if imperfect, adoption of the notion that development—like all political projects—is gendered: that men and women, for a host of reasons, are affected differently and have differing access to the decision-making processes that shape their lives.[11]

Figure 5: Tied aid as a percentage of bilateral ODA commitments of DAC members

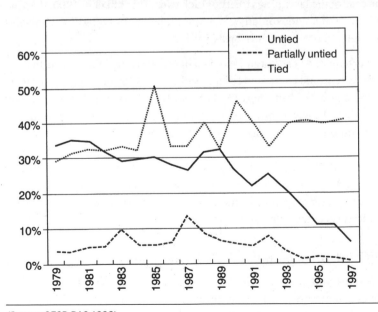

(Source: OECD DAC 1992)

- *Participation of NGOs and community organisations in official efforts is up*: An emphasis on participation has changed the practice of aid implementation (if not yet the design) of most of the bilateral and multilateral donors. The World Bank has a *Participation Sourcebook*; the Inter-American Development Bank (IDB) has a *Resource Book on Participation*, as does the UNDP in its *Empowering People: A Guide to Participation*. While the criticism remains that participatory approaches may be cursory rather than integral, again, the guidelines are an important prerequisite for change.

Many of these trends can be linked to the work of Northern and Southern NGOs in pushing for change.[12] That is a remarkable achievement.

More Southern organisations are at work

Even more Southern organisations are doing even better work at home, in small part through Northern solidarity activity. Of course, there is no way to estimate how many community-based organisations are working in the world; the vast majority are unregistered, local, and in no need of 'relationships' with Northern funding agencies. There are some estimates in particular countries, however, that give a sense of the enormous scale of current efforts (see Box B).

Box B: Some sample numbers

Brazil: Non-profit organisations work throughout the country; there are 45,000 in Sao Paulo alone, and 16,000 in Rio. They employ at least one million people, representing about two per cent of total employment.

Egypt: Non-profit organisations exist across the country; 17,500 are membership-based, 9,500 are charitable, and 3,200 work in development. Included are 22 professional groups, whose members number three million.

Thailand: There are some 11,000 registered non-profit organisations in the country and many more unregistered bodies.

India: At least two million associations are at work in India; Gandhi-inspired non-profit organisations alone employ 600,000 people.

Ghana: 800 formal non-profit organisations are registered, with international groups particularly prominent among them.

(Source: Anheier and Salamon 1998)

Indeed, there is a rise in the number and influence of international (both North and South) umbrella groups that are trying to take the agendas of Southern 'development' NGOs to the international table: CIVICUS is a prominent example. Set up only six years ago, this international body has worked to improve the regulatory, funding, and tax situation of CSOs worldwide, trying to pry open further public space for domestic and international debates. A great deal is going on; and Northerners can take some of the credit.

Humanitarian assistance is quick and effective

Finally, Northern NGOs should be congratulated for the creation of an international system of humanitarian assistance. We have witnessed *unambiguously* efficient and effective short-term international humanitarian assistance (albeit hampered by political indecision) by Northern NGOs, and through the Red Cross and Red Crescent movement, in support of local efforts. Particularly in instances of natural disaster, as opposed to man-made suffering, Northern NGOs (and NGOs from neighbouring countries and regions) have saved countless lives. In the case of Hurricane Mitch in Central America, for instance, at least 58 US NGOs (let alone those from other countries) sent doctors, supplies, money, medical equipment, and volunteers with spectacular speed, and in concert with a host of international organisations.[13] While there are justified criticisms of the political role of humanitarian assistance in prolonging conflict (particularly pertinent in the aftermath of the Rwandan genocide), they do not undermine the spectacular capacity that exists for fast and effective action.

However ...

These successes cannot be claimed without acknowledging certain caveats.

Passive Northern constituencies

Northern domestic audiences remain, in most countries, passive about global issues of social justice, although they are keen contributors to charity (Foy and Helmich 1996). The reasons? Well, in Canada at any rate, global awareness—let alone knowledge about 'the Third World'—is embarrassingly feeble. To be sure, there is a continuing level of public support for overseas aid in Canada. An October 1998 survey showed that some 75 per cent of Canadians support ODA (CIDA 1998), a figure that has been more or less consistent for most of CIDA's history. Yet as long-time aid-watcher Ian Smillie says, public support in Canada is 'a mile wide, but an inch deep'.[14] Writing for the OECD about CIDA's polling records, Smillie noted:

> When asked which they believed was most important for Canada to provide, after 1991 more Canadians chose aid for emergencies over support for long term development. The majority of Canadians were neutral in their opinions on aid. They did not think of aid very often, did not feel it had an impact on them, and did not consider themselves part of the global community. Of neutral Canadians, 40 per cent tended to support aid while 20 per cent tended to oppose it. (Smillie 1998:55)

Further, the proportion of Canadians who feel that the country spends too much on aid seems to be growing, and a majority feels that the demands of domestic fiscal health justify cutting aid-spending abroad.

The shallowness of this support raises alarm bells both within CIDA, concerned that its domestic constituency already favours high-visibility emergency work over longer-term development efforts, and among CSOs themselves, who share the same constituency. One outcome has been notable timidity on the part of many international CSOs. Fears that policy work or non-spectacular, non-televisable, long-term development work would dry up public support have limited their scope of work to 'safer' projects. John Foster, a former head of Oxfam Canada, argues that a number of organisations have engaged in self-censorship for fear that advocacy work may scare away conventional donors who want every charitable dollar to be spent on relieving poverty on the ground.[15]

To counter the shallowness of public support, there is a clear need to mount continuing efforts to increase understanding of global processes and peoples (including the subject of ODA, to be sure, but as a small part). This lack of public understanding (in Canada, anyway, due in part to a lack of global curricula in the schools) may ultimately be most damaging to CSOs' endeavours to bring about change.

Lack of linking

The experiences of *domestic* equity work—homelessness, child poverty, abuse of women—in the North are not changing what is being done internationally. Northern NGOs have, overall, very little to do with anti-poverty work in their own countries: witness the well-publicised disquiet when Oxfam GB or Community Aid Abroad (now Oxfam Australia) took up the issue of domestic work. Specialists in someone else's problems, and not their own, the value of their organisational 'learning' and their credibility begin to wane.

One of the outcomes has been growing interest in direct funding—both for Southern organisations, and for Northern non-NGOs (professional associations, unions)—part of a broad assessment by donors that Northern NGOs may not be adding much to the deal (Riddell and Bebbington 1995).[16] Indeed, in the language of many donors, Northern NGOs are merely 'executing agencies', contractors in the overall business of ODA. Sadly, many NGOs, increasingly cash-strapped in an era of declining ODA, have focused on their role as executing agencies above all else.

Project myopia

NGOs, particularly those heavily involved with donor funding, are organisationally designed to do *projects*. That focus is a historical accident, I think, but one that has become anachronistic: it shapes organisations to manage the manageable (an increasing challenge as levels of ODA fall), and so, inadvertently, to ignore the essential. Alan Fowler, a familiar observer of the NGO world, makes precisely this criticism:

> As a tool, projects are not appropriate for all but the most technical types of development initiative, such as building roads. Where altering human behaviour is concerned, the less appropriate projects become. Many limitations to NGDO effectiveness stem from this fact. Projects serve the bureaucracy of the aid system ... they are time-bound, pre-defined sets of objectives, assumptions, activities and resources which should lead to measurable, beneficial impacts. (Fowler 1997:17)

Development is more than projects, for sure; but what is the alternative? Sociology may have more to say on this topic than development: the study of social movements shows how women's rights and environmental awareness have risen to the fore of the collective conscience, largely without the benefit of projects, funders, and logical framework analyses.

The capitalist challenge

Another caveat concerns the new situation in which many Northern NGOs now find themselves. As currency speculation, foreign direct investment (FDI), corporate social responsibility, and economic ideology dominate the global debate, some NGOs in the North have followed the lead of more activist Southern organisations in engaging with these non-traditional development issues. Particularly as FDI and trade flows now double and triple ODA flows, even to the poorest countries, the challenge of monitoring mainstream economics is even more urgent.

This monitoring role involves engagement with individual companies (Monsanto, for example), with debate about currency regulations (such as the proposed Tobin tax), and FDI policies (the Multilateral Agreement on Trade, for example), and—an illustration of a still-vibrant ideological debate—the growth-based determinants of developmental success (one programme of Focus on the Global South is concentrated on such issues). However, here too the big contributors to the global capital debate are rarely the traditional development agencies (with notable exceptions, such as Oxfam GB). This is another area where non-NGOs such as unions and universities are taking the lead alongside NGO think-tanks (like the Third World Network).

Packing up shop

Why, then, do I think that most NGOs will (and probably should) end their operations? Indeed, most of this article has tried to convince you that NGOs *have* made a crucial difference to the way that international social justice is promoted. The argument, however, is that most NGOs have successfully worked themselves out of a job, both by their success at one level and by their organisational obsolescence at another. The world has changed, and we have not changed quickly enough with it. I see at least four symptoms of this coming of age.

Zeal without 'roots' has inescapable limits

- *Rootlessness — the first symptom*: In a fervour of zeal brought on by the real urgency of need (the conflict is beginning, the children are dying), much of the NGO community began life as public expressions of the Do Now, Think Later mentality. The development of NGO work has produced problems that zeal alone cannot resolve:

- *The inescapable partnership paradox*: North–South NGO relations *are* focused on funding, and so 'partnership' becomes a semantic option for Northerners, but a matter of survival for others (Hately and Malhotra 1997). Of course, there are exceptions (I think that Canada's Inter Pares takes partnership seriously, for example), and the dependency runs both ways: increasingly, Northerners are excluded from donor-funding loops if they do not 'partner' with Southern organisations. Still, the presence of financial support at the core of most North–South relationships makes for a different kind of politics.

- *The funding carrot/stick dilemma*: Much of the time and effort of Northern NGOs is focused on their own governmental or public donors (note: the dynamics governing these two sets of donors are not identical), and this cannot help but distort their own priorities.

- *The existential quest*: Awareness of these debates, but inability retroactively to grow roots, has meant a scrambling for new identity for many organisations. Most of this is only — but understandably — cosmetic.

International work demands a different kind of legitimacy

If the future holds promise for those who do more than projects, for those who engage at the international level or for domestic social justice, then many Northern NGOs are ill placed. Efforts to reform international institutions and norms, let alone those in someone else's country, bring with them a much higher burden of identity. Except for those organisations that can lay claim to a special knowledge or expertise (particularly in human rights or humanitarian assistance), questions are being asked about NGO legitimacy. 'Whom do these people represent?' is often asked of activists from Northern NGOs who are engaged internationally.

Establishment of legitimacy is a matter of far more than proving some simple level of numerical representation. I do think, however, that many Northern NGOs—long engaged in doing projects away from home, chasing development funds from those they seek to influence, and not particularly concerned with internal democracy, in any case—are poorly equipped to meet that challenge of legitimacy. As the stakes are raised at the international level—how trade is governed, how economic policies are set, how borders are protected—these NGOs may not be equal to the challenge.

Northern NGO leadership needs a revolution

Yet another factor of occupational obsolescence is generational. For some countries' cadres of NGO leaders—certainly so in Canada—many have had no other jobs in their professional lives. In Canada, most of today's leaders, now approaching retirement, went directly from university to volunteer posts in Africa in the mid-1960s. Moreover, since the clamp on funding to NGOs in the mid-1990s in Canada, at least, almost no new hiring has taken place. With few jobs, despite a large cadre of development students coming from today's universities, the development NGO community shows distinct signs of ageing.

This personnel profile is particularly relevant if you accept that tomorrow's issues will require different expertise, and different kinds of institution. High-quality economic analysis will be needed by NGO policy units, research organisations, universities, and Southern government bodies. Increased demands will be made on organisations experienced in networking, brokering, and facilitating relationships among domestic and international players. That linking work already takes place in umbrella groups, resource centres, and training units in North and South, but much more will be needed—and will be nearly impossible to fund through the existing NGO funding channels. New skills will be needed in private-sector mediation, interpretation, and negotiation; through the unions, certainly, but also through organisations that can serve as negotiators. The demands for the future are different from the skills that most Northern NGOs, and their leaders, now possess.

New kinds of NGO

This paper suggests a brighter future for social justice. That future, however, does not mean that the same kinds of organisation will be needed: activists must always adapt themselves and their organisations to the world around them. Indeed, parts of the work done by today's Northern NGOs must continue, but there needs to be a real re-mingling of players and functions. Just as the spinning of a kaleidoscope rearranges existing patterns, a juggling of organisations and people would better suit the social-justice demands of the next 50 years.

At least the following functions need to be maintained and reinforced:

* Northern NGOs will need to maintain and improve their coordination of — and capacity for —quick humanitarian assistance, in concert with multilateral bodies.

- Northern NGOs need to expand nascent work with think-tanks, trade unions, and universities to become credible domestic and international macro-economic policy activists.
- Northern NGOs need to hone their relationships and 'value added' as brokers for North–South cooperation, particularly among domestic activists seeking joint purpose at the international level.
- And finally, there is a continuing role for Northern—and Southern—NGOs to maintain a watch on 'global capitalism' and corporate social responsibility.

These four condensed functions—immense as they are—nonetheless hint at a world where justice is being advanced, where 50 years of cooperation have given birth to a genuine global society. The reform, consolidation, and re-organisation of the work of Northern activists is a happy sign that the world we so much want to change is, indeed, changing. I think that is good news, indeed.

Notes

1 One recent example is the Global Partnership for NGO Studies, Education and Training, a consortium of educational centres established by BRAC from Bangladesh, Organisation of Rural Associations for Progress (ORAP) from Zimbabwe, and the School for International Training (SIT) from USA. The centres organise diploma-level and master's-level capacity-building programmes for NGO leaders.

2 According to the Union of International Associations (www.uia.org).

3 In this paper, 'The North' refers to the ODA-providing members of the OECD and OPEC. 'The South' indicates all ODA-receiving countries.

4 The estimates of names and numbers come from my own best guesses; the ODA figures are from OECD Development Assistance Committee sources. Actually, the total is probably higher; the number for ODA to NGOs is what is reported to the DAC, which tend to under-report NGO contributions. A rough guess is that at least 25 per cent of Canadian bilateral ODA—not 8 per cent—goes through NGOs, in addition to what they raise from individuals, a total that would have been some US$478 million in 1997.

5 Among those are Freedom House (http://www.freedomhouse.org/), the Open Society Institutes (http://www.osi.hu), and the Center for Civil Society International (http://www.friends-partners.org/~ccsi).

6 By way of anecdote: at a recent meeting in Canada of officials and NGOs interested in how CSOs could better be involved in international policy processes, one senior official referred to NGOs as 'gorillas' at the table. NGOs in the room responded to the zoological challenge, identifying themselves as ants or as canaries in the mineshaft.

7 See more detail at http://www.worldbank.org/poverty/scapital/bank2.

htm (accessed November 1999).

8 For example, the January 2000 consultations held in Canada in preparation for the World Summit on Social Development Plus 5 were full of loud, organised criticism of Canada's failures to apply WSSD commitments in the five years of budgetary cutbacks at home.

9 More information is available at http://www.worldbank.org/poverty/wdr poverty/conspoor.canany.htm.

10 The North–South Institute held a conference on this topic, where World Bank Senior Economist Joe Stiglitz, among others, spoke (North–South Institute 1999).

11 For a host of examples, have a look at the policies, guidelines, and evaluations of gender and development cooperation organised by ELDIS at http://nt1.ids.ac.uk/eldis/hot/wid.htm.

12 A new and careful study about the World Bank agrees with this assessment, albeit with significant caveats (Fox and Brown 1998).

13 See http://www.hurricanemitch. org/linkages.htm for a list of the efforts of US and other NGO and international organisations to soften the impact of the hurricane.

14 Ian Smillie, personal communication, March 1999.

15 John Foster, personal communication, January 1999.

16 Of course, direct funding is also a politically sensitive bilateral issue. The Overseas Development Institute emphasises that 'Donor funding of southern NGOs has received a mixed reception from recipient governments. Clear hostility from many non-democratic régimes has been part of more general opposition to any initiatives to support organ beyond the control of the state in democratic countries, governme have often resisted moves seen as diverting significant amounts of official aid to non-state controlled initiatives, especially where NGO projects have not been integrated with particular line ministry programmes' (ODI 1995).

References

Anheier, H. K. and L. M. Salamon (1998) *The Nonprofit Sector in the Developing World*, Baltimore: Johns Hopkins University Press.

Chapman, Jennifer (1999) *Effective NGO Campaigning: Summary Paper*, London: New Economics Foundation.

Chapman, Jennifer and Thomas Fisher (2000) 'The effectiveness of NGO campaigning: lessons from practice', *Development in Practice* 10(2): 151-65.

CIDA (1998) 'Canadians and Development Assistance: Environics Poll Results and Trend Analysis', Communications Branch, unpublished mimeo, Ottawa.

Department of Foreign Affairs and International Trade (1998), 'Notes for an Address by the Honourable Lloyd Axworthy', Minister of Foreign Affairs to the NGO Global Forum on the Five-Year Review of the Vienna World Conference on Human Rights, Ottawa, Ontario, June 23, Number 98/47.

Dollar, David et al. (1999) *Assessing Aid: What Works, What Doesn't, and Why*, Washington: The World Bank.

Elkington, John (1997) *Cannibals With Forks: The Triple Bottom Line of 21st Century Business*, London: Capstone Publishing with Sustainability Press.

Foster, John and Anita Anand (eds.) (1999) *Whose World is it Anyway? Civil Society, The United Nations and the Multilateral Future*, Ottawa: The United Nations Association of Canada.

Fowler, Alan (1997) *Striking a Balance: A Guide to Enhancing the Effectiveness of Non-Governmental Organisations in International Development*, London: Earthscan.

Fox, Jonathan A. and L. David Brown (1998) *The Struggle for Accountability: The World Bank, NGOs, and Grassroots Movements*, Cambridge, MA: MIT Press.

Foy, Colm and Henny Helmich (1996) *Public Support for International Development*, Paris: Development Centre, OECD.

Hately, Lynne and Kamal Malhotra (1997) *Between Rhetoric and Reality: Essays on Partnership in Development*, Ottawa: North-South Institute.

Huntington, Samuel P. (1993) *Third Wave: Democratization in the Late Twentieth Century*, Oklahoma: University of Oklahoma Press.

Kruse, Stein-Erik et al. (1997) *Searching for Impact and Methods: NGO Evaluation Synthesis Study*, Volume 1, Main Report, Prepared for the OECD/DAC Expert Group on Evaluation, Helsinki: Ministry of Foreign Affairs for Finland.

Mathews, Jessica T. (1997) 'Power shift', *Foreign Affairs* January/February: 50-66.

Murphy, Brian K. (1991) 'Canadian NGOs and the politics of participation', in Jamie Swift and Brian Tomlinson (eds.), *Conflicts of Interest: Canada and the Third World*, Toronto: Between the Lines.

Najam, Adil (1998) 'Searching for NGO effectiveness', *Development Policy Review* 16:305-10.

The North–South Institute (1999) *Recovery from Crisis: Policy Alternatives for Equitable Development*, Ottawa: The North-South Institute.

O'Brien, Robert, Anne Marie Goetz, Jan Aart Scholte, and Marc Williams (2000), *Contesting Global Governance: Multilateral Economic Institutions and Global Social Movements*, Cambridge: CUP.

ODI (1995) *NGOs and Official Donors*, ODI Briefing Paper Number 8, London: Overseas Development Institute.

OECD, DAC (1992) *Guidelines on Aid and the Environment: Good Practices for Environmental Impact Assessment for Development Projects*, Paris: OECD (available free at http://www.oecd.org/dac/pdf/guid1.pdf).

Putnam, Robert with Robert Leonardi and Rafaella Y. Nanetti (1993) *Making Democracy Work: Civic Traditions in Modern Italy*, Princeton: Princeton University Press.

Riddell, Roger C. and Anthony J. Bebbington (1995) 'Developing Country NGOs and Donor Governments', Report to the Overseas Development Administration, London: Overseas Development Institute, January.

Smillie, Ian (1995) *The Alms Bazaar: Altruism under Fire—Non-profit Organizations and International Development*, Ottawa: International Development Research Centre.

Smillie, Ian (1998) 'Canada', Ian Smillie and Henny Helmich, in collaboration with Tony German and Judith Randel (eds.) *Public Attitudes and International Development Cooperation*, Paris: North–South Centre of the Council of Europe and the

Development Centre of the OECD.

Sogge, David with Kees Biekart and John Saxby (eds.) (1996) *Compassion and Calculation: The Business of Private Foreign Aid*, London: Pluto with the Transnational Institute.

Van Rooy, Alison (1997) 'The frontiers of influence: NGO lobbying at the 1974 World Food Conference, the 1992 Earth Summit and beyond', *World Development* 25(1): 93-114.

Van Rooy, Alison (ed.) (1998), *Civil* ✓ *Society and the Aid Industry: The Politics and Promise*, London: Earthscan, with The North–South Institute.

Riding high or nosediving: development NGOs in the new millennium

Rajesh Tandon

Non-government organisations (NGOs) are today visible, noticed, and acknowledged. The widespread presence of such actors on the development landscape reached its pinnacle at the turn of the millennium. Describing the results of an empirical study in 22 countries, Lester Salomon concludes: 'The non-profit sector thus emerges from the evidence presented here as a sizeable and highly dynamic component of a wide spectrum of societies throughout the world' (Salomon 1999).

This paper attempts to draw some lessons from the performance of development NGOs throughout the world over the past five decades. It starts by describing the meaning of the alternative development paradigm, as practised by NGOs. It then examines some of the major socio-political changes that have occurred in recent years, and their impact on development NGOs. Finally, it outlines some key dilemmas facing development NGOs, and their potential implications for their future roles and contributions at the turn of the millennium.

The alternative development paradigm

Voluntary association and development action have been a part of the historical evolution of many societies. The framework of development, however, is essentially a post-1945 phenomenon. Individuals and groups within the field of development derived their motivation, and continue to do so, from an ideological and spiritual commitment to social reform and change. It is this personal commitment to societal improvement that characterised such non-State actors in the mid-twentieth century. Development NGOs are a contemporary sub-set of the same tradition.

When development NGOs began to be noticed in the 1970s, it was for what was beginning to be called an *alternative development paradigm*. The identification of NGOs with this alternative development paradigm grew stronger over the next decade or so. What were the characteristics of this paradigm, which distinguished NGOs from mainstream development actors? Several significant characteristics can be identified. The alternative development paradigm implied *local-level development*, which was seen to be in contrast to the agenda of national-level development of newly liberated post-colonial nation-States after the Second World War. These States tried to establish certain national priorities that were to be uniformly addressed through a series of development interventions by national governments. The local agenda had local priorities, and looked at the individual village or a slum as a space for improving people's socio-economic situation.

A related characteristic was the *small-scale* nature of these development efforts, something reinforced by Schumacher's proclamation that 'small is beautiful'. This alternative approach emphasised the need to look at development itself as a problem of human development that can be understood, managed, and monitored by small collectives of human beings. Small-scale development contrasted with the large-scale macro-level development programmes which were then being launched with a great deal of vigour and pride – such as the construction of major dams, hydro-electric power stations, roads, and mines.

The third dimension of the alternative development paradigm was an *integrated* approach, which implied looking at the individual, his or her family, and the community as a coherent whole, and bringing together various development inputs to converge in an integrated fashion so that individuals, their families, and their communities could all benefit. This approach contrasted with the fragmented, sectoral development schemes run by most national governments, in which each scheme addressed one aspect of human existence – education, health, drinking water, sanitation, agriculture, rural development, roads, communication, or electricity, for example. These schemes were at times mutually conflicting or even contradictory, and to integrate them required enormous efforts on the part of individuals, families, and communities.

The fourth and perhaps most dynamic characteristic of the alternative development paradigm was its *participatory nature*. This paradigm believed that development cannot be delivered from outside, that people can develop themselves, and that their own involvement, engagement, and contribution are an essential foundation for sustainable development. People's own participation can be enabled through drawing on local knowledge and local resources, and it can be enhanced through a series of interventions leading to their collective empowerment. This dimension was nicely juxtaposed against the externally determined, government-led, functionary-delivered development programmes that characterised many State efforts in the 1970s and 1980s. In the 1970s people's participation was not on the agenda of most governments, nor was it considered relevant or in any case appropriate.

The final dimension of this alternative paradigm was its ideological and inspirational character, which looked at the needs of the target groups in the context of social and economic transformation. Inspired largely by the sufferings and deprivations of the marginalised sections of society, and committed to bringing about socio-economic equality and justice, the alternative development approach relied substantially on conscientisation and the collective mobilisation of the marginalised themselves. Non-formal education, community organisation, and local leadership-building were the kinds of intervention that this alternative development approach of NGOs signified. This contrasted with the mainstream development paradigm, which focused on growth in gross national product and macro-economic development.

The distribution and equity dimension of development was not a major concern of governments in those days. Development was seen as a technocratic professional challenge, which could be managed through expertise and input of resources from outside. 'The technocratic approach, with its emphasis on technological modernisation, managerial efficiency and growth in GNP, held the centre of the stage for over two decades but is now in disrepute' (Mehta et al. 1977:2). Clearly, the NGO development paradigm, described as an alternative development paradigm, contained within itself the seeds of significant future evolutions and had in itself a number of significant analytical dimensions.

The first dimension was to look at the role of the State. Most post-colonial States in Africa, Asia-Pacific, and Latin America and the Caribbean were single-party and authoritarian. Even where democratic forms of political systems were in existence, the hegemony of the State in determining development agendas, mobilising development resources, and delivering development was almost total. The gap between the promise and the reality of how the State functioned, and its inability to change the situation of the poor and the weak in any meaningful way, lent itself easily to a major critique of the very function of the State.

The alternative development paradigm, therefore, was an alternative to the practice of the State. This critique was also influenced by emerging negative consequences of development on the lives and destinies of the poor. In many parts of the developing world, large-scale development projects were resulting in the displacement of indigenous people, poor rural people, and urban slum-dwellers from their land, livelihood, and community. The NGO development paradigm began to analyse such development projects on the basis of who benefits from them and who bears the cost. This critique subsequently led to what began to be called a 'rights-based approach' to development. These human rights were larger than civil and political rights: they included the right to a decent livelihood, the right to life, and the right to life with dignity. 'Thousands and thousands of individuals and groups, all over the world, are engaged in practising such alternatives' (Raise et al. 1997).

In the 1970s, the alternative approach also signified a relative indifference towards macro-economic issues and the production of goods and services. The major focus of analysis was on equitable distribution and on social justice. Agricultural and industrial production was not a major focus of NGO attention. In most situations, private capital, large plantations, and private ownership of industry were considered somehow injurious to the interests of the vast majority of people in developing societies.

While inadequately conceptualised, there were a number of significant elements in this analytical critique which evolved through development NGO practice in the 1970s. These critiques resulted in the emergence of a new agenda in the development paradigm, which subsequently joined the alternative development paradigm. This included concern for the environment, for ecologically balanced and sustainable development, the rights of women and gender equity. It studied the disparities between the Western societies characterised by North America and Western Europe, on the one hand, and the developing societies on the other. The global system was seen as unjust and perpetuating the 'development of under-development' in countries of Africa, Asia, and Latin America (as argued brilliantly by André Gunder Frank and Samir Amin).

Outcomes

After two decades of widespread acknowledgement of this unique alternative development paradigm, which was associated with NGO work throughout the world, a number of significant outcomes could be observed in the practice and discourse of development by the mid-1990s. The first set of outcomes relates to the NGOs themselves. Between 1970 and 1995, NGOs gained a high degree of visibility in almost every country in the world. Their roles and contributions began to be noticed. Their presence, their experience, and their point of view began to be heard by the developmentalists, nationally and internationally. National governments began to take stock of the NGOs in their own countries and of the international NGOs working in their societies. There has also been a significant and manifold increase in the flow of resources to NGOs. From global institutions and national governments, as well as from private foundations and other sources, overall access to resources by NGOs increased significantly over this 25-year period. These resources included those linked to the 'development aid' system, as well as contributions of people (mostly in the North) to emergency relief.

NGOs also gained enormous access to power during this period. They began to be invited to be part of the various official government committees at provincial and national levels. They began to be part of the UN system and of the Bretton Woods institutions. They gained access to the highest level of development decision-making in the UN and multilateral system as well as the national policy-making institutions. UN conferences in the 1980s and 1990s presented unique opportunities for NGOs to influence policy formulations, development debates, and alternative development approaches.

This period also witnessed an enormous growth in the size and diversity of the NGO community itself. A large number of NGOs emerged in different places, and international NGOs began to operate in many more countries of the world. NGOs also began to develop a broader range of internal differentiation – from service delivery to welfare provision, to emergency operations, to policy advocacy, to networking, to research, and capability building. A wide range of thematic and issue-oriented NGOs, as well as general-purpose agencies, gained ascendancy during these 25 years. Describing this variety, David Korten presented the four-generation model of development NGOs, 'The VO [voluntary organisation] with a fourth generation strategy is essentially a service organisation to the people's movement it supports' (Korten 1990).

A second set of outcomes during this period was related to the nature of changes in the political systems throughout the world. By the mid-1990s, many more countries had adopted some form of liberal democratic governance mechanism. As a result, there was an increase in pluralistic and competitive politics with direct popular participation. Countries that had remained under authoritarian and dictatorial regimes became democratic, as exemplified by the Philippines, Chile, and South Africa in the three continents of Asia, Latin America, and Africa. NGOs were seen to have played a significant role in energising the people's democratic aspirations and in fostering the resulting democratic transition of these countries. Throughout the world, the experiences, voices, and contributions of NGOs from these three countries were presented as exemplars.

A third set of outcomes is related to the dramatic shifts in the Soviet Union and the nature of the socialist regime. Eastern and Central Europe went through a period of significant economic and political transformation after the abandonment of Soviet-style socialism. This had enormous consequences world-wide, because the Cold War dynamics of East and West suddenly disappeared, and a new dynamic between the North and the South began to take their place. The response of Warsaw Pact countries to the aspirations of developing countries in Asia, Africa, and Latin America had been in competition with Western Europe and North America during the Cold War period. With the disappearance of Soviet Union, the world became a uni-polar and, therefore, a much more hegemonic political régime than before.

Another outcome of this period was the dramatic change in the status of development of many countries throughout the world. Many countries of Southeast and East Asia, and Latin America, experienced dramatic improvements in income levels and social-development outcomes. As a result, there were significant reductions in poverty and marginalisation, and substantial improvements in education, health, and other social indicators in these contexts. This presented the possibility that the model of rapid economic development represented by these countries could be touted as the model development paradigm for the rest of the world.

The most significant outcome of this period perhaps was in the slow but significant transformation of the development agenda itself. National governments, UN agencies, the Bretton Woods institutions, development think-tanks – the entire development community by the mid-1990s – began to create an impression that the mainstream development discourse had 'absorbed' the principles of the alternative development paradigm that were being promoted by NGOs in the 1970s. Local-level development, integrated interventions, mobilisation of the poor, and participation have become the hallmark of development philosophy. The Declaration and Programme of Action of the UN World Summit for Social

Development held at Copenhagen in March 1995 had governments agree to the following:

Encouraging the fullest participation in society requires:

(a) Strengthening the capacities and opportunities for all people ...

(b) Enabling institutions of civil society ...

(c) Giving community organisations greater involvement in the design and implementation of local projects ... (UN 1995: 98-9)

Champions of economic growth like the World Bank and OECD are talking about balanced growth, sustainable development, and participation. 'Participation is a process through which stakeholders influence and share control over development initiatives, and the decision and resources which affect them', according to the World Bank's 1994 policy statement. Mainstream development discourse at the turn of the millennium looks not very different from the alternative development paradigm that was put forward by NGOs in the 1970s. In some significant ways, therefore, NGOs can claim to have been 'successful': they can claim to have influenced national and international development policies, priorities, and discourse in the direction of their own experience. The big players of development have now incorporated the alternative principles espoused by NGOs more than two decades ago, and mainstream development now reflects that perspective. James D. Wolfensohn, President of the World Bank Group, echoed this in his annual address to the Board of Governors in September 1999, calling for 'Coalitions for Change'.

In some respects, this is a significant achievement and a matter of great satisfaction for NGOs. The fraternity of NGOs can take pride in the fact that, as we enter the new millennium, the global development agenda has been significantly inspired by the practice and perspectives of hundreds of thousands of NGOs world-wide. Yet, in some important ways, it is simplistic to treat this as an unmitigated success. Although these principles have been adopted in the development policies of the major actors, it is only the discourse that has changed: the practice needs much more improvement. The fear that big players will co-opt the NGO agenda remains valid if mere shifts of language are confused with actual practice on the ground. The challenge now is to hold these macro-players accountable to their own rhetoric.

A parallel question is to ask what has been the cost of this success over the past 25 years? Is it fair and analytically sound to compare the efforts of NGOs in the 1970s and those of today? The context has shifted. Countries, people, societies, and the world have dramatically changed in the past quarter of a century. NGOs today operate in a significantly different context from the one prevalent in the 1970s and early 1980s. What are some of the key challenges facing NGOs in today's context, and how do NGOs attempt, if at all, to respond to them? What are some of the directions in which these challenges will shape the future of NGO contributions to our societies?

Daunting dilemmas

At the start of the new century, NGOs are facing certain unresolved, and still daunting, dilemmas. These are issues on which clarity of perspective and decisive action are not very common, although the need for them is periodically emphasised. Six of these contemporary dilemmas are considered below.

Economic growth and private enterprise

As we have seen, the identity of the development NGOs was closely associated with their demand for the equitable distribution of resources – land, forest, water, capital, technology, income, etc. However, experience has shown that basic economic growth in a society is a prerequisite for addressing issues of poverty and deprivation. This does not imply rapid growth, and certainly not double-digit growth, nor does it imply that economic growth alone is the answer. But it is clear that any improvements in the lives of the poor (in Sub-Saharan Africa or South Asia, for example) are inconceivable unless there is economic development and growth in those societies.

Even those NGOs that grudgingly accepted this premise continue to hope that the public sector will somehow drive this economic development. NGOs are still very suspicious of arguments that propose a decent role for private enterprise in the economic development of societies. By its very nature, profit-seeking private enterprise is considered by many NGOs to embody a less than desirable human value. However, the reality on the ground in many societies is that small-scale private entrepreneurship has driven enormous economic development throughout history. This is particularly true for those societies and communities that have encouraged private trading and private initiative in agriculture and small-scale industry over the last 5000 years. India and

China are two prime examples of countries with a rich history of individual private entrepreneurs, families of entrepreneurs, and communities of private economic enterprises. In questioning the very legitimacy of private enterprise for economic development, NGOs are largely focusing on corporate-sector enterprises or multinational corporations (MNCs). While the economic might and global outreach of the latter is certainly a cause for concern as they become immensely powerful, the corporate sector has contributed to the provision of efficient and inexpensive access to a large number of goods and services in our societies – goods that were until only 50 years ago accessible only to the most exclusive élites. Therefore, NGOs' blanket condemnation of significant economic institutions reflects a partial understanding of the reality of economic development and growth. At the same time, the critical analysis of MNCs and the concentration of wealth and consequent exercise of political power by them are new areas for NGO attention and action.

In addition, there is an increasingly problematic contradiction in NGOs' rapidly expanding acceptance of micro-credit and micro-finance as crucial economic development strategies. From the illustrious and much-quoted Grameen Bank in Bangladesh to initiatives in every other part of the developing world, micro-credit has become a new 'mantra' for addressing poverty. While there are some impressive gains made by making available small amounts of low-interest credit to women (in particular), we should not lose sight of the fact that, by its very nature, this intervention seeks to expand the pool of private enterprise for economic development. It also implies promoting greater access to and linkage with the market institutions for the poor, thereby transforming their subsistence-level livelihoods to more modern market-based economic enterprises. In many respects, the outputs of products and services generated from these micro-credit interventions of groups of poor women compete with those offered by other private enterprises, including the corporate sector. It appears in this scenario that the NGOs are wanting to 'have their cake and eat it too' – clearly an untenable proposition.

Governance

The second dilemma relates to the broader issue of governance. In recent years, good governance has become a fad in development discourse. However, as noted earlier, the alternative development paradigm of

NGOs focused a great deal on the 'bottom-up' process of development, which was to be collectively constructed through participatory action. 'Putting people in the centre of development' implied removing the State and its agents from that centre. Participatory development models proposed by NGOs challenged the State-led models of development adopted since the end of the Second World War. Therefore, a logical next step in that alternative development paradigm was to reduce the importance of the State in the governance of natural resources and local development, enabling organised collectives of local communities to become responsible for these things.

This implies that NGOs need to consider the possibility of working to create a more efficient, more transparent, and more accountable apparatus of democratic governance. However, NGOs continue to struggle with the provision of sector-oriented programmes and services – health, education, drinking water, rural development, urban development, environment, etc. The link between poverty eradication and sustainable development, on the one hand, and transparent, accountable, and participatory democracy and governance on the other has not yet been conceptually or emotionally accepted by NGOs.

The need for participative governance has been well expressed in a recent publication by the Commonwealth Foundation (1999):

> Citizens believe that a good society is one in which they can participate in public spheres to make their own contribution towards the public good. Their voices are loud and clear on this. People want a society characterised by responsive and inclusive governance. They want to be heard and consulted on a regular and continuing basis, not merely at the time of an election. They want more than a vote. They are asking for participation and inclusion in the decisions taken and policies made by public agencies and officials.

This raises the challenge of engaging with the formal political system in a given country. But NGOs are unable to agree on whether they should talk to the political parties and political leaders at all, except to those who are government ministers. The growing worldwide trend towards local self-governance through elected local bodies has not been embraced as yet by the NGO fraternity. Questions about their own internal governance become relevant too. Just as government agencies and departments cannot bring in externally designed programmes for local bodies simply to accept, likewise NGO programmes, designed and funded through external resources, cannot be implemented in local communities unless they are reviewed by local bodies to ensure that NGOs are properly accountable to them.

Likewise, there is a question of growing government expenditure on militarisation and defence, and large-scale consumption of public budgets in overstaffed public agencies. Money spent in these areas is money taken away from social development and poverty-eradication programmes. Not many NGOs see this link or are willing to take a stand on issues of militarisation and public-sector staffing, for example. 'While it is time that the future of poor-people centred development programmes has to be approached through a fusion of government and NGO practices, it will be far from easy to bring this about when to do so will erode the power and income of the government officials' (Holloway 1989).

At the heart of the governance issue is the political process. Politics of negotiation and consensus building across diversified interest groups and varied priorities is the basis of democratic governance in any society. But many NGOs fail to understand the political process, and nor are they in a position to deal with it.

Resistance and reform

A third and related dilemma is that of policy resistance versus policy reform. The experience of NGOs, as mentioned earlier, has been remarkably effective in resisting certain policies and programmes that were perceived to be inimical to the interests of the poor and the marginalised. Anti-dam, anti-industry, anti-mining struggles stand out as powerful symbols of successful NGO contributions. When governments and international agencies were unwilling to listen to the NGOs or to consider their experience and voice at all, resistance was a powerful instrument, and adversarial relationships were an effective basis for dealing with harmful or indifferent policies and programmes. However, as governments and international agencies have begun to invite NGOs to work with them in shaping their policies and programmes, NGOs find themselves in a great dilemma as they try to decide what to propose as solutions, what to recommend as models. This is partly a result of the fact that NGO experience has generally been limited to micro-level, small-scale projects from which it is difficult, if not impossible, to extrapolate to macro-level national or international policies and programmes.

In addition, the process of generating these solutions in a democratic framework requires political negotiations and contentious consensus building, which is difficult, if not impossible, given the background of NGO experience. Having taken a specific position on policy issues such as forest management, land reform, or gender justice, NGOs become one party among others, all promoting their own interests, perspectives, and commitments. The NGOs' solutions and recommendations are ranged among the many that are likely to influence policies and programmes. The process of sitting round a table, debating with those who entertain other points of view and negotiating a democratic agreement, often entails accepting only a partial recommendation of the NGO position. In the eyes of many NGOs, this is seen as unacceptable and 'dirty' compromise. The real world, unfortunately, is very messy and dirty. There is nothing pure in it, let alone a pure position. Having taken the moral high ground on certain policy issues, many NGOs face the dilemma of how to reconcile themselves publicly with partial, but more broadly agreed, solutions which seem to indicate a compromise with their original purist position. 'The international development field has now become a marketplace ... A strategic re-orientation means that NGOs must acknowledge the complexity of development and the reality of a more inter-dependent world' (Brodhead and Copley 1988).

Globalisation

A fourth dilemma for NGOs is that of globalisation. In some significant ways, NGOs have benefited from the process of globalisation. As we have seen, they have gained access to global resources and influence in global forums. UN conferences in the last 15 years have promoted the globalisation of development discourse and development policy-making. On the other hand, there are trends in globalisation that reinforce existing inequalities across nations and people. New information technology (IT) opens up enormous possibilities to those who have access to its hardware and software. That access is distributed extremely unevenly in the world today, as described by UNDP's *Human Development Report 1999*. Many NGOs with access to IT are themselves part of the privileged minority in their societies.

NGOs are greatly concerned about poor countries' exclusion from equal participation in the World Trade Organisation, and the dominance of Northern capital flows in the world speculation market. There is increasing evidence that the natural-resource base of the poor and of local industry in many parts of the world is being eroded by lopsided globalisation that favours the rich nations of the North. The common NGO reaction has been to shun and condemn globalisation. But the option of confining oneself within national boundaries carries peculiar socio-political implications, including a return to feudal and parochial systems. Globalisation also offers new possibilities, and widespread citizen aspiration for democratic governance is one such possibility that NGOs can support. The emergence of multilateral mechanisms at the regional level (the EU, ASEAN, and NAFTA trading communities, for example) and at the global level (the WTO, APEC, Davos Summit, etc.) are opportunities to counterbalance bilateralism between the strong and the weak. This ambivalence towards globalisation continues to paralyse NGOs and undermines their ability to take advantage of some of its aspects, while continuing to challenge and resist others. A more reasoned and analytical approach to the issues of globalisation is needed by NGOs:

> Social fragmentation, economic instability, and uncertainty about the future are breeding prejudice, intolerance, and racism. Peace and democracy are not compatible with ever-increasing poverty and exclusion. The social and geographic segregation of a growing number of individuals can only fuel ethnic tensions and violence. From the moral and ethical standpoint, global apartheid is absolutely unacceptable (Darcy De Oliveira and Tandon 1994).

Sustainability

Another major dilemma facing NGOs concerns the question of their own resources. As intermediary agents in their societies, serving the poor and the marginalised, NGOs have historically relied on externally generated resources. Most of their funding has come from development aid. As development aid from Northern OECD countries began to contribute greater resources to NGOs, more and more development NGOs gained access to it and began to become dependent on it. In recent years, a large proportion of this development assistance has been routed through governments, and NGOs have used resources made available to them from large-scale government programmes. This access to large-scale development aid has many serious implications.

Traditional Northern donors are asking Southern development NGOs to demonstrate their financial sustainability. As an increasingly popular prescription, NGOs are being exhorted to enter into partnerships with the corporate sector, on the grounds that this represents an enormous potential source of sustained flows of financial resources to NGOs.

It is obvious that intermediaries of any kind require resources from those who can afford to provide them. On that principle, NGOs' contribution to society may not be fundable by their direct (and indirect) beneficiaries. Yet contributions from traditional development-aid sources are stagnant, if not declining. Their dependence on that aid flow is making NGOs become service providers in a restricted and narrow sense, so depriving them of their ability to maintain autonomous, independent perspectives and positions on a wide range of socio-political and economic issues. As NGOs become more involved in large-scale service delivery and/or become more reliant on official funding, one might expect some fall-off in their flexibility, speed of response, and ability to innovate. 'The orientation of accountability (to donors) away from the grassroots is a particular threat to [NGOs]' (Edwards and Hulme 1995). How does one maintain a sustainable economic base, a material base, which allows NGOs flexible funds and yet keeps them accountable to the society and the community in which they live, work, and practise?

NGOs' legitimacy and accountability are increasingly linked to their resource base. Resource providers can demand a certain limited type of accountability: that which has to do with efficient and purposive use of resources provided by them. But NGOs do not exist only to spend money that they occasionally receive from outside. Rather, they exist to pursue a particular vision and set of development priorities. Therefore, their accountability must translate into the reality in which they intervene, and local communities and society must be the interface through which NGOs define their accountability. It is a difficult dilemma to resolve, but one that is increasingly haunting NGOs as prescriptions for sustainability and local resource mobilisation are being offered in the market at a rapidly increasing rate.

An approach based on local accountability would also enhance NGOs' identity and rootedness in their own societies. As a result, the challenge of sustainability would no longer be posed merely in financial terms. Indeed, the sustainability of NGOs then would also include their intellectual and institutional contributions.

Bridging civil society

Finally, NGOs are facing the dilemma of whom they should speak to. Historically, they have been busy working with the poor and the marginalised. Occasionally, they related to development policy-makers and ideologues. However, over the years, NGO conversations generally remained limited to the 'charmed circles of the already converted'. As a result, only a small section of society in the countries in which they operated was familiar with their approaches and experiences. In some situations, NGOs saw themselves as the only activists in pursuit of such important societal goals. 'Micro movements abound all over the place, but there is not enough of a dialogue between them' (Kothari 1988).

NGOs tended neither to pay attention to nor develop any relationship with other civil-society actors – religious institutions, traditional formations, community-based initiatives, trade unions, or social movements. This inward-looking tendency has been historically reinforced through donors' policies and practices. Issues of accountability, impact, and sustainability are now pushing NGOs to open up their horizons and deal with the rest of society. Talking about their experience and perspectives beyond the coterie of the already converted has become an important challenge for NGOs. 'The role of NGOs in strengthening Civil Society to regain and retain hegemony over the state and private enterprise is a critical strategic function' (Tandon 1991).

This broad-based task of public education is also an essential foundation for bringing about societal transformation within a democratic framework. More and more people have to be persuaded to see the value and the relevance of the work that NGOs are doing. However, dealing with all these other sections of society may strain NGOs and take their resources and attention away from their traditional beneficiary 'target' groups – the poor and the marginalised themselves. It is certainly an issue that most international donors and external resource providers ask: *Are you spending our dollars in directly helping the poor or not?* Thus, NGOs wanting to break ground and expand their 'circles of conversation' find themselves extremely restricted, and hence their experience of working with other civil-society actors is limited. Building a broad-based consensus in society on issues that concern NGOs may require resolving this dilemma sooner rather than later. 'This effective, pluralistic and efficient functioning of development NGOs in the South itself becomes an expression of sustainable development' (Tandon 1996).

The future for NGOs

In essence, the future contributions of development NGOs are linked to their ability to deal with the dilemmas and challenges described above.

The 'niche' for NGO action has historically been in advancing new practices and promoting creative solutions. The new millennium presents a qualitatively different set of opportunities and challenges for NGO action. Re-definition and re-strategising are needed at this juncture, not just individually by each NGO, but by the sector as a whole.

References

Brodhead Tim and Brent Herbert Copley (1988) *Bridges of Hope*, Ottawa: The North-South Institute

Commonwealth Foundation (1999) *Citizens and Governance*, London: The Commonwealth Foundation

Darcy De Oliveira, Miguel and Rajesh Tandon (1994) *Citizens: Strengthening Global Civil Society*, Washington: Civicus

Edwards, Michael and David Hulme (eds.) (1995) *Non-Governmental Organisations – Performance and Accountability – Beyond the Magic Bullet*, London: Earthscan (with Save the Children Fund)

Holloway, Richard (ed.) (1989) *Doing Development*, London: Earthscan

Korten, David C. (1990) *Getting to the 21st Century: Voluntary Action and the Global Agenda*, West Hartford CT: Kumarian Press

Kothari, Rajni (1988) *Rethinking Development*, New Delhi: Ajanta

Mehta N., W. Haque, P. Wignaraja, and A.Rahman (1977) *Development Dialogue: A Quarter Century of Anti-Rural Development*

Raise, Vinod, Aditi Choudhury, and Sumit Choudhury (eds.) (1997) *The Dispossessed*, ARENA

Salomon, Lester M. et al. (1999) *Global Civil Society: Dimensions of the Nonprofit Sector*, Baltimore MA: Johns Hopkins Centre for Civil Society Studies

Tandon, Rajesh (1991) *Civil Society, the State and Roles of NGOs*, Boston: IDR Occasional Paper

Tandon, Rajesh (1996) 'Institutional Strengthening of NGOs in the South', ODA-BOND-CDS Workshop

United Nations (1995) World Summit for Social Development 6-12 March 1995: The Copenhagen Declaration and Programme of Action, New York NY: UN Department of Public Information

International NGOs and the challenge of modernity

Brian K. Murphy

Fifty years after the historic launch of the global development era with the 'Four Points' speech on 20 January 1949 by US President Harry Truman – as *de facto* leader of the 'Free World' – the very concept of 'development' is coming under fierce scrutiny, its most basic premises and tenets fundamentally challenged from all points on the political spectrum, whether the far right, the hard left, or the liberal centre.

Likewise, 30 years after the attempt to re-tool this global development project with the 1969-70 Report of the Commission on International Development, 'Partnership for Development' (or 'The Pearson Report', after its Chairman, Lester B. Pearson), the promise of equal partnership between North and South in promoting global prosperity and equity has been swamped by the more ruthless competitive mechanisms of what has come to be known as economic globalisation.

In the process, the global imperative that was announced in 1980 by the Independent Commission on International Development Issues, North–South, in 'A Programme for Survival' (or 'The Brandt Report', after Commission Chair, Willy Brandt), has been mocked and marginalised, as though its vision of pragmatic global interdependence was just a quixotic and idealistic fancy, rather than the minimal blueprint for global survival that this actually represented.

More recent attempts to bring a modicum of rational constraint to the anarchy of the global market and corporate licence, such as that manifest in the 1995 Report of the Commission on Global Governance (Ramphal and Carlsson 1995) – with its urgent emphasis on promoting global security, defined in terms that included protecting the global commons, nurturing social cohesion, and conserving the natural environment –

have failed to forestall the destructive impact of the forces of globalisation, in spite of a recurring diagnosis of a world gone wrong.

Now, as the twenty-first century begins, professionals and activists in international co-operation for global justice and peace are at the cusp of a fundamental global transition. This transition could possibly signal the end of the traumatic rupture and violence that marked the twentieth century – what Hobsbawm (1994) called 'the age of extremes' – and the dawning of an era that will see the sustained, equitable, and just transformation of the planet to the benefit of all of humankind, wherever we live, and however we envision our communities, our lives, and our livelihoods. Equally possible is a transformation that consolidates the wealth and privilege of a minority, but deepens the misery and malaise of the 'new social majority' (Esteva and Prakash 1998), the permanently marginalised and impoverished people who are the majority of virtually every nation, including the growing underclass in the more affluent industrialised countries.

The latter scenario can only lead to human debasement and a catastrophe that ultimately will swamp even the enclaves of privilege which have been artificially sheltered from the horrors that have engulfed hundreds of millions over the past century. But hope remains for a positive and fundamental transformation that can bring peace, justice, and universal dignity to the human community. This hope is rooted in the reality that around the world, and as never before, people are engaged in dialogue and debate about national neo-liberal economic policies and the effects of globalisation. At the heart of this dialogue is the question of whether it is still possible to bring about a truly free, humane, equitable, and just world, and how such a historic project might be re-launched and realised within this new century. What is the role of international NGOs in this process?

Globalisation revisited

That human society has entered an era marked by myriad phenomena collectively labelled 'globalisation' has become a cliché. Like most clichés, the term describes so much that it defines nothing at all. In any case, from the perspective of international co-operation and social-justice activism, the critical reality lies not in the general characteristics of globalisation, but in the particular and unique conditions of people's lives, and the effects of globalisation in the places where we live: in our homes, our communities, and our natural and cultural environments.

Inescapably, one of the most dramatic effects of globalisation has been the intense localisation of its impact on ordinary people. The more globalised the systems and mechanisms of commerce and finance, the more isolated and marginalised are individuals, their families, their communities, and the more particular are the circumstances of their lives. And yet, within this isolation and 'particularity' are the seeds of the resurgence of community itself, and of the age-old strategies of co-operation and mutual support that have characterised human habitation and interaction throughout history.

This feature of globalisation – what I call 'localisation' – is perhaps its most profound and enduring element. Yet, ironically, while this is starkly apparent in the places where international development agencies and institutions work, it is little remarked upon. Localisation has been obscured by the rhetoric – for and against – of debate about the general and worldwide impact of globalisation. In the final analysis, however, impact is, by definition, local and specific. Theoretical commonalities are no more than abstractions; the concrete reality is very particular.

The forces that have globalised economic systems and restructured societies have generated countervailing forces of increasingly local responses to the effects of globalisation in people's lives. Globalisation makes the world not a bigger place, but a smaller one. It becomes a place in which communities of interest consolidate and become concentrated, locally as well as internationally. As the process of globalisation intensifies, so will the process of localisation – the long-term impact of which will be a dominant characteristic of the new development era.

How does globalisation affect concrete conditions at the local level?

The erosion of governance

Globalisation is not a natural event, an inevitable global progression of consolidated economic growth and development. The specific variation of globalisation that we have created internationally, and its local manifestations and effects, is not even the only variation possible. Rather, it is the option that has been chosen and implemented by the global powers, using as a cutting edge the multiplex instrument known as structural adjustment, which has been imposed as a condition for debt restructuring and IMF loans worldwide over the past twenty years.

The fundamental and explicit goal of structural adjustment has been to liberate international financial and commercial enterprises, and the global markets in which they compete, from the control or influence of individual governments, through the deregulation of trade and commerce and the privatisation of the social functions of the State. A necessary aim of this process has been to diminish the economic independence and sovereignty of nations and integrate them within a global economic system and a trade and investment regime that will regulate and govern national policies in the interests of the 'free' market and international commerce.

This process is virtually complete and has been a resounding and tragic success, so much so that the élite who drive this global regime are now desperate to reverse some of the most disastrous effects of their policies and to stabilise what has become an extremely volatile political and economic global situation. The hand-wringing of corporate and political leaders at the Davos 'economic summit' in June 1999 revealed the growing preoccupation with the need to rebuild and protect the institutions of national governance in order to forestall the crisis and anarchy that international capital sees clouding the horizon.

Meanwhile, the vision of democratic national governments that promote and protect the common interests of their citizens, to whose social and cultural needs as well as their economic well-being they respond, has been destroyed – even as rogue governments hide behind notions of sovereignty to resist international sanctions for their brutal repression of internal dissent. This has not happened accidentally, but as an explicit policy of the international system and of the same actors who now wring their hands at economic summits. Although seldom a reality at the best of times, this notion of good governance has been a rhetorical goal of most national governments throughout the century. Indeed, it was one of the four points of Truman's platform, and the axis of the various proposals for global partnership, from Pearson, through Brandt, to Ramphal and Carlsson – and remains so within the official text of global institutions, even as the resources and tools of responsible government have been diminished and debased in most countries.

Everywhere, the institutions of governance have been eroded and have lost legitimacy with their populations. The primary function of the State has become that of social control within its own borders, along with the imposition of policies to attract and serve the national and international economic interests that are now essential to 'develop' and integrate the national economy within the global system. Yet even this minimal goal is barely realistic, in a system where the strong consolidate and increase their wealth while the weak compete with the weaker and are increasingly diminished.

The result is the abandonment of the poorest and most marginal, precisely at the moment when global events have made them most vulnerable to dislocation and catastrophe. This process of exclusion is accompanied by a dangerous erosion of the institutions of governance, and a vacuum of legitimate and credible political leadership that can deal with the crises caused by the destruction of the social fabric that has accompanied the radical restructuring currently underway.

Destruction of economies of scale

At the heart of the process of economic globalisation has been the increasing concentration of wealth and capital – the means of production and distribution – and economic power. This process of constantly increasing economies of scale and the vertical and horizontal integration of production, marketing, and distribution – what capitalist economists call 'increasing efficiency and productivity' – has effectively destroyed local economies and made smaller-scale artisanal and family-based production and commerce non-viable. In most countries, this process has been formally encouraged by government policy for more than twenty years. Aggressive legislation and regulation have promoted large-scale industrial and export-based production at the expense of traditional economies, as part of the structural-adjustment orthodoxy imposed by the IMF and the World Bank. In many cases, government policies have been complemented by organised violence – literally terrorising people off the land and out of production, as we see daily in Colombia and Brazil, for example. With this dislocation has also come an explosive unemployment crisis all over the world, as growing numbers of people come to depend on wage labour at a rate that far outstrips the capacity of the economy to create even temporary and poorly paid jobs, let alone secure and gainful employment.

The local effect of this economic disenfranchisement is the emergence of the so-called parallel or 'informal' economy. This is the real economy for the majority of people in the South, and an increasing proportion of the underclass in the North as well. While there have been massive attempts to appropriate this phenomenon as part of official international development programmes – particularly through the burgeoning micro-credit movement to promote petty-capitalism – these schemes do not begin to apprehend, let alone influence, the evolution of informal economies, which are extremely localised and diverse. Modern economics, which Heilbroner (1996) describes as the theory and study of the mechanics of capitalism (which is assumed to be all that there is), does not have the tools even to see and identify the elements of the informal economy in its local manifestations. Far less can capitalist economic theory describe and analyse the mechanics and norms of the informal economy, many of which are norms of mutual support and cultural action, rather than of mere acquisition and accumulation.[1]

Restructuring class and privatising citizenship

Not surprisingly, economic structural adjustment had brought with it a restructuring of class within traditional societies, the implications of which have not really begun to be analysed. A society's political-economic structure determines the distribution of wealth, and the distribution of the labour involved in producing that wealth. Structural adjustment, often presented as a technical matter, a mere refinement of an existing, natural system, actually represents a fundamental transformation for most societies in the world, including the industrialised nations of the North. Structural adjustment – and more specifically the neo-liberal economic ideology that underpins it – formally rejects the notion of the 'commons' and the 'commonweal', the well-being of the community as a whole. It reduces the role of the State in promoting the economic welfare of the citizen, and a fair distribution of the common wealth of the nation through basic services such as health care and education. It also declares the logic of the market – and, in particular, the global market – as the motor of society, rather than the logic of society itself determining the mechanisms of the market and the economy. This fundamental inversion increasingly isolates and marginalises those already remote from prevailing market mechanisms, and promotes the concentration of wealth in fewer and fewer hands. It also makes redundant and obsolete the skills and products of entire strata of society, particularly primary producers – farmers, herders, fishers, foresters, miners, artisans – essentially making them economically 'useless' and, therefore, 'class-less', and rendering them economic outsiders even within their own society.

Structural adjustment has entailed the economic disenfranchisement of large swathes of entire societies – often a significant majority of the population – while at the same time promoting the emergence of a new and expanded 'globalised' and affluent upper-middle class, whose outlook and self-interest is influenced much less by local and national conditions than by international events and trends. With the withdrawal of the State from its role as the promoter and protector of general social welfare, and the privatisation of even the most essential social services, this emerging class can purchase all of the services it wishes – whether water or electricity, education or medical care – while the class-less have access to nothing, not even the resources required to respond to their most basic needs. To the limited extent that the State intervenes to provide any meagre assistance to those in need, it is dispensed as charity, not as an entitlement of citizenship.

The result of this restructuring is a formal, rationalised system which reinforces the structures of deep economic and social disparity, and through which the basic rights of citizens are privatised and commodified: available for purchase, but only for those with the means. And while the growing class-less majority are aliens even in their own land, often handled with hostility and aggression by the police and security forces of their countries, the internationalised affluent classes are virtual global citizens, sovereign in their own societies and internationally, easily able to turn their backs on the conditions experienced by those left behind.

De-ruralisation

The most profound change in most societies in this period has been the transformation of largely rural agricultural economies and ways of life. The countryside is being transformed, common lands systematically privatised, peasants driven from their lands, and agriculture concentrated, industrialised, and export-driven. The same process is destroying coastal fishing communities and other primary producers. Those who become socially and economically dislocated drift to the cities and across borders to join the tens of millions of rootless people forced into the international wage economy.

Diminished food security

The triumphant rhetoric about the benefits of globalisation and the integration of global markets implicitly and uncritically assumes that food security has been achieved, and that this new reality benefits everyone. But the bounty benefits only those with access to this food, and with the money to pay for it. For others, there is no such bounty, and often it is their deprivation that subsidises the choices that the affluent urban classes take for granted.

In reality, the world's food supply is less secure today than ever before, even with the remarkable increase in production that has been achieved in the past 50 years. Certainly today there is enough food produced for all; indeed, in many sectors there is vast over-production. At the same time, this unparalleled production devastates landscapes, local markets, and livelihoods. It is a manifestation of the contradictions inherent in global food systems that threaten the security of most poor people every day.

Gains in food production have been achieved through intensive and concentrated cultivation based on chemical inputs, genetic engineering, and monoculture. This process has been exhaustively documented by the Rural Advancement Foundation International (RAFI), and others, most recently in the successful campaign against Monsanto and its 'Terminator' technology – which ultimately saw Monsanto publicly withdraw this technology in early October 1999[2] — and the on-going campaign on the broader issues of genetically modified (GM) food. The resulting loss of genetic diversity and wasting of landscapes is making all basic foodstuffs vulnerable to catastrophe. The cost in terms of lost livelihoods and generations of farming wisdom is even more catastrophic. Tens of millions of small farmers around the world have been driven off the land by the unrelenting competitive pressure of industrial agriculture. Turning our backs on centuries of tradition, knowledge, and stewardship of the land, we are entrusting global food security to a coterie of unaccountable global corporations, such as Aventis, Monsanto-Upjohn, Bayer, Dupont, and Syngenta (Novartis). In a global system that is driven by commercial logic, and where governments have abdicated responsibility for ensuring the basic well-being and livelihoods of ordinary people, food distribution is left to the market. Those driven out of the market – and those who were never part of it in the first place – go hungry.

Internalised social conflict

It is not surprising, given the developments outlined here, to see the phenomenon of conflict and violence in nations across the globe; it is to be expected that the poorer and more decaying the society, the more widespread and horrible the violence. This is one of the most tragic effects of the 'localisation' that comes with globalisation. The contradictions of wealth and power that are manifest internationally are internalised intensely in each country, and at the local level within each country, just as the structures of disparity are manifest both nationally and locally.

Conflicts thus emerge among and between both those who have nothing left, and therefore nothing to lose, and among those who, in the context of the prevalent vacuum in governance, fight for control of the spoils of the devastation caused by the ravages of globalisation. The conflicts that catch international attention are described in many ways, but most often focus on the characteristics of the populations involved, rather than on the root causes of the violence. Internal conflicts are usually described as being tribal, ethnic, or religious in nature, as though primordial antipathies – often fantasies of colonial history rather than real historic antipathies – are merely recurring.

At base, however, it is the fact that contracting opportunity and deepening economic and social crisis inevitably both consolidate local community identity and heighten differences – real and imagined – among those in crisis. The targets of the frustration may be marked by differences – of ethnicity, religion, or origin – but it is not the differences themselves that are at the root of the hostility and violence. Rather, it is poverty, despair, and lack of any reasonable horizon of prosperity and hope for a humane future that are the underlying causes: the dehumanisation that comes with the accumulated erosion of livelihood, community, and culture. It is this dehumanisation that is the legacy of the restructuring enforced by the last decades of the 'development era'. The violence that scars the landscape of so many blighted nations is a predictable outcome, all the more stark because it was predicted, although the official record still ignores the cause.

The other element of this phenomenon is an apparent resurgence of nationalism and fundamentalism. Again, as globalisation proceeds, we see the factionalisation of nationalism and fundamentalism into smaller and smaller local units of sectarian identity, each exploiting the disenchantment and disenfranchisement of people abandoned and set adrift by the structures of governance and power that once guaranteed at least stability and place, if not prosperity. Nationalist and fundamentalist leaders easily exploit dislocation and alienation by casting 'the other' in the role of scapegoat and promising at least a clear identity and the possibility of opportunity in a landscape cleared of competing claims to scarce land and resources.

This process is deepened by the fact that when the opportunities for legitimate economic enterprise are destroyed, they are often replaced by the illicit, especially when the illicit is both the sole avenue into the global marketplace, and immensely profitable. This is most clearly seen with the production and marketing of narcotics, but increasingly involves the trafficking of human beings, which according to the UN will soon be more profitable than drug trafficking. Control of the mining and international marketing of precious minerals, of trees and lumber, and even of the land itself, is also critical in many local conflicts, as are sales of and control over other commodities.

Global apartheid and the diaspora of the poor

In all of this, one of the noblest human instincts – to move on, to explore, to pioneer, to settle and resettle – has been perverted as never before. People, families, and entire communities have been forcibly dislocated by the processes described here. Migration is ever increasing, from countryside to city, from traditional environments to hostile urban slums, across borders and across continents. Untold numbers of people are homeless, often stateless, without identity or identification. A small minority are among the official toll of refugees, the almost 15 million people who are presently the titular wards of the UN High Commissioner for Refugees (UNHCR). At least ten times this number are internally displaced within scores of countries that are racked by internal violence. These people are officially protected and assisted by no one, and often harassed by the State and other contending actors in local power struggles.

But the largest number of displaced communities and individuals are entirely anonymous, uprooted by the social upheaval of economic 'restructuring', on the move to earn the money needed to live and be able to provide even the tiniest opportunity for their children to build a different life. These are the ones who are often called squatters and itinerant workers in their own countries and 'migrant labourers' abroad. Most often they are 'illegals' – illicit human beings, with no rights nor protectors, unwelcome at home, unwelcome abroad, undesirables without place or name. These are the ones who pay the heaviest price for the new world that is being advertised for the new global citizen, but who will never reap the benefit from the restructuring that has uprooted them. A bitter irony is the fact that it is precisely the notion of national 'sovereignty' that allows governments to control the movements of their own citizens, including their right to leave the country or return, as well as to prevent the internal migration of others fleeing violence, repression, or economic hardship in their homeland. While sovereignty is being ceded on all fronts that could assist the poor and promote local development, it is still used to rationalise the arbitrary use of extreme coercion – with virtually no accountability to international sanction or standards – in order to restrict and control the movement of people. In the reality of globalisation, the movement of goods and money is free, but the movement of people is more restricted than ever before – except for the new globalised élite.

A particularly heinous variation in the dynamics of migration and coercion at the dawn of the twenty-first century is the trade and traffic in human beings, now one of the world's largest and most profitable illicit commercial ventures. This trade is dominated by the trafficking of people as indentured labourers, often in hazardous and illegal conditions, and bereft of the minimum of decent conditions or protection, forever indebted to the traffickers and their 'employers'. In its most extreme form, trafficking includes outright slavery, including sexual slavery, which entraps hundreds of thousands of young women annually.

The feminisation of poverty

It is no secret that where there are poor people, the majority and the poorest among them will be women and children. This pattern is as old as history, rooted in structures of patriarchy and male domination, reinforced by women's economic dependence and entrenched gender roles, and enforced by their vulnerability to pervasive domestic and sexual violence.

Modern social and economic restructuring has accentuated this historic injustice. It has fundamentally ruptured the very heart of traditional communities that for women – even in poverty and amid entrenched historic gender-oppression – were a home and haven. And it has undermined specifically the kinds of agricultural production and processing that are the mainstay of hearth and home, the labour for which is provided in the main by women worldwide. The poverty that is deepened and rationalised within the new world economic order therefore particularly affects women and the children whom they have chosen to protect with their own lives. The destruction of communities and the subsistence activity that sustained them, and the transition to cash economies, has inevitably affected most those with the least money and economic power and the least possibility of moving into the cash economy. This vulnerability is intensified by the hard fact that women, often entirely abandoned and on their own, are left with – and embrace with their humanity – the responsibility of looking after children, no matter what circumstances the world has laid at their feet. It is women who assume primary responsibility for the survival of their families, and for the restructuring and reconstructing of the life of the family in the situations of dislocation and displacement described here. Moreover, these women continue to face double – and sometimes triple – social and economic discrimination: as poor and dislocated people, as women, and often as indigenous people.

It would be a mistake to consider women only as victims of these processes. The shared experience of women is that the critical circumstances of war, of economic crisis, of social and natural disaster, all provoke a profound questioning of a social order that manifests itself not only in the misogyny and gender-oppression that they experience, but also in class, cultural, racial, ethnic, and generational conflict. As women have faced violence, insecurity, loss or destruction of their accustomed environment and lives, they have also become protagonists in the struggle to recover decent living conditions, and have taken on new roles both within their families and their communities and towards government authorities. This protagonism of women uprooted and abandoned is a fundamental factor in the resurgence of citizen action described below.

The resurgence of citizen action

As argued earlier, one of the most significant elements of globalisation has been a concomitant and intense localisation of both the impacts of globalisation themselves and the organised response to them. Indeed, the development that may ultimately have the most far-reaching and long-lasting implications is the resurgence of popular organisation and the mobilisation of communities of interest in campaigns of dissent, resistance, and proposition within what has come to be referred to as 'civil society'.

For the purposes of this essay, civil society – a term which, like globalisation, denotes and connotes a wide range of meanings – refers to the sum of citizens organised into formal and informal associations to contribute to their collective lives and communities and to propose and contest social and economic policies with their fellow citizens, their governments, and the State.

The abdication of government and retreat of the State from its role in social welfare and development has led local communities to come together to analyse and create their own solutions to the crises they are experiencing. Citizen action, and greater involvement in governance right down to the municipal level, has reached unprecedented heights and is fast becoming one of the most important political realities around the world. As this grassroots organisation consolidates, we are now seeing local associations reach out to others in their communities, and beyond to the national, regional, and international levels in strategies of mutual support and collaboration on major issues such as ending violence and constructing peace; enforcing government and corporate accountability; promoting democratic governance, human rights, social equity, and economic opportunity; protecting local food security and traditional primary producers; and conserving the natural and cultural environments.

In a remarkable and dynamic development, this element of localisation is achieving a critical mass, such that local groups are increasingly ready and able to take advantage of the shrinking world and the technical tools of global communications in order to reach out for support for their own immediate issues and strategies, and to join with others in solidarity and common cause based on shared issues. This intensification of community has coincided with the expansion of opportunity for collective and collaborative action at wider levels of abstraction both nationally and internationally.

It is simplistic to refer to this process as the 'globalisation of civil society', as some in the NGO world have rather triumphantly asserted. It is, in fact, a profound challenge to the essence of globalisation, and those who promote a global civil society misapprehend and betray the profound roots and essential impetus of this new movement. Rather, what we are seeing is the *amplification of localisation* through a process of concerted local, national, and international action. The focus remains particular, specific, and local; and the strength of community and the impacts of strategies are also local and particular. This is the significance – and the power – of this new civil resurgence.

Indeed, it is this very fact – that the locus and focus are very much local and national as well as international – that leads many governments to allege that such international co-operation to put pressure on local policies and practices is an assault on national sovereignty. They are beginning to feel the pressure and effect of increasingly concerted citizen action. Again, as in the case of the dilemmas concerning the ever-increasing migration of dislocated populations, in matters of citizen action and dissent we experience the belated recourse on the part of the

State to claims of national sovereignty in order to protect existing structures of privilege, even though sovereignty – indeed, responsibility and accountability – in all substantive areas of economic and social policy has been ceded. Sovereignty is at the forefront of the mechanics of social control, but yet is not defended in the arena of social development and self-determination.

Challenging the discourse

How are these phenomena described in the media and in the official discourse of policy makers and international agencies and institutions? Within what framework are the problems that we all face today defined and described? These questions are critical, because how the world is defined and described determines and limits the reality that will be acknowledged and the variables that will be addressed.

Inevitably, the prevailing framework within which world problems are described and analysed is that of 'modernity' and progressive history. The serious and articulate critique of modernity is still largely contained within intellectual circles and (post-modernist) cultural theorists, although its influence is increasingly felt within the 'Critical Theory' stream of political science and feminist social theory.[3] This said, the influence of post-modernism has inescapably seeped into mainstream discourse. The notion of 'discourse' itself is an important contribution, which acknowledges that there are many parallel and competing realities in the world, and the one that prevails – that is, the one that 'rules' – is the one that reflects and serves the interests of those who control how reality is described, what is seen to be 'true', and what is allowed to be talked about.

From this perspective, how are the global phenomena outlined above described in mainstream discourse? What is seen to be true, and how are we allowed to talk about these problems?

The modern age, which began with the Renaissance and so-called Enlightenment period in Western Europe, is now some 500 years old. It has reached its apogee with the extended industrial revolution, the third phase of which – the electronic revolution – we are in today. This (modern) period represents the hegemony of technological objectification of the world and knowledge, and has been marked by a hyper-rationalist, scientific, linear, and reductionist de-struction of nature. It is no coincidence that capitalism, industrialism, and corporatism have flourished in such an extreme and radical fashion in this age.

'International development', as announced 50 years ago by Truman and since promoted by international agencies, including the international NGO movement, is based in this linear and cumulative notion of history, and the complex set of assumptions about 'progress' that goes with it – including the bias of the 'scientific method', and the systems calculus that is used to measure and promote 'progress'. This is typified in 'strategic framework analysis' and its poor cousin, 'results-based management', presently imposed on the voluntary sector by public and private funders who are obsessed with 'inputs', 'outcomes', and 'indicators'. This ethos has been embraced by and is now aggressively – sometimes ruthlessly – promoted by senior managers in many of our leading NGOs, convinced that restructuring our organisations along corporate lines is the ticket to successful integration in the new trilateral global order that sees the public, private, and voluntary sectors somehow as partners in development.

Modernity, progress, and the project of development

The crux is in the paradigm of modernity and the concepts of progress and development themselves. The project of development and modernisation began with the conviction that there is a natural order, design, and progress in things and that humans have the capacity and responsibility to promote and direct progress through the application of science and technology. Hence progress is equated with technological invention and capitalist enterprise, industrial development, economic growth, and the expansion and integration of markets. These have come to be the essential human activities, the normal and natural vocation of all human beings and societies.

Development, and specifically international development as defined since Truman, is merely the concerted programme to bring the entire planet into one clear, concerted, and unified road of progress: the road of liberal capitalism. Within this framework, all problems and catastrophes that emerge within the project of modernity and 'progress' are seen as aberrations in the normal and natural course of things – indeed as abnormal – although these effects are not rare at all, but rather constitute the norm itself. They are in fact an element that marks the development era and its various strategies and false starts.

Yet, social, cultural, and environmental disaster continue to be described as deviations from the march of progress, rather than intrinsic to the project of global development itself. That 'development' is an imposition on those who are being 'developed', and that progress itself is often destructive of what already exists, while offering little to those dislocated by it, is not seriously considered, although the critique has been voiced by serious observers from the outset of the development project, and the effect has been evident for all to see from the beginning.

Fully 15 years ago, Sithembiso Nyoni, then of the Organisation of Rural Associations for Progress (ORAP) in Zimbabwe, declared that the poor are fighting 'an internationally well-organised system of domination and exploitation ... which would rather see the poor removed from the face of the earth than see them change their situation or have them gain real power over their own fate' (Nyoni 1987). She warned that 'we cannot reverse the process of underdevelopment by using the same tools, methods, structures, and institutions which were used to exploit and dominate the poor' in the first place.

Even today, although the wall has been irreversibly breached, and the negative effects of development practice, and progress itself, have come under more intense scrutiny, it is extremely difficult to obtain any more than lip-service to the proposition that the application of the norms and tools of 'progress' – often dangerous and destructive, and always only selectively beneficial – should be a democratic choice in the context of processes of self-determination, rather than an imposition from outside with the collusion of national élites who are already integrated within the global economy and political system.

The politics of utility

Within the discourse of modernity, how are the pervasively negative effects of 'progress' rationalised and justified? At the core of modernity is the ethics of utilitarianism. The criteria of politics and action are utility and pragmatism: *what is useful is true, and what works is good*. The utilitarian principle, 'the greatest good for the greatest number', replaces the golden rule of the ages, 'do unto others as you would have them do unto you', which can be re-phrased as 'guarantee for all what you expect as a right for yourself'.

Cloaked in the language of objectivity and good intentions, utilitarianism is promoted as democratic and inclusive, where the best thing possible is always done and the majority always benefit. On the contrary, it is most often undemocratic and exclusive, and always begins with the assumption that some people – a lot of people – must lose. Utilitarianism is a win–lose proposition, based on the explicit and calculated exclusion of some (often the majority) for the benefit of others, and the cost–benefit analysis is virtually always done by those in a position to ensure their own interests, or by proxies – including international NGOs – operating in professional capacities.

In the context of globalisation, this calculation is even more perverse. Although speaking the rhetoric of utilitarianism, no serious orthodox theorist or senior bureaucrat or politician any longer argues that the restructuring occurring in response to the forces of economic globalisation is beneficial for the majority living on the planet, or that the majority will ever benefit in their lifetime. The new utilitarian mantra is 'short-term pain for long-term gain', and the greatest number are acknowledged to be those 'suffering the worst effects' of restructuring, whose condition the development industry is continually scrambling to 'ameliorate'. Structural adjustment is justified by the promise that in spite of the pain and disruption caused for billions now living and struggling on the planet, the greater good will ultimately be available for a greater number: that is, those not yet born who will inherit in some dim future the brave new world that technology, capitalism, and corporatism create.

But of course, the real issue is: who benefits and loses today, and who decides? When a cost–benefit calculation is made, who makes the calculation, who benefits, and who pays the cost are critical issues. And when we presume to make this choice on some calculation of a greater good for a greater number, what of others – the lesser number – who not only do not benefit, but actually pay the freight for the rest of us, often at the cost of their communities, livelihoods, and their very lives?

The choice of who pays, and who is left out, at the table of globalised progress, is not haphazard. We know who they are, and their characteristics – race, gender, and class – and we know where they live. The sustained project of international co-operation and the international NGO movement must be to empower precisely those who are at the short end of the utilitarian equation, the lesser number – although, at almost three billion souls, they are virtually the majority on the planet – the permanently marginalised who are not scheduled today, or tomorrow, or ever, to be included in the greater good that utilitarian pragmatism and its corporate sponsors promise.

Point of view

The prevailing discourse of globalisation obscures the reality of poverty that continues and deepens for the majority on earth. More than three billion people suffer deep and unrelenting poverty. War and militarism hold sway, and authentic electoral democracy remains the exception rather than the rule. How this state of affairs is described and defined depends upon point of view, direct lived experience, and perceived interests. The project of international co-operation for equity and global justice has to be assessed from the perspective of those most directly affected. Many of these people do not believe that their poverty is a natural state, nor that some must always be poor. They do not believe that war is natural, and that war must always be with us. They do not believe that governance must be the domain of élites, or that tyranny is natural and inevitable.

The question of agency is critical here. People are poor because of the way in which humankind acts and behaves – that is, how we run our affairs, and in whose interests the world is organised and managed. Wars do not just happen: they are declared and waged by human beings. Tyranny does not just emerge: it is the brutal and intolerant exercise of power by a few people over the many. People are not simply poor: they are *impoverished*. That is, the affairs of humans are the acts of humans and the responsibility of humans. We either condone the way in which the world is organised and managed, or we change it. And if we wish to change it, then we must try to describe it accurately.

From this perspective, NGOs and those involved in international co-operation cannot abdicate our right and responsibility to speak out about our experience with the world. Nor can we allow ourselves to be silenced by some code of speech that speaks in the passive voice, and avoids recognising and describing 'agency' — that is, that the conditions which we deplore are created by the identifiable actions of real people, including ourselves.

The world is organised rationally and systematically to work the way it does, and is justified within a finely wrought ideological and moral framework. Real people – Presidents and Prime Ministers, corporate directors and clerks, bankers and traders, industrialists, managers, professors, government bureaucrats, and NGO managers – are the rational and intentional authors of our economic system, and articulate advocates of the ideological and moral framework that justifies and explains this system. At the international level, the World Bank, the IMF, and the WTO are rational instruments with clear policies, reflecting the priorities and interests of those who create and run them. The structural adjustment policies imposed on sovereign nations by these institutions, and the foreign policies of the governments that control them, have had real, demonstrated effects in the world. From the point of view of the international activist for social justice, it is necessary to speak out and to promote and support programmes to challenge and transform these effects, and to change the systems that destroy rather than develop human societies.

Still, there is an instinctive resistance to accepting the intentional and rational nature of these systems. There is resistance to the assertion that those who create and manage systems are responsible for their effects. There is resistance to the implication that we who participate in these systems, or observe them, without struggling to change them, are complicit in their effects. But from the point of view of those who are brutalised by global systems and their local inflections, evil received is evil done, and there can be no neutral act, regardless of the good intentions of those who engage in international programmes.

Diversity and homogeneity

Ironically, it is globalisation itself, in its manifestation of localisation, that is finally revealing the deep fault-lines in the development paradigm, and creating the opportunity for other perspectives and visions to emerge.

Modernity assumes homogeneity: the increasing convergence of quality and interest into one common, global, human future. Within modernity, diversity is seen as a deviation from the central axis of progress and so must be tamed and refined for the project to progress. At its inception, the quest for a unified theory of nature and a unified practice of human society was, and remains today, the impetus of modernism. The concentration of all human endeavour into one consolidated social and economic system is at the heart of the project of modernism. Indeed, some of the prophets of this final stage of the modern age have declared that, with the hegemony of liberal democracy and *laissez-faire* capitalism, the project is a success, and the 'end of history' has dawned.

In this context, while paying lip-service to 'difference' – the superficial characteristics and varying histories of groups – development programmes, including those of international NGOs, have never been patient with diversity. Diversity implies not only diverse pasts, but diverse futures: it assumes diverse visions of the world, of the meaning of 'progress', and of quality of life and ways of being. Diversity assumes self-determination. It assumes that no option is 'natural' and enjoys a special claim to absorb all other ways of being and systems of human community.

Due to the ways in which the effects of globalisation are localised, the social majority who are marginalised by it are reinforced in their diversity and in the particularity of the experience of resistance, adaptation, and survival. The social solidarity required among people in the isolation of their abandonment by the State and the mainstream economy nurtures the very diversity that globalisation promised to absorb and level.

Outside its margins, the influence of the system is marginal, and other norms and values emerge and are tested in the on-going dynamics of communal and personal struggle. With the increasing interaction among those marginalised by the new economic order, and the crisis of national governance, new social and political visions and values are being asserted as never before. The world has become more than a laboratory for political experiment and social engineering; it is becoming once again a garden of social and economic diversity and a celebration of human creativity and ingenuity. It is in retrospect no coincidence that this is happening precisely as the economic project of globalisation is approaching its own material limits. The legacy of this era may indeed be the end of the possibility for any single hegemony to dominate the earth again, since the intensified localisation that has accompanied globalisation has left communities of interest armed with renewed identity, a profound scepticism about absolutes and progress, and the tools to develop, defend, and assert their identity in the wider world.

The role of the voluntary sector

Within the above process there has also emerged an incredible amount of sophisticated, effective mobilisation within civil society around the world. Active, intentional citizenship is increasing, and is increasingly effective. Links between citizens, and citizens' groups – locally, nationally, regionally, and globally – are increasing. People are no longer satisfied to leave governance to the whim and will of politicians and bureaucrats and local party bosses. We are entering a new age of civil and political accountability.

This is the positive side of globalisation, a phenomenon that is largely invisible and only now beginning to be acknowledged and analysed. People are making huge strides in taking control over their own lives, although much of this activity is happening outside the mainstream consciousness and discourse. It is in this context that voluntary-sector agencies have a dynamic contribution to make if we can move beyond our meek and compliant humanitarianism and our cloak of 'neutrality'.

The politics of international co-operation – which means, or at least should include, radical politics – has been obscured by an emphasis on professionalisation and technique. The dilemmas of institutional viability have been reduced to questions of money and comparative advantage – that is, they have been constrained by corporate logic rather than the logic of a clear and explicit political project, vision, and role. Rather than challenging the way the world is, the tendency is to accept and adapt to – and therefore reinforce – the way the world is, as though nothing significant or structural can be changed, so it must be managed and ameliorated. Recall the 'inevitability' of globalisation, and 'the end of history' discourse.

Increasingly, the model for the 'successful' NGO is the corporation – ideally a transnational corporation – and NGOs are ever more marketed and judged against corporate ideals. As part of this trend, a new development 'scientism' is strangling us with things like strategic framework analysis and results-based management, precisely the values and methods and techniques that have made the world what it is today. The 'realist' ethos holds sway, and *Realpolitik* justifies all. It is all very pragmatic and utilitarian.

The role of the voluntary sector is fast becoming, in the new language, merely 'to ameliorate the worst effects', to care for those who cannot adapt, who are left behind, who 'are not prepared'. And in so doing, many in the voluntary sector have become deliverers of (charitable) services, partners of (downsized) government, and handmaidens to the (corporate) philanthropic sector, which sponsors charitable activity, often as advertising. Not only are people increasingly commodified, even in their poverty, but so too are our cherished voluntary organisations, which once were expressions of cultural and political participation.

To mediate this erosion of the original values of the voluntary sector, we have to identify and challenge the corporatisation of NGOs in the name of efficiency and effectiveness, and the utilitarian ethic that emerges from this trend and dominates practice in many NGOs – especially the leading transnational NGOs with their internationally promoted brand names. On the proposition side, we have to recuperate the politics of NGO activism, and the (original) notion of international co-operation as a profoundly political activity. We need to promote a new sense of *protaganismo*. We need a renaissance of transformative NGOs.

Our sector cries for a new season of proliferation, which would see the creation of a whole new generation of NGOs. We need new organisations, new forms, smaller and more political, value-driven, organisations, new voices, new methods, moved by the ethics of common cause and social solidarity. We need diversity, dissent, debate – indeed, a breakdown in the self-interested and stale consensus about the role of NGOs, and a resurgent passion among truly citizen-led voluntary organisations to create the world, and transform it in the interest of everyone on the planet.

We need to challenge some of the current notions of international civil society, and the role of NGOs as a partner of the State and of the multilateral regimes. We have to be critical and wary of notions of global governance, and especially of the idea that NGOs can or should be integral to governance structures. As always the questions are: In whose interest? In whose voice?

We need a renewed openness and space within the traditional NGOs to allow and encourage political activists, young and old, to challenge the hegemony of the professionals and the momentum of tripartitism.

The role of the voluntary sector is to give breath and heart to innovative and alternative ideas for developing and conserving creative, vibrant, tolerant, caring, and dynamic societies. It is a role of nurturing mutual support and social solidarity, of promoting values of social responsibility and reciprocity, of supporting and mobilising citizenship in the interests of the entire community. The essence of this role is participation, is activism – indeed, is citizenship itself. The essence of this role is not service provision, and is not technical support, which are the paths along which the preponderance of voluntary organisations in Northern countries, with the encouragement of government and corporate sponsors, have allowed themselves to be diverted.

The greatest dilemma facing an activist organisation in the domestic or international arena is that the voluntary sector itself has become an intrinsic part of the system that it was once committed to transform. Many mainstream leaders of NGOs have internalised the language and myths of social and economic conservatism. Many NGOs, indoctrinated in the assumptions of neo-conservatism, and convinced that 'globalisation' is inevitable and irreversible – that indeed, we are at the end of history – have joined with its acolytes, ironically without much critical analysis of what 'it' actually is or means. What the corporate PR manager understands implicitly as economic propaganda, NGO people often repeat as articles of faith.

Firoze Manji (1999), writing about the role of NGOs in Africa, says: 'If NGOs are to play a positive role, then it will need to be based on two premises: solidarity and rights.' He continues:

Solidarity is not about fighting other people's battles. It is about establishing co-operation between different constituencies on the basis of mutual self-respect and concerns about the injustices suffered by each. It is about taking sides in the face of injustice, or the processes that reproduce injustice. It is not built on sympathy, charity, or the portrayal of others as objects of pity, nor the arrogant self-appointment as trustees of the poor. It is not about fundraising to run projects overseas, but raising funds that others can use to fight their own battles. It is about taking actions within one's own terrain that will enhance the capacity of others to succeed in their fight against injustice.

The role of the voluntary sector is, fundamentally and inescapably, political, regardless of whether or not this is acknowledged and acted out explicitly. The critical and primary role of the international NGO movement should be to initiate and support actions that promote the right of all persons to be fully human and achieve their full creative potential, and to live creatively and actively as citizens in their communities, their countries, and their world.[4] Strengthening the capacity of marginalised people everywhere to influence the social, economic, and political structures that govern their lives should be the central focus of our movement in the early years of this new century.

The voluntary sector should be a garden of social innovation and change, a locus of organised resistance to and dissent from the excesses of the market and privilege – whether the privilege of class, of race, or of gender. Yet today, when we have such a critical innovative and transformative role to play, the mantra of the established voluntary sector is a new 'realism': the pragmatism of adaptation and 'social partnership'. The vision is not of change, but of charity. And if anything must change, it seems, it will not be the world: it will have to be those whom the world no longer needs or wants, those on the margins of society and the market. All of this is seen as natural, and those who challenge it are often described as unrealistic, ideological, outdated, strident, unreasonable, unco-operative – in other words, marginal.

In her keynote address to the Conference on Economic Sovereignty in a Globalising World, held in Bangkok in March 1999, Susan George declared:

No matter how many disasters of all kinds the neo-liberal system has visibly created, no matter what financial crises it may engender, no matter how many losers and outcasts it may create, it is still made to seem inevitable, like an act of God, the only possible economic and social order available to us.[5]

She continued:

> Let me stress how important it is to understand that this vast neo-liberal experiment we are all being forced to live under has been created by people with a purpose. Once you grasp this, once you understand that neo-liberalism is not a force like gravity but a totally artificial construct, you can understand that what some people have created, other people can change. But they cannot change it without recognising the importance of ideas. I'm all for grassroots projects, but I also warn that these will collapse if the overall ideological climate is hostile to their goals.

She closed her presentation by observing:

> We have the numbers on our side, because there are far more losers than winners in the neo-liberal game. What we lack, so far, is the organisation and the unity which in this age of technology can be overcome ... Solidarity no longer means aid, or not just aid, but finding the hidden synergies in each other's struggles so that our numerical force and the power of our ideas become overwhelming.

It has been said that politics is the art of the possible. On the contrary, politics *could* be the art of the possible. But historically, politics has largely been the business of persuading people that various transformative social visions and courses of action are *impossible*. However, if enough people share a choice, that choice is not only possible, it is inevitable. As Frances Ponge tells us, 'Beauty is the impossible which lasts'.

Many people sincerely believe that some things will simply never change, including many of the realities described in this paper, and that we must work within these constraints. I can only say in response that while we must obviously work in the context of these constraints, it is precisely those things that are believed will never change upon which we as change agents should most relentlessly focus.

Transformational activists, and effective transformational organisations, do not have to be marginal, and we should not allow ourselves to be marginalised. We do not have to be cogs in the machine.

The world is not the way it must be if it is to nurture and protect human health and prosperity. It can be changed for the better, and this can happen best through the direct participation of citizens collaborating to envision better ways, and mobilising to bring their ideas forward in the diverse theatre of proposition and debate that we know as civil society. This is not only necessary, but possible. The international NGO movement should re-affirm its commitment to it. This is our unique role.

Acknowledgement

This paper was prepared with the invaluable contribution of my colleagues at Inter Pares, who provided extensive critical suggestions on early drafts, and of Deborah Eade, whose comments and questions helped to sharpen the analysis as it was completed.

References

Esteva, Gustavo and Madhu Suri Prakash (1998) 'Beyond development, what?', *Development in Practice* 8(3): 280-96

George, Jim (1994) *Discourses of Global Politics, A Critical (Re) Introduction to International Relations,* Boulder CO: Lynne Reinner

Heilbroner, Robert (1996) *Teachings from the Worldly Philosophy,* New York: Norton

Hobsbawm, Eric J. (1994) *The Age of Extremes: A History of the World 1914–91,* New York: Pantheon

Manji, Firoze (1999) 'Rights, Poverty and Development: The Role of NGOs', mimeograph of paper presented at the Third International NGO Conference, NGOs in a Global Future, Birmingham, 10-13 January 1999

Murphy, Brian K. (1999) *Transforming Ourselves, Transforming the World, An Open Conspiracy for Social Change,* London: Zed Books and Halifax: Fernwood Books

Nyoni, Sithembiso (1987) 'Indigenous NGOs: liberation, self-reliance, and development', *World Development,* special issue Autumn 1987 (pp. 51-6), entitled *Development Alternatives: the Challenge for NGOs,* proceedings of a symposium held 11-13 March 1987 in London, sponsored by *World Development* and the Overseas Development Institute

Ramphal, Shridath and Ingvar Carlsson (1995) *Global Neighbourhood, Report of the Commission on Global Governance,* Oxford: Oxford University Press

Notes

1 The discussion of this theme in Esteva and Prakash (1998) is excellent.

2 For information on this campaign – and for much more on the corporate threat to food security and the environment – visit the website of RAFI (www.rafi.org). This website is in a class by itself, easily one of the best, most accessible, and most useful and informative on the internet.

3 An excellent treatment of this theme can be found in George (1994).

4 For an extensive treatment of this theme, see Murphy (1999).

5 'A Short History of Neo-Liberalism: Twenty Years of Elite Economics, and Emerging Opportunities for Structural Change', address by Susan George to the Conference on Economic Sovereignty in a Globalising World, hosted by Focus on the Global South, Bangkok 24-26 March 1999; see also Susan George (1997) 'How to win the war of ideas, lessons from the Gramscian right', *Dissent* 44(3).

Globalisation, civil society, and the multilateral system

José Antonio Alonso

Introduction: the scope of globalisation

At times, words seem to obscure rather than clarify ideas. As Goethe had one of his characters say: 'When the concept is lacking, a word always comes up to save the day'. In economic parlance, some words have acquired such symbolic power that they work as talismans: their mere mention seems to rule out the need for any further analysis. This occurs to a certain extent with *globalisation*, which has become a generic and universal term, used to refer to any factors of change in contemporary society. The word then loses any precise meaning. We therefore need to ask ourselves what the concept really means and implies.

Indeed, the root of the problem lies, at least among romance languages, with the word itself. Does the anglicism *globalisation* mean anything more than *internationalisation*? It would seem that *globalisation* seeks to refer to relations that are more intense and homogeneous among countries and social actors than *internationalisation* would imply. These connect not only across national boundaries, but also above and beyond the institutions – both State and cultural – upon which such boundaries were previously built. *Globalisation* clearly highlights the sense of the world as a system, as an 'entity to be organised', as Mattelart (1997) rightly pointed out. From this perspective, globalisation is more than the simple increase in the flows of trade, finance, or communication between countries. Rather, globalisation represents a new era in the world system, one that is characterised by the dislocation of national economies and nation-states, and their re-composition on the basis of global relations, in accordance with what the market demands.

From this perspective, it is clear that reality diverges from the idea that globalisation is already completed, which is how it is often presented. There is a sort of fetishism, to which some international organisations have contributed when they refer to global tendencies as though these implied the dismantling of the nation-state in the face of inexorable and irreversible market trends, as if globalisation was a *fait accompli*. A detailed analysis shows that globalisation is in fact a process that is asymmetrical, unequal, and certainly incomplete. It is *asymmetrical* because it does not affect all areas in the same way: while certain relationships (such as capital transactions) are highly integrated, others (for example, movement of people or access to technology) are governed by decidedly restrictive regulations. It is *unequal* because it does not affect all countries in the same way: while the degree of integration is high among industrialised countries, whole areas of the developing world – like most of sub-Saharan Africa – remain on the periphery of these trends towards progress and economic dynamism. It is *incomplete* because it is more an on-going process than a thorough-going reality: we should not forget that only one-sixth of the world's production is involved in international trade, nor that most of the national savings of any country in the world are invested in its own domestic market, to take just two examples from the economic sphere.

In any event, we are not talking about an entirely new trend. Authors such as Rodrik (1997) remind us that the degree of openness in international economic relations at the beginning of the twentieth century was very similar to what we observe today, in real terms. It is also true that the coefficient of business openness (exports plus imports over GDP) of the group of rich European countries did not return to 1913 levels until the 1980s. These clarifications and caveats are not to deny, but rather to temper the inclination to view the current phase in the economy as being radically new and irreversible, or meaning that globalisation has been achieved in full.

Globalisation: process and ideology

Globalisation as a process

Like other change processes, globalisation fuels openly opposing positions. While for some it is the very expression of social and economic modernisation, for others it poses an obstacle to the governance of the planet and a threat to social cohesion.[1] While the former group demand that all countries fully adapt to the requirements imposed by international markets, the latter seek to resist this trend, preferring to maintain the scope of national decision making – and State power – of an earlier era. Neither of these options is very convincing (Touraine 1999). There is no reason why recognising the growing presence of a global market should mean that we renounce the possibility of any co-ordinated social action – that is, public action – outside the market. Nevertheless, the scope for such action is much narrower today than it was 50 or 100 years ago.

Globalisation in any case cannot be ascribed in terms of simple value-judgements: it is a process that carries possibilities and threats alike. Possibilities, because it should not be forgotten that the broadening of international markets, which was one of the mainstays of the globalisation process, laid the foundations for one of the fastest periods of growth in the world economy, between 1950 and 1973. The increasing convergence among the developed economies over the last few decades is fuelled by the same trend, and has hinged crucially upon the spread of technology and the opening of borders fostered by moves towards globalisation. Its effects are not limited to the developed countries but have also reached some of the Pacific Rim and Latin American economies. Last in this list of positive factors associated with globalisation is the emergence of an increasingly widespread awareness of what is involved in good governance of the planet and of the rights upon which international action must rest. The series of international summits promoted by the UN, and the fact that a new more precise definition of human rights is beginning to take root, are evidence of this awareness.

At the same time, it must be acknowledged that globalisation also entails threats and risks. Globalisation broadens the bases for economic growth, while at the same time stimulating the polarising dynamic that is implicit in the market economy. The opening up of the economy stimulates processes of economic convergence, but it also fuels the various phenomena of exclusion of those areas or regions that lack the wherewithal to take advantage of the spread of technological changes which underpin such convergence. In addition, opening up to international markets gives a new base for economic dynamism, but this growth also implies greater instability, in that the economy becomes more vulnerable to international pressures, speculation, or market contagion. And in the end, globalisation reduces the scope for State-level decision making and forces governments to justify their interventions in the domestic economy, since these interventions may jeopardise social cohesion at the national level. Thus while on the one hand globalisation raises expectations of income redistribution, on the other hand social spending is reduced, and societies become more unequal.

None of these perverse trends can be viewed as being historically predetermined or inevitable: they are simply risks that need to be countered by active policies to avoid or minimise these risks. There is room both for political decisions and for social policies, even though the weakening and streamlining of the State, and the reduction in its scope (which often go hand in hand with globalisation), diminish the chances of deliberate corrective action in this field.

There is one last aspect of globalisation worth highlighting: its tendency to promote excessively restrictive policies in terms of economic management (Todd 1999). In the context of the nationally regulated post-war economies, the dynamics of demand became a relevant factor in explaining growth. Public spending, through social policies derived from the 'Keynesian pact', implies regulating the economic cycle. The problem is that some of these regulatory possibilities have been lost as a result of globalisation. Two of the instruments of Keynesian intervention – income policy and State activism – have only limited effectiveness when an economy is totally open to international competition. Faced with permeable national boundaries, the tendency is to adopt economic policies with a restrictive bias: restricting demand, controlling costs, reducing public expenditures, and placing principal emphasis on the control of inflation. This search for stability is a process that finds its justification in the need to be as competitive as possible in the international market. But what might be considered a reasonable therapy for an individual country tends to have perverse effects for everyone when it is adopted universally. Economic management is thus imbued with a recessionary bias. Naturally, these restrictions affect the least-developed countries the worst, even though they are precisely the countries that most need a dynamic environment to stimulate growth.

The ideology of 'global'

Even if the 'globalised world' cannot be said to be a fully fledged reality, we can argue that it has given rise to a particular form of ideological outlook which is widespread throughout the world today. It is an ideology that extols the market as the only efficient mechanism for economic distribution and social co-ordination. It thus also views the existence of a single market for the whole planet, without any interference in the free interaction of its constituent parts, as being the height of modernisation and progress in an open and efficient world. The assumption that what is 'global' is also automatically efficient, as an apparently irrefutable argument, does not allow space for examination. This historic fatalism leads to the spiritual and political dislocation that are notable characteristics of modern societies: government and civil society appear impotent and perplexed when confronted with a process which is portrayed as irresistible and irreversible.

Nonetheless, it is worth noting that in every society the processes of distribution and social co-ordination are a combination of three complementary mechanisms and not one, as the globalisers claim. These are the *market*, i.e. distribution through competitive pricing; the *hierarchy*, i.e. distribution through organisational processes; and the *values*, i.e. distribution as a response to accepted ethical principles (Anisi 1992). In every society a combination of these three forms of social co-ordination and distribution exists, and no single form has the unique capacity to mould the social fabric. The greater efficiency of the hierarchy as compared with the market in realising certain transactions has been sufficiently studied by the institutional school (Williamson 1975 and 1985). To these must be added the relevance of values in uniting people, as reference-points for their decisions and for co-ordinated social action. The relative weightings of these three dimensions vary, depending upon the context (see Figure 1), but all three are present in every setting. Even in the business world, for instance, a company operates in the market by buying and selling products in competition with its rivals; it is organised internally in accordance with hierarchical principles – authority – to co-ordinate decisions; and it promotes corporate values among its employees to bring their work into line with the corporate objectives. The characteristic of global ideology – a version of neo-liberalism – is that it seeks to reduce or convert such mechanisms into just one – the market – which is held to be the very expression of efficiency.

In short, globalisation is presented to us both as a type of false consciousness and as an on-going historical process, as both illusion and reality. Today, it is more vital than ever to shatter this illusion, in order to preserve our capacity to act in the social sphere and influence the course of history.

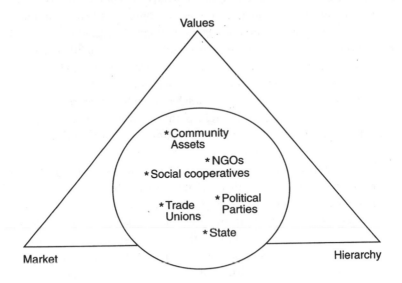

A single policy?

One of the signs of the conversion of globalisation into ideology is the standardisation of the economic discourse. Whatever the circumstances of a given country, the economic-policy recommendations seem to respond to only one pattern: commercial openness and financial deregulation, internal economic liberalisation, streamlining of the State, and disciplined macro-economic management. The constant repetition of this same remedy suggests that this official discourse is irrefutable. Some of these recommendations may well be relevant to the reality of a specific economy. The problem is the imperious, uniform, and irrefutable manner with which such reforms are demanded.

International organisations have played a major role in standardising economic discourse. They did not refrain from mystifying the success of the Southeast Asian countries, converting this experience into a model for reforms elsewhere. The problem is that the reality of the Asian experience has little to do with the reforms advocated in the 1980s by these organisations. Rather, the factors which explain the region's success include an active State, strategic use of selective protectionism, the policy of promoting human resources, and the degree of social equality achieved.[2] In fact, if we wanted to generalise, comparative case studies reveal the existence of four generic factors upon which most successful experiences of international development have depended, namely a high level of investment, a degree of macro-economic stability, human-resource development, and the establishment of sound and efficient institutions for the management of conflict (Rodrik 1999). All these factors were alien to World Bank and IMF policy recommendations, and in some cases even openly contradicted their policy advice.

However, beyond this list of common factors, what the study of history shows us is that there is no single path to development. The paths towards progress followed by specific countries at various times have diverged greatly. There is no theoretical or empirical foundation for the argument that there is but one single and universally valid body of fixed prescriptions. Each country must seek its own route to progress, based on its own assets, taking into account its own history and particular circumstances. In other words, in spite of globalism, there is still scope for national decisions: areas of discretion which can be used in defining a national development strategy which takes particular circumstances into account but which also defines its specific priorities in an autonomous manner. To deny that this is possible is not to yield to the realism of the supposed demands of the market, but rather to accept the fictions put forward by the globalising ideologues.

Globalisation and multilateral action

The need for global management

There are many problems that require a major role for multilateral action in the promotion of development in an increasingly globalised world. First, there is a notable asymmetry in the levels of effective integration between markets and countries, and the possibilities that the multilateral institutions provide for *co-ordinated international action*. But this co-ordination is needed more than ever, given the *interrelated nature* of different economies. Decisions taken in terms of a national economy are very easily transmitted to the international community. Nobody is free from this contagious effect, as seen in the most recent financial crisis. From this springs the interest in developing more efficient co-ordination mechanisms between countries. This co-ordination requires a multi-lateral institutional system with the ability to engage in global dialogue and co-ordinated management; and this in turn means tackling the problems entailed in the governance of the current international system.

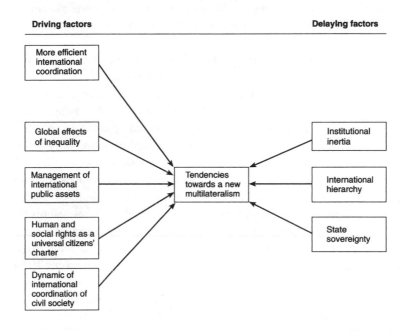

This multilateral system must also be entrusted with the production of those goods that, by virtue of the process of globalisation, can now be viewed as *international public goods*. That is to say, they are goods which are *non-excludable* (meaning there is no easy way to extract payment from the beneficiaries) and are characterised by the *non-competitive nature of benefits* (meaning that one user's consumption does not diminish the benefits available to others) (Kaul et al. 1999; Kanbur et al. 1999). The benefits of a pure public good are available to everyone – payers and non-payers alike – once the good is provided, and are thus susceptible to 'free riding'. Consequently, the management of international public goods cannot easily be left to the market. Nations tend to under-contribute to international public goods, unless there is some kind of organisational structure to co-ordinate their individual contributions. In this sphere, we might mention factors like political and financial stability, environmental policies, and the handling of problems associated with global ecological deterioration or the promotion of primary health. For this reason, the provision of such goods should be entrusted to a multilateral institution which can co-ordinate social action.

Third, the protagonism of multilateral action is also supported by the treatment that should be applied to problems which used to be considered local but which today are *problems affecting the management of the entire international system*. This is the case with many of the indicators of the profound and persistent inequality between peoples. Today, poverty is no longer conceived as an evil affecting only those who suffer it directly, but as a problem concerning everyone, since all people are affected by its consequences. The global problems include phenomena such as environmental deterioration, the pressure exerted by population growth on certain scarce or vulnerable natural resources, tensions deriving from migration, the spread of illnesses that can be prevented or treated, international insecurity associated with drug-trafficking and terrorism, natural disasters and regional armed conflicts. Though not caused solely by poverty, all of these feed off the destitution in which much of the population of the developing world lives. All of these are problems which affect the international community as a whole and whose solution goes beyond what any one nation is capable of doing, however powerful. It requires concerted action on the part of the international community to address the underlying causes of many of these ills, which are rooted in underdevelopment and poverty.

A further expression of this sense of the globalising world can be found in the UN-sponsored series of *world conferences and international summits* which, in a concerted fashion, began to analyse the main issues posed by development itself. A rather imprecise, but nevertheless useful, set of doctrines emerged on how to approach the problems of development, which in turn led the way to a body of consensus-based commitments, some more precise than others, on a range of issues. Perhaps the clearest expression of this shared commitment was at the World Conference on Human Rights which took place in Vienna in 1993, where definitions were reached on the universality, indivisibility, and interdependence of the civil, cultural, economic, political, and social rights of all people (including the 'right to development') as inalienable and intrinsic to all human beings. This principle was later reaffirmed at the Social Summit in Copenhagen in 1995. Essentially, a set of rights that are intrinsic to all human beings was defined, a sort of citizens' charter that transcends borders, nationalities, races, and religions. Hence, the promotion of these rights was no longer to be viewed as a generous and discretionary act on the part of States, but as an international obligation that is binding on all countries and peoples.

However, this new global framework for defining both the problems deriving from underdevelopment as well as people's rights clashes with the preferably bilateral – and discretionary – character of international action in this field. The development-aid system was born in a world of nations, as part of the bilateral policies of the industrialised States, who would freely decide upon the quantity, composition, and purpose of allocating such resources. This way of structuring the aid system runs up against the increasingly global nature of the problems that aid seeks to tackle, and the universality of the right to development held by citizens of the South. It is therefore necessary to give new impetus to multilateral action, if we want to be effective in achieving a more just and integrated world: an impetus that must be preceded by thorough reform of the multilateral system in force today (see Figure 2).

Three stages of multilateralism

The need for a such a programme of reforms is prompted by persistent calls, as much from inside as from outside, to address the mismatch between the real ability of the multilateral system and the demands and responsibilities facing this system in the real world. Over the last ten years there have been a number of particularly creative proposals for reform of the UN system. These include the reports of Urquhart and Childers (1990); the proposals of the UN Association in the USA (Fromuth 1988); the work of the 'Inter-governmental Group of High-Level Experts' – the group of 18 – created by the General Assembly in 1985 (Bertrand 1988); private initiatives, such as that carried out by Khan and Strong, which took shape in the 'Davidson Report' (Lyon 1989); and the ambitious work of the so-called Nordic Project, sponsored by Denmark, Norway, Finland, Iceland, and Sweden. To these largely thwarted proposals must be added the initiatives directly sponsored by UN Secretary-Generals, including Boutros-Ghali's *Agenda for Peace* and *A Programme for Development*, and the recent *Renewal of the United Nations: A programme for reform* proposed in 1997 by Kofi Annan.

Thus, the relevant question is not whether a change is necessary, but rather the magnitude of this change and its implications. In fact, the institutions belonging to the UN system have gone through genuine restructuring and review of their functions over the last few years. The problem is, as Zoninsein (1999) notes, that the outside world has changed faster still. To understand the multilateral order that this changing reality requires, it is useful to refer to three categories based on those proposed by Robert Cox (1992), in setting out the different stages through which multilateralism has passed.

Hegemonic multilateralism

The basis for the multilateral system as we know it was forged in the period immediately following the Second World War, reflecting the conceptions and correlation of forces of the day. It thus gave rise to *hegemonic multilateralism*, which was profoundly shaped by the bipolar world of the post-war period. Within each of the two opposing blocs, a very defined international hierarchy was maintained, set up in a vertical manner and equipped with mechanisms to enable each of them to encourage other countries to join their camp and also to force their allies' compliance. The clash between the two blocs permeated every international confrontation, and so conditioned how each side would respond to every international issue.

The balance of forces between the two superpowers constituted a form of mutual deterrence and a way to contain conflicts; and was a major factor in ensuring cohesion among the countries making up each bloc. In fact, the dynamic of confrontation – the 'enemy without'— made it easier for each member to identify its interests with those of the bloc as a whole, and in turn with those of the hegemonic power. It should be said, however, that the co-ordinating role taken on by the USA within the West was a spontaneous and not a forced outcome of this bipolar structure of contained confrontation.

Such a world order seeks to promote greater economic integration in the North as a prerequisite for economic growth among the members of each respective grouping. Hence the system of fixed exchange rates was set up to facilitate monetary stability, the IMF was established to support this system, and GATT was created to encourage liberalisation and multilateralism of commerce. It is arguable how far these regulatory systems were coherent and rational, but there is no doubt that they contributed to bringing about the period that saw the most intense economic growth ever seen in the West, between 1950 and 1973.

At the time, the designers of the institutional framework were quite happy to allow the South to be cast as subordinate within the international order. The developing world was thus not invited to take part in designing the newly emerging international order; and the South was not fully integrated into any of the most relevant international mechanisms. Rather, the developing countries joined the established order as subordinates, and depended on the discretion of the industrialised countries to concede them any involvement on the international scene. International development aid represents one such concessional mechanism. In fact, the system of development aid began as a function of the newly established order, an instrument to encourage internal cohesion within each bloc by reducing the tensions which might be generated by inequalities in the economic and social situation of the respective member States. This task was all the more necessary, bearing in mind the context in which aid began, which coincided with the great wave of decolonisation as many of the former colonies in Africa, Asia, and the Caribbean gained independence. To ensure that this process would not encourage centrifugal forces within either bloc, it was necessary to introduce mechanisms – such as aid – that expressed the commitment of the countries of the North to the future destiny of a disadvantaged South.

Diffuse multilateralism

The world at the close of the 1980s was very different from that in which the international order was set up in the post-war period. Among the various changes, three seem particularly relevant.

- First, the world changed from being a bipolar world to one in which at least three major blocs can be discerned in terms of the concentration of economic and political power: North America, Europe, and the Pacific. Each of these is in turn made up of a constellation of countries, linked through very different mechanisms. The tension between these blocs is very different from that of days gone by. It is marked more by rivalry than by confrontation, the struggle being directed towards the business and technological spheres, much more than towards ideology or military strength.
- Second, there have been notable advances in the process of integration between markets and countries across national boundaries: a process which, though most evident in the business sphere, is most acutely expressed in the areas of finance and communications. Given that co-ordination mechanisms have not been developed alongside these

processes of change, economic instability today is much greater than in the past. This instability affects all countries, whatever their level of income, but has the severest impact on the developing world, which, with remarkable effort and all too understandable limitations, has succeeded in entering the international market.

- Third, the South has become visibly and increasingly heterogeneous, so that there are growing differences in the socio-economic conditions of different countries in what used to be called the Third World. It is no longer possible to think of developing countries as representing one single reality to which one single diagnosis and one single therapy can apply. On the contrary, they are a very heterogeneous set of countries, representing societies with a variety of needs and opportunities for future growth.

These changes were significant enough to affect the institutional and operational bases of the earlier form of multilateralism. The system itself was introducing changes in its structure, in order to adapt to these new circumstances. Some of these alterations were the result of a tacit process of change, such as the shift within the IMF's role towards stabilisation programmes for developing countries. Others derived from more explicit options, such as the collapse of the system of exchange agreed in Bretton Woods, or the search for more efficient co-ordination forums like those provided by the G7. Others emerged as a result of the response to unexpected crises, such as the redefinition of NATO's activity, following its military intervention in Kosovo.

There are two basic points to make about this phase of *diffuse multilateralism*: the first is that US hegemony is not guaranteed, since it is no longer the spontaneous outcome of the logic underpinning the international system. The second is the mismatch between the co-ordination that the new environmental conditions demand, and what the current multilateral system can offer. If the former point tends to encourage the USA – and its most immediate neighbours – to seek new mechanisms to preserve its leadership, the latter calls for international co-ordination that is as broad and inclusive as possible, given the growing interaction between countries in a globalising world. Clearly, these two objectives are somewhat contradictory: to preserve the hierarchy, exclusion is necessary, but to govern the world today depends on greater inclusion and co-ordination. This is why the tendency has been to opt for hybrid formulas of limited co-ordination, where this does not entail questioning the hierarchy. Regionalism is one such formula, though perhaps the most obvious example of limited co-ordination is the G7. The problem is that, while these options may well be efficient in maintaining the hierarchy in international relations, they are clearly incapable of meeting the equally important objective of international co-ordination. To overcome these inadequacies, a *new multilateralism* is needed.

New multilateralism

New multilateralism is as yet only a proposal for the future, one that seeks to respond to the contradictions within the existing multilateral system, and also embody the autonomous initiatives to generate international co-ordination currently being forged by civil society. The contradictions of 'diffuse multilateralism' have been referred to throughout this paper. Three are particularly serious.

- First, as has been emphasised above, is the contradiction between the level of integration that has been achieved and the degree of inequality between countries and regions. This extreme inequality is the source of problems affecting the entire planet, which can be properly resolved only by addressing the root causes.
- Second is the contradiction between the level of integration that now exists and the capacity to institutionalise concerted international action. The formulas for limited co-ordination, such as the G7, may be useful for preserving the international hierarchy, but they are only marginally effective as mechanisms for global governance. The recent financial crisis showed that everyone – North and South – can be affected by what initially appeared to be highly localised problems.
- Third is the contradiction between the emergence of global problems and the lack of international mechanisms for integrated management of public assets. The environment is perhaps the area that has seen the greatest breakthrough, although this is not to suggest that the situation is remotely satisfactory.

If these contradictions define the limitations of what diffuse multilateralism has to offer, there are current trends which hint at the possibility of an alternative multilateralism that is not conditioned on the mediation of the State. This multilateralism is rooted in civil society itself, whose autonomous international co-ordination initiatives it encompasses. There are numerous examples: professional organisations, interest groups, sports bodies, political and social forces, and development NGOs among others.

Because of these trends, 'new multilateralism' should keep four normative principles to the fore.

- First, instead of the hierarchical and exclusive multilateralism of the past, it must work towards a form of multilateralism that is both inclusive and democratic. Only the capacity to integrate the whole of the international community in a democratic way will enable it to distance itself from conflict-based solutions, and to find consensual ways to manage global problems.
- Second, this same democratic character brings with it the need to draw into the process of re-shaping the multilateral agencies both State and non-State forces and social sectors. The summits in Rio, Vienna, and Beijing saw the active participation – however imperfect – of civil-society organisations; and these experiences point the way towards a radical overhaul and renewal of the multilateral institutions.
- Third, the new multilateralism must build on a charter of human rights that transcends borders and social conditions of the individual person: a sort of universal citizens' charter. This will be a definition of human rights expressed not only in the sense of negative rights but also of positive ones,[3] relating to the social conditions of different peoples and the possibilities for their development.
- Lastly, the new multilateralism must be capable of taking on a wide agenda in line with the multidimensional character of the problems of global governance. What is needed is an agenda that can allow the market to operate in those areas in which it has a proven ability to bring about an efficient distribution of resources, but which retains the scope for well thought-out collective – international – action in the protection of the most disadvantaged sectors, the provision of public goods, and the management of the right institutional and regulatory climate within which to promote international development.

Human rights and new multilateralism

This new multilateralism will take a long time to come into being. Of necessity it must be the product of a gradual process of reform, and the adaptation of the existing multilateral system and the creation of alternative spaces for international co-ordination on the part of organisations that represent civil society, providing a space for voicing and defending their interests in an increasingly globalised world.[4] Particularly relevant is this second process of autonomous action by civil society, at the margins of – or rather beyond – what States do. Indeed, it is in the international projection of civil society that we find the dynamic *locus* for the gestation of a new multilateralism.

This is a process which should be firmly rooted in the idea of a kind of universal citizens' charter which defines and defends human rights – understood not only in the negative sense, as political and civil rights are defined, but also in the positive sense, such as basic social rights. The need for this new multilateralism to centre on this view of human rights responds to two basic considerations. First, it responds to what Plant (1980:38) has suggested as a necessary condition 'to do anything, to carry out any action or achieve any objective'.[5] Certainly, effectively guaranteeing those rights is a prerequisite for moral action; we need a definition of citizens' social rights which is binding upon the international community and not only on individual States.

Second, however, the new multilateralism has to build on this human-rights base in order to guarantee its fully inclusive and democratic character. In fact, in conceiving an international system of human rights, the old order might have generated some of the bases on which to found its own transformation. As An-Na'im (1999:209) argues, the rules and mechanisms of human rights can be conceived 'as a source of empowerment of civil society to articulate and promote its own demands and aspirations, at the same time as providing it with the means of the political struggle to make these effective in practice in order to reach a greater protection of their economic, social and cultural rights, just as of their civil and political ones'.

A final thought

This paper has argued for a programme of conscious action by civil society in the context of an increasingly globalised world. This is not to deny the advantages provided by such a world, but rather to underline the need for organised decisions and ethical values in ordering international relations. The programme that we envisage respects the capacity of the market to operate in those areas in which it has proved effective, but it rejects the idea that the market is the only legitimate institution through which to distribute resources and co-ordinate society. Our programme of action values the possibilities offered by the growing cross-border relations among a range of social actors, but also calls for the establishment of democratic, effective, and inclusive international institutions, in line with the international-level co-ordination and public action that the new world stage demands. A programme, in short, that depends upon the dynamic potential that would be unleashed by the full recognition, in all its dimensions, of human rights, including the right to development.

Notes

1 One example of the debate between these positions can be found in the conversation between Thomas Friedman, author of *The Lexus and the Olive Tree*, and Ignacio Ramonet, author of *Un mundo sin rumbo*, in the pages of *Le Monde Diplomatique*, October 1999.

2 This is one aspect in which, from different perspectives, the following, among others, agree: Amsden (1989), Wade (1990), Young (1995), Rodrik (1997), and Watkins (1998). It was also, finally, partly recognised by the World Bank (1993).

3 Human rights need to be understood, as Plant suggests, by the requirement for moral behaviour: 'The obligation to satisfy these particular needs has to be strict because it is impossible to understand that other obligations might be more important than the satisfaction of these needs, precisely because those who do not have their needs met are not able *ex-hypothesi* to carry out any other obligation, whatever that might be, or to achieve any other objective' (Plant 1980:93). (6)

4 For an alternative vision of the gestation process of this 'new multilateralism', see Zoninsein (1999) and An-Na´im (1999), both in Schechter (1999).

5 For an interesting discussion of the views held by social democracy and liberalism on this subject, represented by Plant and Hayek respectively, see Espada (1999).

(Translator's note: where a title or phrase has been translated from the Spanish which itself was translated from the original English, these translations are likely to differ from the original.)

References

Amsden, A. H. (1989) *Asia's Next Giant: South Korea and Late Industrialization,* New York: Oxford University Press

Anisi, D. (1992) *Jerarquía,Mercado Valores: Una Reflexión Económica sobre el Poder,* Madrid: Alianza Editorial

An-Na´im, A. (1999) 'Expanding the limits of imagination: Human rights from a participatory approach to new multilateralism', in Schechter (ed.)

Bertrand, M. (1988) *The Third Generation World Organisation,* Dordrecht: Martinus Nijhoff

Cox, R. (1992) 'Multilateralism and the world order', *Review of International Studies* 18 (April): 161-80

Espada, J.C. (1999) *Derechos Sociales del Ciudadano,* Madrid: Acento Editorial

Fromuth, R. (ed.) (1988) *A Successor Vision: The United Nations of Tomorrow,* United Nations Association of the USA, University Press of America

Kanbur, R. et al. (1999) *The Future of Development Assistance: Common Pools and International Public Goods,* Policy Essay, No. 25, Washington, ODC.

Kaul, I. et al. (1999) *Global Public Goods. International Cooperation in the 21st Century,* New York: Oxford University Press

Mattelart, A. (1997) 'La nouvelle idéologie globalitaire', in *Mondialisation: Au-delà des Mythes,* Paris: La Découverte

Plant, R. et al. (1980) *Political Philosophy and Social Welfare,* London: Routledge and Kegan Paul

Rodrik, D. (1997) *Has Globalisation Gone Too Far?,* Washington DC: Institute for International Economics

Rodrik, D. (1999) *The New Global Economy and Developing Countries: Making Openness Work,* Washington: ODC

Schechter, M. G. (1999) *Innovation in Multilateralism,* New York: UN University Press

Todd, E. (1999) *La Ilusión Económica: Sobre el Estancamiento de las Sociedades Desarrolladas,* Madrid: De. Taurus

Touraine, A. (1999) *¿Cómo Salir del Liberalismo?,* Barcelona: Paidós

Urquhart, B. and E. Childers (1990) *A World in Need of Leadership: Tomorrow's United Nations,* New York and Uppsala: Ford Foundation and Dag Hammarsjköld Foundation

Wade, R. (1990) *Governing the Market: Economic Theory and the Role of Government in East Asia,* Princeton: Princeton University Press

Watkins, K. (1998) *Economic Growth With Equity,* Oxford: Oxfam

Williamson, O. (1975) *Markets and Hierarchies,* New York: Free Press

Williamson, O. (1985) *The Economic Institutions of Capitalism,* New York: Free Press

World Bank (1993) *The East Asian Miracle: Economic Growth and Public Policy,* Oxford: Oxford University Press

Young, A. (1995) 'The tyranny of numbers: confronting the statistical realities of the East Asian growth experience', *Quarterly Journal of Economics* August: 641-80

Zoninsein, J. (1999) 'Implications of the evolving global structure for the UN system: a view from the South', in Schechter (ed.)

The World Bank, neo-liberalism, and power: discourse analysis and implications for campaigners

Andy Storey

Introduction

Since the beginning of the 1980s, almost all 'Third World' countries have undertaken programmes of economic structural adjustment, involving the liberalisation of market forces (such as abolishing price controls and trade barriers), currency devaluation, institutional reform (such as privatisation and the promotion of foreign investment), and stabilisation (especially reducing government deficits). The dominant forces in framing these adjustment programmes have been the World Bank and, in the case of stabilisation policies, the International Monetary Fund (IMF).

Intense debate rages over the record of structural adjustment. For those aspects of adjustment that have been successfully implemented, the record is, at best, patchy. White (1996) points out that, in the case of Africa, while stabilisation may have improved economic-growth performance in some countries – and even this is challenged in cases such as Mozambique (Hanlon 1996) – there is little or no evidence that the other components of adjustment have yielded positive results.[1]

Adjustment has generated a great deal of lobbying and campaigning effort on the part of NGOs around the world, aiming to highlight the claimed misconceptions, shortcomings, and failures of structural adjustment. This article addresses itself, in part, to that campaigning constituency. However, the central question addressed is not the impact of adjustment, but rather the reasons *why* adjustment took place, drawing in particular on methodologies of discourse analysis. Specifically, I try to explain the adoption by the World Bank of the discourse of neo-liberal economic reform. (I acknowledge that to talk of a *single* World Bank position or discourse is to oversimplify, though I think that the discourse of neo-liberalism has been sufficiently widely held and operationalised within the Bank for the simplification to be acceptable.[2]) I begin by examining the extent to which the Bank's adoption of a neo-liberal discourse has been formed through the interplay of the interests of various policy actors in 'developed' and 'developing' countries.

Factors forming World Bank discourse on economic reform

The influence of Northern governments and interests

Many critics of the World Bank have pointed to its role as, allegedly, an instrument of 'developed country' foreign policy in general, and of US policy in particular (Bello 1994). Gibbon (1995) describes how changing policies at the World Bank can be interpreted in terms of changing interests in the 'developed countries' (the North), especially in the USA. In the 1970s, according to Gibbon, the Bank focused on 'modernising' 'developing countries' (the South) through the promotion of commercial agriculture and industrialisation. This strategy, which tolerated a significant developmental role for the State and which could even countenance levels of protectionism and other such market distortions, required significant exports of capital (loans, aid, investment) from the Bank itself and from the North generally. Thus, Gibbon terms it a capital-export model, and argues that its emergence favoured a number of Northern interests, including the following.

- Private commercial lenders who wished to dispose of surplus deposits and who saw World Bank lending as offering a supportive framework (by developing industry, building infrastructure, etc.) for the deployment of their own loans to the South.
- Manufacturers in the North who wished to develop Southern markets for the export of intermediate goods, especially as recession in the North reduced demand for such goods there.
- Key elements within the US administration who saw 'development' as a way of combating communism without needing to resort to military options.

Gibbon argues that it was changes in these interests that underlay the World Bank's conversion to strict neo-liberalism in the 1980s.

For example, the debt crisis, specifically the threat of default, meant that private commercial banks began to prioritise capital-recovery over capital-export: stabilisation and adjustment had the effect (through measures such as generating government budget surpluses, and promoting exports) of releasing resources for debt repayment. Also, the election of Reagan marked a shift back to a more aggressive US foreign policy towards the South – the 'stick' once again becoming at least as popular as the 'carrot'. This was reflected in a 1980 US Treasury Department review of the World Bank, in response to criticisms from the Heritage Foundation and others that the Bank was too supportive of Southern 'socialism'. While this particular review 'cleared' the Bank of such charges, the right-wing attack upon it continued, leading the Bank to embrace neo-liberalism, in part 'to deflect Reaganite wrath and disarm other critics' (Gibbon 1995:129).

Against this backdrop, the interests of Northern manufacturing exporters became less influential as US policy prioritised the interests of banks, reflecting a perceived generalised shift of power towards finance capital at the expense of industrial capital and workers, and resulting in the estimated loss of hundreds of thousands of manufacturing jobs in the North as Southern markets contracted (George 1992: 93-109).[3] Gibbon's arguments relate to the emerging dominance of the current 'globalisation' paradigm – within which finance capital has exerted a profound influence (Martin and Schuman 1997) – which increasingly prioritised the ability of corporations to move their operations (and their capital) around the world. Against that backdrop, the perceived need to concentrate on the removal of national-level trade barriers (including exchange controls) emerged as a logical policy imperative.

Gibbon is not suggesting a conspiracy-theory explanation of changes in Bank policies, and the interests he identifies as critical may have worked their effects in a facilitative rather than directive way: for example, the constellation of interests which promoted the 1970s capital-export model proved successful because this model coincided with the Bank's institutional self-interest in boosting its lending. (Caufield (1997) also strongly emphasises the Bank's self-interest in shifting vast amounts of money, often on 'objectively' ill-conceived projects.) However, while plausible and persuasive, Gibbon's argument lacks (save in the documented case of the Reaganite offensive) a detailed description of the 'transmission mechanism' through which the interests that he identifies mould specific World Bank policies or shape specific discourses.

A very concrete example of such a 'transmission mechanism' is provided by Wade (1996) in his detailed dissection of how the World Bank formulated its official policy towards East Asian economic development in the early 1990s. Wade locates this policy-formulation process within the context of a debate between the Japanese and US governments about the appropriate role of the State in promoting industrial development, Japan arguing for greater recognition of the developmental potential of the State, and the USA arguing for thoroughgoing liberalisation. Citing the East Asian experience, Japan tried to persuade the Bank (more or less committed to the liberalisation line at this stage) to take account of some of the pro-intervention arguments. The Bank agreed to carry out a study of the topic – published in 1993 as *The East Asian Miracle: Economic Growth and Public Policy* – the result of which 'is heavily weighted towards the Bank's established position' (Wade 1996:5) and, therefore, the position of the US government. Wade provides a detailed analysis of how the final text of the 'miracle' report ended up being what it is, and how the US government was able to influence that final version both in direct and indirect ways.

Wade concludes that 'the Bank forms part of the external infrastructural power of the US state, even though it by no means bows to every demand of the US government' (1996:36). It is Wade's description of the way in which this power relationship is worked out in practice that is most relevant to our present discussion:

> The story of the East Asian Miracle shows the determining importance of essentially American values and interests in the functioning of the Bank. But the influence is exerted not mainly from the American government to the senior management of the Bank – if we look just at this relationship we see considerable autonomy, though the President has always been American. The influence comes partly through the Bank's dependence on world financial markets, and the self-reinforcing congruence between the values of the owners and managers of financial capital and those of the US state. It also comes through the Bank's staffing and professional norms. Not only are Americans greatly over-represented in the professional and managerial ranks but at least as important since the beginning of the 1980s is a second channel of influence – the conquest of managerial positions by economists, and the recruitment of economists, including from the developing countries,

predominantly from North American and British universities (virtually none from Japanese universities). This channel of influence is obscured by talking of 'professionalism' as a source of the Bank's autonomy, without also talking about the *content* of that professionalism and from which member state's intellectual culture it comes. (Wade 1996:35-6)[4]

A commitment to neo-liberalism can thus be interpreted as a *channel* through which the interests of particular powers (the US government and financial capital) are pursued. This channel may be at least as effective as the overt intervention of US government representatives in World Bank policy formulation. For example, the fact that 80 per cent of all World Bank economists in 1991 had been trained in US or British universities[5] (two-thirds in US institutes alone) may well exert a greater influence than any direct phone-call to the Bank President from the US Secretary of the Treasury (Wade 1996:15-6); although, as discussed below, there may be limits to the extent to which the advice of these economists is actually put into practice by loan officers (Wick and Shaw 1998).

According to Wade, the pressure for a certain type of conformity resulting from this 'economistic' culture is such that if economists 'were to show sympathy for other [non-neo-liberal] ideas ... they would be unlikely to be selected for the Bank, on grounds of incompetence' (Wade 1996:31). Reinforcing this pattern is the internal review and in-house editing mechanism through which a document is successively revised by ascending layers of the Bank's hierarchy, with each such layer likely to be more attentive to questions of 'orthodoxy' than that below it. This need not imply a conscious process of distortion, because the forces at work operate, as we have seen, through the channel of orthodox 'professionalism'.

Like Gibbon, Wade emphasises that the Bank also had its own institutional reasons for not wanting to stray too far from neo-liberal prescriptions, including the fact that the Japanese advocacy of State-directed credit programmes in Asia and elsewhere threatened to undermine the market for credit from the Bank itself (Wade 1996:15). Thus, for a variety of 'good organisational and political reasons' (ibid.:35), the World Bank ended up propounding neo-liberal doctrines.

The influence of Southern governments and interests: contesting and appropriating adjustment

While Northern governments and interests may be considered the originators of adjustment, Southern governments and interests are not passive actors in the process. They are not simply forced to adopt externally imposed policies over which they have no influence.

> An implicit or insufficiently explicit premise in studies of the
> political dynamics of adjustment is that economic shifts rarely
> are presented to the state in the form of an unambiguous 'stimulus',
> demanding an invariant policy 'response'. Rather, these events,
> in effect, are appropriated through the interpretative (ideological)
> capacities of domestic actors to reinforce their dominance, or else
> weaken that of rivals. Global shifts *signal* the need for internal
> adjustment, but these signals are converted by ideological mediation
> into programmatic *messages* to the citizenry as to the desired form
> the policy response should take. (Jacobsen 1994: 13)[6]

The type of reduction in State economic power envisaged by adjustment might certainly be expected to pose challenges to 'Third World' (Southern) rulers whose power has often tended to rest on the distribution of State patronage (Chabal and Daloz 1999: 121). Hence, a strategy of contesting adjustment on the part of such State élites is to be expected. In a number of cases, such a contestation strategy was successfully pursued. For example, in the case of Côte d'Ivoire, despite the World Bank's embrace of adjustment at an official policy level, the interests of the Bank administrators who dealt directly with the Ivorian government still lay in disbursing loans, with the result that the government often got away with not implementing the promised reforms (Wick and Shaw 1998). This issue of loan disbursement proceeding even when policy conditions have not been met is by no means unique to Côte d'Ivoire (Nelson 1995: 128).[7]

Rather than (fully) resist the implementation of (all aspects of) adjustment, certain State élites have been able to appropriate it and turn it to their own advantage. This is most obvious in the case of privatisation programmes, where élites have sold State enterprises to themselves and/or their allies (Carmody 1998: 37). Marren (1999: 4), for example, describes how the ruling Suharto family in Indonesia used privatisation to enhance their power: 'Deregulation ... also created growth opportunities for the ... private sector conglomerates and business groups owned by political families including that of President Suharto'. That adjustment can create new opportunities for élite enrichment is also argued by Hibou (1999: 74-5), who points to the role played by weakened regulatory mechanisms, abolition of exchange controls, emergence of new financial institutions, and other such characteristics of adjustment in facilitating a variety of new forms of fraud (see also Hall 1999).

The ability of long-established State-based élites to turn the language and practice of structural adjustment to their own advantage is well illustrated by President Houphouet-Boigny of Côte d'Ivoire. In response to World Bank advice and in the guise of disinterested economic rationality, Houphouet-Boigny dissolved various State companies, abolished some senior positions in the bureaucracy, and brought the Department of Public Works under Presidential control. In reality, each measure served to eliminate rival sources of accumulation and patronage which were within the State bureaucracy but were outside personalised, central control (Bayart 1993: 226). This interpretation of the Ivorian experience, taken together with the earlier description of resistance to adjustment in that country (see above), shows that strategies of contestation and appropriation are not mutually exclusive options.

The 'neutral' State and 'correct' policies

While the initial impetus to the economic reform programmes may have stemmed from Washington, a discourse is never entirely formed by its initial progenitors: it is created and recreated through practice, embedded in organisations and individuals at various stages of policy formulation and implementation. That process of practice and embedding involves, in the case of adjustment, a wide array of actors, some of them with very different interests and agendas.

In fact, a striking feature of adjustment is the extent to which a seemingly clear-cut set of policy prescriptions which would, on the face of it, seem likely to generate clear sets of winners and losers could be adopted by a variety of different actors for radically different reasons. World Bank economists who expressed belief in the efficacy of free-market economic policies obviously supported adjustment. Northern governments anxious to generate debt repayments to Northern financial institutions also had a clear interest in promoting adjustment. Some Bank administrators could get away with expressing nominal support for adjustment, while continuing to lend money to governments not implementing various components of adjustment. Sections of Southern

State-based élites could use adjustment for direct material gain. The discourse of neo-liberal economic reform has been appropriated and moulded by a diverse group of agents.

I argue that part of the reason for this plurality of appropriation and formation is the view taken of the role of the State within the rhetoric of adjustment. There is a growing literature on the extent to which international aid agencies – including the World Bank – tend to portray governments as apolitical, technocratic implementers of policy, with social divisions within a country downplayed or ignored. Ferguson describes how this worked to the government's advantage in Lesotho: the governmental bureaucracy was portrayed as a 'machine for delivering services', rather than as 'a device through which certain classes and interests control the behaviour and choices of others' (Ferguson 1990: 225). As a result, the government was able to use World Bank projects to reinforce its bureaucratic State power over rural areas.

Uvin analyses a similar process at work in Rwanda, when he talks of a 'development ideology' which the State promoted and to which international agencies subscribed:

> [This] basically consists of an argument that the state's sole objective is the pursuit of economic development for the ... masses; as a result, ... [everyone] interested in promoting development should work with the state to make that possible. This ideology legitimises the government's intrusive presence in all aspects of social life, and diverts attention from the very real differences that exist between different classes and social groups. In other words, it diverts attention from all things political, replacing them with a discourse of technicity and collective progress ... [T]his discourse has come to serve as a powerful tool for Third World élites, in their dealings both with their own populations and the international system.
> (Uvin 1997: 99-100)

As noted by Gibbon (1995) and others, the compatibility of the World Bank's discourse with the interests of governments such as those of Lesotho and Rwanda might have been expected to decline, given the anti-statist thrust of the adjustment policies recommended from the 1980s onwards. However, the adoption of the adjustment discourse did not, for the most part, alter the extent to which the State was seen as a neutral force, whose role was to implement policies in a rational, technocratic manner. Referring to the experience of adjustment in Africa,

Gordon notes: 'Ironically, despite their critique of the African state, donor strategies in practice complemented the apolitical rhetoric and hierarchical nature of the existing African regimes: and, in fact, sought to shift from one narrow focus of decision making, i.e., top politicians, to another, i.e., top technocrats' (Gordon 1996: 1529).

The architects and proponents of structural adjustment often saw the implementation of their programmes as requiring skilled (in terms of neo-liberal economics) ministers and civil servants 'detached' and 'insulated' from those 'interest groups' who would otherwise derail the necessary process of reform (Gibbon 1995: 137; Gordon 1996: 1528).[8] Bates exemplifies this tendency when he speaks of the desirability of creating 'strong economic bureaucracies ... able to resist distributive claims and to minimise economic distortions' (Bates 1994: 25). Sandbrook (1996: 8) talks of the desirability of 'technocrats and administrators ... [obtaining] the requisite insulation and competence'; for Sandbrook, the task of government is to 'mediate the many conflicts within society', which is a matter of enhancing 'technical and administrative skills'. There is an implicit assumption that technocrats – once safely ensconced in what Mkandawire (1998:27) describes as 'authoritarian enclaves' such as independent central banks – will neutrally administer the tenets of detached economic wisdom. These policies, however, can be perceived as neutral only 'with respect to those who already accept liberal principles' (Williams and Young 1994: 94).

Indeed, the conception of State neutrality is intimately related to the perceived political neutrality (or technical superiority) of the economic advice itself: the role of the State is to neutrally implement 'correct' (in an abstract sense) policies. Thus, insofar as Bank personnel analyse political issues in the context of adjustment, they tend to do so from the perspective of 'strengthening the domestic constituency for reform', promoting 'country ownership' of reform programmes, and creating the conditions through which governments can 'build consensus' for reform.[9] The actual content of reform is assumed to be beyond argument – the task of politics is simply to persuade people of the merits of implementing reform. To aid in this task, especially on 'complicated' issues like tax reform and trade policy, at least one Bank official recommends the strengthening of 'independent think-tanks' to act as 'voices of authority' in guiding the national debate (towards predetermined, 'correct' conclusions).[10] Some commentators analyse the media in similar terms: thus, Gordon (1996: 1535) describes Nigerian journalism as 'woefully backward' because it is hostile to structural adjustment, whereas Kenyan journalism is labelled 'effective' because it has tended to be supportive of adjustment.

The idea that 'technocrats and administrators', the staff of 'independent think tanks', and 'effective' (because supportive of adjustment) journalists might themselves express the interests (including their own) of certain sections of society is rarely entertained.

Conclusions, and implications for campaigners

I argue that the claimed technical superiority of adjustment conceals a normative commitment to specific (neo-liberal) policies, and that the 'institutional arrangement' which allows different actors to 'buy into' – and help to form – adjustment is the conception of State neutrality in a political sense.

The appeal of such a discourse to World Bank technocrats is obvious. But the conception of State neutrality offers much to Southern State-based élites also because their own power, though perhaps challenged by specific prescriptions of adjustment, is 'naturalised' and, essentially, legitimised. The fact that they will be pursuing their own interests, and/or those of the political constituencies whom they represent – by, for example, selling State companies to family members – is not analysed and is, therefore, facilitated.

Some more specific conclusions on processes of discourse formation in the case of adjustment are the following.

- Interests influencing the adoption of particular discourses are never static – for example, Northern finance capital, which supported neo-liberalism in the 1980s and 1990s, supported an alternative discourse of spendthrift, State-led development in the 1970s. Claims by the 'powers that be' that they are implementing the eternal verities of economic truth, as opposed to a very time-specific paradigm, should be treated with disdain by campaigners.

- Discourses are always the outcome not of unilinear influence or direction, but of a congruence or coalition of interests (most recently including finance capital and the US government). These coalitions are fluid, and members may drop out and reappear over time. This provides campaigners with opportunities to forge seemingly improbable (though perhaps only temporary) alliances.

- While Southern governments are often clearly challenged by neo-liberal economic reform, they are nonetheless able, at least on occasion, to exploit the discourse, and the policies flowing from it, for the purposes of material gain and/or political mobilisation. They may also be able to exploit fissures within the World Bank – for example, between economists and loan administrators – to resist aspects of the adjustment programme altogether. Southern State actors react and adapt to the external stimuli of adjustment policies in order to promote domestic political objectives. Campaigners cannot therefore assume that Southern State actors are automatic allies in campaigns to reform or oppose adjustment.

- The fractures between discourses are not necessarily as dramatic as they may at first appear. For example, the World Bank's earlier discourse of 'statist' development shares with the neo-liberal discourse a fetishisation of the State (or elements therein) as a neutral, technocratic implementer of 'rational' policies. This means that current moves, within the World Bank and elsewhere, back towards support for an apparently more interventionist State role (Stiglitz 1998) should be treated with caution by campaigners. The greatest challenge is not to have more or less State intervention, but rather to resist the depoliticisation of the State which so characterises development discourse.

The World Bank went neo-liberal because it suited the interests of a large range of people for it do so. Part of the reason why that range was so large is that World Bank discourse, while nominally hostile to excessive State intervention, offers little or no political analysis of the State, instead concentrating on 'technical' issues of economic efficiency. Northern and Southern State actors have often been able to continue to pursue their political aims while expressing (and sometimes practising) adherence to the narrow, technical solutions favoured by the Bank. The fact that the received technical wisdom may now favour a somewhat greater role for the State may be welcome news for campaigners, but it does not address the fundamental problem: the absence of a political analysis of who controls the State, and of whose interests it serves.

Notes

1 A former IMF official argues that there has been a turnaround in growth since the mid-1990s, with the 1995-98 sub-Saharan African growth rate four times that of the preceding four-year period; no evidence is adduced in support of the claim that this performance can be attributed to the effects of adjustment (Calamitsis 1999: 7).

2 For an analysis of some recent changes in World Bank thinking, see Fine (1999).

3 A link could also be made here with the attack upon, and decline of, traditional trade union power in the North at this time.

4 Emphasis in original.

5 Wade does not deal with the deeper question of *why* it is that the graduates of British and US universities are disproportionately likely to hold neo-liberal ideas.

6 Emphasis in original. Jacobsen is using adjustment in a wider sense than in reference to the recent experience of neo-liberal reform alone, but the comment applies well to that experience.

7 Another example of contestation is the reluctance to institute full-blooded privatisation in Kenya on the stated grounds that Asians would have been the principal beneficiaries of the privatisation of maize marketing, and that the policy would have been profoundly unpopular as a result (Mkandawire 1994:209- 10).

8 The Bank has been heavily influenced by the so-called New Political Economy (NPE) pioneered by writers such as Robert Bates (1994) (see Williams and Young 1994:91). There is a curious paradox at work here: while Bates recognises that élite groups do use the resources of the State for private ends, and this is a view occasionally recognised by the Bank also (Williams and Young 1994:92), he, and other writers within this approach, appear to believe that this tendency can be overcome by insulation of policy-makers from societal interests, although how they can be insulated from their own interests is never obvious. For a cogent critique of the NPE approach, see Leys (1996: 80-103).

9 The phrases in quotation marks are taken from a talk by Paul Collier, an economist at the World Bank, at the conference on Poverty in Africa – a Dialogue on Causes and Solutions held at the Centre for the Study of African Economies, Oxford, 16 April 1999.

10 *Ibid.*

References

Bates, R. (1994) 'The impulse to reform in Africa', in J.A. Widner (ed.) *Economic Change and Political Liberalisation in Sub-Saharan Africa*, Baltimore: Johns Hopkins University Press.

Bayart, J-F. (1993) *The State in Africa: The Politics of the Belly*, London: Longman.

Bello, W. (1994) *Dark Victory: the United States, Structural Adjustment and Global Poverty*, London: Pluto Press.

Calamitsis, E.A. (1999) 'Adjustment and growth in sub-Saharan Africa: the unfinished agenda', *Finance and Development* 36(1):6-9.

Carmody, P. (1998) 'Constructing alternatives to structural adjustment in Africa', *Review of African Political Economy* 75:25-46.

Caufield, C. (1997) *Masters of Illusion: the World Bank and the Poverty of Nations*, London: Macmillan.

Chabal, P. and J-P. Daloz (1999) *Africa Works: Disorder as Political Instrument*, Oxford, Bloomington and Indianapolis: The International African Institute in association with James Currey and Indiana University Press.

Ferguson, J. (1990) *The Anti-Politics Machine: 'Development', Depoliticisation and Bureaucratic Power in Lesotho*, Minneapolis: University of Minnesota Press.

Fine, B. (1999) 'The developmental state is dead – long live social capital?', *Development and Change* 30:1-19.

George, S. (1992) *The Debt Boomerang: How Third World Debt Harms Us All*, London and Amsterdam: Pluto Press with the Transnational Institute.

Gibbon, P. (1995) 'Towards a political-economy of the World Bank 1970-90', in T. Mkandawire and A. Olukoshi (eds.) *Between Liberalisation and Oppression: The Politics of Structural Adjustment in Africa*, Dakar: CODESRIA.

Gordon, D.F. (1996) 'Sustaining economic reform under political liberalisation in Africa: issues and implications', *World Development* 24(9):1527-37.

Hall, D. (1999) 'Privatisation, multinationals, and corruption', *Development in Practice* 9(5):539-56.

Hanlon, J. (1996) *Peace Without Profit: How the IMF Blocks Rebuilding in Mozambique*, Dublin, Oxford and Portsmouth: Irish Mozambique Solidarity and the International African Institute, in association with James Currey and Heinemann.

Hibou, B. (1999) 'The "social capital" of the state as an agent of deception: or the ruses of economic intelligence', in J-F. Bayart, S. Ellis and B. Hibou (eds.) *The Criminalisation of the State in Africa*, Oxford, Bloomington and Indianapolis: the International African Institute in association with James Currey and Indiana University Press.

Jacobsen, J. K. (1994) *Chasing Progress in the Irish Republic: Ideology, Democracy and Dependent Development*, Cambridge: CUP.

Leys, C. (1996) *The Rise and Fall of Development Theory.*

London: James Currey.

Marren, P. (1999) 'The Asian Crisis and the Indonesian Experience', paper for presentation at ETISC conference, Dublin (20 February).

Martin, H-P. and H. Schumann (1997) *The Global Trap: Globalization and the Assault on Prosperity and Democracy,* London: Zed Books.

Mkandawire, T. (1994) 'The political economy of privatisation in Africa', in G.A. Cornia and G.K. Helleiner (eds.) *From Adjustment to Development in Africa: Conflict, Controversy, Convergence, Consensus?,* London: Macmillan.

Mkandawire, T. (1998) *Thinking about Developmental States in Africa.* Geneva: UNCTAD.

Nelson, P. (1995) *The World Bank and Non-Governmental Organisations: the Limits of Apolitical Development,* Basingstoke: Macmillan.

Sandbrook, R. (1996) 'Democratisation and the implementation of economic reform in Africa', *Journal of International Development* 8(1):1-20.

Stiglitz, J. (1998) 'More Instruments and Broader Goals: Moving Towards the Post-Washington Consensus' WIDER Annual Lecture, Helsinki (7 January).

Uvin, P. (1997) 'Prejudice, crisis and genocide in Rwanda', *African Studies Review* 40(2):91-115.

Wade, R. (1996) 'Japan, the World Bank, and the art of paradigm maintenance: The East Asian Miracle in political perspective', *New Left Review* (217):3-36.

White, H. (1996) 'Adjustment in Africa', *Development and Change* 27:785-815.

Wick, P. and J. S. Shaw (1998) 'The Côte d'Ivoire's troubled economy: why World Bank interventions failed', *Cato Journal* 18(1):11 20.

Williams, D. and T. Young (1994) 'Governance, the World Bank and liberal theory', *Political Studies* XLII:84-100.

Dissonance or dialogue: changing relations with the corporate sector

Judy Henderson

The past decade has seen a significant shift in the influence over development policy between the three groups of global actors – governments, civil society, and the private sector. While, through a series of major summits in the 1990s, UN member States attempted to establish global agreements on common environmental, social, and human-rights agendas, for most of the world's people little has changed in reality, and for many the situation has become worse. However, what the global conferences did, inadvertently, facilitate was a much more extensively networked community of civil-society actors, who, through a combination of technological advances and the formation of alliances North–South and across sectors, are now a much more active force in global decision-making forums. While larger transnational or international NGOs (INGOs) are the most visible, many of these are also linked to grassroots movements. Electronic communication has enhanced this connection and has meant a greater participation of civil society in international debates, as well as a capacity for civil-society movements to hold INGOs more accountable.

At the same time, the emergence of the private sector as a key driver of the development paradigm has become more apparent. Throughout the run-up to the Earth Summit process in 1992, the concept of sustainable development was firmly placed on the table. However, at Rio, the private sector's major achievement was to keep the issue of corporate accountability off an agenda over which it had no control, and away from a concept of which it had little understanding. As Ray Anderson, Chairman of Interface and Co-Chair of the US President's Council on Sustainable Development, said in the foreword to the carpet company's

1997 Sustainability Report: 'Three years ago, the word sustainability meant little or nothing to me. For the first twenty-one years of Interface's existence I never gave one thought to what we did for the Earth, except to be sure that we obeyed all laws and regulations.'

Subsequently, leadership within the corporate sector recognised that the concept of sustainable development was not going to disappear, and that there was an urgent need for businesses to get on the front foot in interpreting what it meant for their activities. And they moved fast. Environmental sustainability has now become a mainstream issue for business. Once industry absorbs a message, it responds rapidly – unlike governments, which are constrained by a paralysing blend of political processes and bureaucratic inertia.

The impact of globalisation

Both the corporate sector and civil society have been transformed by the process of globalisation. National boundaries provide few barriers for the transnational corporations (TNCs) that operate in a global marketplace. Similarly, the organisation of civil society is now much more internationalised, with groups of national organisations forming international affiliations in order to achieve greater impact for their advocacy activities.

With the manifest withdrawal over the past decade of government as a major regulator, monitor, and enforcer of development, the private sector and INGOs have been left eyeing each other rather warily. Of the three sets of actors, corporates and INGOs do have in common the need for a much more long-term agenda. Governments, by contrast, must focus primarily on the electoral cycle. While quarterly returns are important, businesses must plan their investment programmes over an extended time period. At the same time, INGOs are seeking sustainable solutions to global issues. Thus, increasingly, industry and INGOs are finding themselves in a parallel search for long-term certainty.

In March 1999, the oil company Shell launched a series of advertisements in the UK at the start of a US$25 million 'stakeholder consultation' campaign. For a company buffeted by the public-relations disasters of the decommissioning of the Brent Spar oil platform and the judicial execution of local activists in Ogoniland, this may have appeared as just another attempt to gloss over a battered image with an advertising blitz. However, it is increasingly evident that, in what it refers to as a 'CNN world', companies like Shell have begun to acknowledge that corporate responsibility does not begin and end with economic performance, but that in the twenty-first century companies will be judged on a much wider agenda of environmental and social accountability. As Shell's chairman Mark Moody-Stuart (1999) notes:

> In the next century sustainable business will have to be responsible and sensitive to the needs of everyone involved. It will be guided by more than one parameter. The demands of economics, of the environment and contributing to a just society are all important for a global commercial enterprise to flourish. To neglect any one of them is to threaten the whole.

This change at the top in some multinationals has not come about by chance, but has largely emerged as a result of a long and persistent campaign by international pressure groups, calling for more corporate accountability.

The call for enforceable codes of conduct for TNCs was an early, but unproductive, campaign through the 1970s and 1980s for more corporate accountability. Instead, free-trade policies, the expanding importance of foreign direct investment, and less restrictive national laws presented TNCs with an open ticket to seek the most industry-friendly regulatory climate. Although persistent criticism of activities of multinationals by pressure groups has encouraged business to develop stricter self-regulatory codes, mandatory reporting and strict compliance mechanisms have been successfully resisted.

In 1997, the UK-based consultancy firm, Control Risks Group, examined the changing relationship between INGOs and business. It concluded that business had to take INGOs seriously, because, as a force, they were now beginning successfully to interfere with business practice. By the use of technology and strategic global campaigning, INGOs had the capacity to damage a company's most precious asset, its reputation.

Companies recognised that they could no longer afford to ignore this threat, and that they needed to pay more attention to a multi-stakeholder environment. This was risky business, as it meant increased transparency in their activities, with the consequent potential for greater exposure to criticism. While initially the relationship between business and INGOs was characterised by caution and unease, a degree of common ground and mutual advantage has been discovered, such that both sides are recognising the potential for constructive engagement. While corporations been driven by the need to protect their reputation,

INGOs have had cause to reconsider their views about the role of the private sector in developing countries, coming to see it as a critical ingredient of economic development and, in the foreseeable future, the only likely source of the growth needed for social development.

Much of the long-term strategic thinking about the developing world is happening not in Foreign Ministries, nor even as much as before in universities, but in private-sector think-tanks. Notwithstanding the Asian collapse and the discrediting of IMF-imposed monetarist solutions to countries in crisis, there seems little likelihood of the shift towards the market-led paradigm being abandoned in the short to medium term. Moreover, with the change in the relative weight of foreign direct investment and official development assistance to developing countries, the power of TNCs to influence development outcomes has been significantly strengthened. Multilateral development banks are increasingly adopting as a key role the facilitation of private-sector involvement in the development process.

Thus, INGOs concerned with poverty and equity now view the private sector as a significant driver of development, a key engine of growth, but one with little conscious orientation towards the impacts of the increased economic activity on the distribution of wealth. While INGOs on the whole accept that it is legitimate for the private sector to make a profit out of development, it is also held that this right carries with it a social responsibility. For these reasons, sections of the INGO community have made a strategic decision to engage in dialogue with industry in the pursuit of more socially just outcomes.

Taking social accountability seriously

It is clear that enlightened leaders in the private sector are seriously committed to making changes in the sector's ways of working. Indicative of this trend is the growing interest in the 'triple bottom line' – a concept involving economic performance, environmental sustainability, and social responsibility – outlined by John Elkington from the UK-based group SustainAbility (Elkington 1997). The idea of the 'triple bottom line' has begun to invade the consciousness of the corporate sector. In a 1998 survey of the attention given to the 'triple bottom line' agenda in the reports of Chief Executive Officers (CEOs), Elkington concludes that while 'only 11% of CEOs currently show even an embryonic understanding of the emerging agenda in this area … [this is] a dramatic increase on the position 3–4 years ago when the figure would certainly have been zero'. With the private sector's rapid-response capacity, it will be interesting to track the growth in this awareness.

What is apparent is that corporations have been much quicker to embrace the environmental issues than to adopt the social agenda. Senior executives have recognised that good environmental performance is linked to enhanced business outcomes and, with leadership from institutions such as the World Business Council on Sustainable Development (WBCSD), stewardship for the environment has become more central to the thinking of major corporations. While many are now producing excellent environmental reports, including opening up their operations to external verification, there has been much more reluctance to address controversial social and ethical aspects of their company's activities. This should not be surprising, given that the connection between social responsibility and commercial gain has yet to be clearly determined, let alone absorbed.

In May 1999, *Business Week* produced a special advertising section in association with the World Resources Institute (WRI) on finding a balance between social, environmental, and financial responsibilities, with articles written by CEOs of ten major corporations. In his overview, Jonathan Lash, WRI President, urged:

> The social challenge reflects the fact that as the private sector has grown in power and importance, so have the expectations of a diverse group of stakeholders. ... With increased visibility for corporate behaviour and increased vulnerability for companies that run afoul of today's volatile public opinion, no company can afford to neglect its relationships with its stakeholders or escape the need to be part of building a better society.

Despite this call to action, all ten essays from CEOs focused on environmental issues; not one seriously tackled the social agenda. The section on 'Managing for the Future' explained:

> Despite rising interest in corporate social responsibility, there remains considerable confusion about the concept. Terms such as 'corporate citizenship', 'eco-justice', and 'business ethics' abound. ... The challenge is to define business performance in relation to its impact on other stakeholders, including communities, employees, developing countries, and suppliers. Such measures should include business ethics issues such as participatory decision-making, community commitment, honesty, bribery, and corruption.

A dilemma for business is the absence of good social-performance indicators. *Business Week* admits that 'the current state of corporate social performance yardsticks parallels that of environmental performance measures 15 years ago'. As part of the 'triple bottom line' approach, social reporting is on the agenda and, with it, verification. Reports on companies' activities in the social and environmental areas are of little value unless they can be verified. Thus good reliable indicators against which a company's performance can be tracked are essential.

Corporate social responsibility

Leadership in the area is again emerging from the WBCSD, which in 1998 launched a two-year study into corporate social responsibility (CSR). In its first report, *Meeting Changing Expectations*, released in March 1999, the Group identified one of the remaining difficulties as the monitoring, management, measurement, and reporting of CSR. It also noted that much of its work thus far had been in the developed world, and there was a need to gather views from developing countries. Following a round of regional consultations in1999, the second work-in-progress report, *Making Good Business Sense*, was released in January 2000. As well as introducing a broader perspective of what CSR might mean in different cultures, the report includes some early guidelines for CSR indicators. INGOs can be encouraged by this signal of genuine commitment to finding workable solutions to CSR, and thus can be more open to working together with business in developing appropriate and verifiable social measures.

The call for more corporate responsibility with respect to human-rights standards emerged from a much higher level at the 1999 World Economic Forum at Davos, where the UN Secretary-General, Kofi Annan, challenged corporate executives to find 'new ways to embed global market forces in universally shared societal values' by adopting his proposal for a Global Compact. This comprises nine principles, derived from three areas of shared international agreements: human rights, labour standards, and environmental protection. This challenge was taken further in a statement by the UN High Commissioner on Human Rights at the Winconference '99 at Interlaken, where she reminded business leaders that economic, social, and cultural rights were equally enshrined as civil and political rights in the Universal Declaration of Human Rights, and that business was a key partner 'in the drive to consolidate social and economic rights'.

References to human rights were, until recently, conspicuously absent from most corporate policies, with notable exceptions such as Body Shop, Levi Strauss, and Reebok. More recently, sections of the oil industry, spurred by damaging reports relating to human-rights abuses, have addressed the issues more seriously in their company codes; but in general this is not an area where business feels comfortable. However, with more company executives now publicly supporting the importance of corporate social responsibility, a key role for INGOs will be to continue to hold them answerable to a broader human-rights agenda.

Despite the emergence of a new breed of business leaders, in reality companies and individuals embracing the concept of the 'triple bottom line' are still relatively few in number. Market fundamentalism remains the dominant ideological trend, with unquestioning adherence to economic globalisation being the order of the day, despite growing protests from the large proportion of the global community that is being left behind. The profit motive will remain the primary objective, with sections of industry merely seeking to give the impression of change – a 'greenwash' – rather than fully incorporating social and environmental concerns as core functions in their work.

Between co-operation and co-option: walking the tightrope

For INGOs, closer co-operation with industry is a high-risk strategy, with the inherent danger of co-option and being seen giving tacit or overt approval to unsustainable or socially inequitable activities. Constructive engagement can easily slide into complacency on the one hand, with the risk of charges of collusion leading to damaging internal dissent on the other. There is also a danger that INGOs might invest considerable resources and public prestige without achieving desired changes to policies and practices. Valuable time and resources can be taken up by requests to participate in industry advisory panels and consultative groups, only to contribute to the corporate public image without bringing about any real change. Co-option – or the appearance of co-option – by a company or industry may also have a negative effect on the credibility of the pressure groups among their peers.

Thus, it is essential for the radical transformers who place a stake in the ground and refuse to budge to remain outside the process. These groups play a critical role in defining the argument and establishing the benchmarks. There is a role for both transformers and reformers, and it is essential that each recognises and respects the legitimacy of the other's position. Otherwise, the NGO movement can become fractured, and valuable energy can be consumed in attacking each other, rather than being focused on common objectives.

INGOs' approach to the private sector needs to be flexible, with a willingness to engage in dialogue with the more receptive companies or to pursue more aggressive tactics when deemed desirable and productive. Skill in assessing these options and managing the conflicting tensions will be essential to ensure that internal and organisational policies are coherent and give a consistent and accurate message. Mistakes in the accuracy of information can be highly damaging to an NGO's credibility. Despite success with the Brent Spar campaign, the reputation of Greenpeace was harmed by the admission that the organisation had made a mistake in some of its claims. Just as companies are increasingly under the spotlight with calls for transparency and accountability, so business will also be quick to hold INGOs accountable for their statements and activities.

An interesting recent initiative in global public policy making has been the World Commission on Dams (WCD), an independent body established in 1998 by the World Bank and the World Conservation Union with a mandate to develop agreed guidelines for future decision-making over water-resource development. The WCD is an experiment in finding solutions to global disputes and, if successful, could provide a model for further dialogue between the private sector and civil society.

While concepts such as 'the triple bottom line', the 'Global Compact', and initiatives provided by the WBCSD and the WCD can provide convenient focal points around which INGOs and the private sector can have potentially productive conversations, constructive engagement between the two sectors will continue to occur at any level only for as long as both clearly see advantages in doing so. For INGOs, there is no guarantee that closer interaction will in the long term lead to more just and sustainable outcomes. While remaining alert to strategic opportunities as they emerge, advocacy groups will continue to pursue a multi-faceted approach. In a fast-moving world, flexibility will be key to INGOs remaining a relevant influence in the twenty-first century.

References

Control Risks Group (1997) 'No Hiding Place', London: Control Risks Group

Elkington, John (1997) 'Cannibals with Forks: The Triple Bottom Line of the Twenty-first Century Business', Oxford: Capstone

Moody-Stuart, Mark (1999) 'The Values of Sustainable Business in the Next Century', speech delivered at St Paul's Cathedral, London, July 1999

World Business Council on Sustainable Development (1999) *Corporate Social Responsibility: Meeting Changing Expectations*, Geneva: WBCSD

World Business Council on Sustainable Development (2000) *Corporate Social Responsibility: Making Good Business Sense*, Geneva: WBCSD

NGOs as development partners to the corporates: child football-stitchers in Pakistan

David Husselbee

Development partnerships

Partnerships are emerging between NGOs and the corporate sector (as distinct from the private sector, which includes small and micro enterprises), as large companies, and particularly multinational corporations (MNCs), become increasingly concerned about the impact of their activities in less developed countries. Most companies now have voluntary codes of conduct on social and environmental issues which they wish to see enacted, while also wishing to protect the values associated with their products from allegations that they are made using exploitative and hazardous working practices. NGOs in turn recognise the increasing importance of companies in development, both locally and internationally, as private flows of foreign direct investment to developing countries increase and flows of official aid fall,[1] and governments are less able to provide adequate services. Both businesses and NGOs see the need to move from a confrontational approach to one of collaboration, without losing the freedom to be critical when necessary. Whether a close liaison with the private sector compromises an NGO's freedom remains an open question for many NGOs.

Attitudes in the corporate sector to partnerships with NGOs are changing. As large companies use the developing world as a source for their products, so their responsibility – as viewed by themselves and consumers – to be involved in development issues rises proportionately. NGOs are seen as a valuable source of knowledge and experience of social and environmental issues, and as more approachable and trustworthy than government, because they, like businesses themselves, are private organisations. Furthermore, their involvement may also help to neutralise campaigns against the companies concerned.

NGO attitudes to the corporate sector are also changing. The Save the Children Fund UK (hereafter SCF) is involved, for example, in the campaign against Nestlé and other producers of baby-milk formula which is promoted in contravention of the WHO marketing code. Its work has also led to confrontation with the arms industry. Thus SCF has given careful consideration to development partnerships with the private sector, but is now seeking chances of constructive dialogue with a more open corporate sector. This is also rooted, for SCF, in its broad strategic step away from operational work towards partnership with a variety of organisations. This offers the potential for new development opportunities and the scope to influence the international accountability of companies.

There is limited documentation, however, of development projects that involve the corporate sector and NGOs. This article seeks to raise issues about such collaboration, and to assess the essential elements of such partnerships, through the example of SCF's work with some of the sporting-goods manufacturers represented by the Sialkot Chamber of Commerce and Industry (SCCI) in Sialkot, an industrial city 144 km north-east of Lahore, in Pakistan, and their international partner brands, represented by the World Federation of Sporting Goods Industry (WFSGI), which wishes to guarantee that children are not employed in stitching footballs.

The elements of partnership, identified by the Prince of Wales Business Leaders Forum (Nelson 1996), are examined here in the context of the sports-goods industry. They include setting clear and common goals; strengthening intermediary leadership to build bridges between partners; understanding and consulting beneficiaries; ensuring clarity of roles and responsibilities; understanding the resource needs and capacities of the respective partners and their particular contributions to the partnership; improving communication and co-ordination; evaluating progress; and ensuring continuous learning and adaptation. The Sialkot case provides a model of a partnership involving a complex variety of players that will not be found in many partnerships between NGOs and the corporate sector. Nonetheless the approach offers pointers for those considering the possibility of working on the inside with the corporate sector, rather than campaigning from the outside. The issues involved will apply to many cross-sector partnerships and are particularly relevant for international and national NGOs.

Footballs and child labour: an approach to partnership

In Sialkot, child workers and their families would stitch footballs in their rural homes and communities, using panels supplied by sub-contractors who served to link the stitchers with the manufacturers in the city. Football stitching was also done in large factories, but this did not involve children. The manufacturers in turn have relationships with international companies, who acquire about 60 per cent of the world's footballs from Sialkot. This complex set of linkages within the private sector was something that had to be understood by the various partners. In early 1996, pressure groups began to focus international attention on the involvement of children in football stitching in Sialkot, raising the alarm about children being exploited, particularly in punishment rooms at the back of workshops.[2] The international industry invited several NGOs based in Pakistan to help them to develop a response. SCF visited Sialkot with a representative of one of the international brands in July 1996. Its resulting report suggested the need for a cross-sectoral partnership, and warned against hurried solutions which could push children into more hazardous and exploitative forms of work, as had happened in the garment industry in Bangladesh (Marcus and Harper 1996: 46).

Subsequently SCF conducted a situation analysis to obtain a detailed picture of the lives of the children involved, and to ensure that their voices could be heard above the international calls for swift answers. This analysis formed the basis of SCF's contribution to the development partnership which evolved in Sialkot in 1997. It had been difficult for international brand names to gain authoritative information about the role of children in the production processes of their suppliers, particularly as the production was home-based or community-based, rather than taking place in factories. The priority for SCF was to establish the facts about the children's lives and views, and to invest in gathering and moving information, rather than funding over-hasty solutions.

SCF found that football stitching was neither very hazardous or exploitative for girls or boys, nor was it a bonded form of work; and that most children were helping their families to meet basic needs. Children were deterred from attending school by the poor quality of education and not simply by the imperative of having to work. The study also raised concerns about the impact on women's employment of the proposed changes in the industry, and the relatively low rates of pay for adult stitchers. SCF thus decided to establish a programme, in alliance with local NGOs, which would focus on improving education, offering credit and savings facilities and stitching centres for women, and monitoring the impact of changes in the industry on children and their families.

The SCF programme is an integral part of the Sialkot partnership, which is a multi-faceted collaboration between the Sialkot manufacturers represented by the SCCI, SCF, UN agencies (the ILO and UNICEF), Pakistani NGOs (Bunyad and Sudhaar), and the government of Pakistan (GoP), represented by Pakistan Bait ul Mal (a government-funded trust), the Department of Education, and the National Rural Support Programme (an NGO established by the GoP). The international companies are indirectly represented by the SCCI and WFSGI, one of whose members – the Sports Goods Manufacturers Association (SGMA) of America – was closely involved in facilitating the partnership and continues to monitor and promote the project.

The initial negotiations

The formal launch of the project took place in Atlanta in February 1997 at the Super Show, the annual sports trade fair in the USA, with the signing of an agreement defining the goals as follows:

1. *Elimination of child labour in soccer-ball production.* The primary goal of the Project is (i) to assist manufacturers seeking to prevent child labour in the manufacture or assembly of soccer balls in Sialkot District and its environs; (ii) to identify and remove children from conditions of child labour in the manufacture or assembly of soccer balls and provide them with educational and other opportunities, and (iii) to facilitate changes in community and family attitudes to child labour.

2. *Elimination of child labour in other local industries.* The Partners recognise that efforts to eliminate child labour in the soccer-ball industry in Pakistan can best succeed if they are complemented by similar efforts in other local industries, and by the creation of meaningful new opportunities for children in this district. It is the hope of the Partners that the development of the Project shall encourage other sectors of the business community in Sialkot, government of Pakistan, and other important institutions in Pakistan to explore how they might do more to contribute to the end of child labour.[3]

The process of drafting these goals involved compromise on all sides and provided the foundations of the partnership. For example, the sports industry insisted that the initial focus be football production, but SCF and the UN agencies advocated that other more exploitative and hazardous industries should be the target of the partnership's longer-term goals.

The agreement also describes the main elements as being the Prevention and Monitoring Programme, involving the monitoring of stitching locations by both the manufacturers' own monitors and the ILO as external monitors, to ensure that children are phased out of the work over an18-month period; and the Social Protection Programme, involving SCF, UNICEF, and local NGOs, which aims to ensure that children who leave football-stitching work do not have to seek more hazardous and exploitative employment. The agreement also covers the co-ordination mechanisms, the specific responsibilities and contributions of the respective parties, and the resolution of disputes. This programme is particularly notable, because it pays careful attention to the lives of children once they have stopped stitching footballs – in contrast to some child-labour programmes that have concentrated primarily, or solely, on monitoring production processes in order to check that children are no longer involved, and so allowing businesses to convince consumers that their products are not made by children.

The international companies were strongly motivated by the need to create an internationally credible partnership which would be acceptable to its members, as well as to its consumers and to the pressure groups. Hence the involvement of international humanitarian organisations was viewed as essential. Such an industry-wide partnership (55 of the international brands have pledged to order footballs only from the Sialkot manufacturers involved in the project) had to be agreed at various geographical levels. Initial discussions between SCF and the industry took place in Sialkot; but, as the partnership grew, discussions soon took place in the respective head offices. The international company associations acted as the brokers which drafted the partnership agreement, which involved negotiations with the ILO in Geneva, UNICEF in New York, and SCF in London.

The speed at which the partnership developed placed stress on SCF's capacity to respond quickly and adequately. In general, SCF's partnerships are with Southern NGOs whose expectations coincide more closely with those of SCF. This allows relationships to evolve and deepen at a mutually acceptable pace, giving time for primary stakeholders to influence the planning process. In Sialkot, SCF consulted the primary stakeholders – the children and their families – while the Atlanta Agreement was being finalised, thus ensuring that their views influenced the next phase in the planning process. This also helped SCF to be sure that its own role in the partnership would be justified by its protection of the rights of children.

The roles of the partners were further defined when the Partners Operational Framework – a UN project-funding document – was developed in April 1997 by the UN mission to Sialkot. This involved the ILO, the manufacturers, SCF, and UNICEF. This was the first time that the partners had discussed in detail in Pakistan how their respective roles would fit together into an effective partnership. The Atlanta Agreement had been a statement of intent and had set the goals, but the bonds between the partners began to grow during the operational negotiations.

The partnership evolves

The progress of the partnership depended on leadership emerging among people in the partner organisations who shared the vision of the project and were prepared to work collaboratively. These people also developed enthusiasm within their own organisations for the project, in spite of concerns about being associated with such a high-profile initiative.

Initially, the sports industry, both in Sialkot and internationally, felt closer to SCF, because the latter made early attempts to understand both the situation on the ground and the perspective of the manufacturers, and responded more quickly than the other partners. This process was particularly helped by a Punjabi member of SCF's programme staff, whose local knowledge helped to establish a rapport with the manufacturers.

To begin with, SCF played the role of mediator in Sialkot. The manufacturers were troubled by the ILO's institutional links with trade unions, this concern being exacerbated by the international-level negotiations which had limited communication and the development of mutual trust within Pakistan until the UN mission arrived. SCF facilitated communication at the beginning of the mission, based on its understanding of the views of all parties. The private-sector actors relied on this until personal contacts among the other organisations began to build the trust upon which the partnership is now based. SCF could then step back from the bridge-building role, in order to allow direct and strong relationships to grow across the partnership.

At various points in the confrontational stages of the discussions, SCF's role in explaining the perspectives of the corporate sector and the ILO to each other was misinterpreted by both SCCI and ILO as a lack of impartiality on SCF's part. Such issues were not resolved until the UN mission had left Sialkot, and the ILO invited SCCI and its international customers to visit Bangladesh to see the work of the ILO in monitoring the garment industry. Constructive discussion became the glue in the partnership, and confrontation was left behind

Putting children at the centre of the analysis

While the negotiations took place, SCF conducted an extensive situation analysis which focused on the views of the stitcher children and their families and consequently provided a bridge between them and those who were influencing the policies of the partnership. A more constructive balance of power resulted by moving the relationship between the stitchers and other stakeholders. The speed at which the partnership had grown before the signing of the Atlanta Agreement had not allowed time for the participation of the primary stakeholders, so the situation analysis was essential to opening the partnership to their views. This helped to evolve goals for the project which were not identical to the goals of the initial agreement, but would be mutually beneficial and acceptable to all stakeholders, including stitchers and consumers.

SCF's analysis sought to illustrate the complexity of the situation and to test the contentions of pressure-group campaigns which suggested that many children were working as bonded labourers for most of the daylight hours, and were not able to attend school because of their work. It also provided a chance to explain to communities the possible impact of proposed changes in the industry. It was very important for SCF to stress the concerns that it shared with the pressure groups as a result of the study.

Previous reports on the football industry in Sialkot had produced estimates of the numbers of children involved that ranged from 5000 to 17,000. The priority of the SCF study was not to verify these figures, but to focus on the *quality* of the lives of the working children. It was clear that thousands of children were involved in the football industry, but the nature of their involvement needed clarification. A combination of quantitative and qualitative techniques was used. The manufacturers had hoped that SCF would come up with a definitive number of children to be protected by the project, and took some convincing that the rural community-based nature of the work made this difficult. Nonetheless, the report was welcomed as a balanced account of the problem. Details of methodology are included in this document.

The findings and recommendations proved to be a challenge to the proposed re-organisation of the industry, which would have seen all production moved out of rural communities into large factories. However, the views were received constructively by the manufacturers, because SCF was lobbying from within the partnership and from a position of trust. SCF would not have had such influence had it remained outside the partnership. The result was that some football production would stay in smaller production units in villages, which allowed women to continue to work close to their homes and children. Many of these women would have been prevented by cultural norms from travelling to the distant factories.

SCF also stressed that paying adults more to stitch footballs would be the most effective way to reduce children's need to work, although this recommendation has been acted upon by only a few manufacturers. Information about profit margins and whether pay could be increased has not been made available to SCF, but its consultations with children and their families had given SCF a clear and legitimate position on policy issues in the sports industry, and allowed it to retain its independence.

Independent monitoring

The roles of the other partners were fully clarified in the Partners Operational Framework developed by the UN mission; they continue to be refined through the co-ordination mechanisms of the project. A question which is not yet adequately answered for many involved in ethical business issues – i.e. which body should provide the independent monitoring of labour standards – was answered in this case by the ILO, who offered the technical assistance of a senior Dutch labour inspector to lead the independent monitoring of stitching locations. The international sports industry had favoured hiring a private accountancy or investigation firm for this role, but doubts about the impartiality of such organisations were raised by the pressure groups. The ILO was seen as impartial and gained the support of the sports industry because of its experience in child-labour monitoring in the Bangladesh garment industry. The ILO has subsequently accepted a similar role in the surgical instruments and carpet industries in Punjab, although there is now some internal debate about how widely ILO should replicate this model of monitoring.

The formal monitoring of production facilities by the ILO, and by the internal manufacturers' monitors, serves to check that children are not working. It provides the manufacturers with the endorsement that they need in order to protect their reputation, the value of their product, and the image of football as a sport. It also provides information about children who are displaced from work to the social protection programme which involves SCF, UNICEF, and local NGOs in education, credit and savings, and vocational training.

Before the signing of the Atlanta Agreement, SCF had been invited to serve as an independent monitor, but had declined. There was concern that this would involve the NGO in endorsing products that claimed to be child-labour free, rather than representing the broader concerns about the need to improve the quality of children's lives. This was not SCF's area of competence and would have threatened its independence and the value of its name as an organisation which represents the rights of children. However, as a member of the project, SCF shares responsibility with the other partners for administering sanctions against companies that do not comply with guidelines of the programme. Thus SCF's independence is essential, if the project is to claim that it has a viable system of controls.

SCF is developing local capacity in social monitoring to ensure that the rights of children are protected. Changes in the quality of children's lives and the lives of their families through the lifetime of the project are monitored, using indicators relating to their attitudes to and use of education, the changes in family incomes, and changes in the work of the children.

The Co-ordination Committee

The Project Co-ordination Committee was established through the negotiations for the Atlanta Agreement and is responsible, to paraphrase the Agreement, for 'facilitating communication ... promoting cooperation between the partners ... identifying individuals and organisations qualified to implement the various parts of the project ... integrating the monitoring and social protection elements of the project ... providing public reports on the project ... encouraging international sports businesses to support the project ... encouraging other businesses in Sialkot to join in efforts against child labour ... approving plans and proposals for the project.' The Committee works at the policy level, and a team was also created at the implementation level, with a secretariat based at the Chamber of Commerce.

It has not been easy for the Co-ordination Committee to create a shared vision of the aims of the programme. New manufacturers joining the programme have been resistant to the role of the partnership in improving education, which they see as the responsibility of the GoP. The Chamber of Commerce has co-ordinated the response of the 53 manufacturers and encouraged their commitment. It is significant that the most committed manufacturers have been those who receive the greatest encouragement on social responsibility from the international brands that they supply. The other manufacturers have taken a less active role and appear to be waiting for the programme to clear the name of their industry, rather than seeking to be involved in the development of the district. Nonetheless, the concept of corporate citizenship is taking a stronger hold because of the partnership; and this is also serving to develop the organisational capacity of the SCCI to be socially responsible. Internationally, SCF has encouraged the brands to request their suppliers in Sialkot to be active in the project.

Results to date

The programme had resulted, by August 1999, in 53 manufacturers having their production facilities monitored by the ILO; the establishment of a programme of savings and credit, and skills training, for 7500 households; school management committees set up in 104 government primary schools; courses to up-grade the skills of 220 teachers; and the establishment of more than 150 non-formal education centres. Social-monitoring reports assessing the impact on communities are available from SCF. The main outstanding issue for the partnership to resolve remains the institutional arrangements that are needed to ensure the local sustainability of the programme when the international organisations withdraw.

What makes partnerships between NGOs and the corporate sector possible?

The elements of successful partnership identified by Nelson (1996) are exemplified by this case study as follows.

Clear and common goals

The different expectations of the corporate sector and NGOs have to be reconciled in the early stages, if a partnership is to work. The corporate world expects results and the achievement of specific targets, especially when responding to criticism. By contrast, NGOs concentrate on process and encourage communities to define their own targets – something that can take time. SCF played a role in decelerating the process to allow time for primary stakeholders to be consulted, but had to show understanding of the needs of the sports industry and to move more quickly than usual, otherwise the partnership would not have worked. The Atlanta Agreement was signed to publicise the fact that the industry was taking action, and to create time for an appropriate programme to be assembled before further international pressure was applied. The proviso that the programme could be delayed if the 'Coordinating Committee other than SCCI ... agree that this is necessary to protect the best interests of the children ...' was included in the Agreement and helped to create realistic expectations about the speed at which a programme could be implemented.

Intermediary leadership to build bridges

Intermediaries from the respective partners were essential. High cultural hurdles had to be crossed to create the partnership between countries on opposite sides of the world and among organisations with vastly different approaches and aims. Strong intermediary vision and leadership has helped to build bridges between the organisations involved.

Partnerships with the corporate sector are often initiated by companies themselves, as approaches from NGOs to the private sector are frequently treated with mistrust. Companies need to be sure that a partnership will promote their aims and values and they tend to trust partnerships that they have initiated themselves. As cross-sectoral partnerships become more common, and NGOs develop experience with the corporate sector, this will change. SCF was initially cautious, being inexperienced in the implementation of development projects with the corporate sector, and concerned about potential threats to its independence. It therefore helped that the opening gambit was made by business, which provided much of the early intermediary leadership.

The commitment and understanding of individuals within the organisations concerned are what make cross-sectoral partnerships work. They need to understand the concerns and views of all parties and to build the bridges that lead to strong ties. SCF had decided to work with the private sector, but the building of links was made easier by the fact that an intermediary representing one of the brands had extensive NGO experience. She encouraged SCF to accept an invitation to visit Sialkot to assess the problem of children working in football stitching. Other international NGOs declined the invitation, for a variety of operational reasons and because of concerns about possibly compromising their independence.

The partners have seen, as the needs of the programme have become clearer, the importance of appointing people who are inclined to work collaboratively at the interface between different organisations and who are not afraid to share with the other partners the credit for success and the responsibility for problems.

Understanding and consulting the beneficiaries and stakeholders

Business remains competitive if it has access to information and knowledge, and NGOs can act as an important source in cross-sector partnerships by providing an understanding of the primary stakeholders and therefore influencing commercial thinking. Business is good at making and selling products, but has not developed competence in consulting producer communities in a participatory way. This is partly because the vocal groups – the Northern consumers and pressure groups – are accepted by the corporate sector as stakeholders with an influence on the success of the business. By contrast, business is only beginning to recognise the producers and their communities, whose voice is not often heard, as stakeholders. In this case, the gap between stakeholders in this partnership was filled by SCF's situation analysis, which placed the views of children and their communities at the centre of the partnership's agenda. Consulting communities in collaboration with Southern NGOs, and representing their views in detail, also provided legitimacy to SCF and a position of strength from which to influence the direction of the partnership and to advocate policy changes that favour children.

Thus their capacity to glean independent knowledge can be a way for NGOs to inform the internal processes of change within a project, through an on-going dialogue with the primary stakeholders. This knowledge provides the NGO with an independent position, which is respected by business people, and also ensures that the NGO does not have to depend on the private sector for information which may be coloured by commercial perspectives.

Clarity of roles and responsibilities

Clarity was reached once the programme began work on the ground. The initial project documents had outlined the various roles, and this provided a basis for discussion, but eventually these roles were clarified by those responsible for implementation. The initial involvement of people in Sialkot would have resulted in roles being defined more clearly from the beginning.

Understanding resource needs and capacities

The clarification of roles depends on the ability of organisations to recognise the competencies and capacities of each of the partners. Roles cannot be clear if the partners do not recognise the strengths that the others can bring. Given the high profile of the sports industry, each partner in Sialkot has recognised that being accompanied by others provides the best chance of success and reduces the level of exposure of individual organisations. The experience of ILO in industrial monitoring, of UNICEF in education, of SCF in social and children's issues and education, and of the sports industry in communicating and planning, are all valuable aspects of the project.

Resource needs for the project were assessed during the drafting of the Partners Operational Framework. The partnership has provided leverage for the partners to gain funding – a task which would have been more difficult for organisations operating in isolation. SCF, for example, has designed a project for funding by the British government's Department for International Development (DFID) and has also attracted sources of expertise from within Pakistan, such as the National Rural Support Programme, which has strong credit and savings programmes.

Communication and co-ordination

Maintaining understanding among the partners has required regular communication among them through the co-ordinating mechanisms described above, and through meetings with individual partners to resolve particular concerns. The sports industry at times has been particularly demanding of partners to communicate clearly and promptly, and doing so represents a form of increased accountability for all involved.

Mechanisms for co-ordination and accountability provide each partner with equal power to influence and question the progress of the partnership. The possible imposition of sanctions against partners who do not comply to the standards agreed has to be built into the way the partnership works.

Evaluating progress and continuous learning and adaptation

The nature and profile of the partnership involves all the partners in a new form of accountability – to each other and to the project's stakeholders – in evaluating the progress of the project. Both the producer and the consumer will have a stronger influence over the organisations involved, which will benefit the organisations themselves and the children of Sialkot. This new accountability presents a considerable risk which none of the partners would take alone, and encourages thorough evaluation of progress. The partners have become more adaptable as trust has grown. This trust has enabled them to be more honest about the weaknesses of each other's work, as the need to resolve problems collectively has become more apparent.

All the partners are learning from each other and have been prepared to adapt their roles as the project has developed. The way in which the external monitoring component implemented by the ILO emerged against the initial wishes of the private sector is an example, and the evolving approach of the Sialkot manufacturers to ethical issues is another. SCF has developed its analysis of child-labour issues from its involvement in the project, and is now learning about the particular issues arising from work with the corporate sector.

Conclusions for NGOs

- *Corporate-sector policy:* Before entering partnership negotiations, an NGO needs to have clear policy guidelines on engaging with the private sector, particularly on issues such as the endorsement of corporate-sector firms and their products. The absence of such a policy can place considerable pressure on those representing the NGO in negotiations, although inevitably there are times when policy emerges from experience. Particular policies relating to the partnership in question need to be based on the views of the primary stakeholders.

- *Distinctive advocacy:* An NGO needs to have a clear advocacy policy, using the views of the primary stakeholders, on the relevant issues. In this case, this role gave SCF a distinctive identity within the partnership, ensuring that its views would not be confused with those of the corporate partners. (The relationship with local NGOs provided SCF with a vital link to the views of communities.) NGO opinion will, however, often converge with that of the corporate sector, and the reasons for this convergence need to be clearly articulated.

The combination of different organisations can provide a strong base for external communication and advocacy work, something that would not have existed for the respective organisations working alone. The innovative nature of this partnership has attracted wide media coverage, particularly during the launch in Atlanta and during the Oslo Child Labour conference in October 1997, and many opportunities have emerged for SCF to communicate its views on child labour. The partnership has also influenced the GoP, which is seeking to improve education in Sialkot through a government trust, Pakistan Bait ul Mal, and the Prime Minister's Literacy Commission. Members of the partnership have also gained access to policy makers and opinion leaders. One example includes a visit to Washington which included meetings with the Congressional Human Rights Caucus, the Congressional Progressive Caucus responsible for drafting much of the US trade legislation in recent years, and the Child Labour Coalition, which includes the Foul Ball Campaign, labour groups, and consumer groups. The project has also facilitated links for SCF with trade unions in Pakistan and Europe on child-labour issues.

- NGOs need to *build trust externally and internally* through regular and timely contacts with the corporate sector and a willingness to understand their perspective. Initial commitment and reasonably prompt responses encourage confidence on all sides. Staff with local knowledge and language skills can help to break down cultural barriers and build links with the suppliers in a developing country. Confrontational approaches to negotiating agreements delay the growth of trust, but this does not obviate the need to negotiate from a clearly defined independent position.

  Confidence in the partnership within the NGO can be created through consulting trusted external third parties who can assess the value and potential pitfalls of the proposed partnership and assist with the internal debate. The determination of community leaders within the SCCI to develop a partnership to benefit children, as well as their own companies, was important for SCF and had been confirmed by third-party observers.

- *Alliances* with similar organisations in the partnership help to protect the name of the NGO in a high-profile project, and mean that it can avoid the direct endorsement of products that might detract from putting forward the values of the NGO concerned.

- *Continuing public communication:* A project involving an industry of high concern to consumers will necessitate regular communications with those consumers, in order to explain the project and its value to them and to the products that they buy. This degree of public accountability is seldom found in partnerships involving development organisations, and a detailed and co-ordinated communications and media strategy helps to facilitate it. This may involve the NGO in presenting the project at events such as trade fairs, corporate-sector conferences, and press conferences at major events. The NGO can use these opportunities to present its own distinctive advocacy statements, and so to maintain its clear identity in the partnership. NGOs also need to be ready to respond to the considerable media attention that may be drawn to such partnerships. A consistent approach across an international NGO, including the press office, ensures that the NGO's role is effectively communicated. This partnership also has a communications strategy of its own, which includes producing a bi-monthly update and co-ordinated guidelines for working with the media. This strategy mitigates the considerable risk for such a high-profile project of adverse publicity that is based on inaccurate information .

- *Develop consistent response capacity across the organisation:* International companies often do not have staff based permanently in the country that is the source of their products, so discussions inevitably take place at head-office level as well as locally. This increases the danger that the primary stakeholders will not have their views heard, so these have to be communicated at all levels. Participation in a partnership with a private company whose economy may be larger than that of many developing countries can place considerable stress on relatively small NGOs. For this reason, clear policies and advocacy approaches need to be supported by staff who are committed to the partnership approach across the organisation in areas including programmes, policy, research, advocacy, marketing, and public and media relations. The approach also needs to be consistent at head-office level and within the country concerned, and it is best to hold discussions in-country if possible.

- *Maintain links with those campaigning from the outside:* The independence of an NGO on the inside of a partnership can be reinforced through links with NGOs and pressure groups who may be seeking to influence the corporate sector from the outside. The appropriate level of external pressure can push the partnership towards its goals, and the NGO that is working within the partnership can help to influence the degree of pressure applied. The corporate sector needs to be comfortable about the nature of the links between their partner NGO and external groups.

In conclusion, this case study can help companies and international and local NGOs to understand each other's perspectives as they seek to meet the development challenges of the future by working in cross-sectoral partnerships. The international aspect of these partnerships, and consumers' recognition of international NGOs, will ensure that such NGOs have a role to play in such partnerships until Southern NGOs also gain international recognition. The Sialkot case provides some pointers, which would benefit from examination through other case studies, to help NGOs to shape their role in the twenty-first century; and to be sure that they work closely enough with, but not too close to, the corporate sector.

Acknowledgements

This paper contains extracts from a presentation made to the Conference of Business for Social Responsibility – a US non-profit organisation promoting ethical business – held in Los Angeles in November 1997. Though based on his work at SCF-UK, the paper was written in the author's personal capacity, and so the views represented here should not be attributed either to his former or current employers. Thanks to Rachel Marcus and Fiona King of SCF in London for their ideas and suggestions.

Notes

1 In 1996, official aid flows fell by four per cent to US$55 billion, while private flows grew by 40 per cent to US$234 billion. These figures are misleading, however, as 80 per cent of private investment flows went to just 12 countries, with much of the investment being speculative, rather than being invested in productive sectors.

2 The Foul Ball Campaign, part of the International Labour Rights Fund in Washington, took the lead.

3 The full text of the Atlanta Agreement is included in SCF's situation analysis report (SCF 1997), available from its offices in London, Islamabad, and Sialkot.

References and further reading

Crawford, R. J. (1999) 'Two steps forward, one step back', *Financial Times Management Review* June 1999

Department for International Development (1996) 'Managing Business for a Positive Impact on Society', Workshop Report, London: DFID

Edwards, Michael and David Hulme (eds.) (1995) *Non Governmental Organisations: Performance and Accountability – Beyond the Magic Bullet*, London: Earthscan/SCF

Heap, Simon (1998) *NGOs and the Private Sector: Potential for Partnerships?* Occasional Paper No.27, Oxford: INTRAC

Marcus, R. and C. Harper (1996) *Small Hands: Children in the Working World*, Working Paper No.16, London: SCF

Moser, T. and D. Miller (1997) 'Multinational corporations' impacts on the environment and communities in the developing world: a synthesis of the contemporary debate', *Greener Management International, Journal of Corporate Environmental Strategy and Practice*, Autumn 1997: 40-51

Nelson, J. (1996) *Business as Partners in Development: Creating Wealth for Countries, Companies and Communities*, London: Prince of Wales Business Leaders Forum

Raven, H. (1996) 'Report on British Overseas Agencies Group Relations with the Private Sector', London: British Overseas Agencies Group

SCF (1997) 'Stitching Footballs: Voices of Children in Sialkot, Pakistan', London: SCF

Sialkot Partnership (1999) 'Monthly Progress Report', Sialkot: Sialkot Partnership

Wilks A. (1997) *The World Bank's Promotion of Privatisation and Private Sector Development: Issues and Concerns*, London: Bretton Woods Project

NGOs: fragmented dreams

Jaime Joseph A

Southern NGOs: a background to the crisis

It is difficult to discuss the role of development NGOs without first acknowledging some personal feelings and motives.[1] Some twenty years ago, many socially and politically committed Peruvian professionals decided to set up NGOs as instruments to bring about the democratic transformation of a society that is characterised by profound socio-economic inequality and political exclusion. We sought to establish a new democratic order and a new society, one based on justice and equality, and geared towards meeting the interests of the poor and exploited of Peru.

Today, as NGOs confront problems of identity and of survival, we need to take stock. What is it that keeps us founder-members still working in the NGO sector? What roles do or should NGOs play today? What type of discourse, scenario, and inspiration can NGOs offer the up-and-coming generations of development professionals? What challenging new ideas might open up different directions for NGOs?

The overwhelmingly negative situation has led many development professionals to opt out and abandon their commitment to the NGOs. By far the most important factor has been the relatively poor salaries, but working conditions have also become increasingly demanding and uncomfortable. At the subjective level, we feel we are swimming against the tide. And while often it is not even clear in which direction we should be heading, we have the distinct impression that our progress is slowing down. In some regions, Peru among them, our vulnerability and isolation became very intense as NGOs were caught in the crossfire between terrorism and State repression. And now there is a growing feeling of unease that we are alone and unsupported.

Assuming that those of us who have remained in the NGO sector are not here simply as a result of inertia or incompetence, we nevertheless need to re-think our role at the start of the new millennium. There is no logical reason why the turn of the calendar should change our views, but it serves as a useful pretext for taking a fresh look at the future.

At this point, we need to define the scope of our reflections and clarify what we mean by the term 'NGO', given the plethora of institutions that describe themselves as such. Probably readers of this volume will not require a very detailed definition of development NGOs. We know who we are. We are talking about institutions that came into being during the last thirty years, and were born in the search for ways to work alongside and support the most disadvantaged members of society: the poor and their organisations. We have used different terms to identify the poor over the years, depending on our own way of seeing things and on the language of the day: 'the exploited', 'the oppressed', 'the marginalised'. Today we are increasingly aware that the poor are 'excluded' from power or wealth. Driven by political and ethical commitment, our mission was to help to improve the living conditions of the poor, to strengthen them as social actors (if not social classes), and to play a part in the utopian and radical transformation of a world that is based on structural injustice.

We trust that this broad definition of development NGOs is precise enough to show where we are coming from. However, we would add our perception that NGOs are not only losing their role as radical social critics, and their capacity to put forward broad alternatives. They are also, perhaps more seriously, losing their ability to respond to and take political initiatives. Equally worrying is the loss of the flexibility and audacity that will be required in the search for new ways of achieving new goals. The passage of time has rendered us — some more than others — conservative and often uninspired. This situation is not peculiar to NGOs in Peru: numerous workshops, conferences, and research findings suggest that there is widespread self-questioning within the NGO sector and a search for new horizons.[2]

Finally, a critical element in the context in which NGOs are evolving is the role of international and multilateral agencies that work for the development of 'Third World' countries. In some cases, the need to accommodate ourselves to their agenda has resulted in or reinforced the trend towards the loss of autonomy, initiative, and flexibility referred to above. NGOs have 'accidentally on purpose' been absorbed into the flourishing 'aid industry', in which the logic of development *projects* takes precedence over that of development *strategies*. The bureaucratisation of NGOs and cuts in external funding have left us struggling to survive and compete in a tight marketplace. All this has conspired to foster not only our subordination in terms of ideology, but also our financial dependence on the outside.

Globalisation and the one-thought world: *la pensée unique*[3]

We cannot fully understand the crisis of NGOs without some reflection on the global context in which we are working. Without a doubt, our environment is characterised by a form of globalisation that is based on the increased speed with which the free market operates; or, to put it another way, the speed and the freedom with which capital, merchandise, and information can circulate. However, if this type of globalisation was the only significant factor in the equation, we would simply be experiencing an accelerated phase in the expansion of capitalism, and not a situation that is qualitatively different.[4] But the advancing tide of globalisation has brought with it what has been called the *pensée unique*, or the one-thought world. This proposed universal mindset which we have imported, whether by choice or not, along with the neo-liberal development model, has not helped to galvanise us as people or as nations. Rather, this imported ideology has weighed our theoretical, epistemological, and ethical anchors, and left us to drift on the tides of a globalised sea. In the words of the Chilean political analyst Norbert Lechner, '[I]nterpretive codes are crumbling and, as a result, we perceive reality as disorder on a large scale' (Lechner 1998).

We must of course recognise that it is not only the NGOs who have been affected by this crisis and the loss of direction that characterises the contemporary scene. So too have political parties, which have come to symbolise a decadent political order. Likewise, the nation-state which, having retreated from its social responsibilities and weakened the mechanisms and institutions of democratic politics, is now attempting to address the problems of inequality and social discontent by falling back on authoritarianism in various guises. This holds true also for governments that have been legitimised by the formal electoral process and 'delegative democracy' (O'Donnell 1992).

Fragmented dreams and division

This type of globalisation and universal thinking has affected NGOs, as well as the people and social organisation they work with. We invite our readers to seek the origins of this crisis in the actors themselves. In this case, to look within our NGOs and in the mindsets of those with whom we work, to understand the nature of the crisis and to find paths out of it. The fragmentation we have referred to is apparent, for example, in the gulf that separates the recognition of the importance for development of ethics, values, culture, ethnicity, and gender from practices and projects which are shaped by and often serve the logic of neo-liberalism. The award of a well-deserved Nobel Prize for Economics to Amartya Sen has brought attention to the role of ethics and values in development. But there is a risk of such considerations becoming just another rhetorical fad or optional extra, rather than the very basis for human development. NGOs have in the past championed other fashionable concepts and causes such as 'sustainable development', 'citizenship', 'civil society', 'gender equity', 'youth opportunity', and 'consensus building', but often they fail to establish the links between them in a global strategy of change. While important, these aspects of development are neutralised and even distorted, unless they are linked with genuine social processes that have a perspective that goes beyond short-term or sectoral concerns.

It is remarkable that almost all the NGOs use the same terminology: 'participatory democracy', 'local development', 'citizen participation', and 'human rights'. However, there are grounds for fearing that schemes and approaches are being adopted — more in practice than as a matter of theoretical conviction — which in effect restrict participatory democracy and citizenship simply to participation at the micro-level in processes and programmes to combat poverty and other effects of structural adjustment. Hence, there is a tendency to regard any successful poverty-relief programme at the micro-level as 'local development'. The concept of local development thus loses any relation to envisaging and working towards other, more holistic and more human, forms of development.

All of which brings us to the unavoidable question of how we relate people's specific concrete problems and needs to general concerns for human development and democracy. In this globalised, fragmented world we must look for the *public spaces* in which particular interests come together in the 'common good'. This, we believe, can happen only in the political arena. However, NGOs have consciously or unconsciously adopted approaches to development and anti-poverty efforts that are based on a limited — often negative — concept of what politics is about. Furthermore, some even seek to reduce popular political expression to the very minimum, simply in order to achieve their project objectives. We therefore need to ask ourselves why NGOs have disengaged from politics, and to look for ways to restore a political perspective both to development and to our own commitment to the well-being of ordinary people in countries like Peru.

Democracy and development: two halves of a single whole

The Argentinean political analyst, José Aricó, said some years ago that 'we are unable to find a way out [of the crisis] because we are captives of the very terms in which the crisis is defined. We reason from within it, and it is the crisis that imposes a horizon on our ability to see.' And it has become increasingly clear that the misnamed (neo-)liberal model, or Washington Consensus, has imposed on us not merely a set of economic measures, set out in the IMF's 'letters of intent' to which our countries must subscribe should they not wish to forgo the chance to increase their debts, but also a particular vision of development and politics, which leaves the former to the market and reduces politics to almost trivial matters.

To escape from this political, theoretical, ethical, and cultural impasse, we would like to explore two central considerations, democracy and development, and to establish a necessary relationship between them. Our intention is not to offer a theoretical essay, but we hope to show how the current divide within our NGOs between research, lobbying, and consultancy work on the one hand, and promotional and educational work with social actors on the other, derives from our limited and disjointed understanding of the processes of democracy and development. Such an understanding serves the neo-liberal world project. We argue that we need to treat democracy and development as two halves of the same whole, two aspects of a single theoretical concept and process. We will then draw on these notions to suggest a possible fertile starting point for finding a way out of our crisis.

Human development

The development model that underpins the Washington Consensus and has been imposed on the world by multilateral agencies such as the IMF and the World Bank has been criticised by many analysts and even by some of its creators.[5] Denis Goulet has criticised the *reductionist* nature of the model, which measures development only in terms of macro-economic concerns and indicators. In Latin America, Manfred Max-Neef introduced the concept of *development on a human scale*. Amartya Sen, who now speaks to a worldwide audience, has argued the importance and the role of values and ethics in development. The UNDP, along with its *Human Development Reports*, has also played a significant part in encouraging critical appraisal of the model. The criticisms and alternative approaches offered by these and many other analysts have created a fertile basis for the search for solutions to the crisis in which we are trapped. This is not to suggest, however, that our critical analysis or theoretical apparatus have any automatic or straightforward solutions to offer.

There is a danger awaiting us in the way that we approach our critique of the prevailing model of development. The critique that has been developed over the last twenty years has profoundly human origins, inspired by the recognition of the tremendous suffering, poverty, injustice, and marginalisation that is generated by this model of development. This view has led to the emergence of social movements on a world-wide scale, one of the most important of which is the present Jubilee 2000 Campaign for the reduction or forgiveness of the unjust burden of foreign debt that is borne by the poorest countries.

However, we do not all draw the same conclusions from this critique. Many strategies designed to soften the impact of the neo-liberal model of development focus solely on its *effects*, not on the causes inherent in it. We need to ask ourselves whether NGO strategies are also limited to combating effects without identifying and addressing the causes of poverty. For example, it is possible to criticise the narrowness of the neo-liberal model and its exclusive focus on macro-economic indicators, and to include other issues relating to the social dimensions (income, health, food, education), or gender, or the environment – but still remain within the framework of the same model. In this what we might term 'neo-structuralist' approach, ethical considerations and human values serve to correct the defects of the neo-liberal model, but not to criticise the model itself. As Aricó noted, we are still caught within the terms in which the crisis is defined.

Many NGOs, especially those that started out with socialist or Marxist leanings, have often been very cautious and restrained in their critiques of neo-liberalism, because of the loss of their own ideological footing and paradigms, particularly since the fall of the Berlin Wall. Other NGOs (the minority) have maintained a radically critical discourse, but in practice their work on the ground has also been confined to attempts to alleviate the effects of the model. As we see it, in neither case have NGOs succeeded in identifying where to start in order to develop a critical, holistic, and practice-based analysis. The problem of finding a starting point that is both profoundly and radically critical *and* innovative is not exclusive to NGOs. Left-wing political parties, as well as other parties and political movements working for social change, appear to be similarly paralysed, caught between the urgent need to alleviate poverty and the need to find new ways forward. We may indeed ask whether the 'Third Way' is not just another example of an attempt to find a better way of dealing with the effects of the neo-liberal model, rather than searching for a different approach altogether.

Democracy for development

Our critique needs to approach this issue from a different perspective. As mentioned earlier, ethical principles, cultural values, and concern for the quality of life should not be seen as 'optional extras', serving merely to counteract the negative effects of the prevailing model. They should be the starting point for a human and holistic approach to — rather than model of — development. Amartya Sen and many others have shown that we need to understand development as the development of the human person, his or her *freely* determined needs and capacities. It should be remembered that the human person — the starting point and also the subject of human development — creates himself or herself as a person in society, in relationships with others, in and with the community. Hence human development also means the development of society.

We do not intend to embark on a review of the various approaches to human development. The authors mentioned above argue their case quite clearly in their own writings. What is vital, and this takes us to the second concept, that of *democracy*, is that the human person and the societies in which the person exists must of necessity be the very *subject* of development, not merely an object or reference point in our analysis and evaluation of differing approaches to development.

Sen defines human development as the development of the capacities of the human person, capacities that must be *freely* determined. We must underline the critical importance of this definition and everything that flows from it. No one can decide what human development is to mean for someone else. And no society or culture can dictate the perspectives or values of another society. People's role in development should not be limited to participating in decisions about how to address the effects of a given development model. They must be free to choose what development they want, both as individuals and as communities, two dimensions of our identities that are in constant interaction and tension. The means by which this free determination is achieved is essentially the exercise of democratic political activity.

The reader will probably need little convincing in order to agree that the 'democratic' systems with which we are familiar do not deliver real power (*cratos*) into the hands of the people (*demos*), power of the sort that allows them freely to determine the type of development they want. In the first place, our democratic systems are based above all on nation-states, which are themselves now greatly weakened in their capacity to shape the direction of development within their own frontiers. Second, there are increasing signs that the majority — the poor and marginalised — no longer expect the democratic system to provide them with solutions to their problems and basic aspirations. It is no coincidence that the number of authoritarian governments — both elected and otherwise — has increased as the desire to participate in politics has diminished. People are choosing to opt out of politics rather than to participate – choosing the exit rather than attempting to voice their concerns (Hirschman 1982). They prefer to delegate political responsibility, rather than elect people who are able to represent their interests (O'Donnell 1992). The most worrying aspect of this trend towards depoliticisation and the decline of representative democracy is that it is not simply a reflection of the 'backwardness' of developing countries, but is also now apparent even in the developed world.

In many of the poorer countries, most of them former colonies, this divorce between democracy and human development and well-being also has a historical dimension. In the case of Peru, for example, we find that since becoming an independent republic, the country has spent more years under dictatorships and authoritarian governments than it has under democratically elected governments. The indicators of economic and social development reveal that progress is more closely associated with authoritarian government than it has been with democracy. Popular support in Peru for the overtly authoritarian Fujimori government and current developments in Ecuador and Venezuela, a country with a more substantial democratic tradition, suggest that these countries are moving in the same direction: towards authoritarianism and the concentration of power.

From what has been said above, we can surely now draw some preliminary conclusions. On the one hand, if we understand development to mean the development of the person and his or her *freely* determined capacities, then we can conclude that democracy and development are inseparable. Consequently, we cannot pursue development and leave democracy until later, as the Fujimori government argues. Nor can we try to establish a democratic system without linking these efforts to the development process, which seems to be the thinking embodied in the political groups opposed to the authoritarian government in Peru.

On the other hand, if we also recognise that the political mechanisms required for individuals and peoples to exercise freedom of choice (i.e. democratic political systems) have been profoundly weakened, then we can conclude that our strategies for achieving human development must focus on building forms of democracy — participative and representative — that are closely associated with the processes of development. Here again, we find serious limitations in the ways in which many NGOs are approaching the task of strengthening both the democratic system and political and social actors. Simply put, often the programmes and projects that are explicitly designed to strengthen democracy are not based on a critical analysis of the democratic political system itself. Instead, they tend to limit their action to the formal aspects of democracy, which, while important, are not the core of the problem. Hence we find numerous attempts, especially directed towards women, to *build citizenship*, to allow them to exercise their civil and political rights. Such programmes are aimed at redressing the substantial gender imbalance of those registered to vote and generally promoting *citizenship* or civic participation.

What we would criticise in many of these programmes is their apparent failure to recognise that the system of representative democracy that we imported with our constitutions when we gained independence is not the product of inclusive or unifying social and economic processes. A modern political model was superimposed upon a pre-modern market and society. We must therefore recognise that in countries such as our own, where life is so precarious, a solid citizenship must be the result of the social and political practices of the people themselves, rather than the result of laws and rules. If we forget this relationship between democracy and the social processes that are actually at work, we risk building a democracy whose citizens are fragile abstractions, with no connection to the human development process that we are proposing.

In a recent conference, the town planner and councillor of Barcelona, Jordi Borja, described an incident that illustrates our point. Residents in a predominantly working-class neighbourhood of Barcelona organised to oppose the building of a recreation centre for elderly people. According to Borja, the local community rejected the idea of having 'old people in our neighbourhood'. As Borja pointed out, this action was 'civic participation', but participation with a clearly anti-democratic content. This anecdote serves to emphasise the importance of ensuring that our efforts to build a democratic political system do not take place in isolation from the processes of human development, processes which have technical dimensions but which are also about ethics. The basic issue is the political content and direction of the democracy we are putting forward.

Where might we find a solution?

We have tried to establish a theoretical and practical relationship between human development and democratic politics, arguing that human, freely determined development can only be arrived at through democratic political activity. If this is so, we want to ask how and where such political practices can emerge. From our experience we believe that the key is in the social actors themselves, particularly the popular organisations and their leaders.

We assume that readers who are familiar with grassroots organisations will be aware that so far the reference to the 'individual and/or social actor' has been at a level of generalisation and abstraction. Such abstraction and generalisation lends itself to all forms of exaggerated and misleading simplifications. Indeed, there are studies and analyses of these actors that depict contradictory realities and perspectives. Some observers consider that collective organisations have fulfilled their historical role, that political and development processes are now the exclusive domain of the individual, and that political activity is reduced to little more than the *marketing* of policy proposals which politicians offer to the public via the mass media. This political 'market' is analysed in the same way as other markets, using surveys, opinion polls, and ratings.

This kind of assessment of social organisations may be very useful for the purposes of those NGO professionals who prioritise methodological and quantitative research, or who offer their consulting services to government entities and multilateral agencies, or who lobby at the national or international level. Seen from this perspective, the only area in which social organisation has any role to play is in the processes of ensuring basic survival. These processes are seen as important for humanitarian reasons, but are of little relevance as far as political activity is concerned, that is, activities in which the aim is to gain access to public decision making, i.e. to power. The organisations therefore have no place in political activity through which the interests of the individual can be aligned with the country's overall interests, and through which consensus, common interest, and the 'common good' are constructed.

The opposite stance, equally at odds with reality, is taken by those who champion various forms of 'popular protagonism' and stubbornly maintain that social actors have the capacity, almost in and of themselves, to resolve the crisis. This point of view is one that may appeal more to those who experienced the powerful social and class movements of previous decades. However, the optimism inherent in this approach encourages a tendency to exaggerate the benevolence of social actors and their practices. Often such exaggerated optimism tends to deify the people, disregarding their weaknesses and the negative impact that poverty — profound and persistent poverty — is having on the actors themselves and on their vision and the collective consciousness.

We do not share the view that people living in persistent poverty and great deprivation are unable to aspire to anything more than survival. Everyday experience shows that 'post-material interests' (Inglehart 1997) can indeed form part of the aspirations and concerns of the poor. However, it is also true that the widespread and prolonged crisis and the widening gap between the rich and the poor, plus the injustice that this gap reveals, have a negative impact on social actors, on their self-esteem, their desire for progress and their willingness to engage in politics. Poverty in itself has never dignified, ennobled, or motivated anyone: quite the opposite. Poverty and injustice dehumanise, discourage, and demobilise. This demobilisation is intensified by the *universal* discourse of the one-thought world that accompanies the neo-liberal model. According to that discourse, success and development are the fruit of individual effort, of individual competitiveness. Furthermore, it is also true that the social actors in a defeated society have never been the protagonists of historical change. Thus, we need to identify the places and conditions that will allow us to overcome the negative impacts of the crisis.

The emergence of 'public spaces'

In spite of the obvious weaknesses and contradictions that exist in the popular social sectors with which we work, it is to them that we must look for new approaches and strategies. While they have lost ground in the neo-liberal globalisation process, these sectors and their organisations nevertheless possess a valuable wealth of experience, values, and wisdom that we must draw upon. In particular, we believe that recent experiences of consensus building among diverse social organisations may offer the beginnings of socio-political processes that lead to rebuilding democratic forms of political action aiming at integral development. We are calling these experiences of co-ordination for consensus building *public spaces*.

Two caveats are necessary. First, these emerging experiences of broad-based consensus building have attracted a lot of attention and raised considerable expectations, especially at the local level where local governments are playing a central role. The concrete successes, often in the form of local development plans and above all in participatory approaches to the alleviation of poverty, have generated considerable enthusiasm. We can well understand this enthusiasm and the need to see success and encouragement amid the desolate landscape of defeat and retreat in which we are working. But this has also led observers to exaggerate the solidity and obscure the weaknesses of the political and social processes and actors concerned. Excessive enthusiasm may lead to discouragement, and in fact we have seen how fragile many of these ventures have been, virtually collapsing and disappearing simply with a change of municipal authority.

We also need to point out that by *'public space'* we are referring to the specific experience of interaction among the social actors.[6] We prefer *'public space'* to *'consensus building'*, because the latter is used almost exclusively to refer to planning processes organised in conjunction with municipal authorities. As we understand it, the term 'public space' encompasses a much wider range of scenarios and activities, in which actors with diverse and even conflicting interests and characteristics interact not only with a view to dealing with their particular problems but also to building common interests.

Therefore, our definition of 'public space' refers to more than just urban scenarios — parks and meeting halls — for meetings and get-togethers, as used by urban planners. In an urban context, common spaces of this kind are certainly important for creating identities and establishing a sense of belonging. However, our definition of 'public space', while incorporating a geographical or neighbourhood component, refers more to the political processes and to the way actors participate in them.

Another aspect of this notion of 'public space' derives from an interest in and a concern about communication, language, and the creation of common meanings and discourse. Communication is a central and perhaps neglected feature of modern-day democratic politics, and hence we are interested in the role and type of communication that takes place within the 'public spaces' that we wish to observe and consolidate. However our interest is in understanding the particular nature of the relationships, dynamics, and communication that exist among social organisations within the 'public space', and among individuals within their organisations.

Development-oriented political culture

We been studying these 'public spaces' from the viewpoint of concern about the crisis faced by the NGOs and other actors in the poor world. We wish to assess the potential of these 'public spaces' for linking up the processes of democratisation and development that are based on individuals in society, and the crossroads between liberalism and communitarianism. We are concentrating on these 'public spaces' because we have a sense that within them will be found approaches and strategies that will enable us to emerge from our present crisis.

The first way in which we can find out more about such experiences is through direct contact, as many NGOs are doing. However, this is not enough by itself, and there is a danger of either ascribing too much value to what we observe or of being over-critical when we witness any difficulties, complications, or failures – and thus overlooking anything that offers potential or can be remedied.

Here we offer some suggestions and preliminary comments drawn from a study currently being undertaken by a team from Centro Alternativa who have been working in the poorer neighbourhoods of the Cono Norte of Metropolitan Lima. Our study, entitled 'Political Culture and Human Development', began with an analysis of our situation and of various aspects of the crisis. The research team conducted interviews and focus-group discussions, along with direct observation. On the basis of this tentative and open-ended preliminary study, we formulated a series of concepts or hypotheses that continue to guide our research. If our intuitions prove to be well founded, these concepts and hypotheses may contribute to the much-needed process of analysis both within our own institutions and together with organisations that are committed to improving the lot of the ordinary people of Peru.

We grouped our ideas into three categories and then attempted to see how these relate to one another. The first is concerned with the process of individuation and its constituent elements — how social actors perceive themselves as *individuals*; the construction of their identity as persons in relation to their community, history, and traditions; the values to which the subject subscribes, and his/her capacity to argue from the basis of these values; his/her spiritual dimension; and his/her perceptions and attitudes towards his/her civic role. The process of individuation is known to be profoundly related to the values expressed within the community and to the worldviews (or cosmovisions) offered by the environment in which s/he becomes socialised. We are aware that the particular feature of the community or organisation exercises a considerable influence, for better or worse, on the personal development of those individuals who are capable of engaging with the processes of development and democratisation.

The second category describes the vision of development. We want to identify the constituent elements of that vision and its scope; the ways in which needs, capacities, and interests are defined; the common ground that exists within the different ways of thinking, the ethical components and perceptions of time and scenarios. We want to establish whether individual or collective actors share a holistic — human — vision of development, or one that is limited to the macro-economic dimensions, personal initiative, and competitiveness. It is important to know whether the values of solidarity and trust offer a basis from which to approach development, or whether they are merely defensive survival strategies.

The third category of ideas encompasses the political perspective and the construction of 'public spaces'. As we see it, opportunities for reconstructing the 'public domain' and politics exist primarily at the sub-national or regional level. We wish to analyse the relationship that exists between (more or less human and holistic) visions of development and the processes by which new forms of democratic political activity are constructed. We need to know whether social organisations and individuals see politics as being an important, indeed essential, means of achieving human development, or whether they have devolved or delegated that responsibility to others. In particular, we wish to understand the factors that lead social actors to participate in 'public spaces'.

The approach we propose is therefore based on an acknowledgement of the vital interrelationship existing between the person or individual, the community, development, and politics. The linking up of these different elements does not represent a point of departure but, rather, a point of arrival. It relates to our very purpose as NGOs, and hence we need to identify strategies that take account of these central elements.

Ways forward

If these conceptual categories have anything to offer, it is not because they contain unusual or new ideas. Each has been the subject of much study and comment. However, and we believe this is crucial, the tendency has been to consider each category or set of ideas in isolation. When the economic and political crisis began, in the second half of the 1970s, considerable emphasis was placed on day-to-day life, the individual and his or her rights and aspirations. The intention was to restore the balance after an excessive emphasis on collective action, through forms of social organisation, trade unions, and political parties. However, this emphasis on the individual and daily life often left aside the two-way causal relationships at play in the interaction between the individual or community on the one hand, and the vision of development and politics on the other.

Similarly, many studies and evaluations that look at development are concerned with its human dimension. However, these studies often refer to the people involved almost exclusively in terms of the impact of the prevailing model of development on the quality of life of poor communities. As a result, considerable attention has been devoted to defining qualitative indicators of human development. This kind of analysis has often failed to identify the human person or the communities or society in which she or he lives, as the *subjects* and protagonists of the process, and not as an end product. There is also a tendency in human-development approaches to assume that people, their communities and society are somehow a solid and noble entity, a somewhat Rousseauesque notion. But this is not the case, at least in our urban societies that are exposed to the discourse and the universal mindset of globalisation.

Furthermore, in these human approaches to development, there has been little attention paid to the political mechanisms that might lead to human development, the simple assumption being that the existing system of representative democracy is adequate to the task. As we have stated, this assumption is no longer valid. Analyses and programmes aimed at reinforcing and encouraging participation in democratic processes have tended to focus only on the formal aspects of the democratic system: the rights and duties of citizens, institutions and procedures, autonomy, etc. The relationship between the democratic system and the development process is lost, as well as the idea that democracy is a tool for arriving at human development. Consequently, concern for the participation of individuals and civil-society organisations (CSOs) has focused on the rights to and mechanisms for participation in the democratic system, but not on the content and meaning of the participation that is envisaged.

In our own research and work with the people's organisations, we have been trying to understand the interrelationships between our three conceptual categories: individual/community, development, and democracy. Without going into detail, we are finding that where 'weak' individuals with low self-esteem predominate, while they are conscious of what they lack, they do not formulate interests and nor do they consider their own capacities. In such cases, the community or the social organisation is simply a means for dealing with concrete and specific issues, not a basis for development proposals or for democracy building. In weak individuals and organisations we also find a limited vision of development, a short-term perspective without clarity about the role of each actor within the development process. Similarly, where we find weak individuals and a narrow vision of development, we also find a negative vision of politics and a lack of political will. The chain of causality that links all three categories, as is so often the case, is not linear but circular. Our interest is to make the circle virtuous and not vicious.

We suggest, and there is already some evidence to support this proposition, that an approach which takes into account the inter-relationships between these three conceptual categories may both contribute to a better understanding of the nature of the crisis and offer ways out of it. These issues cut across the various specialised areas within the NGOs — research, lobbying, and consultancy on the one hand, promotional and educational work on the other. They may help to build bridges, theoretical and practical, across the divide between the different areas of work and among the people working in various specialised areas, and so help to close the gap that exists between the diverse types of work that NGOs may be involved in at any one time. We are also attempting to discover how far our three broad categories can help us to develop a common agenda for the different actors who are involved with the poor and disadvantaged, especially NGOs and the international aid agencies.

References

Hirschman, Albert O. (1982) *Shifting Involvements, Private Interest and Public Action*, Princeton NJ: Princeton University Press.

Inglehart, Ronald (1997) *Modernization and Postmodernization, Cultural Economic and Political*, Princeton NJ: Princeton University Press.

Lechner, Norbert (1998) 'Las transformaciones de la política' in *Seminario Las Transformaciones de la Política*, Lima: IEP.

O'Donnell, Guillermo (1992) 'Delegative Democracy', Working Paper 172, Notre Dame University: Kellogg Institute.

Ramonet, I. (1997) 'The one and only way of thinking', in M. Rahnem and V. Bawtree (eds.) *The Post-Development Reader*, London: Zed Books.

Indicators of identity: NGOs and the strategic imperative of assessing core values

John Hailey

> As foreign aid declines, new forms of international cooperation are emerging to meet the realities of this changing world, with a focus on rules and standards rather than subsidised resource transfer.
> (Edwards, Hulme, and Wallace 1999)

This quotation comes from the background paper presented at a January 1999 international conference, entitled 'NGOs in a Global Future'. It reflects one of the main themes that underpinned much of the ensuing discussion. Many speakers expressed concern at the consequences of the changing relationship between NGOs and aid donors, and the implications for the role and remit of NGOs in the next century. One such consequence is that there will be increased competition for limited aid funds, and donors thus will be in a stronger position to impose conditions and influence the core values of NGOs.

This article argues that, in the light of this increasingly competitive environment, the distinctive values common to many NGOs give them a particular advantage over other types of organisation. This perspective should be seen in the context of donors' increasing willingness to fund non-traditional development actors, including the military, parastatals, quangos, private service contractors, and consultancy firms. If NGOs, of various types, are to distinguish themselves from other recipients of aid funding, they need not only to be seen to have sufficient organisational capacity and to use such funds effectively, but also to identify, articulate, and nurture their own core values and identity. In order to help this process, this paper identifies some of the key indicators that best reflect values and organisational capacities that distinguish NGOs from other

ideologies and 'performance culture' which dominated much organisational thinking in the 1980s, and the competition for funds and the changing pattern of aid flows that marked the 1990s. The resulting emphasis on value for money, accountability, and cost-efficiency has encouraged the use of mechanistic planning and evaluation tools such as Logical Framework Analysis ('logframe'), and various other assessment mechanisms that rely on measurable indicators of output, impact, and capacity.

One obvious consequence of this changing emphasis is that the particular values that were the hallmark of the NGO sector at its inception are beginning to be diluted. These values, and the intangible social goals that NGOs espoused, are threatened in the rush to achieve tangible, quantifiable measures of development. Many Northern NGOs, such as CAFOD or Oxfam GB, emerged from a climate of humanitarian concern or social activism. Southern NGOs were commonly change agents who gained their legitimacy, and therefore their effectiveness, through their espoused values and their ability to identify with, and work with, the local community. Yet donors increasingly see such NGOs as partners, or even associates, who can be contracted to provide specific services (such as primary health care to x number of children), build physical infrastructure (so many tube wells or watershed projects), or promote income-generating activity (training y number of local entrepreneurs, or running Grameen Bank-like microcredit programmes).

Thus, the very things that made many NGOs distinct and gave them added value are under threat. We have a picture of a sector in which traditional values are jeopardised, and which does not have the management or organisational capacity to cope with the new demands being imposed on it. Most obviously, pressure from donors has encouraged many Southern NGOs to expand their activities, and accept contractual obligations and performance criteria that have led to the marginalisation of the values, tacit knowledge, and cultural sensitivities which differentiated NGOs from other organisations. In hindsight, these are in fact the core competencies that NGOs lose at their peril.

This is not an argument for the abandonment of mechanistic performance criteria or evaluation tools, nor for the rejection of ideas of accountability or cost-effectiveness; but a recognition that indicators of key organisational values, that are particular to many development NGOs, are an essential reporting requirement. They are not project-specific, but should be applied across the whole organisation and be given the same weight as financial accounts or a social audit.

Indicators of key organisational values

If, as this paper argues, such values are key differentiators, then organisational indicators which reflect their role and importance are essential components of any organisational assessment or annual reporting exercise. Among other things, such indicators need to assess the NGO's capacity to promote internal learning, its degree of transparency and levels of accountability; and the extent to which it is participatory in its approach to decision making, planning, or programme evaluation. Such indicators need to be measurable, clear, and precise if they are to be operationally useful. The following capacities and their associated indicators demonstrate the range of measures available, and reflect the diversity of indicators used to assess key organisational values.

Is there any indication that this organisation has been involved in a genuinely participative planning, monitoring, or evaluation process within the local community with which it is working?

- That the phrase 'participation' is commonly found in mission statements and institutional objectives of the NGO, and that the philosophy of participation is articulated in other documentation and staff-training materials.
- That there are clear descriptions of the participatory process in which the organisation is involved which are freely available in local and generic languages.
- That there are visual records (photos/videos/maps/matrices) and written records (minutes/leaflets/posters) of participatory planning exercises freely available which reflect participation by a balanced range of different members of the community by gender, class, education, etc.
- That there are regular public meetings held in the local language, attended by a certain percentage of identified members of the local community and the staff of the NGO, in which three-quarters of the speakers come from the local community.
- That 'group synergy' was observed during meetings and gatherings, reflected in body language, speed of discussion, type of words or jargon used, and a lack of comments that employed divisive language ('us' and 'them', 'our' and 'their', etc.).
- That NGO staff receive training, literature, and manuals, or are paid an incentive to ensure that participatory approaches are applied and that local knowledge is promoted.

The increasing involvement of consultancy firms, private-sector contractors, the military, and new multilateral agencies will fuel this competition and, faced with new conditions imposed by donors, NGOs may feel tempted to dilute their distinctive values. There is, therefore, an urgent need for NGOs to identify and nurture the values that have made them such a distinct component of the development process. If NGOs lose their core values, they lose their role. They are reduced to being just another type of contractor competing for funds, commissions, and projects. If they can identify and develop organisational capacities and management competencies that are rooted in their core values, they will not only have a strategic advantage when attracting funding, volunteers, and staff; but they will also best serve the needs of their members, their supporters, and the communities in which they work.

References

Chambers, Robert (1997) *Whose Reality Counts: Putting the First Last*, London: IT Publications

Clark, John (1991) *Democratizing Development: The Role of Voluntary Organisations*, London: Earthscan

Eade, Deborah (1998) *Capacity Building: An Approach to People-Centred Development*, Oxford: Oxfam

Edwards, Michael, David Hulme, and Tina Wallace (1999) 'NGOs in a Global Future: Marrying Local Delivery to Worldwide Leverage', Background Paper to Conference on NGOs in a Global Future, Birmingham, January 1999

Edwards, Michael and David Hulme (eds.) (1992) *Making a Difference: NGOs and Development in a Changing World*, London: Earthscan.

Edwards, Michael and David Hulme (eds.) (1995) *Non-Governmental Organisations – Performance and Accountability: Beyond the Magic Bullet*, London: Earthscan

Fowler, Alan (1997) *Striking a Balance: A Guide to Enhancing the Effectiveness of NGOs*, London: Earthscan

Korten, David (1990) *Getting to the 21st Century: Voluntary Action and the Global Agenda*, West Hartford: Kumarian

Smillie, Ian (1995) *The Alms Bazaar: Non-Profit Organisations and International Development*, London: IT Publications

Smillie, Ian and Henny Helmich (eds.) (1999) *Stakeholders: Government — NGO Partnerships for International Development*, London: Earthscan

Development agencies: global or solo players?

Sylvia Borren

Emancipation and solidarity: linked or at loggerheads?

The term 'emancipation' is used in this paper to refer to the experiences of any group of people who are disadvantaged, structurally excluded from access to resources, or suffering from some form of discrimination, if they become increasingly able to analyse their own situation, identify the structural forces working against them, and gain access to knowledge, skills, and organisational power to change their situation and work towards sustainable solutions. Emancipation can be achieved by impoverished people, indigenous people, women from a range of social and economic backgrounds, members of sexual minority groups, people living with disabilities, and children – indeed by members of any social sector who identify and organise against the exclusion and oppression that affect them. 'Solidarity', as used in this paper, refers to a conviction of our common humanity that motivates people who are not themselves facing a particular set of negative circumstances, but who identify with those who are. They recognise the need to mobilise against injustice and poverty, because they wish to live in a fairer world, and because they want to support a particular social group or emancipation process.

There are two important links between emancipation and solidarity. First is the cognitive and emotional recognition of injustice, whether experienced oneself or by others, which provides the motivation to work towards change. Cognitive and/or emotional rejection of the reality of injustice, the familiar tendency to 'blame the victim', may be the result of a process of psychological denial. The first step on the road to

equally critically to the ways of working of the agency's partner organisations – organisations which may not respect sufficiently the autonomy or emancipation process of the people participating in their programmes (the intended beneficiaries), or which may not have an effective policy on issues such as gender equity or cultural and social diversity.

The quality of partnership

The quality of the relationship between the donor organisation and its local partner agency depends on the donor's practical commitment to the principle that a local group, organisation, or institution is an autonomous actor, primarily responsible for its own emancipation – and thus also for its own analysis, strategies, ways of working, and management practices. In the same way, donor agencies are also autonomous actors who need to define as transparently as possible what roles they can and cannot play, what their policies and quality standards are, and what they have to offer. They will be sensitive to, and influenced by, a variety of stakeholders and voices in setting these policies, standards, and roles. It is in the interaction between the various autonomous actors (stakeholders) that partnership and co-operation develop. This partnership is based on common values, shared analysis, and the energy needed to find sustainable solutions. Various actors or stakeholders may play differing but complementary roles, depending on the specific problems of poverty and injustice.

Development agencies engage in varieties of partnership. The relationship may well vary, depending on which roles the partners play in specific development situations. Dilemmas and tensions can exist between donor agencies and partners if they are playing several roles at once. Discussion of these issues is needed in order to decide which roles can or cannot be combined, or how checks and balances will be put in place to ensure quality – and to avoid well-intentioned, solidarity-based donor-dominance getting in the way of autonomy, ownership, and emancipation of the real actors of development: the 'beneficiaries', or programme participants.

Roles and functions of development agencies – and their staff

Strategic development funding

Development agencies facilitate change by funding relevant and appropriate actors in the South and (to a lesser extent, as yet) in the North: community-based organisations (CBOs), social movements, trade unions, intermediary or thematic NGOs or organisations, sometimes local governments or other organisations, and possibly individuals on a temporary basis. The aim of the funding is to support and empower organisations and those participating in their programmes who are denied their social, political, and economic rights. Funding provides the financial means for them to organise and construct their own solutions.

'Strategic development funding' involves identifying and supporting social actors who can make innovative and critical contributions to eliminating the immediate and structural causes of injustice and poverty, and who can achieve patterns of sustainable development, mostly in Africa, Asia Pacific, Latin America, the former Soviet Union, and Eastern Europe, but also in Western countries. Such funding might also be considered strategic because these social actors are supported in their core organisational needs and development (rather than simply in their activities and projects). Sometimes it can be appropriate to fund innovative but small and/or risky initiatives, as stepping-stones to something better or bigger. Ideally, partners are also able to network and interact with others to achieve greater impact than they could if they worked on their own.

Strategic development funding requires the skill to undertake contextual and organisational surveys. Replicability and sustainability are two key criteria for any development programme, but individual initiatives can also lead to significant learning and may be supported on that basis.

A common problem is that the funding relationship is unsustainable. Southern partners can be damaged both by a sudden influx of funds and by an unexpected cutback. But donors may similarly be affected by processes that they cannot control, such as fluctuating exchange rates, a change of government, or changes in the policies of their own funders . Partners often try to solve this by spreading the risk among a number of donors. However, these donors seldom co-ordinate their monitoring and reporting requirements, which leaves the partner organisation having to spend a lot of time and energy on reporting.

to dependence, disempowerment, and strategic or organisational problems for the partner organisation in the long term. Good consultants, therapists, and doctors have learned to manage these tensions in their role, and have learned to interrelate with their clients or patients in a way that empowers them, and leaves them real autonomy when making decisions. Development agencies may find it worthwhile to consider some of the professional and ethical standards, codes of conduct, and communication skills that have been developed in those professions.

It may also be possible to design checks and balances in the relationship between partner and donor, to prevent some of the inadvertent donor-dominance described above. It may be helpful to employ more objective ways of working, such as using assessment tools, hiring external evaluators, seeking second opinions, and undergoing mutual appraisal exercises.

A third and related issue is the negotiation of 'minimum standards' between donors and their partner organisations. In part, this has to do with planning, reporting, and financial accountability; but it also concerns value-ridden matters such as gender awareness or a non-partisan ideology. Accountability to the donor often takes precedence over accountability to the participants of any particular programme. There is little opportunity for social organisations or NGOs to compare their performance systematically with that of others. Without accountability to participants, or horizontal accountability among NGOs (benchmarking, or peer comparison), accountability is likely to become donor-driven. This is complicated by the fact that donors may not themselves be accountable institutions with coherent policies, but are made up of individual people who have decision-making power, and their own views and opinions. There are rarely any formal complaint mechanisms in place; nor is there a chance to obtain a second opinion in the case of disagreement. When an individual contact changes in the donor organisation, a partner organisation might face a new set of opinions and requirements. Institutional consistency is not, on the whole, a strong point among donors. Here, then, the power of solidarity-driven individuals over-rides the beneficiaries' or participants' ownership of their development processes.

Operational development work

There are situations, countries, or regions where there are no (or virtually no) local or national organisations, and little or no community organising. Yet the problems faced by people living there may include lack of health care or education programmes, or poor and unsustainable rural development practices. In this context, an international NGO may decide to take on operational development work. In effect, the donor assumes a role that is usually played by a local social actor or intermediary NGO. The donor's field staff will, in operational programmes, usually employ participatory methods, establishing CBOs, and developing responses to local needs alongside them. The accountability of this work, both to the communities themselves and to the agency's domestic constituency, is not in itself different from the accountability required of local organisations: participatory planning, clarity of objectives, efficient and effective working methods, clear monitoring and evaluation are all needed. Field staff involved in operational work will nearly always also be involved in training and coaching local people and organisations to develop their own capacity to take responsibility for the work later.

The issues to be addressed are mostly concerned with questions of empowerment, replicability, and withdrawal – which are again not intrinsically different from those faced by local intermediary NGOs, except that, where these have good governance, democratic practices, and community-based participant-accountability structures in place, they are likely to be more sensitive to local checks and balances. If, for instance, the operational agency has developed a method of engaging with the community, and then structured means of providing water-points, grain mills, housing, primary schools, child-care services, primary health care, animal husbandry, etc., the first tension lies in the balance between involvement and empowerment of the local community and the efficiency or quality of the product or service provided. It can take much longer – and cost more – to involve the community fully in choices about where and how houses are built, water-points installed, etc. The drive for efficiency or lower costs may result in cutting back on such involvement. Similarly, there may be optimal community development, but a very slow process to achieve concrete results. How can we measure the quality of this community process? How sustainable is the service or product when the operational development workers withdraw? There are many examples of water points or grain mills being abandoned through lack of maintenance, and instances of small economic enterprises failing because local markets are not sufficiently developed or accessible, but also there are many examples of inordinately slow processes in situations where social tensions over scarce facilities are growing.

Effective withdrawal systems that leave sustainable CBOs with improved services and economic opportunities can certainly be achieved. The timing and manner of withdrawal are crucial, and necessarily involve the handing over of control/power. Depending on the level of community ownership of the development work, withdrawal can be successfully handled. But experience suggests that it is difficult to do well, and more systematic learning and research may be needed.

Another contentious issue in operational development work concerns how to deal with existing power structures within a community which in themselves replicate patterns of oppression and exclusion. If the agency is to develop and maintain a strong relationship with local leaders, what should be done about marginalised groups, sometimes of a different ethnic background, or groups with specific problems such as HIV/AIDS? What about domestic violence, genital mutilation, child labour, and so on? Often the choice is to leave some of these difficult questions until 'the time is ripe'. This might imply that certain forms of injustice and exclusion are therefore sanctioned. But is it possible for an external agency to be accepted in a community while also challenging that community on some of these deeper issues of human rights? Perhaps operational international NGOs are more likely to alter some of these traditional patterns, because they have less of a vested interest in winning local acceptance; or perhaps they are less likely to question existing power structures, because they need local acceptance, are required to obtain permits to deploy staff there, or are concerned for the security of their staff, and so they cannot afford to upset local leaders. Although the reality will differ from place to place, some research may help here. Certainly some progressive local groups (not least women's groups and human-rights organisations) at times criticise international operational NGOs for excessive compliance with local power structures.

Humanitarian response

Situations that require a humanitarian response frequently arise, and some agencies now have expertise in this area. Humanitarian response is a specialised business, involving both technical and social engineering. It calls for the assessment of physical and social conditions, understanding the social dynamics of a community under extreme duress, and finding entry-points which will bring physical relief, while respecting the good development principles of empowerment, emancipation, and sustainable development. It also requires tremendous strategic and tactical insight to balance an operational response with related advocacy work. The latter may (eventually) make more impact – but the legitimacy for such advocacy lies in having a direct operational involvement.

There are many important issues here. The severity of the emergency must be judged, and local opinions might have to be over-ruled. There have been cases of local denial (at NGO and at government levels), but there are also examples of exaggerated and mistaken intervention by the international community. Very practical issues must be addressed: how to organise hygienic conditions in refugee camps, which might require placing sanitary facilities at the outskirts – thus increasing the risk of sexual violence, which may mean that women do not use the facilities. Operational agencies must decide how to distribute food in an orderly and fair way, especially when there is a terrible shortage. Sometimes this is done via male heads of households, neglecting the needs of women-headed households. Sometimes more vulnerable women do receive distributions, but then have no power to keep the food when, for instance, it is taken for re-distribution by local chiefs.

There are many ethical dilemmas too. How can an agency respond appropriately to human-rights atrocities if speaking out may compromise the personal security of its staff, or may result in its being expelled from the area, so leaving local people without support? The agency may be confronted by political dilemmas concerning its degree of neutrality or partiality, the conditionalities attached to humanitarian aid, and so on. A number of these issues have been addressed by the so-called Humanitarian Charter, which has been signed by many donors (Sphere Project 2000).

The familiar problems of discouraging dependency and devising withdrawal strategies when working with local organisations are all the more difficult and significant in an emergency situation. However, perhaps the task of describing and adhering to gender-sensitive high-quality work in emergencies is the biggest challenge – these being by definition situations that require a high-speed response, while some of the developmental dynamics require much more time to sort out. Some see emergencies as an opportunity to fast-track certain aspects of social development (such as fostering women's leadership, or strengthening the position of indigenous minorities), and in general there are increasing attempts to bridge the gap between humanitarian work, operational development work, and strategic development funding. However, the interaction between these three roles needs more reflection.

Political strategising and advocacy

There are many political questions to address at international, regional, national, and local levels. Essential to dealing with them is the development agency's definition of its mission, which will in most cases commit it to relieving the plight of people living in poverty and suffering, injustice or exclusion.

Important issues and dilemmas are often strategic in nature. When the international or national political community does not accept its own responsibilities, but holds the humanitarian aid and development community responsible for not providing better development results, this is clearly unfair. But if the development community draws attention to this fact, it may be perceived as adopting a defensive stance to justify its inability to prove its own effectiveness.

The strength of development agencies in political analysis and strategic positioning may be their access to information at many different levels and from many different angles. Obviously, it is always vital to consult partner organisations very fully on any given issue. They will not always agree with one another, so development agencies have to be prepared to take responsibility for their own analysis and strategies. Accountability to local and national civil society is often not sufficiently organised, however, and this is another area that requires attention and improvement.

Who is involved in what advocacy, and when? These are critical questions. Development agencies themselves will obviously be most involved in lobbying the parliaments in their own countries or regions. Their partner organisations are fully involved in advocacy at their own national and regional levels – and many are an important force in international forums, such as the UN conferences and (increasingly) at the World Bank and IMF. Often, however, an agency's partners want to be involved in research and in defining the issues and strategies of advocacy – and to take part in or run the advocacy themselves. What happens when development agencies wish to play a strategic role in countries or regions other than their own? When is this appropriate, and when is it problematic? Should local partners be consulted first? Should strategies be co-ordinated with them? What if various partners hold differing ideological, strategic, or tactical positions? Should agencies then 'go it alone'?

Capacity building, organisational consultancy, and training

There is a great need for capacity building, training, and organisational consultancy to foster the development of strong CBOs and NGOs. Aspects of their work that need to be strengthened include management skills, women's leadership skills, organisational development, planning, monitoring and evaluation, and effective phase-out or hand-over systems.

The question of how (in which role) to engage with a particular person or partner organisation is very important, to ensure empowerment and emancipatory learning, rather than unsolicited advice or unwanted interventions. The principle of respect and autonomy in the relationship between trainer and trainee, or between consultant and manager, is a value to which all would aspire but which may in practice be difficult to achieve. There are many examples of relationships of dependency which are not in line with a philosophy of empowerment, and which can lead to undesired effects such as the trainer/coach/consultant becoming a 'distance manager'. Such situations are not sustainable; nor do they foster autonomous emancipated partner organisations or the development of strong management.

Professional issues of this type take on a special character when the agency doing the advising, training, or consulting is also the one that is involved in funding it. These combined roles of holding the purse strings and advising/coaching hardly leave the recipient of this well-intentioned work much autonomous space to develop his or her own strategy, or organisation, or management style. The problem of resolving this tension is not exclusive to international development agencies: it also confronts the larger intermediary NGOs in their relationship to CBOs. Even the most professional donor-agency staff, working with the most sophisticated partner organisation, will encounter this issue. Solutions can be found in the clear separation of roles, ensuring that the recipient manager/organisation has a clear choice about whom to engage with as consultant/trainer, or linking and learning opportunities with like-minded organisations in other countries. In practice, the separation of roles may be more difficult for vulnerable CBOs or newly established NGOs – and yet such organisations are obviously more susceptible to the risk of donor-dependence. Clear quality standards are essential here, as is the need to incorporate checks and balances even in these situations.

One advantage that development agencies may have, if and when they learn to co-operate more fully among themselves, is their access to thousands of partner organisations in many countries. This is potentially a tremendous resource for linking/learning processes. One can always learn from the best practice of others. And there are great possibilities for developing 'good practice' portfolios on specific themes or strategic questions. Development agencies need to consider how much effort they are prepared to invest in organising the available information, ensuring enough depth of material and analysis, and making it accessible. The new information and communication technologies open up great opportunities for development work, but only if information is acknowledged as a means of production, and this would mean donors investing in e-mail and Internet facilities for partner organisations.

Another question is how to motivate staff and partners to want to learn about the experience of others. Although the development business seems to adopt many similar ways of working in different countries (a special kind of globalisation), there is at the same time a strong sense of wanting to pioneer individual programmes. There is seldom so much interest in working on systematic learning, benchmarking, or replicability. There is a clear need for much more attention to be paid to systematic monitoring, evaluation, in-depth analysis, and research into the effectiveness of various development strategies and activities. There is an increasing demand for the development community to prove its effectiveness and efficiency (by doing cost/benefit analysis in the widest sense, studying inputs and outputs, effects and results, and longer-term impacts on people's lives). It is, therefore, vital that the indicators for success (quantitative and qualitative) are set by the development community itself, and not by others who may have a simplistic or unrealistic method of 'measuring' results.

The organisational culture of development agencies and their partners which are well intentioned, value-based, and committed to certain causes and principles may be analysed as 'input'-oriented. Hard work and passionate commitment may sometimes prompt defensive replies to the questions 'Are you making a difference?' or 'Could you work more effectively?', possibly because people who do not commit themselves to working for a fairer world sometimes seem to delight in proving that those who do are naïve 'do-gooders' – implying that poverty and injustice are immutable facts of life. The issue here is how to encourage a culture of open and confident engagement with all shades of critical dialogue.

Domestic roles or global ones?

For many development agencies in the North, their global activities are complemented by domestic programmes that aim to educate and involve the general public 'at home'. This can be done in a variety of ways: most directly through 'accompaniment' projects, and less directly through development education, fundraising, and fair-trade initiatives.

Accompaniment

Accompaniment, or 'being there, living and working alongside people living in poverty and oppression', is a function that implies a recognition of the need to understand fully what happens to people within the processes of poverty and injustice. Empathy, the ability to place oneself in the shoes of another, is a very important skill. Accompaniment allows people to experience the lives of others at close hand and to engage in their reality. It takes various forms, such as sending volunteers or witnesses during certain tense times such as elections. Or it can be combined with the function of protecting people or voicing their plight in situations where it is too dangerous for them to speak out themselves.

Accompaniment can then be a positive experience for the people who do it, because it enriches their experience and deepens their insight and capacity for empathy. Back in their own countries, this experience can have a mobilising effect. It can also be important to those being accompanied, because it offers protection or connections to a wider social movement against poverty and related injustice.

Counterbalancing the positive aspects of this international interaction are some potentially negative effects: for instance, the inadvertent dominance of the one doing the accompaniment, who will in 'being there' affect the dynamics of the particular situation. This influence is often beneficial: an external witness may have a protective effect, and may draw the eyes of the world to a particular situation – but what happens when that person leaves? Is there sustainable change? What if it gets too dangerous, and expatriates are withdrawn, while local people cannot leave? And who stands to gain more from accompaniment? Are the results of such interaction clear, and who benefits most?

Development education

Through public-awareness work that is variously known as development education, global education, peace education, human-rights education, or environmental awareness, the staff of development agencies aim to ensure that children and adults worldwide understand the nature and causes of poverty, that they develop empathy for others, and also that increasing numbers of people use their understanding, attitudes, and skills as part of a global social movement that seeks basic changes in the social and economic systems that perpetuate poverty and injustice.

There are increasing opportunities to include development education in formal education systems and in adult organisations. Learning in schools was traditionally dominated by theoretical training, but more recently there has been a growing interest in action-learning, developing 'emotional intelligence', acquiring social and life skills, and encouraging schoolchildren to do community work. For adults, there is a need to be involved and to take some control over their social and economic destinies.

When development education adopts a highly moralistic or ideological tone, it often fails to engage the intended audience. People resist being preached to: they want to control their own thinking. The challenge facing people who work in development education is to create a process of learning that allows participants to take ownership of their new ideas and understanding of the underlying causes of poverty and exclusion. The same principles of autonomy and equality that are used in developing strategic funding relations with partners should apply here.

Fundraising

Fundraising establishes relations with the general public, small and large donors, foundations, the corporate sector, and government and international institutions. It is significant partly because it is an actual transfer of assets from rich to poor, and partly because it is a vital element in supporting CBOs, social movements, and NGOs – 'civil society' in the widest sense. Social organisation carries considerable costs in terms of human capital, time, and money. Private organisations are considerable players in supporting social movements and NGOs around the world, but they need funds to do so. Finally, raising funds from the general public is one of the surest practical ways for an agency to get feedback on the public's evaluation of its performance: every donation is a vote of confidence.

Fundraising for emergency relief creates a difficult set of issues. Most challenging is the recognition that dramatic cases of human suffering, and their coverage in the media, create opportunities to raise funds for those affected – and for agencies to expand in the process. It requires honesty to keep the humanitarian response to the fore and to manage it in such a way that relief programmes are not driven by the availability of funds. Development agencies must commit themselves to looking beyond the crisis for which there is funding and towards ways of supporting longer-term solutions.

Fundraisers must resist the temptation to rely on sensationalist images and messages in order to galvanise the public to support emergency relief work. Conventional images of the suffering of passive 'victims' contradict development-education efforts and reinforce negative attitudes among the general public. In addition, using the commercial media to convey over-simplified messages in order to reach a wider 'market' involves the risk of commercial slickness, which may alienate those supporters who understand the complexities of social change or humanitarian assistance in the South.

Fair trade

Some development agencies invite members of the public to become ethical consumers – people whose shopping habits are informed by knowledge of the conditions under which goods were produced. Increasingly, the concept of fair trade is being taken up by consumer movements, and by commercial enterprises who market themselves as fair and ethical businesses. Fair trade in agricultural produce (coffee, bananas, etc.) has reached a commercially viable level and is having an effect on general production practices. However, the smaller, labour-intensive fair-trade enterprises that are supported by development agencies are not always sufficiently equipped to run a commercial business. In addition, tastes in fashion and domestic items undergo rapid change, which makes this a risky business.

Getting our own house in order: conclusions for Oxfam International

Oxfam International (OI) is a network of organisations involved in tackling the injustices that cause poverty and suffering locally and globally, and working with others towards sustainable solutions and a fairer world. These solutions are based on a conceptual framework of justice and human rights, including social and economic rights.

The Oxfam group sees itself as part of a global movement that is working towards such aims, and which therefore embraces a wide range of development NGOs, CBOs, and social movements, North and South. Its central philosophy is that people – wherever they are in the world – should regain ownership over their own lives and destinies, and should receive support on the grounds of our common humanity and the need for social justice at all levels.

As a change agent, OI sets out to play a number of different roles or functions, and wants to be clear and coherent about these. Certain OI affiliates have developed and play certain roles more fully than others. This can provide a basis for constructive harmonisation, based on respect for diversity, compatibility, and complementarity. At the same time, all members of the Oxfam group share a common set of values, which are enshrined in common working principles and on the Code of Conduct for humanitarian agencies (Sphere Project 2000), and which serve to guide their work and indicate the limits of acceptable diversity between them.

OI recognises that the injustice that causes poverty and suffering must be analysed in each specific context – and the analysis should be done by or with, and in partnership with, those people who are themselves affected by the context where change is needed. However, the biggest challenge is not so much the analysis of the problems, but the development of sustainable solutions.

The starting-point for these solutions must be respect for the autonomy and diversity of the work, policy positions, and roles of the respective OI members – and of their partner organisations – in various types of co-operative partnership. A power analysis of the positions of the various actors, and of existing checks and balances, can indicate how partnership relationships are being managed. Any power monopoly that does not have or allow for the development of such a system of checks and balances is in itself suspect. This is true of governments, public institutions (such as prisons or mental-health institutions), market monopolies (for example, multinational companies), and forces within politics or civil society that find themselves in a dominant position (political parties, religious monopolies, Mafia-type groups, and so on). Donor organisations run a similar risk of monopolising power, which is why OI is committed to building checks and balances into its own systems of stakeholder interaction and management.

Key values for members of the Oxfam group are respect for the diversity of people and partner organisations, and for their autonomy; the transparency and accountability of their own organisational policy and processes; and a consultative style of decision making to ensure that a range of voices and partners can effectively influence Oxfam's thinking and practice. If development agencies as a sector were to adopt similar principles and practices – and be prepared to co-operate more fully with each other – then an effective global citizens' movement could soon be a dream turned reality.

Reference

Sphere Project (2000) *The Sphere Handbook: Humanitarian Charter and Minimum Standards in Disaster Response*, Geneva: The Sphere Project

Coming to grips with organisational values

Vijay Padaki

A starting point

There are two NGOs. We can call them AID (Action in Development) and DIA (Development in Action). Their programmes have many things in common: main areas of work, the community organisation approach, size, infrastructure, annual budget, geographic location, the kinds of community in which they work, and so on. People often refer to them as twin organisations. Yet the differences between the two organisations cannot be ignored: the contrasts in rates of staff turnover, level of community involvement in the programmes, relations with government offices, among other things. It should not be difficult to see that similarities in the classic '3 Ss' (strategy, structure, systems) cannot predict the 'character' of either organisation as it actually functions. Such differences-over-similarities can be observed in any group of organisations — in government, in business and industry, in educational institutions, in sports. On the other hand, organisational groupings also reveal certain similarities-over-differences — the typicalities within textiles, pharmaceuticals, information technology, railways, banks, and so on, including NGOs in development.

The typicalities in organisational behaviour have been dealt with from various theoretical perspectives. Whether we choose to call it character or culture or climate, it is clear that the common factor being referred to is the *internalisation of norms of behaviour*. The subject of human values appears best suited to explain the phenomenon of organisational culture and, equally, to help us to manage that culture effectively. Values can be seen as forming the core of organisational culture.

A natural first question in approaching the subject of organisational values is: so what? Why bother to understand values in organisational behaviour, as long as the organisation does what it is supposed to do and does it well enough? In other words, is the 'soft' subject of values in any way related to the 'hard' facts of performance? The 'excellence' literature of the 1980s sought to convince us that attention to certain key organisational parameters was all that mattered. (The '3 Ss' extended to '5 Ss' and then to '7 Ss' for poetic consistency.) Further, the inadvertent implication was that the attention to those parameters could be value-free. Imagine the dismay when most of the corporations listed as 'excellent' had plummeted within the decade. In contrast, the 'robustness' line of thinking in the 1990s (without the pushy marketing of the earlier literature) identifies characteristics associated with the long-term health and effectiveness of organisations (Collins and Porras 1994; Ackoff 1994). One such characteristic is a clear organisational value system that provides depth, stability, and consistency to management practices. Far from being contradictory, values and performance may be seen as a necessary unity. The significance of organisational values in management is gaining recognition steadily (Roe and Ester 1999).

A natural second question would be about the relevance of this issue for NGOs, especially those in development programmes. Yet, within only three decades, we have seen shifts in emphasis in development interventions from charity through development to sustainability. Correspondingly, although usually a step behind, the *management* of development NGOs' programmes has also had to evolve, along with changing assumptions of what constitutes good performance and, therefore, good management. Most NGOs, at one time or another, will have confronted conflicts between the requirements of good management and the demands of good development (for instance, the 'product' outcomes versus the 'process' outcomes). At the base of these assumptions are certain core convictions of what is *good* (or bad) and what is *right* (or wrong) about the tasks that we undertake, and how we go about them. In other words, the organisational value system.

The term *values* is used in many varied ways. The first tasks before us are to move away from the realm of catchphrases towards a framework that meets the requirements of internal consistency as well as of operational validity and relevance. To do this, we need to examine briefly the key premises that support a unified concept of values in our social behaviours. For a study of values to benefit management policy and practice, we should ensure, at the minimum, the following:

- an acceptable theory of what values are (for 'there is nothing so practical as good theory');
- an acceptable methodology for observing and assessing these values;
- an empirical base to make comparative statements from the observations made.

Definitions

The highly integrative work of Milton Rokeach (1970, 1973) provides an excellent explanation of values. It begins with a description of the organisation of beliefs in the human cognitive system. There is a strong neuro-physiological basis to the cognitive organisation. However, it seems possible to understand the working of the system in non-technical terms.

Beliefs, attitudes, values in the cognitive system

The organisation of our beliefs as units in a composite cognitive system is understood better if we imagine a global mass of all our beliefs — from the best value for money in toothpastes, through the best ways to bring up a baby, to the best approach in community development. This mass of beliefs can be seen in a *central–peripheral continuum*. In other words, some of our beliefs can be at the periphery of our cognitive system. We shall call them peripheral beliefs. Some beliefs can be at the core of the system. We shall call them central beliefs. The term *system* is used to describe the organisation of our cognitions, because the individual units are seen as being interdependent and interacting. The properties exhibited by the system are summarised in Box 1.

The term *belief* should be used when there is evidence of cognitive organisation (true/false, yes/no, likely/unlikely, very much/very little, etc.), but insufficient evidence of any feeling or emotion aroused (for example, a belief about a pop singer — here today, gone tomorrow). The term *attitude* should be used only when there is sufficient evidence that the individual can be placed on a dimension of emotional involvement (like/dislike, approve/disapprove, good/bad, etc.). An attitude represents an organisation of beliefs (for example, beliefs about singers, bands, and lyrics as part of an attitude to music). The term *value* should be used when there is evidence of a relatively enduring behaviour pattern (would/would not, willing/unwilling, readiness/hesitation, etc.). A value represents an organisation of attitudes. A *value system* is a cluster

- At the periphery, the beliefs can exist with fewer associations with other beliefs, and even in isolation.
  Towards the centre, the specific units of beliefs are integrated through generalisations into more meaningful entities that are interrelated and consistent among themselves.
- At the periphery, beliefs may be transient, fleeting, and 'under test'.
  Towards the centre, beliefs are likely to be 'proven' and enduring.
- At the periphery, beliefs are not accompanied by definite feelings and emotions.
  Towards the centre, beliefs are organised into attitudes and have a definite emotional accompaniment, an 'organismic commitment'.
- At the periphery, beliefs have a low likelihood of being associated with sustained behaviour.
  Towards the centre, beliefs are more likely to be associated with sustained behaviour.
- At the periphery, beliefs are more easily changed or replaced and (because they are associated with fewer others) involve very little change in other beliefs.
  Towards the centre, beliefs are more difficult to change and involve changes in many other beliefs.

For a diagrammatic representation of our belief system, we can think of them as being arranged in a sphere, with increasing density and stronger bonds among units towards the core. Disturbances in the system can occur at the periphery or at a deeper level. Surface explosions cause much less damage than subterranean ones that set off quakes and fissures.

of values, often interrelated, that governs the characteristic thinking-feeling-behaviour pattern of the person (for example, beliefs about music, drama, painting, and dance in an aesthetic value).

Value as an individual attribute

Since the basis is in the organisation of an individual's belief system, the correct and precise meaning of the term 'value' is as an individual attribute. It is formed in the individual, is observable in the individual, and is assessable, too, as an *individual* attribute, (for example, as materialistic value, religious value, or altruistic value).

Organisational values as shared beliefs

The collection of individuals that constitutes an organisation may thus be viewed also as a collection of individual belief systems. The organisation displays a recognisable identity or 'character' when there is considerable agreement, typicality, or overlap among the individual belief systems over and above the differences among them. Typically, this means a small set of interrelated values, rather than any one single value. This composite set of values, internally consistent, may be referred to as the *organisational value system*. The task of assessing organisational values therefore requires the following steps:

* identifying the predominant belief clusters among a critical mass of people in the organisation;
* assessing the extent of consensus among them;
* if necessary, identifying the forces or mechanisms by which prevalent value systems are maintained or may be altered.

Differing organisational value systems

Questions arising here would be:

* Why do organisations differ in their value systems, and how are value systems shaped?
* Why do organisations differ in the extent of consensus in values, and how is consensus shaped?

Values and behavioural fields

In contemporary, pluralistic societies, individuals exist and function in different social organisations that might uphold (and demand conformity to) quite different value systems. Likewise, the organisation itself may exist in multiple 'behavioural fields', each with its own value premises — the financial institutions, the raw-material trade, the NGO network, the community traditions, the environmental movement, and so on. The influence of the external environment on the value system is examined later in this paper.

Value conflicts and resolution

Value conflicts may be regarded as natural, normal, and even healthy in any organisation. However, exactly as with conflict resolution in the individual, the organisation's conflict-resolution modes, too, may be viewed as purposeful and healthy or self-defeating and unhealthy. One way of understanding the 'health' of an organisation's coping mechanisms is in terms of the balance struck between internal processes and the demands from external or institutional forces. Indeed, a diagnostic framework for organisational effectiveness may be constructed on these premises.

Methodology for studying values

Over the last 15 years, the practical value of the theoretical framework, presented in a nutshell above, has been amply demonstrated in numerous organisational settings in both the business and industry sectors and the voluntary and development sectors. The methodology for profiling an organisational value system has steadily evolved (Woodcock and Francis 1989; Padaki and Padaki 1998). Some approaches found useful by the author are given below.

Individual values

The values prevalent in an individual can be visualised as being of two types:

- *Terminal values*: the end-states considered highly desirable, such as material comfort, freedom, religious bliss, i.e. the ends.
- *Instrumental values*: the best ways to conduct oneself, often to achieve the desired end-states, such as honesty, hard work, discipline, i.e. the means.

An individual value system may thus be viewed as a combination in a matrix of terminal and instrumental values. Table 1 presents lists of terminal and instrumental values identified by Rokeach (1970, 1973), and Figure 1 illustrates how an individual value system may be clustered in the matrix.

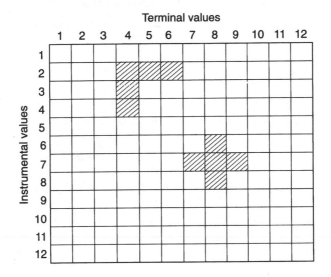

The shaded cells represent the combination of the strongest terminal values with the strongest instrumental values in the person.

In addition to individual predispositions, there are the values upheld by the organisation as a whole, which can also be viewed in terms of terminal and instrumental values. Some examples:

- **Organisational terminal values**: for instance, contributing to quality of life in society, being a model corporate citizen, achieving social justice.
- **Organisational instrumental values**: for instance, continuous innovation in products or services, transparency in management, activism in plans and programmes.

Organisational values

In an organisational setting, people carry within them two sets of values:
- **Personal conduct values**, such as: *I believe that honesty is the best policy ... I must excel in everything I do ... Life must be enjoyed ...* etc.
- **Task-related values**, such as: customer-centred; committed to equal opportunities/empowering structures/targets at any cost, etc.

Table 1: Terminal and instrumental values	
Terminal values	**Instrumental values**
A comfortable life (a prosperous life)	Ambition (hard-work, aspiration)
An exciting life (a stimulating, active life)	Broad-mindedness (open-mindedness)
A sense of accomplishment (lasting contribution)	Capability (competence, effectiveness)
A world at peace (free of war and conflict)	Cheerfulness (lightheartedness, joy)
A world of beauty (beauty of nature and the arts)	Cleanliness (neatness, tidiness)
Equality (brotherhood, equal opportunity for all)	Courage (standing up for your beliefs)
Family security (taking care of loved ones)	Forgiveness (willingness to pardon others)
Freedom (independence, free choice)	Helpfulness (working for the welfare of others)
Happiness (contentedness)	Honesty (sincerity, truthfulness)
Inner harmony (freedom from inner conflict)	Imagination (daring, creativity)
Mature love (sexual and spiritual intimacy)	Independence (self-reliance, self-sufficiency)
National security (protection from attack)	Intellectual rigour (intelligence, reflectiveness)
Pleasure (an enjoyable, leisurely life)	Logic (consistency, rationality)
Salvation (saved, eternal life)	Love (affection, tenderness)
Self-respect (self-esteem)	Obedience (duty, respect)
Social recognition (respect, admiration)	Politeness (courtesy, good manners)
True friendship (close companionship)	Responsibility (dependability, reliability)
Wisdom (a mature understanding of life)	Self-control (restraint, self-discipline)

The task of assessing organisational values is a challenge, because it includes:

- identifying the set of values prevailing in the organisation;
- identifying areas of conflict between individual predispositions and organisational positions;
- identifying areas of conflict between different groups of people — between levels, between functions/departments, between different units, and so on;
- identifying internal inconsistencies within the organisational values — i.e. conflicts between the practices from one value and the practices from another. (For example, '*People are our greatest assets*' and '*No one is indispensable in this organisation*'.)

Value reinforcement

Organisational values can exist in the form of a strong consensus, or be superficial and weakly shared. The absence of consensus has often a diagnostic value in itself. The organisational analysis should attempt not only to assess the extent of consensus on an organisation's stated values, but also to examine the organisational factors that might explain either the reinforcement of the value system or its weak consensus. This is precisely the exercise in the Motorola Ethics Renewal Process, undertaken regularly and seriously by the corporation (Moothy et al. 1998).

The sources of organisational values

Most of the literature is polarised towards two main explanations of organisational culture: the *micro*, looking at factors within the organisation, with a heavy emphasis on the leadership, especially the characteristics of the leader; and the *macro*, looking at historical, political, and even religious traditions in the society, seeking common features in all socio-cultural groups.

Considerable work in India has shown that there is an intermediate level of analysis that may be both relevant and significant, namely, the *sectoral field* in which the organisation exists (Padaki and Padaki 1998). For instance, most textile mills in Western India have remarkably similar management practices and top-management 'styles'. Attempts to introduce certain 'modern' management practices have generally failed. Management trainers and consultants tend to see this 'resistance to change' as located in the short-sightedness of the top management, i.e. the chief executive. What is not seen is that the same chief executive displays a quite different 'style' in another business of the same corporate entity — in electronics or pharmaceuticals or petrochemicals. In other words, the leader is the same, but the leadership process is different.

Each sectoral field makes its own demands on the management of the enterprise and, therefore, calls for an appropriate configuration of core practices that characterise the sector (Padaki and Radhakrishnan 1984). The similarities-over-differences are clearly recognisable. The work of the author's team has shown that it is possible to identify a cluster of values that are predominant in a sector. This mapping can be done for almost any sector.

What are the values most likely to be found in the NGO sector? The extensive exploration of organisational values in India has revealed that all NGO work is covered by a 'spectrum' of values (see Table 2). The spectrum applies to all types of NGOs in development — donor agencies, operational NGOs, resource/support NGOs, grassroots organisations. Each NGO is likely to have a smaller set of closely related values, drawn from the spectrum that constitutes its characteristic culture. The explanation for this characteristic set should interest us. It might well be traced to internal factors, such as the leadership in the organisation. In most cases, however, it is likely to be the product of an interactive process between internal and external factors. The spectrum itself represents the similarities-over-differences in the NGO sector.

Combinations of three primary colours give us an amazing range of hues. Combinations of three primary emotions give the human species a range of emotional states that are still not fully categorised, but are nevertheless the basis for a lot of personality categorisation. The 'personality' of an organisation, too, can be derived from combinations of value positions. As with the charting of human personality, no two organisations are likely to be exactly the same. Yet organisations may be seen as falling into certain clusters, based on the predominant value orientations.

Organisational values in management

It must be recognised that organisational values form the core of all management practice. This recognition is typically absent or weak, because the values usually operate silently, without direct articulation. Values are also likely to be regarded as 'soft' matter, and not given serious attention. However, the intimate connections to 'hard' management practice cannot be denied. For instance:

- **Values and performance**: What constitutes good performance, satisfactory achievement? What kinds of 'output' receive reward, recognition, reinforcement? What is unacceptable, punishable?
- **Values and organisation structure**: Is it possible that we need teamwork and co-operation but the organisation structure reinforces individualistic or competitive behaviours? When an organisation is not 'walking the talk', the gap can usually be explained by an inappropriate, unhelpful structure for the desired process. The interesting question that arises is: Can features of organisational structure influence the values in an organisation? Or do espoused values invariably shape structure? NGO managements are often surprised when they discover that the 'models' of structure and

Table 2: NGO organisational values

Given below is a list of values that an organisation may stand for. They refer to an organisation's beliefs and convictions, as reflected in policy and practice.

- **Achievement**: To set high standards of accomplishment, to persevere in their pursuit, to take risks if necessary, along with innovation and enterprise.
- **Accountability**: Responsibility for organisational objectives with full recognition of the constituencies — donors, partners, communities; evaluative reflection, ownership of what is said and done.
- **Conflict resolution**: Acceptance that there are inter-group and inter-organisational conflicts in all human transactions, along with the determination to confront conflicts and resolve them.
- **Conservation**: Simplicity in appearance, restraint in consumption, awareness and concern for long-term consequences of resource wastage.
- **Empathy**: Sensitivity to needs and emotional states of people concerned, along with the desire for positive action.
- **Equality**: Relationships and transactions that respect and accept differences among people (class, community, faith, etc.) but provide equal opportunities for all.
- **Gender equity**: Equal opportunity and affirmative action with respect to gender, in the conviction that true development will come from gender equality.
- **Non-violence**: Confrontational but constitutional, people-based political processes as a powerful methodology for social change.
- **Participation**: The involvement of all in the organisation in its functioning, especially in policy and direction, with democratic and open styles of communication and supervision.
- **People development**: A policy of deliberately developing people's abilities, skills and competence, along with investment of time and resources in actual practice.
- **Secularism**: Pursuit of programme objectives without consideration of religion or creed, but with understanding and respect for the importance of religious faith in people's lives; acceptance of diversity of faith.
- **Self-reliance**: To work towards levels of competence and resource mobilisation by which an organisation may be relatively free of exploitative manipulation by other groups or institutions.

systems that they brought into the organisation have actually been influencing their lives silently, powerfully.

- **Values and strategy**: One of the most important requirements in an organisation's strategic plan is its clear position about why it is pursuing this line of work, the core convictions about it. What are vision and mission statements, after all?

Organisational aim + values = vision

Organisational goals + values = mission

Without shared clarity and conviction about values, vision statements and mission statements become exercises in writing clever copy.

- **Values and partnership**: Organisational effectiveness, viewed either in the short term (operational achievements) or in the long term (institutional achievements), depends to a great extent on the combined ability of several people in the organisation to work with other organisations in a collaborative mode — the community organisations, government agencies, donor groups, support NGOs, and so on. Conventional 'capacity building' methods often succeed in enhancing within-group competencies, but in the process inadvertently retard between-group competencies for collaborative behaviours. The work of the author's team has shown that partnerships and inter-organisational effectiveness are the most important tasks in NGO management (Padaki 1995, 1999) and need to be viewed as a strategic requirement in development intervention itself, as institutional development beyond organisational development (OD). In facilitating effective partnerships, it is seen that the most important process is that of clarifying the values underlying the tasks at the interfaces between organisations. This seems particularly crucial in cross-cultural partnerships in large development programmes.

Going back to the two NGOs, AID and DIA, can we see how the differences in their observed 'character' can be traced to the inescapable bind between organisational values and management practice? Table 3 attempts the comparison.

Dealing with organisational values

The exercise of exploring organisational values is a useful and relevant *gateway* for an Organisational Development (OD) process. A strategic planning exercise sometimes provides a timely opportunity to initiate an OD process. Interestingly, the concept and practice of OD itself is based

Management processes: sampler	Organisation 1: AID	Organisation 2: DIA
Performance or behaviours rewarded	• Achieving targets • Adherence to laid-down procedures • Contribution to internal co-operation	• Facilitating processes • Innovation and exploration • Contribution to external co-operation
Organisation structure	• Group-based • Unidirectional accountability • Emphasis on individual role clarity • Single-point leadership, decision making	• Team-based • Multidirectional accountability • Emphasis on role interdependencies • Multi-point leadership, decision making
Participatory methodology in programmes and systems	• To get things done • As a technique • As steering	• To empower people • As a commitment • As learning
Strategic perspective	• Maximisation — operational efficiency	• Optimisation — systemic effectiveness
Transactions — external	• Task-specific • Turf protection	• Empathetic • Collaboration
Transactions — internal	• Conforming	• Adaptive
Project management	• Blueprint approach	• Action-research approach
Vision or Mission Statements	*Both organisations claim that they are people-oriented, working for social justice through sustainable development programmes.*	

on certain value premises that are likely to be congruent with the spectrum of NGO values (Miles 1975, Padaki 1997). Understanding the prevailing value system, appreciating its implications in organisational realities, and working towards an alternative values–practice balance, can all be part of the exercise. Needless to say, although the exercise benefits from a starting framework and some structure, the process is highly participatory. Two illustrative case studies are presented below.

Case study 1: internal and external realities at MYRADA

The list of organisational values relevant to development work (Table 2) can be examined by an NGO to arrive at its own profile. The typical procedure would involve a critical mass of opinion makers using a valid scaling technique to reveal (a) the differences in significance among the values, and (b) the extent of consensus within the group. The exercise can be repeated to derive comparative profiles.

MYRADA is a large, multi-project NGO in India with several integrated rural development projects spread over several States. The organisation receives funds from various donor agencies and, in turn, has several programme heads within the project areas. Over the years, the organisation has earned a reputation for successfully combining a good development perspective with hard professionalism in programme management. Always open to new ideas and developments, MYRADA has experimented with several management systems and techniques.

In an attempt to understand more fully the dynamics of donor–partner relations, the organisation decided to first examine the prevailing internal value system. After a charting of individual value profiles from a wide cross-section of staff, the management team undertook an exploration of values prevalent at the system level of the organisation. For this purpose, nine values were first identified as the most relevant for MYRADA, out of the twelve in the spectrum for NGOs (Table 2). Next, members of the management team ranked the nine values under four organisational conditions:

1 *Within* the organisation: as it *is* currently, in internal practices and conventions;
2 *Within* the organisation: as it *ought* to be;
3 *External*: as it *is* currently, in the organisation's development perspective and what is promoted in the communities being served;
4 *External*: as it *ought* to be.

The sample size of the managers' team was adequate to derive approximations of interval scale positions from the rankings of the nine values in each of the four conditions.

Figure 2 shows the four value profiles derived from the assessment. Readers are welcome to draw their own inferences from the two profiles. The organisation itself benefited greatly from this 'mirror' on the following counts:

- understanding inconsistencies within the 'internal' and 'external' profiles;
- understanding inconsistencies between profiles;

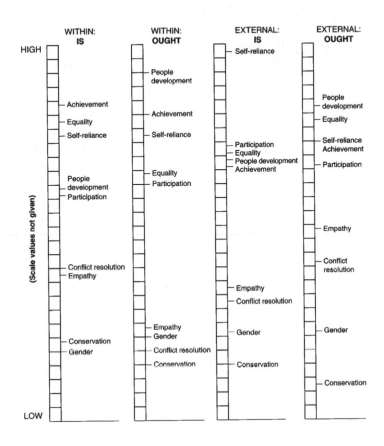

- seeking causes for the differences in consensus between profiles;
- seeking the connections with organisational structures and processes.

Case study 2: Oxfam (India) Trust in transformation

In one of the most elaborate and multifaceted exercises in organisational restructuring, involving the eight offices in India of Oxfam (UK) (now called Oxfam GB), the Oxfam India Trust (OIT) found itself tackling such sensitive issues as grades, salaries, tenure, job descriptions, performance standards, and career paths, all at once, and with all the ramifications of interconnectedness. The single most important operating principle throughout the exercise during a period lasting almost three years was the complete conviction in the rightness of consultative processes, involving every category of staff, from Office Attendants to the Regional Managers. The Staff Association played an especially constructive and facilitative role, ensuring full collaborative effort from all staff. The restructuring was completed and implemented with remarkable thoroughness, although it was extremely taxing for many involved in the process.

At the core was the obvious egalitarian organisational value — practised, not preached, noticeable in such mundane everyday events as meetings and greetings, as well as in policy-driven practices such as equal opportunities, gender relations, joint reviews, and the role of the Staff Association in management.

In the second phase of the OD process, the offices opted to move towards a team-based performance management system in which the Regional Manager was seen as part of the office team and therefore would have his/her own performance reviewed and goals set by the team in the quarterly review and goal-setting cycles; and the National Director was part of the team of Managers and, therefore, would have his/her own performance reviewed and goals set by the Management Team.

The introduction of the system was preceded by an exploration of the values of Oxfam-in-India, using the same instrument as in Table 2. The process revealed an internal polarisation around two nodal clusters: the *task-related values* (achievement, accountability, etc.) and the *people-related values* (empathy, participation, etc.). This is a common occurrence in many organisations, resulting in two sub-cultures. In NGOs that are old and large, the polarisation is more likely to be associated with a 'generation' difference — between the older, people-oriented staff and the younger, management-oriented staff. The difference is viewed very often as fundamental and irreconcilable (Padaki 1995). The management team-building process in OIT succeeded in viewing the value clusters as *complementary* rather than conflicting. More importantly, the management team was able to identify the organisation structures and systems by which the complementarity could be achieved.

A model workshop in organisational values

There is obviously no one correct way for an organisation to work towards a congruence between values and practice. However, it seems possible to visualise a minimum coverage in a first exercise in coming to grips with organisational value systems. A two-day workshop has been seen to serve the purpose rather well.

Day 1

- A critical-incident methodology is used to identify highly satisfying and highly frustrating experiences. This data pool is analysed to identify both the typicalities and the inconsistencies in management practices.
- An exploration of the concept of values follows, to ensure a shared understanding: the bases in individual cognitive organisation, the types of value, the presence or absence of consensus in groups and organisations, and the mapping of organisational value systems.
- A first exploration of the organisation's value system is undertaken, using the framework described above.

Overnight

An individual, semi-structured exercise for exploring one's own value system is done by all participants.

Day 2

- An extension of the overnight exercise is undertaken to examine the organisation's expectations from its members.
- The group attempts a convergence from the analyses so far towards producing a profile of the organisation's value system.
- The areas of congruence and conflict between the organisation's value system and the prevailing management practices are examined.
- A first action agenda is adopted, including timeframes and responsibilities.

Organisational values in action

Every system of management — made up of methods, tools, and techniques — has underlying assumptions about what *ought to be* the way of doing things in the organisation. Many of these assumptions have implications in terms of how people ought to relate to other people in the various roles they play. Whether stated explicitly or merely implied, these central beliefs and assumptions may be identified in all the prescriptive models of management, from the earliest ones in the

What are the *value premises* in Quality Circles and Total Quality Management (TQM) for the line manager (also brought into NGO management in recent times)?

- *The person on the job knows the working conditions better than I do – hence the value of suggestions.*
- *My best efforts on the job are meant for the benefit of others – hence the customer orientation, both internal and external.*

Without these central beliefs, the motions of quality drills can never produce results. When TQM fails (which is not uncommon), one does not have to look far for the explanation.

What are the value premises in systems like ZOPP and PRA? What is the 'sense of ownership' or the 'feeling of participation' without the real things in experience?

industrial engineering era to the most contemporary attempts to humanise the workplace. A system of management is invariably a product of its time and, therefore, a carrier of a value system (Box 2).

On the other hand, there is in every organisation an existing culture — some traditions, conventions, outlooks, norms of conduct, ways of relating with others — that have their own *ought to* assumptions. It is important for the two sets of assumptions to be compatible. It is, therefore, necessary for an organisation deliberately to examine the value implications of a management system before installing it in the organisation (Padaki and Padaki 1989).

When there is an incompatibility between prevailing organisational values and the value premises of a management system, we have the all too common phenomenon of parallel systems at work in the organisation: the ritual of the formally introduced system, co-existing with the 'real' system by which decisions and actions take place. The frustration arising from maintaining the parallel systems is as inevitable as the dysfunctional state that follows in the organisation.

A prime requirement in any organisational intervention is to create the awareness among all stakeholders concerned of one inescapable fact in management practice: *the need for compatibility between organisational values and the management systems adopted.*

In seeking the necessary compatibility, do we choose systems to match prevailing organisational values, or can the values be altered to match the system? What should we look at first, the values or the system?

The essence of the expression *paradigm shift* is in the realignment of basic assumptions and premises in order to be able to adopt a new way of doing things. In planned interventions, we have a few simple but reliable guidelines:

- If the organisation already maintains values compatible with the value premises in the management system being considered, this might be the ideal situation and it is therefore a good bet that the new system will succeed.

- If the organisation maintains values diverging significantly from the value premises in the management system, it may be best to leave things alone and keep the new system out.

- If the organisation shows inconsistency in values or an absence of clear value positions, there is likely to be inconsistency in management practice as well. The organisation is best assisted to clarify its value positions before tampering with management systems.

- If the organisation shows a clear predisposition towards a set of values, it can be assisted to arrive there and reinforce the value system through actual practice, i.e. by introducing the new or more appropriate management systems.

In sum, organisational values are too important to be taken for granted. They need to be identified, articulated, and revisited periodically. The compatibility between organisational values and management systems (as they actually work) must constantly be verified. Indeed, exercises in changing organisational structures or management systems must be seen as serving the purpose of reinforcing the organisation's value system.

References

Ackoff, R.L. (1994) *The Democratic Corporation,* New York: OUP.

Collins, James C. and Jerry I. Porras (1994) *Built to Last: Successful Habits of Visionary Companies,* New York: Harper Collins.

Miles, R.E. (1975) *Theories of Management: Implications for Organisational Behavior and Development,* New York: McGraw Hill.

Moothy, R. S. et al. (1998) *Uncompromising Integrity: Motorola's Global Challenge,* Scaumberg, IL: Motorola University Press.

Padaki, R. and V. Padaki (1989) 'Towards Effective Organisational Diagnosis' in *Towards Organisational Effectiveness Through HRD,* proceedings of National HRD conference, Jamshedpur: HRD Network.

Padaki, V. (1999) 'Social Institutions in Development Interventions', unpublished workshop position paper, Bangalore: The P&P Group.

Padaki, V. (1997) 'Organisational development: yesterday, today, tomorrow', *Search Bulletin,* XII, No. 1:24-25.

Padaki, V. (ed.) (1995) *Development Intervention and Programme Evaluation: Concepts and Cases*, New Delhi: Sage.

Padaki, V. and R. Padaki (1998) 'Organisational Value Systems: an alternative perspective in OD' in S. Ramnarayan, et al. (eds.) *Organisation Development: Interventions and Strategies*. New Delhi: Response Books (a division of Sage Publications, India).

Padaki, V. and T Radhakrishnan (1984) 'Management by Values', *Management and Labour Studies*, October, pp. 55-71.

Roe, Robert A. and Peter Ester (eds.) (1999) Special issue on 'Values and Work', *Applied Psychology: An International Review* 48(1).

Rokeach, Milton (1970) *Beliefs, Attitudes, Values*, New York: Jossey-Bass.

Rokeach, Milton (1973) *The Nature of Human Values*, Glencoe: Free Press.

Woodcock, Mike and Dave Francis (1989) *Clarifying Organisational Values*, London: Gower.

We NGOs: a controversial way of being and acting

Cândido Grzybowski

Like it or not, we NGOs are now increasingly present on the social and political scene worldwide. As the name implies, we are not governmental, but we do claim a role in promoting the common good and defending public interest. We are heterogeneous: we come in many shapes and sizes, and we are generally minuscule when compared with governmental or multilateral agencies. Embracing apparently lost causes, we are often rather more committed and militant than efficient in what we do, and above all we are an irritant to the establishment, be it the State or the private sector. The question is, however, are organisations like these still needed?

My reflection on NGOs is from an insider's perspective (derived from my experience in IBASE, based in Rio de Janeiro) in terms of our relationships and alliances – with other NGOs, with other civil-society organisations, with social movements, and with governments and companies in Brazil and abroad. Our personal circumstances inevitably affect our perspectives. I recognise, then, the limitations of my viewpoint, but I would argue that it is a legitimate and important one, in that it contributes to an analysis of the factors that shape the existence and purpose of NGOs.

I shall focus on various questions that I consider essential to an understanding of NGOs. On the one hand, we have the changes in our social relationships and social structures; the problems of exclusion and inclusion, with the concomitant persistence of poverty and greater inequality; the expansion of public space and the new context for political action. These circumstances are fundamental to an understanding of how NGOs have emerged and evolved. On the other hand, I will try to show the specificity of NGOs in the context of the development of civil societies, and the challenges and agendas that they will need to face in the near future. I will then highlight the conditions that underlie the legitimacy and impact of NGOs as autonomous political actors.

Societies change: looking beyond the neo-liberal wave

It is particularly opportune today to remind ourselves of Galileo's words, *eppur si muove* ('and yet it does move'), to affirm that amid all the economic and financial turbulence and uncertainties that hang over us, there are alternatives to the *pensée unique*[1] and its model of globalisation, given that human beings continue to change and create, producing their own lives and history. What we need to identify and free up is the potential of the movement that is being born and is renewing itself through a whole range of struggles to affirm humanity itself. In other words, we need to transfer our attention from the agenda of the 'global casino' and cast our eye on real societies, in which human beings are re-inventing living conditions in the here and now. If NGOs are as buoyant and optimistic as they are, it is simply because they are conditioned from birth to look at the world in this way. This is one of their secrets.

It is beyond our scope here to make a critical analysis of globalisation. I start from the premise that such an analysis is a common reference point for the readers of this volume, and that the more important challenge here is to point out the possibilities that present themselves at the start of the twenty-first century, particularly to NGOs. It is important, however, to stress that the neo-liberalism which spurs the current form of economic and financial globalisation, in spite of the power of the discourse and its real impact, is in fact the expression of a crisis of capitalism, not of a durable 'solution' for it. Right now, the cracks are more than visible. In almost three decades of neo-liberal policies, what stands out is the crisis of destruction, of demolition, the fragmenting impact of the need for 'flexibilisation', all in the name of the market and large corporations. Maybe the clearest image of neo-liberalism is the violent tide of the market, with its terrifying waves crashing on to the beach, and destroying the very protection system that humanity had been setting up to deal with the wounds of capitalism. Much has been destroyed; there is much to rebuild. Alongside the all too real threat that this has meant, and still means, for at least 80 per cent of the world's poor, the worst effect has been the risk of dismantling more universal ideas and values. It is worth highlighting the need to rebuild a utopia of a more egalitarian society, one that is just and participatory. NGOs have a role to play in this task.

As Eric Hobsbawm reminds us, in terms of human history the twentieth century started late and finished early. Before the official end of the century, we were experiencing the movement of crisis for humankind at the birth. What is this movement? Where is all this taking us? 'Solutions' are always human inventions and need not be followed slavishly. Not even history repeats itself. If what moves us is a universal humanistic perspective, founded on the values of equality, liberty, and solidarity, then we need clearly to define the tasks that we have ahead of us and get involved in achieving them. We need, above all, to understand the essential newness of the moment: that new problems are being confronted and that new solutions are being born in the struggle of human beings to create decent living conditions at the beginning of the twenty-first century. These questions are particularly crucial in understanding the reason for NGOs' existence.

Destruction, inequality, poverty, and social exclusion

One of the most visible paradoxes marking the emergence of this new century is the contrast between the extreme ease and speed with which financial capital circulates around Planet Earth and the barriers of all kinds that are erected to impede the migration of human beings. The question of migrants is only the most visible tip of the iceberg of the globalisation-driven exclusion of the greater part of humanity. It is an exclusion that repeats itself from the global to the local level. There is not room for everyone in the world of economic and financial globalisation. The inclusion of a minority, their access to goods and resources, implies the exclusion of the majority. Among the included are those who, in effect, are deepening inequality and poverty, thereby generating social exclusion. Apart from this, this 'exclusionary inclusion' is based on the degradation and destruction of the environment, the very basis of all life on earth. The appropriation and use of natural resources from a perspective of gain at any price, and on a global scale, exacerbates environmental destruction and generates unsustainability and social exclusion.

This is something new, as much in terms of structure as of awareness. The logic of inclusion–exclusion is structural; it is a basis for the functioning of the system. For this very reason it is unsustainable, if it is not actually producing massive destruction. At the same time, an opportunity to promote a new awareness of the excluded is being developed by the recognition of the global nature of the problem, an awareness that exclusion is not a temporary state, something between a previous situation and a new, but as yet unresolved, situation; that it is indeed a permanent way of being and living in the South, North, East, and West (notwithstanding the huge asymmetry in power and riches). More radical still, one has the basis for bringing together creative struggles of societal alternatives for a new century, when one realises the relationship between the logic of structural social exclusion and the destructive forms of the production–consumption system. In fact, this is what is happening throughout the world, via social movements that are constituting real barriers to environmental destruction, exclusion, and poverty at the local level. Struggles are mushrooming all over the place, fragmented and dispersed, coloured by the cultural and political diversity of their societies. However, we cannot fail to grasp their core significance: they are struggles that enable us to foresee a 'global-ness' based on human beings and planetary citizenship.

We are faced with new relationships and forms of socialisation. It is no longer only inclusion in the processes of production that opens up one's chances of being a part of society. The struggles against this very exclusion and environmental destruction take on a fundamental role in defining the basic conditions for belonging to real societies. The question of poverty and the struggle against it demand particular attention here. Essentially, we are no longer faced with an absolute lack of goods and resources, but rather with a denial of access to them, be it through the concentration of resources within the control of a minority, or through a predatory form of production and consumption. To be poor is above all to be excluded, because without the power of access and influence in the use of (what should be) collective goods and resources, the economic and political system works to serve only a minority.

Human rights, sustainability, plus democracy: basic points of reference

The emergence of a planetary awareness capable of feeding new dreams and social projects for a new humanism will not be automatic. But it is possible. Indeed, behind the diversity of the current struggles, we can gather the threads and identify a common point of reference that will be needed in creating a broad movement of opinion, a wave of triumphs and constructive changes. I would highlight in particular the significance that human rights and the question of sustainability are assuming as common threads running through struggles throughout the world.

My concern here is not with the yet unresolved debates relating to human rights. What I want to hold on to is their universal adoption as points of reference for those who are actually struggling for rights. In this sense, in immediate terms, more important than the philosophical and judicial formulation of human rights is their transformation into a practical category, an ethical and moral reference point for millions of human beings, especially the poor and excluded majorities. This is a new and fundamental fact in terms of the social relationships that have become possible at this stage in our history, and which is of particular importance for civic action concerned with constructing alternatives to the prevailing (dis)order. Like it or not, human rights are a global reference point with a huge capacity to mobilise and transform our societies. They are a common platform. The work of NGOs has a lot to do with this. We turn human rights into a basis for a global movement. Indeed, the greatest merit of human rights is to show the mass of humanity that we are united, even across our diversity of gender, age, race, culture, and context.

I highlight three practical dimensions of human rights that can be identified from different struggles that are taking place in the most diverse settings. In the first place, human rights tend to be a reference point in the building of awareness. It is in the light of human rights that groups of the poor and excluded organise their perception of reality. Second, human rights tend to be a barometer against which to measure and evaluate the social relations to which these groups are subjected. For this reason, they are an instrument with which to identify and define the problem that the group wishes to address. Finally, human rights bring the struggles of various individual groups under one banner, which is the struggle for rights that have been either denied or stolen.

The other basic reference point, which also emerges from real, living movements, is that of sustainability. Again, more important than the conceptual debate is its mobilising capacity as a political issue. In reality, what actually mobilises people is not the difficult notion of sustainability itself, but the widespread perception today that the exploitation of the environment is a fundamental issue, affecting the lives of everyone.

This new awareness is one indisputable success of the environmental NGOs, since the concept of sustainability embodies any proposal for what should be done and what can be done. The challenge is to weave together the perception of the importance of the environment, in terms of the quality of life for the majority of the world's poor and excluded, with the concept of sustainable production and consumption of natural resources. Once again, we can identify important indicators which are coming out of actual social movements. A new socio-environmental awareness is starting to develop, centred on human rights, where the right to environmental resources is also a fundamental right.

Together with the radicalisation of democracy – a civilising task par excellence – human rights and sustainability seem to me to be the basis for a post-neo-liberal reconstruction. The very existence of these concerns within our social movements should be attributed largely, though not exclusively, to NGOs. This achievement alone would already be sufficient to justify the existence of NGOs, and their renewed mission at the start of the new century.

Expansion of public space and the new conditions for political action

Antonio Gramsci developed the concept of civil society to take account of political action beyond the politico-military sphere of the State proper. The idea of 'trenches' to characterise these new forms of struggle, taken from the experience of resistance in the First World War, does not however account for the huge complexity that struggle and political action have acquired in our societies. The development of civil societies, as a space for public rather than State action, is one of the most striking features of recent political history. It should be emphasised that this did not happen either by substituting for – or dispensing with – the State, but as a result of a significant increase in public space. The undeniable crisis of the nation-state model is not the result of the development of so-called civil societies, but of policies derived from the neo-liberal focus on the globalised market as the basic mechanism to regulate societies. In this sense, neo-liberalism also threatens the very development of civil societies as an autonomous political space, something that is essential for the radicalisation of democracy.

The point to underline here is that NGOs should be seen both as one of the products and as one of the contributory factors in this expansion of public space. What I am referring to here is the increased organisation and action arising from the diverse initiatives of different social groups, of ordinary men and women, be it to defend their immediate interests or to work for the common good. This has heightened the tension in the contradictions implicit in social relations, and is transforming these into possibilities for the emergence of new kinds of citizen, the building of social identities, of proposals, of new organisations, and forms of struggle. Civil society is enriched through the very diversity of social, political, and cultural life. It is, however, far from representing an alternative in and of itself. We are simply witnessing a political manifestation, not exclusively of political parties or of the State, but rather of the diversity of contradictions and subjects that make up real-life society.

NGOs are a minute fraction of the organisational and active universe that constitute civil societies. To confuse them with civil society itself is to ascribe to them capacities and a legitimacy that they do not possess, in addition to making it impossible to see what their real role is. Worse still is to project civil society as an alternative, in itself, to the dominant processes in our societies. In fact, civil societies are simply contradictory and tense spaces of non-State political action, wedged between the State (power) and the private sector (economy).

It is undeniable that new spaces and new conditions for political action are opening up. The dismantling of the State practised by neo-liberalism and its accompanying form of globalisation is a huge challenge today. An urgent task is to re-establish the State as the underlying basis for those universal public policies of which only it is capable. There are, however, tasks above and beyond the State, which are specific to civil societies and their process of transforming human beings into collective entities, diverse and contradictory as they are. NGOs are merely a part of this. However, within their limits as political actors, they do have some potential.

We are faced with both constraints and opportunities. A citizenship which promotes a new democratic universalism based on human rights and sustainability is now coming face to face with real processes, be it the dismantling of the State and its policies, or a market logic that is both exclusionary and destructive. To address social exclusion, poverty, inequality, and environmental destruction requires either a State that is committed to doing so, or organised citizens struggling to achieve such a goal, or, better still, that they both work together. In any case, the processes that generate exclusion, poverty, and destruction, as well as generating their eventual transformation, are situated beyond the local sphere. The latter fragments, disperses, and localises processes that are wide-ranging and multifaceted. The structuring thread of citizen action needs universal reference points, given the destructive and exclusionary dominant logic that it must confront. In practice, such a historical perspective has to be constructed beyond the local level. Needs can only be perceived as a denial of rights if one has a universalising and global perspective that casts them in this light. Action is effective – and NGOs know this very well – when it influences the local level in a practical way and with real results. However, its effectiveness commonly depends on the links between this concrete local level and the structuring processes that extrapolate from this and are shared more widely.

This is a real tension that the expansion of the public sphere and new forms of political action bring with them. NGOs feel it particularly sharply, given that their own action is permeated with such tension. They have a somewhat more far-reaching strategic perspective, but this does not mean that they do not get involved in local-level, practical struggles. The more universal reference points do not always serve to galvanise action at the local level, in such a way that marginalised groups or sectors explicitly challenge the issues of democratisation and sustainability. However, we must recognise the possibilities for new ways of 'doing' politics, in order to understand the new century as well as to see what real scope we have to shape its development within our perspectives of justice, liberty, solidarity, and participation.

The NGO way of working: support, monitor, defend, promote, unsettle

The notoriety and political presence of NGOs in our societies cannot be separated from the emerging struggles in a world that has been globalised by neo-liberalism. There are certainly NGOs that have been in existence for much longer. However, it is over the last decades that they have multiplied and diversified, and acted with greater significance and impact. Proof of this is in the cycle of major international conferences convened by the UN, which were a privileged opportunity for NGOs to have international influence. It is also worth mentioning the events organised alongside international governmental meetings, at which NGOs were not welcome but where they made their presence felt as a counterpoint; as for example in the Uruguay Round of GATT, the creation and implementation of the WTO, the recently aborted Seattle meeting, the regular meetings of other large multilateral organisations (the World Bank, the IMF, the Inter-American Development Bank), and in the always closed-door sessions of the G7. This is without taking account of all the regional processes, such as the EU, Mercosur, and other regional economic blocs. Despite their involvement at the very local level, NGOs are out front in promoting an unprecedented form of civil internationalism.

But what do we NGOs bring to real-life societies? Obviously, we don't change anything, and don't have the capacity to do so. Or rather, we are only part of the changes, no more than small links in a process that can only be one of huge mass movements. That we unsettle things I have no doubt. For lack of a better metaphor, I would compare us to fleas. As NGOs, we are minuscule political animals, sometimes difficult to locate, but who bite and irritate. In other words, we annoy the established elephantine system. As we annoy it, we make it walk or move itself, even if this is to fight us. Governments, multilateral organisations, companies, and huge civil-society organisations, small local powers, politicians, and the media, all of them may be bitten by the little NGO fleas. Indeed, we form a 'colony', and so can really make them itch. We are there where we are least expected, and we attack without warning.

Beyond this flea metaphor, however, I believe it would be a big mistake to think that our influence on societies is due to any special financial or organisational capacity. Perhaps what we have is a certain degree of creativity mixed with big ideas, peculiar to activists, which find strength when combined with our fundamental quality of uniting ethics with analytical capacity. What characterises us is the capacity to identify uncomfortable but nevertheless undeniable causes of social problems. We identify and construct our reading of these causes on the basis of ethical precepts and analysis, data, experiences, etc., to support them. We create arguments for political action from these causes, which the public then take up, demanding actions of all those who have any involvement in the issue. Our weapon, our bite, is this mix of ethical argument and analysis. We do not represent anything, other than the groups of men and women who unite around the cause. However, we argue, appeal, provoke, suggest options, and support the organisations of those who are affected by the problem. We give value to the issue being fought for, and we monitor and put pressure on those who are supposed to be in a position to solve the problems. We are, in a word, both promoters and defenders of the causes of the dispossessed.

Activism, the strength and weakness of NGOs, cannot be compared to the grandiose and sometimes destructive sectarianism of cultural and religious fundamentalists, or to what in general fires the social movements themselves, i.e. the legitimate defence of their members' interests. Neither is it pure activism of the type akin to that of party-political ideology. NGOs tend to constitute themselves around the concerns and shared values of a collectivity. It is vital also to stress that NGOs have no monopoly on the values of justice, equity, solidarity, and participation; nor on a strategic vision of democratic and sustainable human development for Planet Earth. However, we would not be NGOs if such values and strategy ceased to be our driving force. This radically and fundamentally distinguishes us from very many other organisations, be they State or business, or other non-NGO civil-society organisations. Many consider us to be part of the so-called Third Sector, but above all we are citizen bodies, practising direct and participatory democracy. We are not a homogeneous bloc, and we do not wish to be, but we do defend our common identity, built on the basis of values and a way of acting that are essentially and exclusively oriented to fighting for the public interest. This does not mean to say that we do not make mistakes, or that we are not shot through with contradictions in our way of being and doing. On the contrary, we NGOs want to be held to account for the things we claim to be, and for what we actually do – but not for what others attribute to us.

The 'NGO way' should not be confused with the supply of goods and public services when the State or other organisations stop providing them. When we do take on a service-provision role, we try to build visibility; that is, we 'rescue' the causes of marginalised or excluded groups, of people who are wretched, so that society as a whole recognises its responsibility to them. Thus, we work as an amplifier for these groups. We transform their problem into a question for our own organisations, and through them to governments, politicians, journalists, intellectuals – in short, to the élites with decision-making power and influence over our social processes. We want to contribute to the movements for change in society and not merely to 'compensate' for what the dominant paradigm cannot do.

The best of NGOs is their action as a 'colony' through the networks and forums in which they participate. The strength of minuscule NGOs lies in their involvement as very local points of a vast network, a social fabric of monitoring and denunciation, proposal and action: networks with clear universalising trends, as a result of their global reach; voluntary and horizontal networks of information and strategy formulation, that feed on local action and give it potential, giving it a more global and universal dimension. This movement back and forth from the local to the national to the international ends up as being the basis for NGO action.

The examples are numerous, but what come to mind first through my experience in IBASE are the Social Watch network and SAPRIN (Structural Adjustment Participatory Review International Network). Indeed, it is through participation in various networks and forums that NGOs create a global dimension in the non-State public space. Further, it is through them that common reference points are being drawn from diverse and dispersed struggles across the Planet. NGOs, without monopolising these fragmented struggles, are drawing them together into a perspective of universal citizenship and sustainability.

By way of conclusion: some immediate tasks to be faced

Seeking to demonstrate our *raison d'être* as NGOs, I have been pointing out the challenges and a concrete agenda that this new century sets out for us, and emphasising what seems to me to be the essential. However, there are three elements that I would highlight as a way of concluding a reflection which is, above all, an effort to take stock of what I myself am doing. These are immensely challenging tasks, and they need to be tackled immediately and collectively.

Our perspective, which stresses the importance of concrete social struggles, needs to be put into action. We must therefore equip ourselves to bring out into the open what we see in the areas where we work. I sense a lack of research, reflection, and especially, strategy among NGOs. I have argued elsewhere for the need to make a map of the world of citizens' struggles. We need to develop the capacity to put forward our point of view. For example, it is possible to point to concrete struggles for resources throughout the world: struggles which involve very specific groups of poor and excluded people or those who suffer threats of destruction; struggles that stand out as much for their needs and immediate problems, as for their particular cultures and way of life; but struggles nevertheless that are profoundly universal in what unifies them. We need to develop an awareness of this. A map of such struggles can help to strengthen our approach, our points of reference. But most of all, it could give us a powerful means of demonstrating the universality of the causes that we defend and promote.

As NGOs, we cannot deny that our most intimate *raison d'être* is solidarity. We ourselves are the tangible fruit of solidarity, since no NGO as such has its own resources. We carry out public action with the resources of those who believe in us, resemble us, and are together with us in the causes that we defend. In this way we are part of a chain of solidarity between the societies of which we are a part, and of the world. Today's solidarity has a clear international dimension. International co-operation is, for many of us, its concrete expression. We have an ethical obligation to contribute to the re-establishment of solidarity at the beginning of this century. In the context of globalisation, co-operation has tended (and still tends) to be a prisoner to the production–market agenda, which reduces the ideas of equality, liberty, solidarity, and participation to competitiveness and efficiency of economic production. We must not fall into the trap of looking for immediate results without taking into account the causes that motivate solidarity. We need to recover – and this is the challenge ahead – that sense of complicity among international activists as a basis for co-operation among people driven by common values and ideas. The aid agencies of the North and the NGOs of the South are pivotal axes of the same movement, a call to renew the task of planetary citizenship against all forms of destruction and social exclusion.

Challenging the philosophical and theoretical order is at the heart of what NGOs do. In the final analysis, it was the NGOs who lent their radical nature, and above all raised the banner of equality in diversity, which has since been taken forward by many movements. Indeed, on the basis of concrete struggles at local level, and through their networks, NGOs gave more visibility to the idea of diversity and equality as a right. But in diversity of gender, race, age, culture, or any other difference, we do not accept an exclusionary view of inequality. NGOs' action and proposals have also contributed to condemning any interpretation of equality that crushes people, or denies the right to be different.

This is not as simple as it seems. A humanist utopia of equality, liberty, solidarity, and participation cannot be reconstructed today without also being criss-crossed by the dimension of diversity. More than anything else, diversity is life. It is through diversity as life's driving force that, in philosophical, political, and historical terms, we bring in the dimension of sustainability, which is fundamental today in conceptualising our humanist utopia. This is obviously a huge challenge. The question is: are NGOs responding to this challenge with enough urgency? Our future existence largely depends on our answer.

Acknowledgement

Translated by Frances Rubin. An electronic version of the Portuguese original is available from the Editor, on request.

Note

1 The phrase '*pensée unique*' was coined in 1995 by Ignacio Ramonet, editor-in-chief of *Le Monde Diplomatique*, and refers to 'the translation into ideological terms that claim to be universal of economic interests, particularly those of international capital' (Ramonet 1997:179).

Reference

Ramonet, Ignacio (1997) 'The one and only way of thinking', in M. Rahnema and V. Bawtree (eds.) *The Post-Development Reader*, London: Zed Books.

Northern NGO advocacy: perceptions, reality, and the challenge

Ian Anderson

Perceptions

Northern NGO advocacy[1] has come a long way since the early 1970s campaigns, which John Clark describes as being 'poorly financed and run by highly committed but inexperienced volunteers but [which were] highly effective at capturing the public imagination' (in Edwards and Hulme 1992: 197-8). NGO advocacy has become more focused, more strategic, and has made more effective use of the media. NGOs have learned to gain access to and use the political processes, structures, and institutions of their home countries, as well as those of the multilateral agencies. This evolution of NGO advocacy has led to more effective interaction between NGOs and official agencies; to alliances between Northern and Southern NGOs, as those in the South have expanded their advocacy into the international arena; and to alliances between the broad-based development and relief NGOs and specialised campaigning groups and networks, including environmental organisations.

NGO policy-reform successes are widely acknowledged; Clark (1991), Salman and Eaves in Paul and Israel (1991), Edwards (1993), UNDP (1993), and Smillie (1995) all recognise that Northern and Southern NGOs, often acting together, have materially contributed to influencing policy changes by Northern and Southern governments. Clark (1991: 150), tracing NGO campaigning from its origins in the 1970s, notes the baby-milk marketing code, the drafting of an international essential drugs list, trade liberalisation for clothing manufactured in the South, an EEC emergency food reserve for the provision of famine relief, action on global warming and rainforest destruction, debt relief to African countries, and the imposition of sanctions to combat apartheid. To Clark's listing, Edwards (1993: 116) adds: influence on World Bank policies in relation to gender, participation, poverty, and the environment; cancellation of, or modification to, World Bank projects (notably dams and associated resettlement schemes), movement away from vertical interventions in health-sector investment (especially immunisation), improvements in food regimes for refugees and displaced persons, modification of IMF-imposed structural adjustment programmes to take greater account of their social consequences, and country-specific issues such as reconstruction aid for Cambodia and EU access for bananas produced in the Windward Islands. Smillie (1995: 229-30) notes NGO activity and influence at major UN environmental conferences, evidence given by NGOs to parliamentary studies and international inquiries, significant changes in African agricultural policy, and the improvements gained by Save the Children Fund (UK) in the standards of care required of organisations operating children's homes in Uganda. Salman and Eaves in Paul and Israel (1991), writing in a World Bank publication, cite examples of influence on a number of its projects. UNDP (1993: 84-99), in a chapter generally critical of NGOs, cites numerous beneficial advocacy initiatives by Southern NGOs, as well as gains by Northern NGOs. Amnesty International is singled out as having 'amply demonstrated the power of information to protect the rights of individuals and groups'. In referring to pressure from NGOs, which has brought about changes in the actions of multinational corporations, UNDP acknowledges that '[a]dvocacy clearly is – and probably will continue to be – the NGOs' greatest strength' (op.cit.:88 and 98).

More recently, NGO campaigning has been extended to representation at major UN conferences, starting with the 1992 Earth Summit held in Rio de Janeiro, where some 1500 NGOs were accredited to participate, through to the 1999 World Trade Organisation (WTO) meeting in Seattle, where, apart from the violent disruptions that attracted most media attention, NGOs concerned about the economic and social aspects of WTO policy and their impact on the environment, human rights, labour, and development were present and active. The recognition, through the award of the 1997 Nobel Peace Prize, of the achievements of the coalition of NGOs that formed the International Campaign to Ban Landmines, and the award of the 1999 prize to Médecins Sans Frontières for its highly visible public support to people in emergencies, and the present outcome of debt relief as a result of NGOs' work on the Highly Indebted Poor Countries (HIPC) initiative are further evidence of the growing effectiveness of NGO advocacy.

Notwithstanding these accepted gains, much of the literature is severely critical of NGOs and their advocacy. Principal among the criticisms of shortcomings of Northern NGOs are relationships with official donors (which NGOs are seen to be afraid to criticise, while being heavily reliant on their funding); the absence of a clear advocacy strategy; the limited allocation of resources to advocacy programmes, resulting from pressure to be seen to be applying resources to more tangible, marketable humanitarian relief and development projects; the failure of NGOs to demonstrate, through evaluation of their advocacy, its effectiveness and impact; the failure of NGOs to build the alliances needed to broaden and strengthen their advocacy voices; and the failure of NGOs to develop credible alternatives to neo-liberal growth-oriented economic orthodoxies which, critics suggest, requires more research by NGOs and a more conscious linkage of NGO field experience and the development models adopted by them. In addition, Northern NGOs' role as legitimate advocates for the Southern poor has been under scrutiny, as Northern NGO advocacy has evolved and Southern NGOs have themselves become increasingly involved in advocacy beyond their national borders. Northern NGOs are being challenged on issues that include the changing nature of relationships between Northern and Southern NGOs and demands for new forms of alliance between them; Southern expectations of their Northern counterparts; and tensions concerning who should determine the development agenda.

There is in the literature a broadly accepted recognition that structural macro-reforms are essential, if the fundamental causes of poverty are to be redressed. Watkins (1995: 216 and 217) summarises the need for reforms as 'requiring a transformation in attitudes, policies and institutions' and 'a fundamental redirection of policy on the part of other foci of power including the UN, international financial and trade organisations, corporations (TNCs), official aid donors and NGOs'.

This is the challenge facing Northern NGOs in their advocacy: how, by employing strategies which maximise their effectiveness and impact, they will be able to 'address the structural causes of poverty and related injustice' (Oxfam International 1999: 4).

The reality

In the course of conducting doctoral research on the policy impact of the Washington Advocacy Office (WAO) of Oxfam International (OI), I surveyed larger Northern NGOs for the purposes of testing generalised criticisms of their advocacy. I obtained data covering the period 1981 to 1996, to provide benchmarks for detailed research into the WAO and its advocacy programme since its establishment in 1995; and to place the OI affiliates in the context of Northern NGOs, especially those with substantial international networks and affiliations.[2] For this purpose the survey sought data in respect of the allocation of income from government and private sources; the allocation of expenditure between development and relief programmes, advocacy, and other expenditures; advocacy strategy, policy objectives, staffing, and selection criteria for issues and alliances; the topics upon which NGOs had advocated; evaluation of advocacy; and, in the case of national Oxfams, the nature and extent of co-operation between affiliates, and with the WAO.

The relationship between income from government sources and advocacy expenditures

By attempting to establish a correlation between official donor income and the resources allocated to advocacy, the survey sought to test the criticism that the increasing proportion and scale of NGO funding from official donors creates a dependency which constrains NGO advocacy. The survey sought to establish whether there is a correlation between official donor funding and advocacy resource allocation, without attempting to assess whether, as Edwards and Hulme (1995: 20) argue, NGOs' dependence on official funding 'emasculate[s] NGO attempts to serve as catalysts for the poor'.

From the response data, no correlation between government funding and advocacy expenditures could be established, and in fact significant apparent contradictions were indicated. As might be reasonably expected, respondents whose institutions received the highest levels of government funding generally reported the lowest levels of advocacy expenditures. However, among the Oxfams, Intermón, the affiliate which over the survey period reported the highest rate of growth in government funding (80.4 per cent per year, to 52.3 per cent of total expenditures in 1996) also, over that period, increased its advocacy expenditures to the highest proportion of all the OI affiliates (11 per cent). Conversely, Oxfam America, which accepts no government funding, halved its advocacy expenditures as a proportion of total expenditures over the survey period (from 10.4 per cent to 5.3 per cent in 1996), and on a non-inflation-adjusted basis barely increased advocacy expenditures over that period. Further support for the proposition that it is the NGO's policy orientation rather than dependence on official funding which influences the level of its advocacy activity is found in the case of the two Canadian OI affiliates: they are similarly reliant on government funding and may be expected to be subject to similar government influences, yet one has consistently spent more than 5 per cent of total expenditures on advocacy, while the other's advocacy expenditures declined from 2.3 per cent in 1984 to 1.2 per cent in 1996.

Advocacy as a proportion of total NGO spending

It is Clark's hypothesis that, notwithstanding the broadly accepted view that advocacy is the strategy most likely to contribute to achieving significant reductions in poverty levels, NGOs have put few resources into it (Clark 1991:147).

This proposition would seem to be supported by the levels of reported advocacy spending. By 1996, when NGO advocacy might be expected to have reached a level of maturity, reported advocacy expenditures (which excludes grant expenditures for Southern or partner advocacy) among both OI affiliates and other respondents were overall 4.1 per cent of total expenditures, with the range varying from five respondents who reported zero or negligible advocacy expenditures, up to one reporting 12.5 per cent of total expenditures.

These levels of advocacy expenditures would support the view that NGOs themselves do not have sufficient belief in their advocacy to challenge the alleged constraints on their allocation of resources into advocacy. This allocation of resources to NGO advocacy may be compared for example, with Greenpeace, which embraces an action-oriented strategy, which exists as a 'catalyst for change', and which has demonstrated the ability to mobilise large numbers of people in pursuit of specific achievable objectives (Greenpeace 1996:1 and 3).[3] Greenpeace therefore employs a wholly advocacy-focused strategy, compared with development and humanitarian relief NGOs whose level of advocacy-resource allocation through to 1996, despite mission statements which include addressing the structural causes of poverty, at least appears to confirm Clark's view, expressed as follows:

> Advocacy may be seen as important but it is not urgent.
> Consequently it is easily squeezed out by the day-to-day dilemmas and crises arising from the project activities, from donor pressures and from media enquiries. (Clark 1991: 147)

Advocacy strategy and staffing alliances: issues for advocacy

Much of the literature is critical of NGOs for being slow to adopt and clarify advocacy as a strategy. In particular, Edwards (1993: 165) identified a failure to combine 'different forms and levels of action in mutually supportive and reinforcing ways within a single strategy for change ... working simultaneously and in a co-ordinated fashion at local, national and international levels, both in detailed policy work and public campaigning, educational and media activity'.

Of the respondents providing data, 17 out of 23 claimed to have an advocacy policy. In addition to the 'yes/no' response in this respect, information was sought on the rationale, objectives, and policy for selecting topics for their advocacy. Predictably, the responses on advocacy objectives referred to influencing decision makers and public opinion to bring about change to the benefit of the poor. In selecting issues or subjects for advocacy, most respondents linked their advocacy to field experience, to their assessment of the prospects of successfully bringing about positive change, and to influencing opinion within their home-country constituencies. However, despite the linkage of advocacy with field experience, only two indicated that they consulted with Southern NGOs in selecting topics for their advocacy; a fact which would tend to support the questioning of Northern NGOs' legitimacy to claim to speak as advocates for the Southern poor, and criticisms of their failure to build effective partnerships with Southern NGOs.

Consistent with generally increased advocacy expenditures over the survey period, in every case where NGOs reported employing dedicated advocacy staff, total staff resources were greater in 1996 than in 1984, and generally the proportion of specialist advocacy staff at middle and senior management levels rose over the survey period.

Notable from the responses was the growth in the number of NGO advocacy topics over the survey period, and the very wide range of topics covered by their advocacy. In the period 1993–1996, several issues emerged around which Oxfams and other NGOs have coalesced: debt advocacy (in which almost all Oxfams reported active co-operation with the WAO since its establishment in 1995, and on which six non-Oxfams also reported advocacy), trade-related issues, and landmines.

Unsurprisingly, the survey responses in relation to advocacy alliances were overwhelmingly positive, with all respondents indicating some form (without being asked to comment on the depth and effectiveness) of co-operative advocacy relationships within their home country or region, and with Northern umbrella bodies or their own international network. The least-reported form of alliance was with Southern organisations, with which only 14 of the 23 respondents on this topic indicated an advocacy alliance.

In summary, the survey responses suggest that for the majority of participating NGOs advocacy has – through a combination of the allocation of human and financial resources, the recognition of advocacy as a strategy, and advocacy alliances – been integrated into the fabric of their organisations in pursuit of their missions to reduce poverty and offer humanitarian relief. While the survey findings therefore suggest that over time NGOs are to a progressively greater extent recognising, integrating, and providing resources for advocacy, they do not shed light on the effectiveness or impact of that advocacy.

Evaluation

A recurrent theme in published criticisms of NGOs is the need for them to be more thorough, rigorous, and objective in evaluating their work, and the need to publish evaluation results as an essential component of NGO transparency. Among others, Clark (1991), Edwards and Hulme (1995), and Saxby in Sogge (1996) argue that this is necessary and, in Clark's view, to the advantage of NGOs. Edwards and Hulme (1995) and Smillie (1995) stress the need for greater attention to evaluating NGO advocacy as a prerequisite for NGOs being able more effectively to communicate their advocacy achievements. Without this, NGOs will be unable to win greater private and official donor support for the allocation of resources to advocacy.

In the survey, NGOs were asked to advise whether they consistently evaluate their advocacy (or at least claim to), the basis used for evaluation, and to which stakeholders the results are made available. The findings support the criticisms noted above. Only half (11 out of 23) of the NGOs which responded reported that their advocacy is formally evaluated, and of these only four stated that their advocacy was always evaluated. Survey responses indicate that release of evaluation results to stakeholders is much less of a priority to NGOs than commentators believe would be useful as a means of demonstrating effectiveness and transparency. Apart from funding agencies, to which six respondents reported that they made advocacy evaluations available, the survey responses indicate very little release of advocacy evaluations within

NGOs' own networks, to donors, Southern partner organisations, researchers, or the media.

Summary observations from the survey

Within its limitations, the survey has provided useful insights into Northern NGOs and their advocacy. The number of NGOs that recognise advocacy as a strategy to be employed in pursuit of their objectives, the increasing resources being allocated to advocacy, and the specialised and more senior staff being employed in advocacy all suggest that NGOs are heeding the calls for increased strategic priority to be given to advocacy.

The responses indicate that, although they clearly have some way to go, NGOs are increasingly addressing two[4] of the strategic weaknesses identified by Edwards (1993:168): the absence of a clear coherent advocacy strategy and the allocation of resources necessary effectively to implement that strategy; and the failure to build the alliances needed to broaden and strengthen their advocacy voices.

The third strategic weakness identified by Edwards, the 'emasculation' of advocacy for fear of reductions in official funding on which many are so dependent, was not substantiated by the survey. The lack of correlation between official funding and advocacy expenditures, and, indeed, the contradictions noted above, suggest that it is the organisational culture and its priorities, rather than reliance on official funding, that determines the emphasis placed upon advocacy, and resources allocated to it. While the survey found no correlation between official funding and advocacy expenditures, it was beyond its scope to examine the nature of the advocacy and the extent to which the advocacy messages may be influenced by dependence on official donors. Thus, it is possible that the content of advocacy, rather than the decision to engage in and allocate resources to it, may be influenced by dependency on official donor funding (Minear 1987: 207).

The further major flaw in NGO advocacy that was identified in the literature is the failure of NGOs to demonstrate to themselves and their stakeholders, through evaluation, the effectiveness of their advocacy as justification for the financial and human resources dedicated to it. Evaluation, documentation, and publication of advocacy experience, in addition to helping to demonstrate both the effectiveness of NGOs' advocacy and their accountability, may help to 'facilitate scaling-up by others' (Edwards and Hulme 1994; Edwards and Hulme 1992: 224; Archer 1994: 232). Without the foundation provided by consistent, thorough evaluation of their advocacy, NGOs will be unable to assess its effectiveness, or address the criticisms made of it. Without being able to demonstrate their advocacy achievements through evaluation, NGOs are unable to fully commit the strategic priority and resources needed to realise the structural macro-reforms which are acknowledged to be essential if they are to have a substantial impact on world-wide poverty and related injustice. Until NGOs themselves have sufficient confidence in the effectiveness of their advocacy both to communicate and demonstrate their advocacy achievements, advocacy will surely remain a relatively minor component of NGO strategy, notwithstanding its potential contribution to their stated missions. If consistent, thorough evaluation of their advocacy is a prerequisite for such a level of informed confidence, the survey responses suggest a need for much greater priority to be given to advocacy evaluation by NGOs.[5]

The challenge

This then is the challenge to NGOs' advocacy programmes: to evaluate the effectiveness of their campaigning, lobbying, and development education so that they are able confidently to demonstrate their advocacy achievements. By so doing, NGOs would be liberated from the constraints imposed by the beliefs of private and official donors that resources ought not be diverted away from tangible, currently more marketable, humanitarian relief and development projects. Having reached this level of demonstrable knowledge of their advocacy achievements, NGOs will be much better placed strategically to assess and determine the issues upon which they should be advocating, to set their advocacy goals, to plan desired outcomes, and to make more informed judgements about the people, organisations, and institutions that they should be seeking to influence, and the methods and forms of organisation and alliance that will be most effective. This increased level of confidence in their advocacy will enable NGOs to invest greater resources in advocacy programmes which contribute to the realisation of their poverty-reduction goals. Anything less will consign NGOs to being no more than bit players in the necessary transformation of the institutions, policies, and practices which sustain poverty and powerlessness.

Notes

1 For these purposes, advocacy is assumed to incorporate campaigning, lobbying, and development education as the three principal streams of activity by which NGOs have sought to influence structures and policies and to bring about change in the interests of eradicating poverty and its underlying causes.

2 The survey was distributed to all 11 OI affiliates, plus 54 development NGOs listed in the 1992 Organisation for Economic Co-operation and Development Directory, whose entries referred to advocacy activity, and whose 1990 budgets were not less than that of Oxfam Canada, which in that year was the lowest of OECD country-based Oxfams, and so indicative of a Northern NGO which encompassed the full range of development NGO activity. Further, because the OI affiliates include Oxfam Hong Kong as the only one not based in an OECD member country, two members of international NGO networks based in Newly Industrialised Economies were included in the survey, making a total of 56 NGOs not related to Oxfam. Fifty-two of the 67 (77 per cent) of the surveyed NGOs responded, although 29 of the NGOs not related to Oxfam did not provide data.

3 It may be argued that this comparison is unfair, because Greenpeace and other organisations such as Friends of the Earth and Amnesty International have effecting change as their sole *raison d'être*, without the 'encumbrance' of development and humanitarian relief programmes, which were the purposes for which Northern NGOs were generally founded. Nevertheless, NGOs which claim to address the structural causes of poverty in the course of pursuing their mission and employ advocacy as the strategy for effecting change to improve the lives of people living in poverty have a duty to do so most effectively. Advocacy is not an optional extra for those NGOs, but is essential to bringing about the change in structures, policies, and practices which institutionalise poverty.

4 Of the four strategic weaknesses of NGO advocacy identified by Edwards, their failure to develop credible alternatives to neo-liberal economic growth-oriented orthodoxies was beyond the survey's scope.

5 Roche (1999), in a chapter devoted to impact assessment and advocacy, outlines current approaches to evaluating advocacy, by reference to number of case studies. This work, which makes the case for assessing advocacy (applicable to both development programmes and humanitarian emergencies), presents a number of qualitative, quantitative, and participatory approaches to evaluation. Through these case studies Roche therefore demonstrates that at least some NGOs are giving greater priority to advocacy evaluation than is indicated by the survey responses. Roche (p.193) recognises the need for NGOs to be able to demonstrate the effectiveness of their advocacy by stating: 'NGOs need to demonstrate that their advocacy work is not only effective but also cost-effective and has impact in the sense of making positive difference to people's lives. They must show that lasting change in policy and practice actually results in improving the lives of men and women living in poverty and that this achievement is due, at least in part, to

their research, capacity-building, and lobbying efforts. NGOs also need to know under what conditions they should advocate on behalf of others and when they should be strengthening others to speak for themselves. They have to demonstrate that they are going about this work in a professional and competent manner, and use the monitoring of this work to learn and to improve future performance.'

References

Archer, D. (1994) 'The changing roles of non-governmental organisations in the field of education (in the context of changing relationships with the state)', *International Journal of Educational Development* 14(3)

Clark, John (1991) *Democratizing Development: The Role of Voluntary Organisations*, London: Earthscan

Edwards, Michael (1993) 'Does the doormat influence the boot? Critical thoughts on UK NGOs and international advocacy', *Development in Practice* 3(3): 163-75

Edwards, Michael and David Hulme (eds.) (1992) *Making a Difference: NGOs and Development in a Changing World*, London: Earthscan

Edwards, M. and David Hulme (eds.) (1995) *Non-Governmental Organizations – Performance and Accountability: Beyond the Magic Bullet*, London: Earthscan

Greenpeace International (1996) *25 years as a Catalyst for Change*, Amsterdam: Greenpeace International

Minear, Larry (1987) 'The other missions of NGOs: education and advocacy', *World Development* (Supplement) 15

Organisation for Economic Co-operation and Development (1992) *Directory of Non-Governmental Environment and Development Organisations In OECD Member Countries*, Paris: OECD

Oxfam International (1999) 'Strategic Plan 1999-2000', unpublished

Paul, S. and A. Israel (1991), *Non-governmental Organisations and the World Bank*, Washington DC: The World Bank

Roche, Chris (1999) *Impact Assessment for Development Agencies: Learning to Value Change*, Oxford: Oxfam

Smillie, Ian (1995) *The Alms Bazaar: Altruism Under Fire – Non-profit Organizations and International Development*, Ottawa: International Development Research Centre

Sogge, David (ed.) (1996) *Compassion and Calculation: The Business of Private Foreign Aid*, London: Pluto

United Nations Development Programme (1993) *Human Development Report 1993*, Oxford: Oxford University Press

Watkins, Kevin (1995) *The Oxfam Poverty Report*, Oxford: Oxfam

Campaigning: a fashion or the best way to change the global agenda?

Gerd Leipold

Even bankers want to campaign

A new investment fund was recently launched in London. Climbers abseiled down the building of a financial institution, while unfurling a banner to advertise the new fund. A casual observer could have turned wearily away from what looked like another routine Greenpeace banner-hanging event.

Most NGOs these days want to do more campaigning.[1] Recent studies of the effectiveness of NGO campaigning to date (Chapman and Fisher 1999, 2000) identify the following reasons for this trend: the need of Northern NGOs to find new roles, as Southern NGOs take over project work; the recognition that projects will have limited effects without structural changes; an increasing call by Southern organisations for Northern NGOs to do more campaign and policy work; and the desire among NGOs for public profile. The latter has two distinct aspects: the belief that media coverage is necessary and crucial for policy change,[2] and the somewhat sounder assumption that it helps fundraising.

Campaign organisations and organisations that also campaign

Campaigning is not a new phenomenon: it has been around for centuries. A characteristic of campaigns is that they spring up when legality and legitimacy find themselves at odds with each other, so that certain groups claim legitimacy for their cause and deny this legitimacy to the prevailing powers. Campaign organisations, whose very reason for existence is to campaign, have existed for a long time. Anti-slavery International (formerly the Anti-Slavery Society) is one of the oldest such organisations, while Greenpeace and Amnesty International are probably the best-known modern ones.

The success of modern campaign organisations has stimulated organisations which had previously tended to limit themselves to project work to extend or build a campaigning arm. These organisations have quite distinct characteristics. A good campaign organisation is highly interactive, being able both to create an agenda and also to take advantage of existing agendas. It will spend a major proportion of its resources on communication, communication being its core business and not just a tool. Campaigning is a dialectical process, so campaign organisations tend to be confrontational and in turn attract confrontational people. Campaign organisations have to be opportunistic, not in terms of their beliefs and values, but in terms of reaching audiences. They derive their legitimacy from the popular support that they enjoy and from the quality of information that they provide. In a campaign – especially if it is directed at the general public – tactics are as important as strategy, a characteristic which campaigns share with politics.

Organisations that also campaign would obviously want to impose their existing organisational procedures on their campaigning activities. Their campaigning results will, therefore, be less than impressive. Alternatively, they will have to live with two different organisational cultures. Real conflicts of interests between campaigns and project work can arise where no compromise will do justice to both. Campaigns which are undertaken mainly for fundraising purposes may make it possible to avoid such conflicts, but generally at the price of a weak campaign.

Three contemporary campaigns

Three examples will help to identify characteristics of campaigns and to address the difficult question of what campaigns can achieve.

Brent Spar

Few campaigns in recent years achieved such a public resonance as Greenpeace's successful attempt to prevent the dumping at sea of the disused Brent Spar oil platform. Originally it was conceived as a medium-sized action to attract attention to a forthcoming meeting of the Oslo and Paris Convention. (Interestingly, the communication specialists of the organisation were opposed to the action, predicting that it would have little resonance.) It was not considered a campaign *per se*, only as a tactic within a long-standing lobbying strategy.

It rapidly took on a life of its own. Brent Spar gripped the attention of the European public. Individuals and organisations felt compelled to become active, and were soon followed by a number of governments. Organisations called for a boycott of Shell. Some individuals even firebombed a petrol station. European governments pressured their UK counterpart to reverse its position. Greenpeace occupied centre-stage in the media, but it certainly did not control what happened in the public and political arena. This loss of control – anathema to traditional management approaches – is typical of a successful public campaign. Truly activating people – probably the proudest achievement that a campaign could hope to claim – means that those people will decide largely on their own about the next steps.

The Brent Spar campaign effectively put an end to the dumping of decommissioned oil platforms. The environmental significance of this is low, if one looks simply at the amount of pollution entering the oceans through dumping. However, the symbolic importance is much higher. The oceans can no longer be considered as a convenient and cheap dumping ground far away from where the waste was created.[3]

After Shell abandoned its plan to dump the platform, Greenpeace experienced a severe setback when it admitted – on its own initiative – that it had overestimated the amount of oil left in the platform. For the central argument, this fact was of secondary importance. It was only brought up towards the end of the campaign, when people were already strongly supporting Greenpeace; and in some countries it was hardly mentioned. However, it tainted Greenpeace's success with the suspicion that the organisation had got its facts wrong: a serious problem for any campaign. Greenpeace's mistake and its ensuing apology were probably reported out of proportion to their real significance, but after the publicity it had received throughout its action, the organisation could hardly complain.

Brent Spar and – equally important – the execution of Ken Sarowiwa were watersheds for Shell and other big oil companies. A large number of senior managers were replaced by a newer generation. The companies conceded that the legality of their action was not enough: they also needed public legitimacy. They committed themselves to listening more to the public. They withdrew from the Global Climate Commission – an industry group which denies the threat of global warming and has resisted all moves to reduce carbon dioxide emissions. Respect for human rights and a commitment to sustainable development were added to the companies' objectives. Investment in renewable energies multiplied. BP even conceded that the company would eventually have to move out of fossil fuels.

The oil companies reacted incredibly fast, more so than a government or for that matter a major NGO would have been able to do, and so demonstrated the degree to which campaigns can affect corporations. The deeper question of the extent to which these changes are more than a cosmetic make-over to reduce external criticism and restore reputation, however, is hard to answer. Even if the changes are for real, it is too early to judge what effect they will have on the global environment, on human rights, and on poverty. The impact of campaigns is generally extremely difficult and sometimes impossible to judge. One will usually have to wait a long time to tell, and then many other factors will also have had an influence.

Landmines

Landmines appeared on the public agenda less than 15 years ago and the campaign to ban them became one of the most popular causes ever. Eventually, it was awarded a Nobel Peace Prize. The icon of the campaign was Diana, Princess of Wales. Had she been still been alive, she might have been honoured with the Nobel Prize herself. Her importance for the campaign is hard to gauge. Her involvement was as much the effect of the campaign itself as the cause of its success. Rarely do famous people get involved in an early stage of a campaign, with the exception of ageing rock stars who are bored with their own music and worried about their dwindling pulling power.

Once the landmines issue had reached a threshold of public interest, someone like Princess Diana almost naturally appeared on stage – and this is not to deny her seriousness or her importance. The popular media demand the personalisation of issues: they want figureheads and personalities, and they appoint their 'spokespeople', even if campaigning organisations do not nominate them. Popularisation should not be dismissed. On the contrary, it is an important aspect of campaigns, especially in their later stages. Not only does it create pressure: it also gives the cause a democratic legitimacy. Popularisation can be just as difficult as other aspects of campaigning. It requires different skills and also a new type of campaigner.

In the case of landmines, Robin Coupland from the International Committee of the Red Cross (ICRC), who provided the first comprehensive field data of mine injuries, and Ray McGrath, founder of the Mines Advisory Group (MAG), who worked in Afghanistan and pioneered mine clearance, probably most deserved to be honoured with the Nobel Prize. But in campaigning as elsewhere, those who sow the seeds rarely reap the harvest.

What was the harvest? Undoubtedly the landmines campaign created a huge awareness of anti-personnel devices and their effects. A sense of solidarity was created, and a call for action was the result. This awareness is not confined to rich countries. A recent study by ICRC (ICRC 1999: 65) in countries that have experienced war revealed a very high awareness of landmines, even in conflicts where they were not used.

The landmines campaign led directly to the Ottawa Treaty, which was negotiated, signed, and ratified unusually quickly. It bypassed the established institutions typically responsible for such a treaty, such as the UN Committee on Disarmament. What was, in the eyes of governments, a security issue best left to military specialists was transformed into a humanitarian issue, with ordinary people displacing the specialists.[4] NGOs exercised unprecedented influence in the negotiations, finally catching up with their counterparts in international environmental forums. Mine clearance became accepted as a major task and is now a well-funded activity, and the medical treatment of mine victims has also much improved.

On the other hand, key countries such as the USA, Russia, and China have not signed the Ottawa Treaty. The number of landmines used has declined, but if one disregards Afghanistan, Angola, and Cambodia – where landmines were most heavily used, and which were the sites of Cold War-related conflicts – then there is probably not much change in practice. Some cynics have even claimed that the campaign provided the best propaganda for landmines. The campaign also failed to make it clear who carried responsibility: the weapon system was demonised, but its producers and users remained anonymous.

A by-product of the landmines campaign (not uncommon in campaigning) was the ban on blinding laser weapons. It happened almost overnight in 1995, inspired by a combination of three factors: an original report by Human Rights Watch, the concern of the US government about China and other countries developing such weapons, and public concern about inhumane weapons, created by the landmines campaign. Just a few months before the ban was agreed, no one, including the opponents of landmines, thought that such an outcome was possible. Campaign successes can happen overnight and can also produce completely unanticipated results.

All in all, the landmines campaign had tangible humanitarian benefits, but it failed to take the weapons out of use. Its real success lies in the awareness created and in the resulting shift in international politics. The secrecy of security and military issues was challenged, the process of negotiations 'civilianised', and the burden of proof shifted to the military side. Military need is no longer automatically regarded as more relevant than humanitarian necessity.

So: the campaign was a success, still more so in terms of its potential for the future rather than in terms of real change now. As Chapman and Fisher (1999: 15-16) point out, campaigns have limits. Real and lasting impact, implementation, and monitoring require tools other than national legislation or international conventions: education, involvement of the grassroots, or fundamental changes (addressing the causes of conflict), for example. If they don't happen, the legacy of the landmines campaign may just be another part of the Lady Di folklore.

Debt and Jubilee 2000

The debt issue is more than 20 years old. Its was originally raised by Southern NGOs who observed the effects of spiralling debt on their countries' development. In the West, the argument about debt was highly politicised. The left was in favour of debt relief; the rest of the political spectrum saw the demand for relief as ideologically motivated, communist propaganda under a thin veneer of concern for the poor. The argument was mostly confined to circles of experts and hardly ever reached a broader public.

Somehow – and it is difficult to identify how and when the transformation happened – the debate about debt changed in the 1990s.The minority position that debt relief was essential became the mainstream view. Active politicians and ministers joined their retired colleagues and NGOs in calling for debt relief. A paradigm shift had taken place.

A number of factors caused that shift. A constant stream of reports on the effects of debt kept the issue alive. The quality of field research by NGOs improved (or, as likely, or even more likely, it conformed more to Western standards and adopted the language of economics), so it was harder to reject it out of hand. The end of the Cold War reduced the ideological content of the debate. Heavily committed banks had had time to reduce their exposure. The World Bank, under the assault of its critics, began to change its policy, while the IMF discredited itself through the patent failure of its own doctrines.

The argument for debt relief had probably already been won when Jubilee 2000 was formed. Jubilee 2000 had the task of further popularising the issue and forming and co-ordinating an international network to create pressure for substantial debt relief. To do so, it needed to demonstrate the widest possible support; so it rightly embarked on widespread coalition-building.[5]

Winning the argument, however, is a double-edged sword in campaigning. The new consensus that develops is typically less radical than the original campaign position. By adopting the new consensus, the mainstream also demands the authority to define it. Once finance ministers are in favour of debt relief, they will also assume the authority for defining the level and form that it should take. Those who campaigned over the years now find themselves easily sidelined, their arguments portrayed as the predictable response of special-interest groups which are never satisfied. Whether Jubilee 2000 managed to avoid this pitfall and achieve full success is probably a contentious matter, even within the campaign. The debt issue serves to illustrate that campaigns are an excellent, possibly even the best, tool to gain symbolic victories, but they cannot by themselves guarantee political and economic change.

Challenges and opportunities for campaigning

The examples selected illustrate some general features of campaigns. Today's political environment poses additional and specific challenges and opportunities.

Challenges

NGOs increasingly work as agents of governments and intergovernmental organisations and they seek co-operation with business. Even with the best possible will, such an approach reduces their independence. Campaigns are by their very nature mostly confrontational, and as such they are constrained if the campaigning organisation is too close to government or business.[6] Politics and politicians have a bad name the world over, though this reputation is probably unfair. NGOs, by contrast, are still mostly perceived as having integrity and compassion, albeit mixed with naïvety. As and when their influence increases, they could easily become engulfed in the crisis of the political system.[7]

As more and more NGOs want to campaign, the competition for public interest becomes stronger. For the campaign issues themselves, this competition is mostly beneficial. However, there is also an underlying (and often unacknowledged) competition among the organisations involved, which can weaken a campaign. In most international forums, NGOs appear united. But this unity is obviously a fractious one, given their highly diverse underlying interests. Once the globally operating NGOs fragment – or appear to do so – their collective claim to the moral high ground is damaged.

For most established NGOs, it is more cost-efficient to concentrate on 'upgrading' their members (that is, increasing the contribution per member) than on maximising the numbers of supporters. More members, however, give campaigns greater legitimacy. So an unfortunate choice has to be made between the two: the most cost-efficient fundraising method, on the one hand, and greater legitimacy on the other.

For a long time, campaigns were mostly for 'progressive' causes (which today may be more difficult to define). However, the instrument of campaigning is not necessarily restricted to progressive causes. Right-wing groups campaign against immigration, while inter-governmental organisations increasingly incorporate campaigns into their own agendas. Chris Rose[8] suggests that in the future campaigning might even become a commercial activity. Indeed, one could imagine a major coffee importer offering fair-trade coffee and at the same time campaigning for girls' education.

Opportunities

The much-cited New Media (not to be equated with the Web) offer the possibility of a close and interactive relationship with members and supporters, and consequently the chance to mobilise and activate people very quickly. The cost of communicating with members is also much lower, which removes the need to have to choose between efficient fundraising and broad-based support.

Organised consumers can exert substantial pressure on companies and can produce quick results in a campaign. New technologies enable consumers to organise efficiently and effectively.

NGOs are used to forming coalitions based on shared objectives and values. Coalitions increase legitimacy, but they are slow and tend to create positions that reflect the need for internal compromise rather than relevance to the external world. The Jubilee and landmines campaigns could not, of course, match the speed of movement of the tightly co-ordinated Greenpeace organisation in the Brent Spar campaign. But then Greenpeace would not have succeeded without the wave of spontaneous and independent support from many quarters. It is certainly rare that such mobilisation happens, so there is a need deliberately to build wider constituencies in most campaigns.

It may be useful for NGOs to think more about strategic alliances based on shared interests. Shared interests have the advantage that they are more likely to lead to action. They reduce the need for co-ordination and allow for independent activities. They can help to push an issue to the contre of the stage (and increase the 'market' and thereby the profile of all involved). Strategic alliances are pragmatic, are intended to last for limited periods, and should ideally involve members from various areas (development, environment, and human rights).

For Southern NGOs, New Media offer the opportunity to find members and raise funds globally, reducing potential financial dependency, and so dramatically increasing their independence. Pilot tests show that this can be very successful, particularly if the Southern NGO is part of a global organisation.

Can campaigns change the global agenda?

One of the most important objectives for development organisations is to achieve a fair global economic system.[9] Campaigns alone cannot achieve this objective, but they can make an important contribution. They can raise awareness and create symbols of the problem. They can activate millions of people and bring together organisations from around the world. They can raise and win the arguments about defining what is fair and what is patently unjust. They can develop a new narrative for development. As Maggie Black once remarked, NGOs are not good at making waves – indeed, they may even waste energy in trying to create waves – but they are good at riding them.[10] This is less a criticism of NGO campaigns than it is an acknowledgement of the limited political and economic might of NGOs.

We will see many organisations campaign for a new global economic system. The most dynamic and most original of these campaigns will originate from small, radical, young groups. They will spring up where the problem is most urgent and visible. After all, riding waves is for young people. In the end, however, bigger organisations – and societies as a whole – will have to learn to make waves.

Notes

1 This article does not make a distinction between campaigning and advocacy, and for simplicity it consistently uses the term *campaigning*. Only campaigning by NGOs, mostly large organisations in the North, is studied. Commercial campaigns are left out, for obvious reasons, but also political election campaigning, as it is substantially different from the campaigning considered here. Key differences are the much shorter timespan, the clear demarcation of winners and losers, and the fixed stages in an election campaign.

2 'Public profile' is often used as a euphemism for media coverage. The importance of media coverage in campaigns is probably over-estimated. While important in later stages of a campaign, it is in all likelihood not essential before the popularising phase.

3 This was not just a symbolic result. Under the direct influence of Brent Spar, in line with long-standing campaigns on behalf of the oceans by Greenpeace and others, and following a trend among most European governments, European countries agreed strong restrictions on waste disposal at sea, coming close to a complete prohibition.

4 This was well expressed by Princess Diana's response to being criticised for meddling in political questions: 'I'm not a political figure, nor do I want to be one. But I come with my heart.'

5 Typically, coalitions in earlier stages of a campaign are less useful, sometimes even detrimental, because they reduce mobility and blunt the sharpness of the argument.

6 One should remember that neither governments nor business are monolithic. It is not impossible, therefore, to combine confrontation and co-operation.

7 NGOs would be ill-advised simply to join the blanket condemnation of politicians and politics. Politicians are probably less corrupt than business people, but are also under higher scrutiny. A weak political system will make it harder, not easier, for most campaigns to achieve real change.

8 Personal communication. Chris Rose is a campaign adviser to Greenpeace International.

9 Barry Coates, director of the World Development Movement, speaks of a 30-year campaign to regulate the global economy.

10 Maggie Black (1992) made this remark to the Oxfam Assembly.

References

Black, Maggie (1992) *A Cause for Our Times: Oxfam – The First Fifty Years*, Oxford: Oxfam

Chapman, Jennifer and Thomas Fisher (1999) 'Effective NGO Campaigning', unpublished report, London: New Economics Foundation

Chapman, Jennifer and Thomas Fisher (2000) 'The effectiveness of NGO campaigning: lessons from practice' *Development in Practice* 10(2): 151-65

ICRC (1999) *ICRC Worldwide Consultation on the Rules of War*, Geneva: ICRC

The international anti-debt campaign: a Southern activist view for activists in 'the North' ... and 'the South'

Dot Keet

The anti-debt campaign goes public

It is an enormous relief to anti-debt groups in the 'global South' that the crisis of external indebtedness has at last moved centre-stage in global public awareness. Whether based on the Christian principle of 'jubilee' renewal – the liberation of the bonded poor and debt-enslaved at the start of the new millennium – or on similar principles espoused by other religions, or on the basis of secular ethics against the exploitation and subordination of the poor and weak by the rich and strong, millions of people are joining the international campaign for a definitive solution to the scandalous extraction of the resources of the world's poor into the overflowing coffers of the rich.

Of course it was – as always – only after influential churches and other religious groups, development agencies, and NGOs in the North took up 'the Third World Debt' that it became 'an issue', something that causes the usual wry observations among researchers and activists in the countries directly concerned, who have been working on debt issues for almost two decades.[1] Nonetheless, this growing recognition is welcome, and the research and information campaigns, political lobbying, and media interventions by anti-debt coalitions in Europe, North America, and Japan must be commended. They have made significant gains in terms of media coverage of the scale and effects of the debt, if not the complex causes. Some anti-debt groups have achieved advances in their respective governments' positions on payments owed to them by countries in the South. The campaign has even compelled the IMF and the World Bank to modify their implacable opposition to debt cancellation (above all, the cancellation of debts owed to themselves). It is mainly in an attempt to deflate growing public criticism, and deflect the full potential thrust of the campaign, that these institutions, in conjunction with the G7 countries, belatedly offered some 'debt relief' for the most Heavily Indebted Poor Countries (HIPCs).

All this is evidence of the impact of the international campaign against the growing 'Third World' debt.[2] The paradox is that, as public information expands, and the campaign makes ever greater gains, the options and issues are actually becoming more complex. As the number and range of participating organisations and countries grow, the discussions of objectives and tactics become more complicated. These debates relate not only to the methods and purposes of engaging with creditor governments, nor only to the aims and implications of, and appropriate responses to, the HIPC strategy. Within and among the anti-debt groups – particularly between some in the North and others in the South – there is a deepening debate on many of the common concepts and implicit assumptions, the tactics and strategies, and the fundamental aims and purposes of the campaign.

Deepening debate on key issues

The IMF/WB offer of debt *relief* (or partial debt 'forgiveness', as the US and other governments refer to it) has been supported multilaterally by government creditors, but accompanied also by certain unilateral decisions on selective debt *reduction* by governments such as Canada, Norway, and Denmark. Meanwhile, non-government anti-debt groups in Europe and North America called for the *cancellation* of the 'unpayable' debts of the 'poorest' countries by the year 2000. However, there are some worrying ambiguities in their position. For, while public campaigns call for a 'halt' to the debt crisis, and for the debt to be 'dropped now', when grappling with their governments and with the IMF/WB, anti-debt groups repeatedly slip into the language of debt 'relief' or 'reduction', and resort to compromised calls for 'more substantial' debt cancellation[3] – that is 'wider, deeper and faster'.[4] The danger is that such arguments could become an implicit acceptance that debt cancellation need not be immediate or total. Yet debt cancellation is what radical activists in the debtor countries seek, and is the vision that is attracting millions of people to the campaign.

One problem is that the terms debt 'relief', 'reduction', and 'cancellation' are used interchangeably by different actors. 'Relief' can refer to relieving the burden-carriers of their burden, but may also mean alleviating rather than terminating the problem. 'Reduction' implies only partial removal of debt repayments. And, unless explicitly defined as 'partial', 'cancellation' should mean the definitive ending of all debt. There needs to be greater clarity and consistency on the part of debt analysts and campaigners in their use of these terms, and the same must be demanded of official spokespeople, in order to prevent unintended ambiguities and misunderstandings, or indeed the deliberate 'fudging' of what is on the table.

More problematic is the interpretation of what is 'unpayable'. The IMF/WB argue that debt is 'sustainable' as long as debt payments are being kept up without default. Some Jubilee 2000 (J2000) groups also base their proposals on 'sustainability' criteria.[5] Others point out that such payments are sustained only at the expense of essential social spending and to the heavy cost of the populations of debtor countries.[6] They argue for an approach based on 'development criteria', meaning that governments have the right to spend on essential primary education and health needs before repaying debts. This begs the question: what is 'essential'? Where are the limits to be drawn when essential social needs are also developmental necessities? Surely, there can be no *a priori* expenditure levels set on what are, and have to be, open-ended and ever-expanding resource requirements for full (not token) education for all, and fully effective (not minimal) health care. These are both a key measure and fundamental means towards self-sustaining development. Nor does the 'basic needs' or minimalist approach take on board the many other social needs – which are also human rights – such as housing, clean water, decent sanitation, accessible and safe transport systems, social and physical security, as well as the right to life-sustaining employment. So, at what level, or when, does Third World debt become 'payable'?

Don't owe! Won't pay!

To anti-debt groups in the South, the very suggestion that their countries' debts are 'payable' is outrageous. And this is the moral position of many of their supporters in the North. In fact, the debts that these governments incurred, by whatever means and for whatever purposes, have in real terms already been repaid – in some cases, many times over. They have also been paid in the incalculable terms of social and environmental damage, political unrest, conflict and wars, and profound human insecurity and suffering. In January 1999, Latin American and Caribbean anti-debt campaigners declared in Tegucigalpa that not only do their countries not 'owe' anything, but that there is a moral, political, social, and environmental debt owed *to* them. The African non-government debt declaration, made in Accra in April 1998, similarly denounced any further debt repayments, and pointed to reparations due to Africa for the damages inflicted by the centuries of slave trade, colonial, and neo-colonial exploitation. The myth of vast external 'aid' flows into Africa is exploded by the fact that US$1.41 in debt payments leave the continent for every dollar received in grants in 1998. This is quite apart from the vast sums that have long been flowing out of many countries in the South, in the form of super-profits on foreign direct investments,[7] dividends on foreign-owned equity, and unequal terms of trade.[8]

From such perspectives, any requirements for any further debt repayments are immoral and illegitimate. Not one cent more should be added to the prolonged outflows of precious resources from South to North: the indebted countries of the South 'don't owe, and won't pay'. For this to become the position of their governments is the challenge to anti-debt campaigners within these countries. However, it also has to be accepted and energetically pursued by Northern anti-debt campaigners in order to bring pressure to bear on their own governments.[9] Minimally, Northern groups must recognise the position of their counterparts in the South and so not contradict it, either explicitly or implicitly. For instance, it is deeply problematic when prominent J2000 spokespeople warn creditor agencies that they must act promptly or 'poor countries will take matters into their own hands'.[10] Rather than trying to pre-empt such possibilities, anti-debt campaigners should be actively helping to make debt renunciation a central component of international discourse. Influential anti-debt campaigners in the richest countries should be using their skills and contacts to prepare international public opinion — and through this the governments of both North *and* South – for this legitimate resolution of the debt crisis.

Different approaches

Other differences within the international anti-debt campaign also need to be admitted. Many development NGOs,[11] although supporting the debt campaign, have been trying to 'improve' the HIPC initiative to embrace more than the current half-dozen qualifying countries, and to be implemented more rapidly than originally planned. However, intensive research by UK Jubilee 2000 revealed[12] that, even if applied to all 41 designated HIPCs, the IMF/WB terms would largely provide 'relief' only on debt that is already not being paid, and which the international finance institutions know will never be paid. In fact, some HIPCs would be paying out more than they are already; and there would actually be an overall gain for creditors from this 'debt relief' exercise. However, the more fundamental objection is that the IMF structural adjustment conditionalities driving the HIPC programme have been a major factor in the deepening economic and social crises in the South, and a powerful reinforcement and aggravation of their external financial dependence and subjection to external controls. HIPC *and* its conditionalities are unacceptable, both in their aims and effects and in principle. Anti-debt groups that do not assimilate this are failing to understand some of the basic causes of the debt crisis, and they may in fact be helping to sustain the debt-bondage of the very countries and peoples they want to assist.

In entering into 'debates' with the IMF/WB – whether in order to 'change' or to 'challenge' them – and in engaging with their own governments to persuade them towards more advanced policy positions, Northern anti-debt groups are also in danger of accommodating themselves to the creditors' selective and divisive approaches towards debtor countries. This is creating discrepancies, not only within the positions of such groups but between them and their Southern counterparts. The International J2000 Coalition explicitly focuses on 'the poorest countries', identifying 52, with a combined population of almost one billion, that are in urgent need of debt cancellation. In practice, however, many J2000 groups and development NGOs are drawn into the focus of the IMF/WB and their own governments on the most heavily indebted Least Developed Countries (LDCs). This is not necessarily wrong in itself, but it begs the question as to where the 'qualifying' line – other than simplistic quantitative GDP measures – should be drawn. Does a country such as Brazil, which is not an LDC but has the very worst income disparities in the world, and dire social and environmental crises, not qualify for debt cancellation? At what real cost will Brazil 'sustain' debt repayments? Similarly, does South Africa, supposedly a 'middle-income developing country', but with income disparities and social problems as acute as those of Brazil, not need debt cancellation in order to apply all possible resources to dealing with the continuing legacy of apartheid? And what of the dozens of other deeply indebted, socially and environmentally stressed, countries?

More countries, more than 'poverty alleviation'

Anti-debt groups in the South need to take a wider and more strategic approach to the country coverage and adopt broader arguments for the debt cancellation campaign. They are aware of the divisive and potentially weakening effects of selective and exclusionary debt-relief proposals and so must maintain a united front among themselves. This does not mean that all national anti-debt campaigns will be identical. There are clear differences in the scale and the structures of specific country debts, and these have to be carefully researched, the targets identified, constituencies mobilised, and diverse tactics employed. However, debt campaigners do need to agree on a set of common principles and maintain the broadest unity and strongest joint positions and common actions possible. Indebted countries cannot allow themselves to be played off against one another. Nor should there be any acceptance of arguments that debt cancellation for some countries can only be done at the expense of others that are more urgent or 'deserving'. Such issues were at the heart of the November 1999 South–South debt summit in South Africa. Already, the official position of the African non-government anti-debt campaign is that its call for total debt cancellation applies to all African countries, irrespective of the size or structures of their debts or their official economic categorisations by the IMF/WB or other international bodies.

Anti-debt campaigners in the South have also to prevail upon their Northern counterparts to take on broader arguments for debt cancellation than 'poverty reduction' alone. Even if employed tactically in arguments to expose the contradictions between the official 'poverty reduction' and 'debt reduction' policies of the rich countries in the OECD,[13] the mere use of such notions can give additional prominence, and legitimacy, to the very limited proposals on offer in the dominant discourse on world poverty. This is counterproductive to the broader need to challenge the OECD's approach, which is to call for a 50 per cent reduction in the numbers of those living in absolute poverty, by the year 2015. It needs to be absolutely clear in any engagement with the OECD that poverty 'reduction' is a totally inadequate aim, and that debt 'reduction' will simply perpetuate the outward flow of 'poverty reducing' resources. Otherwise, such notions can – unintentionally and imperceptibly – displace the South's call for poverty *eradication* and debt *cancellation*. The alternative is to legitimise the 'half a loaf is better than none' approach, which leaves both the half-fed and the unfed in ongoing hunger and misery. And, once again, it begs the question of where the line will be drawn between those to be alleviated of their misery and the remainder, who must continue in 'absolute poverty' – for how long? Fifteen years? A generation? A century?

Wider arguments and perspectives

There are other strong justifications for debt cancellation. Most of these were endorsed in the International J2000 Declaration in Rome in November 1998, but have been inadequately projected in practice. Anti-debt groups need to promote, for example, the proposal to cancel debts incurred through ill-conceived, poorly implemented 'development projects', mainly World Bank-supported, that entailed onerous repayment undertakings without generating appropriate financial returns, or without confirming the availability of other financial resources to meet those obligations. Countries struggling with post-conflict reconstruction and rehabilitation – of which there are many in Africa, Asia, and Latin America – require the same sympathetic and enlightened consideration as was accorded European countries, victors or vanquished, after the Second World War.[14] In fact, such countries in the South require even more generous understanding, since they are labouring under more adverse circumstances, with far poorer human and technical resources.

Southern groups are also insisting on the illegitimacy of debts incurred by military dictatorships and other repressive regimes, which are left for successor governments, and the victims of the former regimes, to pay off. The illegality of loans wittingly made to illegitimate régimes – like those in Argentina, Chile, and Brazil, or Mobutu in Zaïre, Marcos in the Philippines, and a host of others – is enshrined in the Doctrine of Odious Debt, already part of international law and precedent. The creditors of such regimes – whether governmental, commercial, or institutional – have to be confronted with the legal, as well as legitimate, right of subsequent governments to renounce responsibility for such debts. The illegality as well as the illegitimacy of the debt inherited by democratic South Africa from the apartheid régime falls squarely into this category.

These arguments constitute a more comprehensive and just approach, although a politically more challenging one. Some argue that bringing up all these other dimensions will simply cloud the main issue and confuse the majority of supporters. This is debatable. The more real danger is that anti-debt campaigners – North and South – might allow themselves to be drawn into the questionable proposition that the respective country debts have to be broken down so that such 'illegitimate' debts can be clearly identified and dealt with.

Political illegitimacy and illegality

It would be an extremely complex exercise to isolate 'illegitimate' debts, and would hardly be possible without the fullest co-operation of all the parties involved. Further, the guilty banks and governments could deliberately prolong the process. More significantly, such an approach could be falling into the trap of implicitly accepting that the other, or remaining, parts of the debts are somehow 'legitimate'. The main point about the different aspects or components of national debt is that they apply in different combinations in the respective countries, and precisely because these different dimensions and sources of indebtedness are extremely difficult to unravel, these considerations should not become the basis of 'technical' investigations and legal processes. They would have more effective impact if they were marshalled as part of the argument for straight debt cancellation *tout court*.

A further set of problems relates to the use of international law and judicial bodies to pronounce on the 'illegality' of specific cases of odious debt. There are undoubted campaigning uses to be made of this concept, and of selected cases, to highlight a significant source of indebtedness in many countries. But there are also questions about using odious debt as a legal weapon *per se*. There are manifest problems within most countries in pursuing such processes through biased and discredited judicial systems. However, even within somewhat more reliable international judicial bodies and processes, experience has shown that in cases between rich and poor, strong and weak, an essential precondition for equity and justice is that disadvantaged complainants are provided with all the financial, legal, technical, and other backing required to pursue such processes. Such considerations would have to be an integral part of any legal strategies by national or international debt campaigns in this direction, and would still not guarantee full success.

There is an argument which holds that achieving success in even one such case would be a powerful deterrent against further and future irresponsible and illegal lending practices.[15] This assumes, somewhat naïvely, that, under the threat of possible legal action against them if they are uncovered, banks will desist from their traditional *modus operandi* and refrain from using their vast financial and legal resources to continue evading the law as long and as far as they can. This is made all the more likely with the proliferation of dubious banks around the world. Skilful evasions of legal actions are even more feasible with the extensive deregulation of the global financial system, and the uncontrolled, weakly supervised, and poorly monitored practices of banking organisations in the global economy. In fact, campaigners should not rely on the voluntary compliance of banks with national or international legal pronouncements. Nor should they be trying to encourage better 'self-regulation' by banks. The grossly irresponsible behaviour of banks exposed by the Third World debt crisis, and the success of any 'odious debt' legal process, should rather be used – in combination with much broader global campaigns – to call for the international public re-regulation of all financial institutions. This requires closer supervision of banks and related financial organisations, and their subjection to full national and international public scrutiny, social and environmental responsibility, and democratic accountability.

Roles and responsibilities

Clearly, the above considerations raise challenging questions and pose broader tactical and strategic possibilities for the international anti-debt campaigns. Unfortunately, not all of them have yet been taken up with conviction by Northern anti-debt groups, let alone by the general public in the North. Most of these activists are still mainly motivated by the traditional desire among (undoubtedly well-meaning) people in rich countries to alleviate the suffering of the 'helpless poor' elsewhere. This may be sincere, but it will not end the suffering of the poor as long as it does not tackle the multiplicity of causes of that suffering, which include the roles of their own governments, banks, and other lenders, as part of the sources, and not only the 'solvers', of the crisis.

This failure of understanding is evident in the tendency of some influential development organisations in the North[16] to focus mainly, like their home governments, on the roles and responsibilities of Southern governments for the indebtedness of their countries. And they see the improvement of such governments, or 'governance', as the priority condition for – and even before – debt cancellation. There are certainly sound arguments for improving the technical reliability and the political accountability of government, and these go way beyond the requirements of debt (re)payment. However, even within the framework of debt cancellation, this is not a simple or straightforward matter. None know better than the long-suffering peoples of the South the self-serving abuses of power, irresponsibility, indifference, incompetence, and gross corruption that characterised most of their governments most of the time. However, not all governments are totally or equally guilty of such abuses. It is a sweeping generalisation, and shows a superficial understanding of the real process, simply to hold debtor governments responsible, let alone solely responsible, for the predicament of their countries. It is ironic that many Southern campaigners, strongly critical of their own governments, find themselves having to point out to NGOs as well as official agencies in the North that many such governments were both victims *and* culprits in the process. In most cases, the debts escalated due to factors beyond their control, such as dramatic rises in international interest rates that were caused by economic processes and self-serving decisions in the richest countries, particularly the USA. At the same time, countries of the South were handicapped by declining incomes, due to the deteriorating prices for their commodity exports: the harder their people worked, and the more they exported, the lower prices fell. Some governments tried to diversify their national economies to reduce such commodity dependence and vulnerability, but that often entailed further external borrowing. Many indebted governments tried in vain, and somewhat naïvely, to appeal to their creditors to lessen the burden. Others did not even attempt that. Most often, cash-strapped governments feared the reaction of their populations more than they resented their own dependency upon their creditors, and thus they kept returning, year after year, for their next financial fix, just to keep going. And each year they would be rewarded with another 'debt-rescheduling', and another tranche of 'aid' in the form of loans and grants – but only if they had dutifully followed the right policy prescriptions. Whatever their approach, all of them were inextricably tied down by their creditors' payment demands and heavy macro-economic conditionalities. And these were upheld and secured by the mutually reinforcing 'cross-conditionalities' between the bilateral (governmental) and multilateral (institutional) lending agencies.

What needs to be underscored is that there are many causes for the deepening of debt, and responsibility rests on many 'culprits' on all sides. Some argue that much of the problem of developing countries can be attributed to the 'objective workings of the market'. But active agencies include not only commodity brokers, stock-market speculators, and currency dealers, but also legal and illegal (odious) commercial lenders, together with their clients, and industrialised-country governments, along with the multilateral financial institutions that they control. Thus, if anti-debt groups in the North support their governments' demands, as many do, for proof of 'good governance' by erring debtors, as a political condition for debt relief or reduction, they should also call for equally demanding conditions to be placed on the whole range of self-serving, unprincipled, and irresponsible financial agencies, whether governmental, inter-governmental, or commercial.

Conditions and counter-conditions

To be consistent, effective, and fully legitimate in the South, anti-debt campaigners in the North should demand that conditions be placed also upon their own governments, the banks they support, and the institutions they control. A major factor in the creation of the debt crises and democratic deficits in the South derives from the geopolitical, as well as financial, motivations of Cold War governments in bank-rolling highly dubious (but useful) governments in Africa, Asia, and Latin America. Criticisms can also be made of many of the creditor governments which supplied 'tied' grants and loans to promote the interests of their own producers; and which provided (and continue to provide) guarantees to their own exporters, and protections to avaricious and irresponsible banks. And yet these same governments now self-righteously demand that debtors prove their probity. If such developed-country 'democratic' governments now eschew responsibility for the negative practices of their predecessors, they must allow the same latitude to today's governments in the South, who bear little responsibility for the acts of their predecessors in creating their countries' debts.

The leverage that is being incorporated in proposals for debt 'relief' is a blunt instrument to deal with the complex combination of domestic and international factors underpinning governmental abuses and failures in many countries of the South. The domestic factors are many and varied, and arise both from objective factors and subjective failings. The latter include inadequate self-organisation and self-assertion by independent civil-society forces and information media, to challenge and correct the harmful practices of their political, bureaucratic, managerial, and business élites; or to counter their own suppression by them. But, most often, these ruling élites were able to behave as they did by courtesy of the indifference or the conniving *Realpolitik* of the dominant international forces, governmental and entrepreneurial. As the Accra

Declaration states, accountability, transparency, and democracy must be established in all government institutions in Africa, but also in the structures and operations of international lending agencies. This includes both public and private, governmental, commercial, and institutional actors. Without such international regulations and institutional controls, attempts to stop debt crises re-emerging just by disciplining current debtor governments will simply not suffice. Conditions and controls do have to be set, but they must be effectively designed, internationally agreed, transparent in operation, closely monitored – and applied to *all* involved.

In this respect, a further guarantee is in the effective role and rights of popular civil-society organisations (CSOs) in the indebted countries to monitor and help to determine the social uses to which the financial resources released by debt cancellation will be applied. This is supported by anti-debt groups in both North and South, although a particular responsibility rests on Northern groups to give all the support they can to the strengthening of popular organisations in the debtor countries. Without this, the role of civil society in the South could be largely tokenistic, and the task will, in effect, be carried out, as so often, mainly by well-positioned, powerful (and sometimes self-promoting) NGOs in the North 'on behalf of' the South. A case in point is the proposal by some Swiss development groups that the 'savings' made by Swiss-government debt relief in Africa be channelled through 'debt swaps' to the projects of Swiss NGO groups working there. This would in effect divert to themselves resources that should be within the purview of independent local groups and national governments. In this way, well-meaning – but frequently paternalistic and often self-serving – Northern development agencies effectively displace local people from determining how their own resources recovered from external debt drainages should be used.

The real empowerment and effective role of local groups and social movements in the South is even more difficult with respect to proposals for the inclusion of 'all stakeholders' in a future international debt summit under the auspices of the UN. The same applies to the role and 'right of local organisations' to be heard in the proposed Debt Review Bodies,[17] or in relation to other debtor–creditor arbitration panels, as proposed by UNCTAD. Given existing patterns in many such international processes, the role and rights of 'civil society' will largely be enjoyed by the better resourced and strongly organised Northern CSOs 'on behalf of' all global social forces, whose needs and aspirations they do not necessarily understand or represent.

Resources and reimbursements

Much of this whole debate resolves around ensuring that the 'resources released' by debt cancellation will be turned to good social use and not mis-applied or squandered by incompetent governments, or stolen by the corrupt, as has so often happened in the past with monies received from abroad. Campaigners in the South note this new-found concern about such abuses with some irony. It would have helped to control irresponsible external borrowing if the lending agencies – governmental or commercial – had been more scrupulous in their choice of those upon whom they bestowed their loans in the first place. However, the more crucial point now is that the financial resources being 'released' are from the resources of the debtor countries, their own export earnings, which would then be available for essential external expenditures requiring foreign exchange (such as medicines and medical equipment) and other needs within their own economies. *In other words, debt cancellation amounts to 'allowing' these countries to keep and use their own hard-earned money!*

The second point relates to the argument constantly posed by creditor governments, and implicitly or explicitly taken up by many non-government groups, that debt cancellation will somehow carry 'costs' and even require 'new resources'. There may well be costs to creditor governments, and some will undoubtedly have to forgo some income. The alternative is to argue that government coffers in the rich countries should continue to receive such inflows – which, though minuscule within their overall revenues, are huge within the revenues of debtor governments. More importantly, many of the so-called costs or losses will actually be incurred by commercial banks. This would be income forgone rather than real losses, since most have already been fully reimbursed for the loans they provided. However, even if some have not totally recouped their outlays, loan defaults are part of the calculated risks that creditors have to take and plan for. In fact, most such banks have long ago written off many of the 'bad debts' owed them in the Third World, although, in order to maintain the myth of the 'inviolability' of banking principles and the inescapable 'obligations' of creditors, they do not publicise this. Any talk by Northern governments about 'new resources' needed to compensate banks for their losses is a matter between them and their banks and other financial bodies. Alternatively, if the public assumption of responsibility for private debts is unacceptable to Northern tax-payers, then it is a domestic issue between citizens' campaign groups in these countries and their governments. This is not the responsibility, nor the concern, of the victims of these processes in the South, and it should not form part of the international negotiations on debt cancellation.

The 'losses' that will be incurred by the multilateral financial institutions entail two other considerations. The first is the formal issue that the statutes of the IMF, World Bank, and related financial bodies prohibit them from writing off debts, as private banks do all the time. This is a question to be resolved between them and their main financial under-writers and decision-makers, the G7, and other rich countries. The same applies to the regional banks, such as the African Development Bank and its counterparts in Asia and Latin America. All these multilateral financial institutions have to be made to take responsibility for their wrong decisions in the past, their poor project assessments, and, above all, their bad policy impositions. If not, they will continue with the practices and the policies that have contributed to creating economic decline and debt crises in their client countries.

The more immediate issue for countries in the South, above all in Africa, is the proposal[18] that the losses incurred by the international finance institutions should be off-set by the sale of some of the IMF's gold reserves. On the one hand, this may merely be used by the IMF to ensure that its Enhanced Structural Adjustment Facility (ESAF) receives the necessary financial resources to become self-sufficient and self-perpetuating.[19] On the other hand, such massive gold sales will affect yet another area of the commodity-export earnings of a whole range of countries – from relatively 'rich' South Africa to poverty-stricken Burkina Faso in Africa, and others elsewhere. Of course, such dependence upon commodity exports and vulnerability to international commodity-market price fluctuations is a fundamental problem in itself. However, what this (well-meaning but ill-conceived) proposal means is that, once again, what is purportedly (but not actually) being 'given' to the countries of the South with the right hand is taken away with the left.

Unilateral, bilateral, and multilateral approaches

There are various proposals for multilateral debt-negotiation forums, processes involving the UN, or the creation of international arbitration bodies where debtors and creditors can be brought together. There are also innovative proposals for the establishment of international and national legal instruments enshrining the right of effectively bankrupt countries to have recourse, like struggling companies, to insolvency procedures and protections from their creditors. This is part of the legal approach to the debt problem, which could also include the use of Bisque Clauses that entitle debtors unilaterally to suspend or defer debt payments. These are not 'revolutionary' proposals, but core principles and well-established procedures within the capitalist economic system. They are designed to encourage the entrepreneurial endeavours that are supposedly at the very core of the market dynamics that drive capitalism; and to do so by underpinning risk-taking business ventures with guarantees and protections in the event of operational difficulties or business failures.

Some argue that these proposals – and the recourse to the Doctrine of Odious Debt – are overly legalistic, compromising, and constricting. They hold that governments should simply go into unilateral *de facto* default, as some have done even in the recent past (although this is not widely publicised by their creditors, in order not to encourage others to do the same). But, unless a number of countries happen to do so simultaneously, debt default could expose weaker economies to financial, trade, and other reprisals. The more radical and definitive solution would be for all Third World debtor countries explicitly and collectively to renounce or repudiate their debts – but they would also have to be prepared to stand united against counter-actions by the world's financial and political forces. This strategy would require both political will on the part of such governments, and informed popular support and preparedness for the probable short to medium term economic consequences. It would also require extensive prior preparation and mobilisation of international public opinion. Thus, recourse to the collective repudiation of their debts by the countries of the South, as a legitimate, definitive, and last-resort resolution of the debt crisis, needs to become part of international discourse and campaigning activities. Getting there will have to be an incremental political process, although culminating as joint public action. The political ground must be laid to encourage ever-wider – if unpublicised – commitment by increasing numbers of governments to a joint public declaration.

Another collective approach is to make debt cancellation an integral part of international economic negotiations in multilateral institutions, such as the World Trade Organisation (WTO). Already there are tentative proposals that developing countries should insert the 'trade-related' aspects of indebtedness, along with 'trade-related' commodity-price instabilities and other issues of concern to them, into their negotiating packages in the multilateral processes. In this view, such demands could be used as possible trade-offs in the multi-sectoral 'Millennial Round' of WTO negotiations that was to have been proposed by the developed countries at the WTO meeting in Seattle in December 1999. The problem is that this approach proposes trading off the essential needs of developing countries and relatively limited concessions to the weaker economies, in exchange for major gains in the restructuring of the world economy in the interest of the strongest economies and 'their' global corporations. Hence the increasing demand by many developing-country governments, and a growing international campaign by non-government forces, against the proposed 'Millennial Round' altogether.

Needless to say, virtually all debtor governments are still counting on continued bilateral agreements, or continued multilateral negotiations, between themselves and their creditors in the Paris Club to alleviate their debt burdens. Even the 'collective' position of the Organisation of African Unity (OAU) does not go beyond appealing for 'better' HIPC terms and more 'understanding' of Africa's problems by the creditor governments and institutions.

Varied tactics and targets

Radically different as these approaches are, they need not all be mutually exclusive, but nor are they equally useful. Many, such as the moderate appeals for further debt relief and re-schedulings, have long proven ineffective. Other approaches can be utilised simultaneously, or at different phases, by differently situated actors for different targets or specified purposes. However, these multiple or parallel tactics are not without their dangers. For example, skilled researchers who can analyse and expose the fallacies in the arguments of the international financial institutions can certainly make an important contribution. Anti-debt campaigners situated in influential development organisations and social/religious bodies in the North should indeed use their influence with their national media and lobby their governments. But individual researchers or lobbyists, however effective, cannot substitute for organised public opinion. And organised public opinion in the North cannot substitute for organised popular mobilisation in the South.

Although all useful to differing degrees, such varied players, tactics, and targets are not of the same order of significance. Organised popular forces in the North can help to create a propitious climate within and through which governments can be persuaded or pushed towards the required positions. Intellectual efforts and information should be aimed primarily at informing and activating increasing numbers of people. The cogency of technical arguments and the weight of the data amassed are simply not enough, in and of themselves, to impel governments towards making real policy changes. Similarly, popular mobilisation in the South is of a qualitatively different order from that in the North. Northern groups are important in influencing the media, general 'public opinion', and their own governments; and thereby even influencing the governments of the debtor countries to adopt more assertive positions. It is an unfortunate fact, and testimony to their level of political and psychological dependence, that many governments in the South take more notice of such developments taking place in the North than within their own countries. But the empowerment of the people of the South is both a crucial means and has to be the ultimate end of such a campaign. This is essential, if they are to be truly 'liberated' from their bondage and poverty with and through the process, and if their countries are to break out of, and move beyond, economic and political subordination.

As we have already seen, however, there are other real problems when individuals or groups mainly focus on directly 'influencing' government or media figures, or institutions. Although projected as mere differences of tactic, or as a neutral 'division of labour' between different forces in a campaign, the gradualist 'tactical engagement' approach has dangers in itself, and can pre-empt its more far-reaching aims and potential.

The focus on government structures, or even specific official or 'entertainment' figures, can achieve some gains. But these efforts can also distract attention, energies, and resources from the broader public information and mobilisation that is the most fundamental way to bring 'influence' to bear upon governments, both in the North and the South. Among the tried and tested tactical responses by governments to growing popular campaigns, partial concessions – used skilfully by government 'spin doctors' and institutional PR operators – are presented as being much more than they actually are, in order to placate and effectively demobilise campaigners, and to undermine the campaign's potential and fundamental aims. Such 'engagement' tactics invariably entail conscious moves by campaign strategists towards the positions of governments and related institutions, so they can operate within their frameworks and use language that is 'acceptable' to them.[20] The aim may be to draw their adversaries towards the intended objective; but this approach generally has the contrary effect of imperceptibly drawing leading campaign figures into their adversaries' 'logic', rather than the other way round.

Similarly, anticipating where adversaries will draw the final line, and preparing in advance for accommodations or compromise positions, are measures that invariably assume a dynamic of their own. 'Fall-back' stances rapidly become 'front-line' positions, or are drawn to the fore by perceptive adversaries on the basis of how they assess the susceptibilities of leading negotiators or spokespeople on the other side.

The alternative to accepting piecemeal 'gains' through 'engagement' tactics is for campaigners to adopt advanced bargaining positions, using creative initiatives and energetic pro-active strategies to draw or impel governments forward. This is integral to the planning and organisational debates among campaigners everywhere and represents the perennial dilemmas and tactical options that face trade unionists confronting employers, NGOs dealing with governments or their own funders, or even governments negotiating with other governments or institutions. Tactical choices reflect assessments of the nature of the adversary; the mood, potential force, and direction of action of supporters; the real and perceived balances of power; and so on. But such choices are also a function and reflection of the underlying strategic aims and objectives – that is, whether these aims are minimal and reformist, or radical and transformational. In the anti-debt campaign, many of the *tactical* choices being made reflect differing conceptualisations of the overall *strategic* aims and objectives.

Strategic aims and objectives

At one end is the view that (some sort of) debt cancellation is an important – and achievable – end in itself, as long as the campaign remains suitably focused as a 'single issue' campaign, with simple or straightforward demands. In this view, the general public in the developed countries who have taken the debt question to heart would be confused by more complex analyses of all the contributing factors, or would be put off by attempts to add legal, political, and economic dimensions to what they see as a clear moral or 'justice' issue.

At the other end is the view that even if the total debt were to be cancelled immediately, this would not solve the profound socio-economic and environmental problems of the debtor countries, and failure to take this into account could be fundamentally counter-productive. It would be seriously disillusioning and demobilising if inadequately informed debt-campaign supporters in the North were to see their efforts, even their success in getting the debt fully cancelled, fail to solve the poverty problems in the South. And it is the people of these poverty-stricken countries who would bear the brunt of the ensuing general defeatism, or specific 'Afro-pessimism', or 'poverty fatigue', or 'donor fatigue' in the North.

Focusing only on debt is addressing a symptom, rather than the underlying causes of financial dependence and economic subordination. Tackling the debt problem is necessary but totally insufficient as a response to the long-standing structural features of these economies and the nature of their role and location in the global economy. The underlying causes of dependence certainly reside, in part, in economic factors internal to these economies – limited technical and management resources, structural distortions, and sectoral disarticulations, with heavy orientations to external markets and extreme vulnerabilities to external shocks. But these, in turn, are produced and aggravated by factors and forces in the international system. Industrialised-country governments and international companies constantly act to reinforce such external dependence, and their own trade and investment access to, control over, and exploitation of the countries of the South. More recently, the international financial institutions have been marshalled to place pressure on these economies to 'open up' to global investors, exporters, TNCs, and service companies. And it is in this context that the indebtedness of countries is important not merely, or even mainly, for the financial returns produced – although these are substantial. More critically, indebtedness is an effective way to exert political controls or 'policy leverage' (as expressed by the World Bank) which it secures for creditor governments and financial institutions over other governments and economies throughout the world.

The strategic approach lying somewhere between or linking the differing approaches would argue that the issue of debt *is* important in itself. But, because of its very clarity, debt provides an excellent prism through which to expose to wider public view the full spectrum of international financial relations, particularly North–South relations, the functioning of global financial institutions, and the global economic system. If perceived in this way, the anti-debt campaign could carry many millions of indignant and already mobilised people towards these broader issues and to a deeper and fuller understanding of the nature and sources of the poverty and injustice that so move them. They would be activated not only by the plight and needs of millions of poor people in the world, but by the underlying inequitable and exploitative nature of relations between the rich North and the poor South. Millions of people would see more clearly the nature of the relations, or collusion, between rich governments, banks, and other financial agencies, the driving forces and motivations behind the increasingly liberalised global economic system. And the exploitative, damaging, and polarising essence of the global free-market system dominating all peoples and countries would become the active concern of many more millions, North and South.

Related issues and campaigns, alliances, and coalition building

The corollary to this is that anti-debt campaigners have to include such explanations and arguments in their campaigns, and must link up with other related international campaigns, such as that against MAI (the Multilateral Agreement on Investment), and for the international imposition of the Tobin Tax and other instruments for re-regulation and controls on global financial forces. The problem of indebtedness and the demand for debt cancellation must be inserted into the debates, decisions, and demands of these various campaigns; and these constituencies must be drawn into supporting the debt campaign. And *vice versa*. This can be done without necessarily reducing their main focus on debt *per se*, while wider alliances will certainly help to strengthen their efforts. It is through such multi-faceted, mutually supporting coalitions that the range, combination, and weight of inter-national popular forces will become commensurate with the challenges posed by the unaccountable power of gargantuan TNCs, the vast resources of international banks, and the global institutions they use in shaping the 'global economy'.

Building such global coalitions demands political skill and strategic vision on all sides, as is clear from the challenges of building North–South cooperation and mutual support even within the international anti-debt campaign. Engagement in the same campaign, and even fundamentally shared concerns, do not automatically translate into mutual understanding and unity. This paper has highlighted some of the differences between some groups located in the North and others in the South, although, it must be stressed, these divergences and convergences of tactic and strategy also cut across the North–South divide. However, a basic difference that must be recognised is that anti-debt groups in the North can opt out whenever they feel that they have done what they can (and some J2000 groups indeed plan to 'close shop' in December 2000, whether total debt cancellation has been achieved or not), whereas their counterparts in the South will still have to live with, and continue to struggle against, the causes and consequences of economic exploitation and subordination, of which indebtedness is just one symptom.

This is what gives anti-debt campaigners in the South such an important political role. It is their unequal burdens and respective roles and responsibilities that require groups in the North to give full weight to proposals and demands emanating from the South. (It is interesting to note here that there are significant differences between many Northern development agencies acting somewhat paternalistically on behalf of the South, and political solidarity groups in the North that tend to be somewhat more sensitive to the nature of such relationships, and rather more realistic about their role and 'rights'[21].)

However, 'moral authority' and 'political principle' are insufficient bases upon which anti-debt groups in the South should expect their Northern counterparts to take their lead. This role and these relationships have to be securely underpinned by their own research and analyses, mobilisation of their own peoples, and actions within their own countries. Groups in the North cannot expect their counterparts in the South to do this rapidly or easily. They often operate under extremely difficult economic and political circumstances, and require all the support they can get. Certainly, groups in the South should not have to contend with divisive interventions into their initiatives by their counterparts in the North, some even using the familiar 'neo-colonialist' method of promoting and using their own 'client' groups. While there clearly are differences of method and objectives between anti-debt groups in and of the South, there are also intense debates going on among them and an emerging consensus on strategic objectives and common principles (see the box on the following pages). It would be seriously divisive for groups in the North to pick off specific groups in the South – particularly any that choose to stand outside the nascent South–South consensus. Nor should groups and coalitions in, and of, the South have to contend with defensiveness and possessiveness over the global campaign by longer-established and relatively well-endowed groups in the North that, consciously or unconsciously, resent their 'leadership' being encroached upon.

Extract from South–South Summit Declaration, 'Towards a Debt-Free Millennium',
Johannesburg, 18-21 November 1999. (Full text available at www.aidc.org)

The External Debt of countries of the South is illegitimate and immoral. It has been paid many times over. A careful examination of the origins, development, effects, and consequences of this debt can lead us to no other conclusion. We thus reject the continued plunder of the South by way of debt payments.

Peoples and countries of the South are in fact creditors of an enormous historical, social, and ecological debt. This debt must be repaid in order to make possible a 'New Beginning'. In the spirit of Jubilee, we demand restitution of what has been taken unjustly from us, and reparations for the damage wrought.

We forcefully denounce the growing concentration of wealth, power, and resources in the world economy as the essential cause of the increase in violence, impoverishment, and 'indebtedness' of the South. The elimination of extreme poverty cannot take place without the elimination of extreme wealth. We thus demand the eradication of extreme wealth and the vicious system that generates such inequalities. In this context, we reject the perpetuation of external debt collection and debt payments which are Life or Death matters for the millions of persons who are exploited and excluded in our societies.

The External Debt is an ethical, political, social, historical, and ecological problem. It entails responsibilities at different levels and demands imperative and comprehensive action so as to resolve in a permanent and definitive manner. There can be no piecemeal solution to the 'Debt problem'. We thus welcome the momentum that Jubilee 2000 initiatives around the world have generated on this issue and we call on them to broaden and deepen their understanding, educational efforts, and mobilisation beyond the year 2000, in order to achieve our overall aim of a Debt-free Millennium, including the repayment of the debt owed by the North to the South.

Debt is essentially an ideological and political instrument for the exploitation and control of our peoples, resources, and countries by those corporations, countries, and institutions that concentrate wealth and power in the global capitalist system. The accumulation of Foreign Debt in countries of the South is a product of the crisis of that very system and it is used to perpetuate the plunder and domination of our nations often with the acquiescence, if not active collaboration, of local élites.

The neo-liberal global economic system is destructive and genocidal in its workings and effects. Women suffer disproportionately its consequences, as do children, the elderly, and the environment. The same institutions and system responsible for its creation cannot bring about a lasting solution to the 'Debt problem'. That system must be changed and can be changed.

In the process of addressing the 'Debt problem' and changing the neo-liberal global economic system, we must continue to develop an ever closer understanding of the linkages between debt and other related aspects including trade, finance, investment, consumption patterns, food security, environmental depredation, and diverse forms of military and anti-democratic, neo-colonialist intervention and repression.

Many working-class and impoverished and excluded peoples' groups and movements in both the South and the North are engaged in different ways to challenge and transform this system of domination and we must join with them. As Jubilee South we will add our voice and support for the strengthening and creation of alliances and coalitions deeply rooted in historical struggles against all forms of oppression within the long-standing anti-imperialist framework and tradition.

Resistance to debt-related domination unites us as social movements and organisations throughout the South and provides us with an historic opportunity to organise ourselves as part of a broader movement. As Jubilee South, we are born and rooted in Africa, Asia, the Pacific, Latin America, and the Caribbean, but we reach out to all who are part of this historical, political, and ethical South.

Respectful of our different identities and traditions, as well as our varying forms of struggle, we must be united in a common determination to achieve Justice for all: a New Beginning in the New Millennium. In this way South–South and South–North solidarity can be strengthened, as we exercise our collective human right to determine our own future and engage in the struggle to build and defend inclusive and comprehensive alternatives to the present global system that are:

- from the bottom-up

- reflective of different sectoral needs

- respectful of cultural and biological diversity, and

- conducive to new modes of democracy and development that are respectful of human rights, justice, and wellbeing for all.

The North cannot act without the South, even if it is argued that the industrialised countries have a particular responsibility because the chief culprits are 'their' governments, corporations, and banks, and the global institutions controlled by them. This understanding is to be welcomed, but such groups in the North must also recognise that 'their' governments, banks, and international institutions are also 'ours', and indeed 'everyone's' in today's highly integrated global system. We have to find ways to oppose these dominant forces together. Northern groups cannot substitute for and certainly cannot continue to act paternalistically 'on behalf' of the South, particularly as the South becomes more organised and enters more fully into international campaigns. However, while campaigners in the South need to develop a strategic vision based upon their own experiences, understanding, and unity, they must also acknowledge the vital role that supporters and counterpart forces in the North can and must play. Popular movements in the South need allies in the North, because of the strategic positioning of the latter nearer the centres of global power, their accumulated experiences, considerable skills, and greater resources. These are invaluable in supporting organisational development and campaigning endeavours in the South.

In the final analysis, however, what must unite all such movements are not mere tactical considerations or pragmatic calculations about the mutual or respective gains to be made. The quintessential basis of North–South people's solidarity and united action has to be the strategic understanding of the vital importance of people's global coalitions and unity, on the basis of our common humanity and in the interests of our common planetary home.

Acknowledgement

An earlier version of this paper was produced by the Alternative Information and Development Centre (AIDC) in South Africa. There have also been translations into Spanish, German, and Japanese (details from AIDC).

Notes

1 With some pioneering writers in the North such as Susan George.

2 This paper assumes that readers are familiar with the statistics of Third World debt. Further information is available from the UK J2000 Coalition.

3 'Crumbs of Comfort', UK J2000 Coalition, June 1999.

4 World Development Movement, 'Stop Sapping the Poor', June 1999.

5 Jürgen Kaiser, J2000 group, Germany – electronic communication 5 June 1999.

6 UK J2000, Christian Aid, and others.

7 UNCTAD's 1995 study on foreign direct investment (FDI) in Africa points to extremely favourable rates of return to foreign investors – up to 25 per cent. This is much higher than their profit ratios in both developed and developing countries for most years from 1980 to

1993. This pattern was borne out by the 1999 UNCTAD analysis, which revealed rates of FDI profit in Africa of 29 per cent; compared with six per cent even in most of the Asian 'emerging' economies.

8 The terms of trade for Africa declined every year during the 1980s, with losses of US$19 billion in export earnings in 1985-86 alone. It is estimated that sub-Saharan Africa lost potential exports earnings of some US$278 billion between 1980 and 1994, according to studies by UNCTAD and the African Development Bank.

9 Such as the UK J2000 'Don't Collect! Won't Collect' call to the British government.

10 Anne Pettifor, Director of UK J2000.

11 The most notable, in this respect, being Oxfam GB.

12 Joe Hanlon, 'What will it cost to cancel unpayable debt?', UK J2000 Coalition, March 1998.

13 Ibid.

14 Joe Hanlon ' We've been here before: debt default and relief in the past – and how we are demanding that the poor pay more this time', UK J2000, April 1998.

15 Patricia Adams *Odious Debts: Loose Lending, Corruption, and the Third World's Environmental Legacy,* London: Probe International.

16 Such as Oxfam GB, Bread for the World-USA, and others.

17 Anne Pettifor in the *New Internationalist,* No. 312, May 1999.

18 Originally formulated and promoted by development agencies such as Oxfam GB and Christian Aid.

19 This would free the IMF from having repeatedly to go back to its financial under-writers and 'would equip the IMF with a permanent ESAF that will keep it forever involved in the poorest countries and their economic policies', according to Carol Welch, Friends of the Earth (USA), writing in *Economic Justice News,* Vol. 2, May 1999.

20 This has been explicitly stated to this writer by a leading J2000 researcher and strategist.

21 Although in this respect there is often a tension over whether they 'take their lead' from counterpart CSOs or from the governments of the countries with which they are in solidarity

Heroism and ambiguity: NGO advocacy in international policy

Paul Nelson

Heroism and ambiguity

NGO policy activism has been widely portrayed in a heroic light. Campaigns to abolish anti-personnel landmines, restrict child labour, enforce marketing codes for infant formula, protect dolphins and whales, and extend political and civil rights have been covered favourably in the media, studied by a handful of political scientists, and even honoured as Nobel Peace laureates.

These campaigns have mobilised moral outrage into political action on topics where the targets are clear, the cause obviously just, and the abuses graphic. Yet the policy victories of NGOs in these areas (like those of States) are often tenuous and difficult to assess in practice, and securing their implementation generally requires continued political pressure.

Because NGO alliances rely on public participation and the mobilisation of values-based action, they need clearly identified opponents and results in order to motivate public action. But campaigns targeting the World Bank, especially on matters of economic policy, often encounter ambiguity and uncertainty. The Bank affirms that it shares NGOs' agenda of poverty reduction, sustainable development, empowerment, and partnership. Have NGOs made a difference to the Bank's economic policy? How can they know?

In 1997 I evaluated a campaign against orthodox structural adjustment policy, carried out between 1994 and 1996 by the London-based development NGO Christian Aid. The campaign, and the evaluation, offer a chance to reflect on these questions and on other issues of self-governance that face NGOs as they become more prominent political actors.[1] NGO advocates have little record of critically assessing their own impact. Evaluating impact is difficult, and the results are usually ambiguous and debatable, but the process is essential to NGOs' effectiveness and credibility. The article suggests an approach.

NGO advocacy with the World Bank and the International Monetary Fund (IMF) is, I believe, ethically essential, substantively important, and politically relevant to the relationship between the international financial institutions (IFIs) and national policy. But there is a danger that NGO advocates and friendly observers could be seduced by the heroic image that they and others have created. I am not arguing that the heroic image needs to be erased, but that NGOs need to adjust to their new prominence and to the political–economic environment in which they operate. This involves adopting a second generation of advocacy strategies, one that places greater emphasis on implementation of policy, on institutional changes at the IFIs, and on national-level strategies.

This paper is organised as follows. The second section examines NGO campaigns and the sources of ambiguity in their evaluation, and introduces a campaign entitled 'Who Runs the World?' (WRTW). The third section focuses on the process of NGO advocacy, drawing lessons from some recent criticism, and from WRTW. The final section returns to the question of impact and uncertainty, and suggests an approach to ongoing NGO evaluation.

A note on the IMF. WRTW targeted the IMF as well as the World Bank, but contact and results at the IMF were slender. Information and opinion from the IMF were hard to obtain: an IMF public-affairs officer observed that the Fund is more centralised than the Bank, and that, for the public, 'all roads lead to me'. This officer himself declined to speak on the record about the campaign. Advocacy with the IMF is an important and difficult effort for NGOs, and this article will not attempt to add to excellent papers by Scholte (1998) and Polak (1998) of the Center of Concern.

Campaigns on economic policy

NGOs have campaigned to influence the World Bank on issues including dam construction, indigenous people's rights, energy policy, micro-credit lending, structural adjustment, human rights, popular participation, gender, and corruption.

Development NGOs have become regular participants in discussions of popular participation and social-sector projects, areas in which they are considered to have special expertise or delivery capacity that makes it necessary to listen to their concerns. Their substantial and growing efforts to influence the Bank are evaluated less fully and frequently than other NGO activities. Foundations and interested observers have however produced some reviews (Nelson 1995; Fox and Brown 1998; Sogge 1996).

The campaigns of environmental NGOs have had the most visible impact. Alliances and networks originating in struggles to modify or stop particular dam and highway projects have pressed for reforms in sector policies, information disclosure, environmental assessment procedures and accountability mechanisms. NGOs have had particular difficulty in influencing the World Bank on the subject of macro-economic policy. Fifteen years of structural adjustment lending has produced strong dissent from NGOs, both North and South, but the principal impact of their criticism at the Bank has been to help to motivate increased investment in compensatory Social Investment Funds.

NGOs' reform agendas have, in general, succeeded when the agenda or strategy calls for the World Bank to do more – to expand, not curtail, the range of its influence. The Bank has responded to criticism on environmental and social issues by accepting new roles in national environmental planning, project planning, managing the Global Environment Facility, financing pollution abatement, providing training and technical assistance, supporting micro-finance lending, poverty assessments, and post-conflict rehabilitation.

The critique of adjustment lending has usually called for a reduction in the World Bank's role (Nelson 1996). But the critique's most tangible success resulted from NGO support for UNICEF's call for social safety-net programmes to accompany adjustment loans. More fundamental criticism of privatisation, export promotion, and the political impact of the adjustment conditions may have helped to persuade Bank staff to promote wider national 'ownership' of adjustment plans. But the critique has not persuaded any major actor to promote heterodox alternative strategies, and the crisis in Southeast Asia does not appear significantly to have weakened the official consensus on neo-liberal economic strategies.

Economic structural adjustment is an inherently difficult policy area for NGOs to influence. Most economists believe that the best evidence of its impact comes from complex economic models that are outside the expertise of NGO advocates. NGO protests are often viewed as exactly the kind of political pressure that World Bank intervention is meant to correct: the ability of interest groups to sustain their claim to entitlements from government.

'Who Runs the World?'

Christian Aid's two-year campaign aimed to promote greater accountability and change the nature of structural adjustment policies (SAPs) promoted by the World Bank and IMF, particularly in the Philippines, Jamaica, and Zimbabwe. The campaign coincided roughly with the World Bank's 50th anniversary, and with the appointment of James Wolfensohn as President. Its principal objectives were as follows:

1. to get SAPs changed in some countries and ... influence the design of new SAPs;
2. to make the World Bank and IMF more open and accountable to governments, taxpayers, and the poor;
3. to show that there are people-friendly alternatives to SAPs (Christian Aid 1994).

Many of the campaign's initiatives gained the attention of decision-makers in government or the IFIs. It supported the position of key internal reformers, stimulated the media to pay attention to adjustment and debt issues, mobilised a segment of British public opinion, encouraged parliamentary inquiry and government reporting of its policies and votes in the Bank and the IMF, facilitated other NGO coalitions and initiatives, and helped NGO and church partners in Jamaica, the Philippines, and Zimbabwe to gain increased access to World Bank officials.

Ambiguity

But the campaign's actual influence on World Bank policy and practice is obscured by several sources of uncertainty. The organisation is far from static, and has undergone a major change (in style, at least) since James Wolfensohn became President in June 1995. The relatively slow process of developing and financing new projects creates a 'pipeline' of projects in various stages of development, unequally influenced by new policies (Fox and Brown 1998). Interrelations among the Bank, governments, and the IMF further complicate the picture, and Bank staff members have no incentive to acknowledge that confrontational strategies are effective, even if in fact they are.

Most development NGOs encounter another sort of ambiguity as well: even fierce critics of the World Bank support at least the principle of multilateral development finance, and often the continued funding of the Bank itself. Development NGOs may be more affected in this regard than advocates focused on human rights or environmental issues, whose policy agendas are less likely to include support for multilateral lending.

The large number and loose co-ordination of NGO initiatives further complicates the task of distinguishing effects of various initiatives. NGO advocates are not always in agreement or closely co-ordinated, and there is no certain way to differentiate their various effects. Consider the difficulty in assigning 'credit' for institutional and policy changes made by the Bank in Jamaica, including an NGO liaison role in the Bank mission, the creation of the Public Information Centre (PIC), and NGO representation on the board of the Bank-financed Social Investment Fund (SIF). Participants in WRTW note these changes as results of their efforts, but the first two are also tied to larger trends in the Bank's reorganisation, and the Jamaican regional PIC was initiated by an innovative World Bank Resident Representative.

Monitoring the *process* of NGO advocacy is one partial solution to this problem of uncertainty. This is the focus of the third section of this article.

Process: what can NGOs learn from recent criticism?

Most criticism of NGO advocacy has been aimed at NGOs based in industrial countries, which co-ordinate most network campaigning. The criticism raises the question of how campaigns balance five important sets of variables:

- *choice of political arenas*: balancing national and international advocacy strategies
- *self-governance*: balancing strategic leadership with broad participation
- *mass mobilisation*: balancing mass political strategies with insider approaches
- *strategy*: balancing confrontational and co-operative approaches
- *perspective*: balancing short-term campaign goals and long-term constituency building.

Balancing national and international strategies

A coalition involving international NGOs and NGOs based in the World Bank's borrowing countries must choose and balance strategies that target national governments and international institutions. When NGOs choose strategies that use international organisations to gain influence over governments, they may contribute to shifting key policy decisions (and authority) into international arenas.

Jordan and van Tuijl (1997) outline several distinct types of international campaigns, and distinguish the international, national, and local political arenas in which the actors operate. They show that some campaigns, particularly in politically volatile situations where local participants are at risk, suffer from inadequate communication, co-ordination, and acceptance of risk and responsibility by international NGO partners. Cleary (1995) argues that international NGOs favoured confrontational strategies in several instances in Indonesia, when local interests might have been better served by negotiation.

But these are relatively well co-ordinated campaigns based on environmental issues, and indigenous people's rights and human rights. In advocacy on economic policy, links have tended to be less tightly formed, and participants' lobbying strategies less tightly co-ordinated. Much of the NGO advocacy on adjustment in the international arena has addressed the issues globally or regionally, rather than at a national level. WRTW continued this approach, linking agendas only loosely with Southern partners. WRTW promoted its own agenda for policy change, but the ties between the campaign in the UK and Washington and NGO partners' national agendas were loose and flexible. Local partners defined their lobbying objectives, so much so that there is some inconsistency between the radical rethinking of adjustment called for in WRTW materials, and the more limited efforts for debt relief and changes in the administration of the SIF that were the substance of the lobby effort in Jamaica and the Philippines.

The international campaign, said one member of Christian Aid's staff, was 'partner-informed', not 'partner-directed'. In the Philippines, the Freedom from Debt Coalition focused on the IMF programme, arguing to government and the public that the country needs not IMF direction but a domestically rooted programme of 'fundamental reforms'. Jamaican partners noted three objectives: lobby the Government to recognise the 'social debt' and pursue debt forgiveness; persuade the World Bank and government to compensate 'losers' in the reform process; and press for expanded citizen involvement in decisions about spending and borrowing. These objectives overlap with Christian Aid's campaign goals, but criticism of the adjustment model itself does not feature in the partners' stated priorities.

Internationalising economic policy

Do international NGO campaigns assign too much importance to the World Bank? Critics within the Bank and others charge that NGOs blame the Bank for social ills that actually result from bad government policy or global economic change. By doing so, it is charged, NGOs can delay the process of calling governments to account for inept, self-seeking, or corrupt practices.

This criticism was levelled at WRTW from its launch. A commentary in the *Financial Times* faulted the campaign's monograph 'Who Runs the World?' for ignoring African governments' responsibility for their countries' economic and social ills. The criticism is a difficult one for international NGOs based in the industrialised countries, who – with few direct routes to influence the governments that borrow from the World Bank – have seized on donor lending and aid policies as among the most effective approaches. The Bank's institutional self-confidence and influence also seem to have invited attack.

Heavy reliance on international solutions, particularly the Bank, has had an effect on the level at which key political battles are fought. By moving some authority over national policy decisions into the international arena, NGOs could actually reduce the significance of local participation by eroding the policy-setting power of borrowing governments. Some environmental safeguards that were proposed to restrain the World Bank's lending for environmentally questionable projects have also expanded the Bank's influence and justified an increasingly intrusive approach to lending and conditionality (Nelson 1996).

NGOs are only secondarily responsible for this internationalising trend: the increased external influence on national decision-making is a product of larger trends. But NGO advocates should carefully weigh any strategies that increase the leverage of international agencies. Aid donors impose demands for accountability on governments – demands that can reduce their effective accountability to their own citizens. Harrigan (1998) argues that IMF and World Bank influence has had this effect in Jamaica.

Liberalisation and privatisation may often be forced on populations where opposition is broad and unheeded. But adjustment plans are not generally any longer programmes foisted on unwilling governments. Substantial support for liberal reforms has grown in most governments, and much government resistance to the IFIs' macro-policy influence now amounts to delaying implementation of agreed-upon loan conditions.

NGO coalitions should give careful consideration to whether a strategic focus on the IFIs reduces the pressure for government accountability. An ongoing global dialogue between NGOs, governments, and the World Bank offers a possible approach to integrating the national and international dialogue. The Structural Adjustment Participatory Review Initiative (SAPRI) is an experiment with nationally based advocacy co-ordinated at the international level. Growing out of Washington-based negotiations with the Bank, SAPRI now involves governments, NGOs, and the Bank in nationally based discussions and investigations of adjustment policy. The international effort is co-ordinated by a committee with NGO representation from every region. National reviews in the participating countries are planned and co-ordinated by joint committees involving NGO and government participants. Reviews have begun in Ghana and Hungary, and are planned in Uganda, Zimbabwe, the Philippines, Ecuador, and Bangladesh.

Advocacy with national institutions and by national interests is likely to become more important in promoting NGOs' agendas. Dialogue with responsible Bank staff in country operational departments is increasingly important, as the Bank expands its country offices' responsibilities, and implementation of hard-won policy changes often requires co-operation by the national authorities that implement projects.

Balancing and integrating mass action and insider lobbying

NGOs, sometimes praised for opening decision-making processes to a flood of popular opinion and local knowledge, also employ strategies that rely more heavily on careful research and documentation, and direct lobbying by NGO staff. Often, advocacy combines strategies that rely on expertise with others that rest on representation. NGOs generally treat these as complementary, and sometimes this is so. But at other times they collide and conflict. Both occurred during WRTW.

Roe (1995) has criticised international NGO advocacy on environmental issues as a debating exercise between members of a 'New Managerial Class', in which NGO professionals debate with other members of the same global class, posted in the international financial institutions. The critique raises the concern that NGO lawyers, scientists, economists, and anthropologists based in the industrial capitals, with class origins and academic training similar to those of the World Bank's staff, can force policy-making processes that are open to their own participation, without assuring access for excluded communities. This charge merits a full review, but my purpose here is solely to touch on how WRTW balanced broad participation with élite lobbying. The campaign relied jointly on staff reporting and lobbying, public actions by Christian Aid's activist members in the UK and Ireland, and initiatives by Southern NGO partners.

Broad-based public advocacy was most effective when it targeted the British government. The grassroots lobby of Parliament won improvements in transparency and accountability, including greater disclosure of the British Executive Directors' work on the boards of the World Bank and IMF. Letters and postcards from constituents appeared to spark a level of interest from MPs that surprised some knowledgeable observers. Christian Aid supporters sent mass mailings of postcards to World Bank and government officials. The strategy benefited in one case from exquisite timing and a bit of luck. British Chancellor Kenneth Clark used a stack of postcards that he received just before a 1996 G-7 Summit to bolster the UK position in favour of IMF gold sales and a generous multilateral debt-relief initiative.

At their best, public and high-level approaches are mutually reinforcing. Sustained public pressure may help NGOs to secure access to ranking officials, and a successful report, press release, or public event that draws media attention can inspire further public confidence and action. Public pressure may lead to a point at which high-level negotiation is necessary to secure the political gains made possible by public actions, as in the debate over multilateral debt relief during 1996. Early in his presidency, Wolfensohn called for a study of the needs and options for multilateral debt relief that led, via tortuous negotiations, to the now-adopted HIPC initiative. When an internal initiative emerged within the World Bank, NGOs' principal task was no longer to persuade management to take the issue seriously, but to shape the initiative. Bank staff who had paid little attention to NGOs' concerns were suddenly open to NGO input on the details of the process.

Public pressure remained important, but shaping the details of the initiative called for a new level of knowledge and analytical skills. NGOs were prepared, despite their relative shortage of macro-economic expertise, by having developed and stated in advance their minimum standards for a multilateral debt-relief initiative.

Broad-based public strategies sometimes have unanticipated, positive effects. Before the World Bank/IMF 1995 Annual Meeting in Madrid, Christian Aid circulated a statement calling for changes in the IFIs' governance and their policies on adjustment and debt. The Declaration was adopted by church groups in Canada and the USA, and thousands of religious leaders had signed on before it was delivered in Madrid. The Declaration helped to energise a fledgling Religious Working Group on the World Bank/IMF in the USA.

Christian Aid's presence at official international meetings during the campaign – Annual Meetings of the Bank/IMF, Copenhagen Social Summit, G-7 Summits – appears to have yielded the campaign's greatest successes with the media. Two-person teams of Christian Aid staff, armed with a newly released report on a relevant topic, were among the most successful of the many NGO representatives present in interjecting alternative perspectives into financial and mainstream press coverage of the meetings. Outspoken NGOs attract media attention in such meetings, and particularly so in the British media when the UK Treasury was the leading government proponent of a new debt-relief proposal.

The reports produced for the campaign were timed for release at these summits, and were directed both to the media and to policy makers. They sought to present issues simply enough to motivate campaigners, but with enough sophistication to avoid demonising the IFIs. Within the Bank, however, the reports were generally viewed as lacking rigour, and treated as public-relations problems.

Media advertisements, too, illustrate the tension between public campaigning and insider influence. The campaign used advertisements to reach the British public, through national and local dailies; and to draw attention to the issues at the time of World Bank Annual Meetings in 1994, through advertisements placed in the *Financial Times*. The advertisements are the best example of the many meanings of 'influence' in the campaign. Some within the World Bank say the advertisements earned Christian Aid a reputation as a 'head-banger', and harmed its dialogue with the Bank, but others acknowledge that the advertisements brought a higher level of attention to the campaign. The advertisements also increased reporters' recognition of the issues and of the campaign.

Balancing and integrating confrontational and co-operative strategies

NGOs have forced the Bank to learn to manage external criticism. Many within the World Bank acknowledge that NGOs' public criticism in the 1980s called the attention of governments and the Bank to serious and neglected issues. But now that NGOs have been admitted to the dialogue, some argue, the high-volume, public critique is at best background noise, at worst a distraction from serious dialogue. Exposure to criticism has raised the threshold of sensitivity: an open letter or public protest that might have attracted much attention at the Bank in 1985 may now be regarded as a routine matter.

Like many public agencies, the World Bank favours dialogue with 'constructive' critics. Balancing confrontational and co-operative approaches involves both co-ordination between different campaigns and initiatives (such as SAPRI and Women's Eyes on the World Bank), and strategic choices within an organisation or network. Does confrontational campaigning compromise co-operative approaches, or strengthen them? Can a single organisation be effective and credible in both kinds of discussion? The experience of WRTW suggests that it can. But maintaining the balance requires careful attention, as demonstrated by Christian Aid's involvement in three more cooperative initiatives.

NGO Working Group on the World Bank

In the early 1990s, Christian Aid was a member of the 26-member NGO Working Group on the World Bank (NGOWG). The NGOWG's meetings with Bank staff have been, since the early 1980s, a forum for its policy dialogue with development NGOs. Discussion is generally collegial and rests on the premise that the NGO and Bank representatives share common aims and need more open discussion to arrive at shared strategies. Some NGO activists have characterised the Working Group as unfocused and unrepresentative.

Christian Aid's representative played a leading role in re-energising the Working Group and encouraging its recent reorganisation, which aims to broaden Southern NGO involvement and facilitate Southern leadership.[2] The experience of the NGOWG suggests that co-operative strategies may be most effective when backed by broad NGO participation and linked to other, more confrontational, campaigns (Covey 1998).

The Lesotho Highlands Water Project

Christian Aid has worked with the Highlands Church Action Group in Lesotho since 1992 to help to improve the social impact of a major hydro-electric and water-diversion scheme, funded in part by the World Bank. NGOs involved in a global campaign against major dam projects, and against the Bank's role in such projects, are also involved in advocacy.

Christian Aid won high praise from World Bank staff close to the project as a 'credible, professional, engaged critic of the project'. Bank staff implicitly criticise other NGOs whose arguments they characterise as part of a global anti-dam campaign, drawing criticisms from a checklist accumulated elsewhere. Critical campaigning (such as WRTW) may actually increase the effectiveness of such a dialogue. The World Bank's task manager noted that colleagues tended to give attention to measured, 'constructive' comments from Christian Aid, because they thought the NGO had been predisposed to attack the Bank (telephone interview with the author, December 1996).

Appreciation for the 'constructive' dialogue over social policy issues, however, did not prevent the World Bank from proceeding with finance for a new phase of the project, without ensuring that demands for compensation of resettled communities were satisfied.

The politics of aid: a critical constituency

NGOs are among development aid's most consistent advocates, and, at times, aid's most trenchant critics. This position as a 'critical constituency' for aid is considered untenable by some in government and at least a few in the NGO world. One British official succinctly charges that 'the NGOs' message is: "Aid is terrible! And we want more of it!"' (interview with the author, November 1996). The issue is a perennial one for NGOs, and, in a period of dwindling aid budgets, WRTW attracted particularly harsh criticism.

Three government and Bank officials told me similar versions of a rather dramatic morality tale of the good and bad NGOs. Oxfam GB and Christian Aid, the story went, held somewhat similar positions on the World Bank before 1994, but Oxfam appreciated the danger that confronted the Bank and particularly IDA (International Development Association), and perceived that NGO advocacy could potentially 'bring down the whole system' (interviews with the author, November 1996). Oxfam emphasised support for IDA as the framework for any criticisms, while Christian Aid launched a highly critical public campaign.

World Bank and British aid officials charged that critical campaigning plays into the hands of opponents of multilateral aid, including those in the US Congress. Officials asserted that criticising adjustment lending undermines efforts, including Christian Aid's own, to build a constituency for aid. (Conversely, one might argue that an NGO's support for aid spending, even when couched in a critique of aid practice, weakens the incentive for official donors to change policy or practice.)

Was WRTW ill-timed, given the perceived crisis of IDA concessional financing? It seems likely that both risks are real: criticism could strengthen opponents of development aid spending, and knowledge that an NGO will ultimately support its government's contributions may weaken an NGO's leverage in pressing for changes. But from the perspective of many NGOs, full, unconditional support for aid spending would be dishonest, while opposition would be counter-productive. Organisations that choose to criticise and conditionally support aid programmes will appear inconsistent at times. They need to be skilful in judging when to emphasise their criticism or support, and they need to cultivate close relationships with more radical NGO critics, in order to avoid undercutting their efforts to press for reforms.

World Bank staff and government officials may not like the criticism, but staff interviewed all affirmed that public campaigning does not diminish their willingness to discuss and learn from an NGO's alternative perspectives.

Short-term campaign objectives and long-term network or coalition building

Like other political activists, NGO campaigners have both short-term and long-term needs and objectives. Their campaigns are urgent, aiming to relieve immediate human suffering and create opportunity. But they also often give attention to the longer-term processes of coalition- and constituency-building for expanded impact.

Christian Aid's work in coalitions during the WRTW period included facilitating and/or hosting roles in the Bretton Woods Project, the Debt Crisis Network, and the NGO Working Group on the World Bank. The early experience of these coalitions suggests three reasons to emphasise such coalition work.

First, coalitions around specific institutions (Bretton Woods Project) or issues (Debt Crisis Network) allow a focus and specialisation by staff that few individual NGOs can afford to maintain. Their specialisation may better equip NGOs for technical discussions with the World Bank when such dialogue is needed. For NGOs in the UK and Western Europe, effective coalition building helps to compensate for the obvious advantages of access that Washington-based NGOs enjoy.

Second, NGOs can hardly afford to forego potential sources of influence by dividing their efforts on issues such as the IFIs. The World Bank is a skilled participant in dialogue with NGOs and the media. The creation of a new office in London was rightly taken as a sign that the campaign had gained the Bank's attention, but it also calls for a new level of sophistication and unity from NGOs.

Third, building longer-term support from public constituencies may sometimes justify campaign strategies that would not be chosen purely for short-term policy change. Press advertisements and published reports that gain press coverage, for example, can bolster the confidence and enthusiasm of a political constituency, even when the advertisements' direct impact is questionable.

Conclusions and recommendations

The charges that NGOs are not sufficiently reflective and self-critical in assessing the significance and impact of their advocacy (Sogge 1996) have come mostly from sympathetic observers, and should prompt NGOs to more deliberate and consistent assessment of advocacy projects. Results are difficult to discern, but candid self-assessment is important, both to promote effectiveness and to practise transparency. This paper closes with some principles for improved monitoring and assessment.

Work with a model of institutional change

It is difficult to trace and verify impact in a major international organisation. But there is a set of factors that are consistently important for achieving significant policy change, and where change is often at least somewhat easier to monitor and attribute. NGOs can use these factors to sketch a model of the components of change in the target institution. With such a model, advocates can strategise and evaluate their efforts, in part by assessing their impact on the key factors in winning institutional change.

Policy advocates have often noted that there is a process of gaining influence at the World Bank, whose steps include official acknowledgement that an issue is within its scope or mandate; consideration and adoption of new policy; and implementation by staff and borrowers. Recent developments in the debates over debt and adjustment suggest four key strategic factors in motivating significant policy change: support from senior management, initiative by major shareholders, active internal leadership, and external pressure.[3]

- *Support from senior management*: Wolfensohn's direction has opened new opportunities in the debt and adjustment debates. The sometimes embattled President has made common cause with the Bank's NGO critics on some issues, and sought their co-operation in funding discussions. Senior management has in the past been able to block consideration of initiatives on debt and adjustment.
- *Initiative by major shareholders*: NGOs are quick to note their own leadership role in some policy areas, but major changes at the World Bank require action by its Governing Board. The USA has championed environmental initiatives and the information-disclosure and inspection-panel reforms, and the UK's leadership on debt was essential to winning consideration for proposals supported by NGOs. NGOs can help to open new space for innovation by staff who share their concerns and priorities, but such change cannot be institutionalised without the Board's assent, and Board action usually requires leadership by one of its major shareholders.
- *Active internal leadership by individuals committed to change*: Such internal leadership was essential in advancing the popular participation agenda within the World Bank, and in the development of the HIPC debt-relief initiative. When such leadership is present, external advocates may devise a mix of strategies that expand the space for new initiatives internally, while maintaining political pressure on senior management and the Board. (Active staff leadership has not been enough to win rapid change in issue areas such as gender equity and family planning (Siddharth 1995; Conly and Epp 1997).)
- *External pressure from NGOs, other observers, and the media*: The kind of pressure needed may vary with the stages of policy change, and the strength and interest of other actors (management, shareholders, internal leadership). Public political pressure that threatens the image of the IFIs appears to be the key factor in establishing an issue as a concern, and remains important at later stages of a successful advocacy effort. At another stage, the pressure may also require the analytical and negotiating skills to engage in discussions over the

details of new institutional and policy alternatives, as in the debate over multilateral debt relief in 1996.

By holding a model such as this one clearly in mind, policy advocates can plan and assess their own efforts, asking how effectively they advance one or more of the essential ingredients of change.

Make the terms and agendas of NGO partnerships clear

It is often assumed that NGO coalitions should speak with a single voice on the details of their target issues, and often this is the appropriate goal. But expectations among NGO partners may sometimes be more flexible, as in WRTW, and it is important that these understandings be as clear as possible among participants. Within a campaign on structural adjustment policy, for example, there is room for different priorities between advocates focused on the World Bank in Washington and advocates focused on national policy in Jamaica or the Philippines.

What is important is that the agreed, shared agenda is well defined and carefully adhered to, so that the coalition is not easily split if government or the Bank co-operates more readily with one participant than with others. International advocates must also be clear and explicit in stating for whom they speak when they advance a criticism or proposal.

Focus on changes in practice and on institutional change at the World Bank

Aspects of the NGO agenda (such as participation, gender equity, poverty reduction, sustainability, or energy efficiency) are being accepted into the World Bank's vocabulary and policy apparatus. NGO advocates have been well aware of the gap between policy and practice, but winning institutional changes in practice has proved difficult.

The next generation of advocacy priorities and strategies should shift emphasis from global-level policy to institutional mechanisms and to the implementation of policy commitments. Tried and tested advocacy methods for winning policy change have been joined by new approaches required at a new juncture. The environment/infrastructure campaign emphasises institutional changes for accountability and transparency, monitors rule revision in the Bank, and presses for the extension of safeguards to loans for private-sector projects. Debt campaigners are monitoring country-by-country implementation of new rules for debt relief, as well as initiating a public campaign for more radical debt relief.

Some adjustment critics are participating in the national-level SAPRI joint review.

Test the model, and strategies, against experience

Political, intellectual, and institutional commitments have led academics and practitioners to focus on demonstrating NGOs' efficacy as political actors, more than to subject the campaigns to rigorous review. But a more rigorous and candid review of advocacy strategies and impact would benefit NGOs, by helping them to identify effective strategies, and by demonstrating their commitment to the principles of transparency and accountability.

As NGOs attract more attention as political actors in international arenas, they can expect more critical review. They will do well to initiate and encourage such studies themselves.

Be attentive: influence flows both ways

The World Bank has accepted the legitimacy of NGOs' participation in policy discussions and its own obligation to respond to NGO and civil-society interventions. The Bank, in turn, uses its liaison with NGOs skilfully to signal its affiliation with aspects of the NGOs' agenda. The World Bank now presents itself as the leader among major donors in areas such as public participation, social safety nets during economic reform, debt relief, and involuntary resettlement. Some NGO advocates tirelessly point out the limits of the Bank's practice in these areas, but they have learned that a reputation is sometimes more easily won than substantive change.

NGOs themselves are also influenced through their interaction with major donors. Planned, deliberate co-operation in even a single component of a World Bank-financed project is often a major undertaking for an international NGO or its country or regional office, and for national or sub-national NGOs. Critics of the Bank have long recognised that NGOs which accept major support for project work or participation in a conference or committee may open their priorities and practices to its influence.

But the same is true of participation in a policy dialogue, even when NGOs imagine themselves to be the agent of change and the World Bank the target. The political realities of the institution and its political environment can shift NGOs' agendas towards the politically feasible, and the content of the Bank's contributions to the discussion can influence NGO conceptual frameworks as well. NGOs should take care to assure that such change is deliberate and in line with their own mission and commitments. Without careful attention, the Bank's expanding 'partnerships' with a variety of civil-society organisations will only accelerate the already rapid homogenisation of organisations and strategies in the development industry.

Notes

1 This article draws on the author's evaluation report (Nelson 1997), in which references to interviews and personal communi-cations may be found (available from Christian Aid, PO Box 100, London SE1 7RT).

2 Christian Aid participated in the NGOWG as a representative of the Association of Protestant Development Organisations.

3 This line of thinking was suggested by Justin Forsyth, then of Oxfam International.

Acknowledgement

I thank Christian Aid for encouraging publication of the results of the evaluation of their WRTW campaign. Thanks to Paul Spray, Roger Williamson, and an anonymous reviewer for helpful comments either on the evaluation or on this article.

References

Christian Aid (1994) 'Who Runs the World?', campaign folder, London: Christian Aid

Cleary, Seamus (1995) 'In whose interest? NGO advocacy campaigns and the poorest', *International Relations* 12(5): 9-36

Conly, Shanti R. and Joanne E. Epp (1997) *Falling Short: The World Bank's Role in Population and Reproductive Health*, Washington: Population Action International

Covey, Jane G. (1998) 'Critical cooperation? Influencing the World Bank through policy dialogue and operational cooperation' in Fox and Brown (eds.) 1998

Fox, Jonathan and David L. Brown (1998), 'Assessing the impact of NGO advocacy campaigns on World Bank projects and policies,' in Fox and Brown (eds.) *The Struggle for Accountability: The World Bank, NGOs and Grassroots Movements*, Cambridge MA: MIT Press

Harrigan, J. (1998) 'Effects of the IMF and World Bank on public expenditure accountability in Jamaica', *Public Administration and Development* 18:5-22.

Jordan, Lisa and Peter van Tuijl (1997) 'Political Responsibility in NGO Advocacy: Exploring Emerging Shapes of Global Democracy', unpublished paper, June 1997

Nelson, Paul J. (1995) *The World Bank and NGOs: The Limits of Apolitical Development*, London: Macmillan

Nelson, Paul J. (1996) 'Interna-tionalising economic and environmental policy: transnational NGO networks and the World Bank's expanding influence', *Millennium* 25: 605-33.

Nelson, Paul J. (1997) 'Who Runs the World? A Partial Evaluation of a Two-Year Policy Campaign', London: Christian Aid

Polak, Jacques J. (1998) 'IMF Study Group Report: Transparency and Evaluation', report and recommendations by the Center of Concern, Washington DC: Center of Concern

Roe, Emery (1995) 'Critical theory, sustainable development and populism', *Telos* 103: 149-62

Scholte, Jan Arte (1998) 'The International Monetary Fund and Civil Society: an Underdeveloped Dialogue', paper presented at a Workshop on Global Economic Institutions and Global Social Movements, Centre for Economic Policy Research, London, 26 February 1998

Siddharth, Veena (1995) 'Gendered participation: NGOs and the World Bank', *IDS Bulletin* 26(3): 31-8

Sogge, David (ed.) (1996) *Compassion and Calculation: The Business of Private Foreign Aid*, London: Pluto Press.

Dissolving the difference between humanitarianism and development: the mixing of a rights-based solution

Hugo Slim

Some months ago, I spent a morning in the public gallery in Courtroom One of the UN's International Criminal Tribunal for Rwanda in Arusha. Sitting behind the gallery's glass windows, I watched three UN judges holding court in front of an enormous UN flag, listened to the prosecution questioning an anonymous Rwandan woman, Witness J, who was hidden from view and protected by armed guards. I met the eye of the former Bourgmestre of Mabanza Commune, who was being tried on eight counts of genocide, murder, extermination, crimes against humanity, and grave breaches of Common Article 3 and Additional Protocol II of the Geneva Conventions.

A few days later, having driven a few hundred miles north, I sat observing a meeting of elders from a pastoralist community in Kenya. Gathered under a tree, they sat together on land which had once been held in common by their people and been grazed accordingly by their cattle. Bordering a river, this land was an important route to a valuable water source for their herds. Meeting in this spot where they, their fathers, and grandfathers had grazed their herds in years gone by, they were now trespassers. Some years ago, as part of the increasing privatisation and sub-division of so much pastoralist land in Kenya, this land had been demarcated without consulting the great majority of pastoralist elders and was now the property of the wife of the former Minister of Land — the same Minister who had overseen this policy of land 'reform'. As the meeting went on, passions rose about the continuous threats to pastoralist grazing lands from such misplaced land policies and their attendant abuses of political power. As speakers warmed to their theme, a number of elders reminded the meeting that they were a warrior people and that, while they would continue to pursue legal and peaceful means to secure their land rights, they would eventually resort to violence if their efforts were persistently frustrated.

NGOs have been, and continue to be, intensely involved in both Rwanda and Kenya, working in the aftermath of genocide and in the struggle for land rights respectively. Responding to the Rwandan genocide with relief assistance to civilians and with advocacy to support the indictment and trial of *génocidaires*, NGO actions are labelled 'humanitarian'. Working with pastoralists on matters of land rights and livelihood, their activities are characterised as 'developmental'. This distinction is an old one. It is also an essentially unhelpful one, which implies that these two activities represent different professions with distinct values. For too long, using these terms has played into the hands of that dreadful tendency to dualism which dogs the Western mind and has led to the pernicious idea that humanitarianism and development are radically different moral pursuits. The ethic of the humanitarian has been presented unthinkingly as a sort of temporary, morally myopic project which limits itself to meeting urgent physical needs before hurriedly abdicating in favour of development workers and their much grander ethic of social empowerment and transformation. Such conventional assumptions have often been most fervently encouraged by humanitarian workers themselves. But the stereotype helps no one in the long run.

Perpetuating a rigid distinction between humanitarian values and development values opens the door to absurd questions of comparison between the two. Is humanitarian work only about saving life? Is development work 'long term' and humanitarian work 'short term'? Is one apolitical and the other political? The answer is, of course, that both humanitarianism and development are concerned with saving life, both are short and long term, and both are political, in the proper sense of being concerned with the use and abuse of power in human relations. The idea that there is an implicit distinction in values between humanitarianism and development, which is encouraged by relief–development dualism, is misconceived. Poverty and violence both proceed from a common root in a human nature which finds sharing profoundly difficult, and a tendency to dehumanise the 'otherness' in potential rivals all too easy.

If the Arusha courtroom embodies a fledgling international justice system seeking to respond to inordinate violence and suffering with humanitarian and human-rights law, the pastoralist meeting witnessed the possible seeds of a struggle against sustained and iniquitous injustice which may yet produce political violence or war, which will demand a humanitarian response. The impoverishment and violence caused by political oppression and injustice which development seeks to prevent and transform is the same as that which humanitarianism seeks to restrain and abolish when it has overwhelmed a whole society. And the fundamental value that the humanitarian and the development worker bring to different manifestations of injustice is the same: the belief in human dignity and in the essential equality of all human beings.

Politically and legally, the dominant discourse for addressing equality and dignity is now voiced in terms of human rights. And it is in human rights that we can finally dissolve the unhelpful dualism between humanitarianism and development – a process which is already happening, as donors and NGOs alike become 'rights-based'. In doing so, we are really only making good another unfortunate fallout from the Cold War period, which for various reasons found it important to distinguish rigidly between humanitarianism, development, and human rights, so creating a widespread false consciousness on the subject.

In his detailed and very readable account of the five years of negotiations and diplomatic conferences that produced the Geneva Conventions of 1949, Geoffrey Best tells the intriguing story of the 'missing Preamble' (Best 1994). The post-war development of inter-national humanitarian law under the auspices of the ICRC in Geneva took place in parallel with the development of human rights law at the UN in New York. The UN Convention on the Prevention and Punishment of the Crime of Genocide and the Universal Declaration of Human Rights both appeared in December 1948 a few months before the four Geneva Conventions of August the following year. These two bodies of law emerged from rather different roots: human-rights law from the political tradition of 'the rights of man' (sic) and international humanitarian law from the military tradition of chivalry and the 'laws of war'. But in the heady days of the late 1940s, the values they had in common were obvious to all. Because of this, a Preamble to the IV Geneva Convention on the protection of civilians was drafted which 'would solemnise and strengthen it by explicitly proclaiming it to be a human rights instrument and in particular a protection of basic, minimal human rights' (Best 1994:70).

When the Preamble was brought to the final diplomatic conference in Geneva, no one objected to the reference to human rights, and it looked set to be agreed – until a group of countries working with the Holy See decided that the Preamble should affirm such universal principles of human rights still further by relating them directly to God as 'the divine source of human charity'. At the proposal of this amendment, a row ensued which saw the newly organised, and ardently atheist, communist bloc at odds with the religious alliance of key countries. To break the stalemate and move forward with the wider process, it was decided to drop the whole idea of a Preamble. Sadly, therefore, the opportunity to recognise international humanitarian law firmly and explicitly within the wider body of human rights was let slip, not because of a dispute about the affinity between the two bodies of law but as the collateral damage from a dispute about the existence of God!

In the decades that followed, there were those in the Red Cross movement in particular who were probably much relieved that the Preamble never materialised. As authoritarian régimes on both sides of the political spectrum increasingly equated human rights with subversive politics, many humanitarians capitalised on the lack of explicit human-rights discourse in their project and its Conventions and were able to distance themselves from human rights and so make their cause less politically charged. A distinction between human rights, humanitarianism, and development was allowed to emerge which had never really existed in the minds of those who produced the 1948 Universal Declaration or the 1949 Conventions. But this false distinction came to be corrected in the 1990s as human rights, humanitarian law, and rights-based development have made increasingly common cause. Indeed, the recent 'Humanitarian Charter', set forth by the many NGOs involved in the Sphere Project, could be seen as a second attempt at the missing Preamble (Sphere Project 2000: 6-10). Grounding humanitarian action firmly in a rights-based framework which takes account of international humanitarian law, human-rights law, and refugee law, this new charter serves to enfold humanitarian action and the laws of war within the embrace of human rights.

If humanitarianism is once again catching up with the idea of human rights, so too is development. In recent years, the dominant under-standing of poverty and suffering among 'thinking NGOs' has come to fix on power, its abuse and its imbalance, as the essential determinant in the construction of poverty and suffering. And as poverty and violence have become increasingly conceived of in terms of power, development has been re-framed – by NGOs and Western governments alike – in terms of human rights, which provide a countervailing force to challenge and make just demands of power. (See, for example, Oxfam GB's 1994

Basic Rights Campaign, of particular note in view of the fact that human-rights work as such is not regarded as a charitable activity under the law governing the behaviour of charities registered in England and Wales.) The development of universal human rights, whose fundamental value is a human dignity founded in individual equality, personal freedom, and social and economic justice, easily encompasses humanitarian and development activity and shows them to have common ends. The (re)discovery in the 1990s that both humanitarianism and development are 'rights-based' ended, once and for all, the distracting dichotomy set up between the two and it will, one hopes, silence the succession of debates about the differences or links between relief and development which have dominated so many conferences and occupied so much management time in agencies since the 1970s.

The schema of human rights, which development has found so late and which humanitarianism lost so early but has now rediscovered, is the common practical framework for elaborating values which underpin both humanitarian action and development work. Both ethics – the humanitarian ethic of restraint and protection, and the development ethic of empowerment and social justice – value the same common goods and embrace the same ideal of full human dignity. If, in the new century, humanitarians and development workers could both take the bold step of recognising that they are all human-rights workers, then the theory, management, and practice of relief and development work would be relieved of one of their most mesmerising and exhausting distractions – the false dichotomy between these two professions and their common values.

References

Best, G. (1994) *War and Law Since 1945*, Oxford: Oxford University Press

Sphere Project (2000) *The Sphere andbook: Humanitarian Charter and Minimum Standards in Disaster Response*, Geneva: The Sphere Project

Aid: a mixed blessing

Mary B. Anderson

Over the years of providing humanitarian and development assistance, international aid agencies have become increasingly concerned to avoid paternalism and work with, rather than for, those in need. The evolving shift in aid providers' awareness and in their programming approaches is captured in the serial re-naming, over the past decade and a half, of the people for whom aid is intended, beginning with 'victims', then 'recipients', then 'beneficiaries', then 'counterparts', and now 'participants' or, sometimes, 'clients'. Increasingly, NGOs 'partner' with local agencies (and donors require it); programmes are designed to 'build'[1] local capacity; and community 'participation' is encouraged (or, at least, talked about) in all phases of aid delivery, from planning through to evaluation.

Nonetheless, in spite of efforts to put those who receive aid at the centre of aid programming, recipients' reactions are mixed.

Mixed messages from aid recipients[2]

A crisis occurs, and the television cameras focus on the following kinds of image.

- Smiling children in a refugee camp in Kenya jostling, laughing, and joking as they press for handouts – or a stricken Kosovar mother, for whom reaching the international aid agency across the border is a matter of life or death for her injured baby
- A Turkish earthquake survivor thanking the international rescue team for freeing him from the rubble of his former home – or wailing women

in Macedonia demanding more aid, crying, *'There is not enough; the food is insufficient; the shelter is overcrowded; we need more, or our children will die.'*

- A professor in Bosnia-Herzegovina citing statistics of his country's poverty and need, and instructing the international community about its obligation to correct these conditions – or a Sierra Leonean who says, *'You save my life today, but for what tomorrow? Isn't a dignified death preferable to continued life dependent on the uncertain generosity of the international community?'*

- The flood survivor in Bangladesh recounting the two crises experienced by his village, *'the first, a flood that washed away our homes; the second, international aid that turned us all into beggars'* – or the village food committee in Southern Sudan, telling an international NGO to stop food distributions, because *'though we need food, if we receive it, our village will be raided by militias, and then we will have even less food and be even more insecure.'*

- The women in a northeast Thailand village shrugging to express their frustration that *'... the aid agency keeps insisting we plan activities by consensus, but we're too busy for endless meetings that they call "community participation"'* – or the Guatemalan refugees in Mexico, demanding the establishment of refugee committees to plan all camp activities.

Such 'voices' of aid recipients convey a complicated and mixed message to the international community of aid donors. Some demand 'more', while others say 'no more'. Some want greater involvement in the decisions and planning of assistance; others want only to get the funds or the goods and go on with their lives. Some focus on a history of inequality that obligates the international community to an active role in overcoming poverty; others believe that international assistance is always tainted by less-than-honorable motives for external control. Reactions range from heartfelt appreciation to extreme suspicion; from an attempt to get more of it to contempt for donors' wealth; from disgust at outsider control to adoption of insider control; from acceptance of outsider expertise to rejection of dependence on the delivery of aid.

How does one understand such mixed messages? How can we – the 'outsider' aid community – attend to the concerns and demands of those who receive aid, and respond thoughtfully when they don't agree with each other? Furthermore, how should we interpret the fact that, in spite of the cacophony of difference, there is a common theme of unease or dissatisfaction among many of the comments, including even some of those who express appreciation for aid? Why is it that something *feels* wrong to many of the intended beneficiaries of aid? What can we do about this?

The issues underlying this unease do not appear soluble through improved aid techniques, better aid goods, or greater logistical efficiency. That is, they cannot be addressed through the 'stuff' of aid alone. Rather, these issues are essentially relational in nature and, thus, require a revisiting of the difficult inequality that exists, inevitably, between international givers and receivers.

Inevitable inequality

The relationship between (on the one hand) international donor communities and the aid-providing NGOs, and (on the other hand) the people who, because of crises, find themselves unable to sustain or improve their lives without outside help, is by its nature unequal in three important dimensions.[3] First, there is an essential inequality in power that derives from the ability of one side to give because it enjoys a surplus of goods and abilities, while the other side is in need. Second, there is inequality of optionality, arising from the fact that one side can choose whether or not to give, while the other side has little or no choice about accepting aid if they are to survive. Third, inequality arises from the fact that the giving side of the relationship is primarily accountable to communities and powers outside the crisis and only secondarily, if at all, to insiders, the people who receive aid.

There is no way within the systems and structures of international aid that these three inequalities can be overcome. They are inevitable, so long as some peoples are able to give while others must receive. However, the tensions inherent in the giving and receiving of aid need not be antagonistic and destructive. Recognising their inevitability, we might develop a process by which these tensions become dynamic and creative.

Creative tensions

What might such a process entail? Though they do not represent a full solution, I suggest here four areas for consideration and action that acknowledge tensions between giver and receiver as inevitable, and accept and incorporate them to achieve healthier, more productive outcomes from aid.

Identification of areas of innate equality and inequality

A first step for addressing the giver/receiver tension is for aid donors and recipients both to reaffirm their essential human equality on the one hand, and to acknowledge openly the innate inequality in their circumstances on the other. Fundamental humanitarianism is based, in large part, on the belief that all humans, as humans, have a right to and deserve help when they face difficult circumstances. Underlying this belief is the basic tenet that as human beings we are bound to each other in reciprocal valuation of individual dignity and worthiness. That is, we humans are fundamentally equal to each other, at least in principle.

In fact, however, we are deeply unequal by circumstance. To pretend otherwise, or even to try to create protocols and aid structures that attempt to approximate circumstantial equality, may actually undermine the dignity, worthiness, and humanness of both giver and receiver.

When funds and goods flow in one direction and decisions about how much, and when and where such flows occur are lodged outside the community of recipients, no number of 'consultations', participatory meetings, or partnership arrangements can change these facts. Perhaps a more honest and, strange as it may sound, humble acknowledgment on the part of the donor side of the relationship of their good luck[4] in being well-off could provide a better basis for interaction with recipients (who certainly know this anyway). If we manufacture aid structures to obscure this reality or to establish a pretence of equality, a degree of honesty is lost, undermining mutual respect, genuine sympathy, the dignity of life whether poor or rich – all values which might form a healthier basis for the enterprises of aid giving and receiving.

Acceptance of and clarity about the division of labour

Second, givers and receivers of aid should accept the importance of (and define) an appropriate division of labour in their functions. Who knows most about what? Who is better prepared to take which actions? Who is capable of or responsible for which decisions?

This step must be based on local realities, rather than idealised preconceptions or hopes. It is, of course, always true that people within a society in crisis know their society better than any outsider. However, this does not mean that insiders should assume any or all of the responsibilities for aid delivery in all situations. A valid division of labour incorporates an assessment of who has what to offer as inputs (who has what knowledge or other competence?) and an assessment of likely outcomes from the interactive process (what combination will achieve the goals most effectively?).

Sometimes local knowledge (a superior input) can involve also local prejudice (distorting outcomes). For example, experience in conflict settings shows that, very often, local individuals and institutions are embroiled in the inter-group divisions that define the conflict and, thus, not likely to apportion aid impartially or fairly. Sometimes this is a result of their preferred alliances; sometimes the conscientious commitment of local people to serve all sides is subverted by the pressures applied on them by colleagues, family members, militias. In either case, it may be preferable for outsiders to assume responsibility for allocating aid.

Alternatively, in other aid settings, local structures may exist for wise and sensitive decisions about how to allocate limited aid. There may be existing systems for physically distributing aid goods or for identifying when aid is no longer needed. Where this is the case, the assumption of these responsibilities by outside aid-givers only undermines existing local capacity (possibly weakening it) and wastes aid resources on the creation of unnecessary parallel systems.

A well thought-through division of labour would, similarly, acknowledge that, in virtually all international aid situations, external donors know better than local recipients the dangers of too much aid, too long. Broad experience of providing aid has educated donors and international NGOs about the dangers and downsides of aid. First-time recipients do not know these potential costs. A healthy division of labour between giver and receiver should acknowledge these differences in 'aid expertise'. Clarity about roles can be a vehicle for acknowledging capacities that exist within recipient communities and, thus, for affirming the dignity of recipients' humanness. It also can provide the mechanism for clarifying the differences in circumstances that, unacknowledged, can lead to distrust and resentment between givers and receivers.

Defining the goal of aid as 'None Needed'

Third, a re-shaping of the relationship between givers and receivers could be furthered by agreement that the sole purpose of aid is to enable people not to need it. This should be the goal of both humanitarian and development assistance, even though in both dimensions need is shaped to a greater or lesser extent by events outside the control of aid.

A corollary to this is the further acknowledgment that long-term aid relationships are often unnecessary, and often damaging. Short-term aid can, under many circumstances, both be effective in tiding people over a crisis and have a positive developmental impact, in that it does not impede recipients' resumption of full responsibility for their own survival and welfare.

It is important, here, to distinguish between a long-term commitment of aid providers to aid recipients (entailing a full sense of continued caring for people's welfare) and long-term aid programmes. A firm commitment to long-term caring may best be realised through short-term inputs of external material assistance, coupled with sustained engagement in promoting the changes in the world order that allow extreme poverty and wealth to coexist. Not all (or even most) 'root causes' of poverty and suffering are located in the place where poverty and suffering occur.

Managing anguish and joy simultaneously

Finally, our handling of the tensions inherent in the donor–recipient relationship might be improved through more skilful and thoughtful management of the contradictions encountered daily in aid work – namely, the contradictions between the horror and anguish of suffering which prompts aid, and the importance of affirming the joy and pleasures of life if aid is to be worthwhile. In the process of helping and being helped, it is easy to focus on pain and loss. However, if life is to be proferred over death (that is, if saving lives through humanitarian assistance or helping improve the chances of sustained lives through development aid is worthwhile), then life should be, daily, enjoyed.

Philosophers and theologians have told us that suffering is not, in itself, demeaning and demoralising. However, responses to suffering can make it so. Somehow, among aid workers, there is a widely accepted sense that a frenetic pace of exhausted response is the right way to do emergency aid or, equally, that long-term, slow, and tedious plodding is required in development aid. But suffering can be demeaned by harried efficiency or working tedium, just as much as by pity or denial.

In all societies and across all societal differences, genuine friendships are possible. Everywhere there are people who are fascinating, engaging, loving, and fun. There must be some other step we can take as aid providers and aid recipients to maintain inward composure in the face of grim realities so that we allow time for talk, exchange of family lore, sitting together to rest and reflect, and doing 'recreational' things together. Mutual enjoyment should not be confined to enclaves of aid givers, but must also be sought among recipients. Aid providers may be able to redress some of the innate imbalance in their relationships with recipients if they find ways to be empathetic with the latter's sad experiences and, simultaneously, affirm that life is to be enjoyed.

Our Sierra Leonean friend reminds us of this when he asks his difficult question: '*You save my life today, but for what tomorrow?*' To his query I would only add: if life is worth saving today, then it should also be livable, worth living, today (as well as tomorrow). The processes of providing and receiving international assistance need to be re-humanised by enjoyment.

The mixed messages so honestly conveyed by the multiple and varied recipients of aid carry one clear and common text. Another great challenge − perhaps the most important of all for aid providers and recipients − is to accept both our innate human equality and our circumstantial inequality and, in the face of both, to establish relationships of mutual respect and contemporaneous enjoyment of each other. The mixed messages remind us that humanitarian and development assistance are not only about timely deliveries of needed goods (critical as these are). International aid is, fundamentally, about relationships.

Notes

1 Personally, I avoid the phrase 'capacity building' because it risks the same dangers found in earlier 'needs assessments'. That is, too often outsiders define which capacities are missing in a society and, hence, which ones they are going to 'build'. Far preferable, and emphasised years ago by my colleague, Peter Woodrow, and me is the idea of recognising the capacities that *exist* in societies and, as outsiders, supporting and building *on* these rather than assuming a capacity deficit that we, as aid providers, need to fill (Anderson and Woodrow 1989). Of course, there are other writers and thinkers (for instance, Eade 1997) who also use the idea of building capacities to refer to efforts to be responsive to local people who, specifically, request technical or other outsider help.

2 Each quotation here is based on comments made to me directly or to colleagues who have reported them to me. Before I wrote this paper, I reviewed with several other aid-workers their impressions about how recipients feel about aid. Interestingly, among us, we could think of few instances in which we had heard unambiguous praise of aid from any recipient. This is not, of course, a scientific sampling of opinions, but it seems to support my sense that messages from recipients are, at best, mixed.

3 I thank my colleague Hizkias Assefa for helping me to think through these ideas of inequality between outsiders and insiders, in a series of personal conversations.

4 The word I really want to use here is 'grace' which, I learned long ago in my Presbyterian upbringing, means 'unmerited favour'!

References

Anderson, Mary B. and Peter J. Woodrow (1989, new edition 1998) *Rising from the Ashes: Development Strategies in Times of Disaster*, Boulder CO: Lynne Rienner.

Eade, Deborah (1997) *Capacity Building: A People-Centred Approach to Development*, Oxford: Oxfam.

The Local Capacities for Peace Project: the Sudan experience[1]

Abikök Riak

'Do no harm': The Local Capacities for Peace Project

In the mid-1990s, the Local Capacities for Peace Project (LCPP) was launched to investigate the relationship between aid and conflict. The Project is a collaborative effort, involving international and local NGOs: the International Federation of Red Cross and Red Crescent Societies (IFRCS), Catholic Relief Services (CRS), World Vision (WV), UN agencies, and European and American donor agencies (USAID, CIDA, SIDA). Spearheaded by Mary B. Anderson of the Collaborative for Development Action (CDA), the LCPP set out to answer the following question: How can humanitarian or development assistance be given in conflict situations in ways that, rather than feeding into and exacerbating the conflict, help local people to disengage and establish alternative systems for dealing with the underlying problems? Lessons learned from the field experiences of aid providers working in conflict situations around the world were compiled into a booklet, and more recently into a book (Anderson 1999).

The LCPP is based on the premise that when international assistance is given in the context of conflict, even when it is effective in doing what it is intended to do, it not only becomes part of the conflict but it also has the potential to feed into and exacerbate it. In February 1998, WV Sudan joined the LCPP to investigate the effects of its aid programme on the conflicts in the south of the country, and to demonstrate how the field-based lessons learned through the Project could be used to improve the design and implementation of WV Sudan aid programmes.[2]

The LCP process is iterative. It begins with an analysis of the environment and looks at which groups are in conflict, both historically and potentially. Aid workers (assisted by external facilitators) identify the dividers, or capacities for war (for example, different values and interests, the apparatus of war propaganda, systems of discrimination) that separate groups in conflict, and the connectors, or capacities for peace (such as common history and language, shared infrastructure and markets) that bring them together. In this exercise, the dividers and connectors are prioritised according to those that are in WV's sphere of concern (like the north–south war in Sudan) and others in WV's sphere of influence (for example, inter-ethnic conflicts). Through this analysis, we can design programme alternatives that reduce negative impacts and strengthen connectors.

Our involvement with the LCPP has provided a solid foundation for the long-term process of addressing and monitoring the relationship between aid and conflict in Sudan. It challenged us to think about the obvious ways in which our aid can unintentionally contribute to the conflict, as well as the subtler impact of our attitudes and actions and how these can influence the perpetuation or negation of war. Most importantly, LCPP has provided us with the opportunity to improve the quality of our work in Sudan.

The operational environment in southern Sudan

The civil war in Sudan has the dubious distinction of being the world's longest-running civil war, having raged for most of the past four decades. The current fighting has lasted for the past 18 years. An estimated 1.9 million people have been killed since 1983.

WV operates in Yambio in Western Equatoria, and Tonj and Gogrial counties in Bahr el Ghazal (BeG), areas controlled by the Sudan People's Liberation Army/ Movement (SPLA/M). In these areas WV works with the Sudan Relief and Rehabilitation Association (SRRA), the humanitarian wing of the SPLM. In 1994, a civil structure was set up, distinct from the SRRA. In mid-1999, tensions between the SRRA, civil authorities, and traditional leaders became more pronounced.

Tonj and Gogrial counties are close to the front line and are subject to fighting between the Government of Sudan (GoS), southern factions, and independent warlords; and to inter-ethnic struggles. The relationship between civil and military authorities, NGOs, and the local communities is a tense and potentially dangerous one, especially in Gogrial.

A thorough LCP analysis necessitates a keen understanding of the dynamic operational environment in which WV works. One of the key elements of the methodology is the constant reassessment of this environment and the links to WV's programmes. The focus of the LCP analysis in Tonj and Gogrial is on the targeting of food and non-food aid to genuine beneficiaries, and the potentially harmful impact that distributions of food and commodities can have in a conflict.

After the army, WV is the largest employer in the two regions. Therefore, the questions of whom we hire, whom we target as beneficiaries, and how these benefits feed into a war economy are vital. Who benefits from WV programmes and on what level can have tremendous impacts on the conflict and on the economy of the region. We purchase grain from farmers in Yambio for food distributions in BeG, we distribute seeds, tools, and survival kits, we provide drugs in clinics, and we drill boreholes. All of these and many other activities, if not managed appropriately, have the potential for misuse and re-direction to military endeavours. Every day we face armed soldiers requesting food, drugs, and seemingly innocuous rides in vehicles. How do we deal with these challenges without demonstrating either belligerence or powerlessness?

In the first assessment of Yambio, in 1998, a conflict was identified between the community and the local authorities that had developed out of a hiring procedure. The analysis showed that WV was inadvertently contributing to this conflict through a recruitment and hiring policy that depended almost entirely on the SRRA and was, therefore, subject to abuse. Ways to address this included recruitment through churches, open advertising, and committee interviews. These changes provided the community with the opportunity to participate in staff selection, to seek employment, and to represent to a greater extent the diversity of Yambio county. The committees are responsible for interviewing and hiring, and their role has developed to include supervision of employees.

Lessons learned

The LCP analysis was extended to Bahr el Ghazal in late 1998. Some lessons could be transferred from one region to the other. The issues of staff-hiring practices and of abuses associated with currency exchange were common in both regions. During this first phase, an emphasis was placed on training, and analytical discussions were refined.

The focus in the second phase was on incorporating the methodology in the design, implementation, and evaluation of WV Sudan programmes. The dissemination of lessons learned through our involvement with LCP to the WV Partnership more broadly, and the aid community at large, is critical at this stage.

The lessons learned from the implementation of the LCPP are valuable, given the growing size of WV operations in southern Sudan, the increasing complexity of the conflict, and the challenges posed by the interaction between the two. We learned that the appreciative contribution and leadership of senior management are paramount importance to the success of any new paradigm. High staff turnover is common in emergency programmes, and this may jeopardise the capacity and consistency required for the LCP process to make an impact over the planned three year implementation. Training is crucial, and staff in the field and in Nairobi were targeted for basic training and to act as 'champions'. Influential staff were given extended training.

Collaboration among those involved in the LCPP allows dialogue and exchange. Regular meetings give partner agencies the opportunity to discuss the lessons learned and their operational implications. The relationship between WV, CDA, and other partners has provided something rare in the relief community: a forum for critical discussion about the impact of humanitarian aid on conflict that has also emphasised learning and reflection.

Having analysed the impact of their programme on conflict, field staff were eager to make programmatic changes to correct negative impacts. The potential danger is that they may act too quickly, without adequate analysis of the alternatives that they identify. This tendency was checked with more active co-ordination between programme headquarters and field staff. Training was restructured to focus on the iterative process of developing programme options and analysing their potential before making operational changes.

We have become good at identifying ways in which our aid can feed into and exacerbate conflict, but it remains a challenge to develop viable programme options to address the more difficult issues raised. Some issues, such as recruitment and hiring practices for local staff, the setting up of feeding centres, and targeting of beneficiaries, were straightforward, and the programme options developed for them were equally direct.

The LCP framework has been used primarily as a tool to improve programme quality. Staff are now more aware of the impacts that aid can have on existing and potential conflicts. In relief and rehabilitation interventions, aid workers, struggling under the 'tyranny of the urgent', tend to focus more on the what (such as food and water) than on the how.

Through our work with the LCPP, WV has been given the opportunity to take a step back and focus on the neglected 'hows'. What we do is often less important than how we do it. Examining the conflict environment and how WV programmes feed into the connectors and dividers provides a unique tool for implementers to sit and discuss our interventions with stakeholders. This facilitates participation by local authorities and beneficiaries, with whom LCP has created increased understanding as well as communication between the community and WV. The inclusion of beneficiaries and Sudanese staff in the analysis has contributed to a better working environment in Yambio.

LCP as a peace-building tool

WV Sudan entered the LCPP collaboration with the knowledge that aid does not cause wars, nor can it end them; and that we as outsiders cannot create lasting peace in Sudan. At the same time, however, we acknowledged that the work we do, not only the services we provide but how we provide them, can have negative or positive effects on existing tensions and conflicts. After 18 months, we were able to see how interventions can support or undermine Sudanese efforts to build the conditions for their own peace.

The LCP framework is not a peace-building tool *per se*, but many aspects of the process have peace-building elements. The next step is to take our experiences with LCP one step further and explore their links to peace-building. Peace in southern Sudan must be created locally, but WV can facilitate the process. Given our large operational presence and our consequent impact on governance, WV is in a good position to support civil society and local peace initiatives. The key is that the processes are not WV's: in order to be lasting, they must come from the grassroots.

We now have a foundation from which we can begin critically and systematically to explore the potential of our aid programmes to encourage a peace-building environment. By building on this, we can fulfil our mandate to save lives and work with the poorest of the poor, while at the same time providing aid in a knowledgeable and thoughtful way, aware of the complex layers of our role in communities.

The way forward

As we move into the second phase and the third year of our involvement with the LCPP, we wish to pass on lessons learned and so to ensure that the methodology is embedded in the design, implementation, and evaluation of WV Sudan projects. Our ultimate goal is better aid and more accountability. We want accountability at all levels. Our experience is that the LCP methodology is a tool that can help us achieve this.

LCP is only one of several tools that can be useful in programme management, and it of course has its limitations. Though it helps us to organise and process information, it does not answer the questions for us, nor does it make critical decisions. In the end, it comes down to our making better choices and better decisions in our programming. What LCP has done is to provide us with a systematic way of addressing the impact of our aid on conflict and the many programme-quality issues that surround the discussions. Clearly, the LCP framework has benefits, not only for the Sudan programme but also for other organisations working in conflict areas.

Notes

1 An earlier version of this paper was published in the October-December edition of *Together,* a journal of the World Vision Partnership.

2 The LCP initiative in Sudan was funded by World Vision Canada and CIDA.

Reference

Anderson, Mary B. (1999) *Do No Harm: How Aid Can Support Peace — Or War*, Boulder CO: Lynne Rienner

NGOs, disasters, and advocacy: caught between the Prophet and the Shepherd Boy

Alan Whaites

Conflict and disasters haunted the 1990s, challenging the complacency of a world which, official development assistance figures suggest, is increasingly bereft of any kind of internationalist ideal. Complex Humanitarian Emergencies (CHEs), famines, and civil strife have forced themselves on to the media agenda, and then on to that of the politicians, thus creating a more dangerous and unstable environment for NGOs. From Bosnia to Rwanda and beyond, those same NGOs have been successively wrong-footed by the policy analysis and advocacy implications of each emergency. Too often, aid agencies are essentially responding to the last emergency, and so fall short of the mark.

The implications of the increase in internal conflicts have not been lost on the relief capability of the NGOs involved, nor on theoretical thinking – which, thanks to writers such as Hugo Slim and Mark Duffield, has largely been transformed. The flowering of work designed to research conflict, and new methodologies in reconciliation have also seen some aspects of NGO adaptability at its best. But, as this paper will argue, in the field of advocacy, NGOs have failed to reconcile the implications of CHEs with the underlying obligations of humanitarianism.

NGOs have become trapped by conflicting fears, each apparently equally valid and historically real. There is the spectre of Rwanda and the failure to raise the alarm over a situation that resulted in the slaughter of hundreds of thousands of people, and to this day still deeply traumatises survivors, as well as NGO workers who were involved. After Rwanda, a new concern for early warning led aid agencies to enter a field of policy analysis designed to create the potential for early action.[1] This became known as *preventive advocacy*: the articulation of a potential or imminent disaster with the intention that policy makers, whether local or international, will act to avert a crisis. This was the NGO community seeking to act as Old Testament Prophet, standing up to proclaim the potential for disaster should the world fail to change its ways.[2]

This new approach was given its first real test in 1996. By the late summer of that year, some agencies, notably Oxfam GB and World Vision, were already predicting a serious escalation in the conflict in eastern Zaïre – with potentially serious consequences for civilians. Large numbers of Hutu refugees within reach of the Rwandan border, plus the deteriorating situation within Africa's largest State, seemed to suggest that preventive advocacy was justified. In the weeks that followed, NGOs grew increasingly concerned about the potential fate of hundreds of thousands of refugees, cut off in remote areas or confined to camps that were receiving no supplies. The prospect of wholesale massacres seemed real: at best, acts of indiscriminate revenge against Hutus trapped in isolated refugee camps; at worst, the death by neglect or disease of civilians and *interahamwe* militia alike.

Oxfam GB, World Vision, Médecins Sans Frontières (MSF), and others called for the world to intervene to secure safe access for humanitarian workers to these refugees. The international community, its new-found interventionist tendencies tested by Bosnia and Somalia, seemed reluctant to concur.[3] In the heat of the advocacy drive, NGO opinion split – with the Save the Childen Fund (SCF) in the UK declaring intervention unfeasible and unwise. Alex de Waal was equally sceptical, although he pointed more to the apparent over-dramatisation of events by NGOs in order to raise their own profile, influence, and cash.[4]

The charge that NGOs had exaggerated in order to fuel public appeals was inevitably difficult to refute: stories of impending genocide had failed to materialise (though massacres did occur later), leading to a sense that the public had been misled. Some in the NGO community began to point to the dangers of preventive advocacy; fears were raised which were also ultimately disproved, i.e. that NGO credibility would be lost, which would make advocacy of any kind more difficult. By 1998, when the famine in Sudan was coming to light, this concern was being given full voice: for instance, Mark Bowden of SCF explained to the press the dangers of raising the alarm 'before the facts are fully known'.[5] NGOs were warned not to be the Shepherd Boy, crying wolf too often until finally unable to raise any alarm at all.

This is the continuing dilemma for all advocacy-oriented NGOs. Is it preferable for aid agencies to honour their prophetic calling and risk their hard-earned credibility, or should NGOs instead be wary of calling wolf too often? Written from the perspective of an advocacy practitioner, this paper considers the conflicting pressures on the one hand to scale up, and on the other hand to limit advocacy during disasters. Any discussion of this rapidly growing area of activity must also address the need to evaluate the motives of NGOs and the impact of what they achieve: whenever advocacy is an issue, questions of accountability, veracity, and legitimacy are never far from the surface. The paper ends with a plea to NGOs to view their credibility as a resource that *should* be risked, where necessary, as part of the overall humanitarian ethic of saving lives. The dangers of appearing self-serving and misleading are shown to be real, but ultimately the potential to change dire events is too important to be surrendered lightly.

Advocacy and disasters

We are increasingly told that advocacy and awareness-raising are the future of NGOs (particularly Northern NGOs), although precise definitions are rarely offered. The rising numbers of NGOs that are adopting advocacy as an approach, coupled with the diversity of views within the development community, have created considerable room for divergence. It is not surprising, therefore, that any reference to advocacy automatically raises numerous – perfectly appropriate – questions along the lines of: *what is the aim of advocacy, on whose behalf is it undertaken, and with what legitimacy?*

Advocacy is in theory related to one of the higher ideals of the NGO world: the search for justice. At a more prosaic level, advocacy is simply a tool or set of tools – mechanisms by which NGOs try to push their own concerns on to the agendas of others. Most NGOs would state that this tool is used to support Southern communities, whether through specific requests for action at the local level, or through the call for changes to the macro-context which shapes the lives of the poor. Like all tools, advocacy can be dangerous as well as useful, both for an NGO's own staff and for the poor whom it is trying to help. This is especially so in a disaster setting, where background analysis can be rushed, and the agency may be completely unfamiliar with the context.

Indeed, for much of the 1990s, pressures on NGOs to be seen to be involved as well as informed (not least the pressures of fundraising) led to a considerable increase in NGO comment on each new geopolitical problem which arose. De Waal (1994:2) neatly summarised the situation:

In recent years, international relief organisations ... have become increasingly significant political actors, both in the African countries where they work, and in western countries where they undertake publicity, lobbying and advocacy. They have expanded their mandate to encompass human rights and conflict resolution.

The call for foreign military intervention is perhaps the most striking example of 'humanitarianism unbound': liberated from the Cold War straightjacket, international relief organisations in strategically unimportant countries like Somalia and Rwanda can make an extraordinarily bold call, apparently unimpeded by limits on their mandate and expertise, or by accountability. In an ever wider arena, relief agencies are now empowered to make important political judgements, implicit and explicit, which go far beyond their traditional role.

Hugo Slim has also written of the crisis in values affecting NGOs, a crisis that had become particularly stark in those situations where saving lives might not be enough: 'when wider human rights abuses endanger that life in the first place'. Slim (1997:15-16) notes that:

In their choice of position, more and more NGOs and UN forces are adopting a robust form of impartiality which allows them not just to dish out relief in proportion to needs, but also to dish out criticism (advocacy) or military bombardment in proportion to human rights wrong-doing. This hardened impartiality may be the NGO posture of choice in the future, but it will have operational implications and no doubt be met by an equally hard response on occasion.

The retreat from advocacy

The current crisis of confidence among NGOs regarding this more 'robust' position has been largely a result of their attempt to rein in the excesses identified by de Waal. Critics have been helped both by NGO naïvety in geopolitical matters and by the reality that preventive advocacy can easily be seen as (or become) an attempt to play up a crisis as part of an appeal for funds. Valid criticism has also arisen from the temptation for each agency to comment on every conflict, regardless of experience, qualifications, or sometimes even presence. This paper argues that the negative reactions to these dynamics, both internal and external, are healthy, but create their own dangers if they are pressed too far. If NGOs' motives are not always pure, neither are they always bad. The need for preventive advocacy remains.

The primary concern here is that the current loss of confidence may cause a retreat from preventive advocacy (i.e. those actions taken to raise awareness in time to avert the fulfilment of the worst-case scenario). CHEs are not static; they are in reality a sequence of events forming an often lengthy process.[6] Within this context, external action usually arrives late in the day. It is this problem which early warning and preventive advocacy have the potential to change (see Keen and Wilson in Macrae and Zwi 1994).

This paper thus calls for renewed commitment to undertake policy work in terms of complex emergencies, albeit with increased professional rigour and accountability. Perhaps one of Slim's most thought-provoking recent works (Slim 1998) is particularly apt for NGO advocacy workers who are considering the future role of preventive advocacy. He offers a call to humanitarian organisations to step back from 'excessively' institutionalising the humanitarian principle, i.e. the desire, in the formulation of ICRC, 'to prevent and alleviate human suffering wherever it may be found ... to protect life and health and to ensure respect for human beings', which lies at the root of our work. He sees this institutionalising trend as a priestly, ritualistic role, in contrast with the prophetic urge to confront 'society with a truth and [which] is concerned with personal, social, and political transformation'.

The prophetic function of humanitarianism, urging the world to face its least appealing characteristics, cannot be done simply on the basis of currying favour with the media[7] or maintaining harmony among NGOs. It is here that Slim's work speaks acutely to those in the advocacy field. To take his analogy further, we should remember that prophets are rarely popular in their own time. Indeed, Slim comes close to reminding advocacy workers to be wary of the potential conflict between popularity and prophecy:

> The humanitarian prophet will better be a prophet who can move
> at the very centre of events and penetrate the very heart of the
> institutions concerned. But she or he must still be a prophet.
> She must still challenge and call. He must not be calmed into
> straight priesthood by those who would see him cordoned off
> again to pursue the rituals of faith alone. (Slim 1998:2)

Preventive advocacy: a risk worth taking?

Preventive advocacy lies at the heart of this prophetic function and has been an increasing feature of NGO campaigns. The roots of this trend lie firmly in changes in the global context, which have affected conflicts as well as food security. Concern for the latter area produced one of the first overviews of the realities and 'barriers' involved, whether political, institutional, or logistical (Buchanan-Smith and Davies (1995), especially Chapter 2 and pp.19-23). Indeed, preventive advocacy at its best is an NGO's primary means of overcoming the problem that these authors identify, i.e. inaction in the face of available and credible early-warning information – inaction that George and Holl (1997) termed the 'warning-response gap'.

Preventive advocacy is, therefore, heavily dependent upon early-warning studies. For complex emergencies, often rooted in conflict, the concept of early warning has given rise to a mini-industry of forecasters and analysts; new specialists seeking to identify the next bout of civil strife before it occurs. Despite such developments, the most reliable information available to most NGOs remains the local knowledge and understanding of their own local counterparts in the South, who are able to read the signs of poor harvests, rising tensions, and governmental change. It is usually where such local partners are absent, i.e. where agencies lack ongoing programmes, that the NGO community has faltered in its operational and advocacy responses.

Articulating the fears and concerns raised by such local partners in the hope of securing international or local action is, as Slim suggests, something which can often be done within the corridors and meeting rooms of foreign ministry and UN buildings. The increased access of NGOs to governmental, multilateral, and UN actors is encouraging. But this lobbying approach, focused mainly on OECD governments, is not always enough. Reality dictates that making OECD governments listen can sometimes require NGOs first to change the agenda of the general public. Using the media to put pressure on governments is nothing new; but, where preventive advocacy is concerned, it is an inherently risky approach.

This kind of public preventive advocacy involves putting an NGO's name on the line, and with it to some degree the reputation of the aid-agency sector. Not surprisingly, therefore, it is due to this need to mobilise the public through the press that many of the underlying issues of legitimacy and accountability break through to the surface of the discussion. Risks to credibility are compounded by the potential for advocacy efforts to be hijacked for the sake of premature fundraising appeals. Advocacy standards can become easily blurred; the need for the option of articulating the worst-case scenario can lead to prediction being presented as fact.

Even those who are deeply committed to risk-taking preventive advocacy must recognise these dangers fully. In the heat of the situation, advocacy staff, like their relief colleagues, can be exasperated by the fine hairs that are dissected in the discussion of what statements are, or are not, acceptable. But standards matter in advocacy, just as they do in relief work. Advocacy workers, like all NGO staff, have to recognise that there is a fundamental obligation of due diligence owed by every humanitarian worker towards the people whom they aim to assist. Humanitarianism does include the need to put pressure on policy makers to bring about change, but change based on our best available analysis of the needs and aspirations of the poor, not on an eye-catching and opportunist guess. Acknowledging the question of standards means that words are important. Thus, advocacy must mean weighing public statements and risking our credibility strategically, not negligently.

Preventive advocacy: unleashing the spectre

Perhaps the most revealing debate about this question of standards has revolved around the use of the emotive word *famine*. This was an issue that became one of the least edifying parts of the debate surrounding the 1998 emergency in Sudan. 'Famine' is a powerful word; it is right to protect its force and not use it for every food shortage that comes along. Nevertheless, agencies that are observing realities on the ground must also be able to make clear the dangers, and to use language which captures the potential scope of the tragedy taking place. The failure of agencies to agree a definition is unhelpful. For SCF, famine appears to include population movement – which would rule out some of the great famines of history – whereas for MSF it is linked to a distinct geographical area.

Each agency must consider its criteria and measure its desire to articulate any fears against its onus of responsibility (particularly the need for confidence in their understanding of the issues and also of their motives for engagement). Even so, clarifying the nature of famine may be long overdue. NGOs are aware of academic work – whether Sen (1981), Dyson (1991), or Swift (1989) – on causes and characteristics. Perhaps we have now reached the point at which we must come to a consensus on the technical definition of the point at which a humanitarian crisis becomes a famine.[8]

In mid-1998, the pressure from some observers to refrain from talking of famine in Sudan without proven data was reminiscent of earlier criticism of warnings regarding North Korea. In reality, after considering the issue of due diligence, the risk must sometimes be taken, and the spectre unleashed without full empirical proof. For all those engaged in relief advocacy, Becker's work (1996) makes salutary reading. Becker discusses the famine in China between 1958 and 1962 – an event virtually unreported at the time. Lessons for advocacy work might also be drawn from studying the Great Bengal famine or even that of Ethiopia in the early 1970s.

Early-warning advocacy must be responsible and diligent, but it cannot live by a burden of absolute proof. If such an approach were taken, the concept would die. Instead, it needs to survive on the basis of a commitment by NGOs to seek out the best information available and to divorce advocacy and awareness-raising from the fundraising impulse. The experienced hunch, the instincts of partners on the ground, and the risk-taking of Slim's prophetic humanitarianism must be given their due.

Accountability and credibility

Support for risk-taking and a prophetic function in advocacy should not be read as carte blanche for the well-meaning mistake. Without a balance of responsibilities, such an argument can degenerate into the simplistic perspective that we 'have to do our best and make the most informed judgement possible'. It is in the interest of NGOs to go beyond such thinking and to establish a broader understanding of advocacy and its risks. Partly this is a question of protecting our credibility. More importantly, however, it is an extension of that critical obligation to donors and the poor alike: the need for accountability, transparency, and impact.

Advocacy has sometimes been less scrutinised in relation to these standards than have other NGO efforts. Yet advocacy, like any area of NGO activity, should live or die by its usefulness to the poor. An emphasis on clear and measurable objectives must be complemented by a willingness to monitor and evaluate results. It is likely that almost any agency could benefit by comparing the evaluation techniques used for development programmes with those designed for advocacy. The infrequency with which NGOs tend to consult either donors, policy makers, or partners on the effectiveness of their advocacy work raises questions of its own, questions which the rapidly developing nature of CHEs often allows to be quietly left behind. It is, however, precisely during CHEs and concomitant public appeals that transparency and accountability should become an acute NGO concern. Perhaps NGOs might learn from the model set by the evaluation of the media's role in Congo/Zaïre (Philo 1997).

Part of the reason that advocacy has too often been able to escape the accountability challenge has been the difficulty of quantifying what is by nature a complex and sometimes reactive chain of events. But in establishing objectives, and devising strategy, clarity can sometimes be brought by introducing an equal concern for the medium term. CHEs happen within a context of global policy. With policy makers gradually learning the lessons of humanitarian disasters of the past, NGOs, as well as the poor, have vested interests in the right lessons being learned in good time. Ongoing work in partnership with organisations such as the UN Office for Co-ordination of Humanitarian affairs (OCHA) to create a better context for assistance should not be limited to policy makers alone. NGOs will have a critical role if the constituency for timely interventions is to stretch beyond Washington, London, and the UN Security Council to the wider public in both the North and South.

Credibility for whom?

Those who argue that accuracy must be the predominant factor in any advocacy or awareness-raising work during emergencies do so for a number of reasons. For some it is a question of jealously protecting the power of the NGO message, power which rests on the credibility of the commentator. There can be no doubt that we ignore the need for credibility at our peril: NGOs have no divine right to the ear of the public or of policy makers. Our right to be heard has to be earned. We must also, however, be conscious that credibility can become an end in itself – rather like money, it can be permanently hoarded and never put to good use.

Inevitably there are those who will be quick to point to what they perceive to be scare-mongering and inaccuracy on the part of NGOs; the article by Karl Maier (1998) is a noteworthy example. Potential criticism is inevitable, but it should not silence those NGOs who believe that their own credibility can be used to draw attention to crises that threaten large numbers of civilians. Declaring on CNN that a silent famine is occurring in North Korea will of essence be unprovable in a country in which information is a preciously guarded resource. The alternative, however, is for NGOs to make a commitment never to seek to raise international concern regarding humanitarian crises in North Korea, Iraq, Burma, or indeed any context in which accurate statistics remain more a hope than expectation.

This paper argues that credibility is simply a resource – something to be marshalled for future use. The protection of NGOs' credibility becomes an offensive luxury when it is placed above the inherent obligation which rests on all humanitarian NGOs to save lives. In replying to Maier (1998), Stewart Wallis of Oxfam GB stated that it is on the issue of *how* aid agencies make choices in facing the ethical dilemmas of disasters that they should be judged. The public positioning of agencies is equally a question of choosing between perceived obligations, duties, and expectations – of which few would question that the profile and income of the NGO itself should be considered least. Credibility must occasionally be put on the line if the humanitarian principle is to be real. Perhaps Bryer and Cairns (1997:370) offer a view of more over-riding goals:

> ... we argue that we all have humanitarian responsibilities. The real individual in the real internal conflict has a claim on us all to uphold the rights enshrined in humanitarian law. The claim is also on humanitarian agencies ... Thus, though Oxfam does not have a role in directly protecting civilians from violence, it does have an obligation to report violations of humanitarian law to the State parties to the Geneva Conventions, and an ethical duty to advocate for those States to provide the necessary protection.

This is not to suggest that NGOs should conform to an ideal vision of selfless compassion, free of self-seeking motives. But competitive forces emerge fully only once the media are involved – indeed, a recognised emergency can at worst become the aid-agency equivalent of a sharks' feeding frenzy, each one attempting to take its share of public support. Competitiveness should not be confused with the genuine humanitarian urge to raise awareness. Neither should the protection of credibility become the NGO community's new peer pressure to silence those with whom we disagree. While recognising that credibility is a prerequisite for our right to be heard, we must accept that advocacy inherently means risking reputations. They are usually, after all, our only collateral.

Preventive advocacy and motives for raising the alarm

The newly re-organised Disasters Emergency Committee (DEC) in the UK, which combines NGOs and the media, faced its first significant test with the conflict-induced crisis in the Sudan in early summer 1998. The DEC prevaricated for weeks before eventually being pushed into an appeal by the pointed criticism of television journalists filming in feeding centres. The lasting impression for many was of a degree of inter-agency competitiveness that was strange in a group intended to co-ordinate efforts during crisis. Accusations of agencies briefing the press both against other agencies and against the DEC itself were followed by suggestions from the British Secretary of State for International Development, Clare Short, that the motives of the agencies concerned were to a large degree financial.

There is nothing new about the issue of motives and competitiveness in situations in which the public are known to give generously. Indeed, de Waal (1997) develops the theme from his earlier work at some length, seeing the agencies' reaction to potential massacres in 1996 not as a reaction to NGO self-criticism in the aftermath of Rwanda, but rather as being 'anchored in the institutional imperatives of the humanitarian international', stating that '[t]he humanitarian agencies needed money'(p.204). His suggestion that a 'humanitarian Gresham's Law' will lead debased humanitarianism to drive out the 'authentic' version is premised on the reality that aid agencies are indeed competitive beasts. A succinct summary of some of the pressures comes from Storey (1997: 391):

> Part of the answer must lie in the institutional position of NGOs in terms of competitive fundraising: once a disaster (in this case, massive outflows of people) achieved international attention (through the media), all NGOs had to be seen to respond. Failure to do so would have lost an individual NGO credibility and profile at home, even if it believed that such an intervention was misguided or not a priority. One NGO worker stated that, for reasons of publicity surrounding the cholera outbreak in the camps of Zaire, it was a case, for the NGO, of 'be there or die'.

The criticisms made by Clare Short in relation to Sudan were different perhaps only in their implication that the competition for funds was somehow at the expense of, or incompatible with, proper education and advocacy aimed at the UK public on the issues at stake. Although the two activities need not be mutually exclusive, there is a real danger involved. De Waal's argument about competitiveness is true, but only to a degree. The idea that fundraising drives organisational agendas is not new, but it remains an over-simplification of the internal dynamics involved; particularly the relationships between fundraisers and desk officers (see also Suzuki 1998). In reality, the drive to raise funds during emergencies is both market- and field-driven; responding to emergencies is expensive, as is the rehabilitation phase that follows – for which funds are far harder to raise.

External critics such as de Waal provide an essential corrective to NGOs, but can too easily fall victim to the temptation to have it all ways. Had NGOs remained silent in the late summer of 1996, and had massacres ensued, would external observers have commended the agencies for their restraint? Previous experience suggests not.[9] Equally the move to a multi-mandated, highly vocal NGO environment – neatly summarised by de Waal – is without question a poor substitute for an authentic voice for the poor. NGOs have their own agendas and suffer from many faults. Even so, the pronouncements of NGOs during disasters, and the partnerships with the media which they forge, may also be the only way to press for the issue of saving lives to be added to the policy agenda. The recommendations may be flawed – and unfortunately there are no easy ways to guarantee NGOs wisdom. Nevertheless, pressure for action to prevent avoidable fatalities creates a concern that is both invaluable and life-saving.

Conclusion: the impetus to advocacy

This paper has argued that in the field of NGO advocacy and awareness-raising, the humanitarian ethic is not entirely without meaning – 'even' during disasters. Aid agencies do not exist to raise money, although cynics can easily believe otherwise and will find support for their view in every appeal and all home-country expenditure. But in reality, few Northern aid agencies do not connect their ultimate purpose to the improvement of lives in the South. In emergency-relief contexts, the humanitarian ethic increasingly means a willingness to deal with complex external demands, rigorous monitoring, and physical danger. The deaths of ICRC workers in Chechnya served to underline the altered reality of relief assistance in a world in which NGOs are no longer considered to be neutrals.

It is important to recognise inherent problems and dangers. This is a complex area and a major contributory factor in the unrealistic expectations facing today's relief workers, who must now provide policy analysis as well as managing interventions on the ground. Recognition of the dangers, however, does not diminish the usefulness of the tool. Advocacy does have the potential to bring the attention of policy makers to bear on an issue, and ultimately to secure action. It is, therefore, not a tool to be given up easily. Rather, it is, as Storey (1997) has pointed out in relation to former Zaïre, a question of NGOs needing to examine carefully both the level of understanding that underpins their statements and their motives for engaging in a public debate.

The internal drive within NGOs is to respond to a crisis as it is seen on the ground. In an ideologically driven industry, heavy with its own ideas of correctness, the concept of being led from the South is a powerful force. Hence, the original attempts to persuade the DEC to appeal on Sudan originated not in aid-agency fundraising departments, but with those desk officers who were receiving field reports. Indeed, World Vision, the first agency to raise the situation with the DEC and the provider of most of the footage for the appeal, was aware that, under the complex DEC funding rules, its own share of any joint appeal would be less than from launching an advertised appeal of its own.

The importance of recognising the place of the humanitarian ethic within aid-agency responses to disaster is partly, therefore, a need to reflect the real links between headquarters staff and people on the ground. Equally, the humanitarian ethic, and the impetus from the field, should be the driving force behind the advocacy work (including media awareness-raising) which may be essential if early warning is to be made real. As an industry, NGOs should safeguard (even if for some it is a question of 'tolerating') preventive advocacy, whenever such advocacy is based both on the best information available and on a genuine desire to save lives.

A pressing burden of responsibility on NGOs that are involved in relief work is, therefore, to view advocacy as going beyond the immediate and local. Advocacy strategies should be coherent and medium-term in their scope, and so based on a fuller appreciation of successive international responses to emergencies than can be provided by a single incident. SCF has provided a useful example of the thinking that is needed (Macrae and Zwi 1994). Within this medium-term global framework, the individual reality of each situation can be discussed against the backdrop of a more telling context. In this way, we can learn to see how the experience of

Somalia and Liberia can have fatal consequences of inaction for those living and dying in the Great Lakes region. The commitment to relief as an ongoing advocacy issue rather than a series of rapidly developed *ad hoc* messages also offers some hope of addressing the reality that:

> ... the humanitarian response – at varying levels of generosity – has been the only meaningful expression of most governments' concern about internal conflicts. As the Rwanda evaluation put it, we see a 'policy vacuum' in which aid policy becomes not part of a coherent international response, but almost the entire response. Aid policy replaces foreign policy towards those countries in which donor governments perceive little geo-political interest. Indeed, the deepest problem of humanitarian aid in internal conflicts is that it may let the 'international community' off the hook of its responsibilities to uphold international law.
> (Bryer and Cairns 1997:370)

NGOs remain a central voice in the battle to seriously address the world's response to CHEs. New foreign-policy initiatives and any willingness to take rapid action to avert humanitarian disaster remain dependent both on the work of the media and on NGOs' ability to interpret events. The potential not only to save lives in the immediate term, but also to affect long-term thinking on how best to respond in other situations, makes the contribution of NGOs to the discussion a critical part of our humanitarian work. We cannot, therefore, shun the risks involved in such preventive interventions; but neither can we afford to avoid the responsibilities entailed in such engagement.

Notes

1 For some of the thinking behind these moves, see Rupesinghe (1994; 1995) and NCDO (1997).

2 In London the trend became a coalition as International Alert co-ordinated a group of 15 agencies which sought specifically to ensure that genocide such as that which was perpetrated in Rwanda could not happen so easily again.

3 The pressure, however, did ultimately have an effect. International public opinion moved slowly towards the NGO position, and a succession of military planning options was put in place, providing time for Western powers to use their influence instead.

4 De Waal later described his 20 October 1996 *Observer* piece as 'somewhat cynical'. See also de Waal 1997: 205. For criticism of NGO advocacy at the time, see Alex de Waal: 'No bloodless miracle' in the *Guardian*, 18 November 1996.

5 Mark Bowden, as reported by Jeremy Laurance in 'Is there really a famine in Sudan?', The *Independent*, 7 May 1998.

6 See the chapters by Joanna Macrae and Anthony Zwi and by David Keen and Ken Wilson in Macrae and Zwi (eds.) (1994).

7 For an interesting analysis of some of the dynamics involved, see Philo (1997).

8 Cuny with Hill (1999: 37) offers a table of famine indicators that include prolonged drought; onset of a natural disaster (floods, insects, infestation, etc.); increase in the price of staples; rise in price ratio of staple grain to prevailing wages; increase in lending rates in the informal sector; increase in sales of livestock and decrease in average sale price; increased distress sales; increase in deaths among livestock; unusual sales of possessions such as jewellery, ornaments, etc.; seed shortage or increased cost of seeds; widespread sales of land at abnormally low prices; increased hoarding of grains by dealers; consumption of animals by pastoralists; and consumption of famine foods.

9 For a discussion of the de-contextualisation of disasters and some of the wider related issues, see Middleton and O'Keefe (1998).

References

Becker, Jasper (1996) *Hungry Ghosts: China's Secret Famine*, London: John Murray Publishing

Bryer, David and Edmund Cairns (1997) 'For better? For worse? Humanitarian aid in conflict', *Development in Practice* 7(4): 363-74

Buchanan-Smith, M. and S. Davies (1995) *Famine, Early Warning and Response – The Missing Link*, London: IT Publications

Cuny, Frederick C. with Richard B. Hill (1999) *Famine, Conflict and Response: A Basic Guide*, New York, NY: Kumarian

Dyson, T. (1991) 'Demographic responses to famines in South Asia', *IDS Bulletin* 24 (4).

George, Alexander L. and Jane E. Holl (1997) *The Warning-Response Problem and Missed Opportunities in Preventative Diplomacy*, Report to the Carnegie Commission on Preventing Deadly Conflict, New York: Carnegie Corporation

Macrae, Joanna and Anthony Zwi (eds.) (1994) *War and Hunger: Rethinking International Responses to Complex Emergencies*, London: Zed Books with SCF

Maier, Karl (1998) 'The spoils of humanitarianism', *London Review of Books*, 19 February 1998

NCDO (1997) 'From Early Warning to Early Action: A Report on the European Conference on Conflict Prevention', Amsterdam: NCDO

Middleton, Neil and Phil O'Keefe (1998) *Disaster and Development: The Politics of Humanitarian Aid*, London: Pluto Press

Philo, Greg (1997) 'The Zaire Rebellion and the British Media: An Analysis of the Reporting of the Zaire Crisis in November 1996', a report undertaken by the Glasgow Media Group for the 'Dispatches from Disaster Zones' conference held in London in June 1998

Rupesinghe, Kumar (1994) 'Early warning of communal conflicts and humanitarian rises', The Journal of Ethno-Development 4(1)

Rupesinghe, Kumar (1995) 'Towards a Policy Framework for Advancing Preventative Diplomacy', International Alert Discussion Paper, London: International Alert

Sen, Amartya (1981) Poverty and Famines: An Essay on Entitlement and Deprivation, Oxford: Clarendon Press

Slim, Hugo (1997) 'International Humanitarianism's Engagement with Civil War in the 1990s: a Glance at Evolving Practice and Theory', Briefing Paper for ActionAid, Oxford: CENDEP

Slim, Hugo (1998) 'Sharing a Universal Ethic: Spreading the Principle of Humanity beyond Humanitarianism', talk given at ECHO/ODI conference held in London, 7 April 1998

Storey, Andy (1997) 'Non-neutral humanitarianism: NGOs and the Rwanda crisis', Development in Practice, 7(4): 384-94

Suzuki, Naoki (1998) Inside NGOs: Learning to Manage Conflicts between Headquarters and Field Offices, London: IT Publications

Swift, Jeremy (1989) 'Why are rural people vulnerable to famine?' IDS Bulletin 20(2): 8-15

de Waal, Alex (1994) Humanitarianism Unbound: Current Dilemmas Facing Multi-Mandate Relief Operations in Political Emergencies, Discussion Paper No5, London: African Rights

de Waal, Alex (1997) Famine Crimes: Politics and the Disaster Relief Industry in Africa, London: African Rights and The International African Institute

Capacity building: shifting the paradigms of practice

Allan Kaplan

' ... *development must start in somebody's sense; development is not about things you see* ... , *it is about the way somebody is developed in their thinking'*.(Rural fieldworker, cited in Oliver 1996)

So here we are again, once more pursuing the elusive concept of capacity building with a dogged relentlessness which would be amusing, were it not charged with such a sense of responsibility and commitment. There is an image which comes to mind: the concept of capacity building as a captured member of a foreign people (perhaps called Development), about whom we would like to know more but who remain a strange and elusive tribe, forever beyond the borders of our realm. We have captured this one member called Capacity Building, we have thrown him into prison, interrogated him, starved and beaten and isolated him, cursed and abused and threatened him to find out what he knows; but he looks back at us, silent and resentful and unforthcoming. In his silence he remains beyond our abilities to bully, and the very flailings of our desperation seem to build rather than sap the strength of his resolve and the ramparts of his defence. He may lie naked and bleeding in the corner of his cell, but the very silence of his presence mocks and belittles us. After so much battering at the doors of his knowledge, still we seem to have gleaned very little.

What if we were to change tack, to alter our approach? What if we were to treat him with respect, even deference? What if we were to give him his freedom, to demand nothing from him, to release him from the burden of our despair and simply allow him to live among us, and to come and go as he would choose? Perhaps friendship and trust would allow his real self to emerge. Perhaps he might even allow us to walk beside him when he went back to visit his people. Perhaps, under these circumstances, a simple question would elicit an honest answer. And we might even discover that the answer was obvious from the beginning, that in fact it had been staring us in the face all the time, but that we had been unable to see it, because we had obscured our own vision through our desperate battering of the messenger. Is it possible that we are pushing the answers that we seek ever deeper into obscurity through the frantic complexity of our search? In our attempts to unravel the knot, are we in danger of drawing it ever tighter?

Is it possible that capacity building demands such a radically new form of practice, such a radically new form of thinking, that our current approaches are doomed to failure — not because we lack adequate models or 'technologies', but because our very approach to the issue is inadequate? The image presented above, of course, is pure fantasy, but the questions that it prompts are not. This paper is an attempt to outline some of the fundamental shifts that such a new form of approach would entail. It is an attempt to look honestly at the phenomena as they present themselves to us, without presupposition or assumption.

In a previous paper (CDRA 1995) the Community Development Resource Association (CDRA) described organisations as open systems, comprising a number of interlinking and interdependent elements. We noted that these elements form a hierarchy of importance, and that therefore certain elements are more central than others in the attainment of organisational capacity. Thus we noted the following.

Elements of organisational life

A conceptual framework

The first requirement for an organisation with capacity, the 'prerequisite' on which all other capacity is built, is the development of a conceptual framework which reflects the organisation's understanding of the world. This is a coherent frame of reference, a set of concepts which allows the organisation to make sense of the world around it, to locate itself within that world, and to make decisions in relation to it. This framework is not a particular ideology or theory, it is not necessarily correct, and it is not impervious to criticism and change. It is not a precious, fragile thing, but a robust attempt to keep pace conceptually with the (organisational and contextual) developments and challenges facing the organisation. The organisation which does not have a competent working understanding of its world can be said to be incapacitated, regardless of how many other skills and competencies it may have.

Organisational 'attitude'

The second element concerns organisational 'attitude'. An organisation needs to build its confidence to act in and on the world in a way that it believes can be effective and have an impact. Put another way, it has to shift from 'playing the victim' to exerting some control, to believing in its own capacity to affect its circumstances. Another aspect of 'attitude' is accepting responsibility for the social and physical conditions 'out there', whatever the organisation faces in the world. This implies a shift from the politics of demand and protest to a more inclusive acceptance of the responsibilities which go with the recognition of human rights.

Whatever the history of oppression, marginalisation, or simply nasty circumstances that an individual or organisation has had to suffer, these 'attitudes' are the basis for effective action in the world. This is not a question of morality, or of fairness or justice; it is simply the way things work.

Vision and strategy

With clarity of understanding and a sense of confidence and responsibility comes the possibility of developing organisational vision and strategy. Understanding and responsibility lead to a sense of purpose in which the organisation does not lurch from one problem to the next, but manages to plan and implement a programme of action, and is able to adapt this programme in a rational and considered manner.

Organisational structure

Although these elements are not gained entirely sequentially, we may say that, once organisational aims and strategy are clear, it becomes possible to structure the organisation in such a way that roles and functions are clearly defined and differentiated, lines of communication and accountability untangled, and decision-making procedures transparent and functional. Put slightly differently, 'form follows function'; if one tries to do this the other way round, the organisation becomes incapacitated.

Acquisition of skills

The next step in the march towards organisational capacity, in terms of priority and sequence, is the growth and extension of individual skills, abilities, and competencies — the traditional terrain of training courses. Of course, skills also feature earlier; they can, in and of themselves, generate confidence and a sense of control. Development cannot be viewed simplistically; these phases overlap. Yet what emerges clearly from extensive experience is that there is a sequence, a hierarchy, an order. Unless organisational capacity has been developed sufficiently to harness training and the acquisition of new skills, training courses do not 'take', and skills do not adhere. The organisation which does not know where it is going and why, which has a poorly developed sense of responsibility for itself, and which is inadequately structured cannot make use of training courses and skills-acquisition programmes.

Material resources

Finally, an organisation needs material resources: finances, equipment, office space, and so on. Without an appropriate level of these, the organisation will always remain, in an important sense, incapacitated.

This perspective on what constitutes a capacitated organisation has been developed through years of reflection on the interventions that we have made to assist organisations, and through years of reflecting on the differences between those organisations which appear in some measure capable, and those which do not, or which appear less capable. But the most important insight it offers for capacity building is not simply a list of indicators which we can use as a framework for understanding capacity. Rather, it yields two far more radical insights with far-reaching consequences for practice.

First paradigm shift: from the tangible to the intangible

If you look towards the bottom of the hierarchy, you will see those things which are quantifiable, measureable, elements of organisational life which can easily be grasped and worked with. Material and financial resources, skills, organisational structures and systems — all these are easily assessed and quantified. In a word, they belong to the realm of material and visible things. If, however, we turn our attention to the top of the hierarchy, we enter immediately an entirely different realm: the realm of the invisible. Sure, organisations may have written statements of vision, of strategy, and of value, but these written statements do not in any sense indicate whether an organisation actually has a working understanding of its world. They do not indicate the extent to which an organisation feels responsible for its circumstances, or capable of having an effect on them, or the degree to which an organisation is really striving to become a learning organisation, or to what extent it is developing its staff, or manifesting a team spirit or endeavour. Furthermore, they do not indicate the extent to which an organisation is reflective, non-defensive, and self-critical. In short, the elements at the top of the hierarchy of elements of organisational life are ephemeral, transitory, not easily assessed or weighed. They are observable only through the effects that they have, and largely invisible to the organisation itself as well as to those practitioners who would intervene to build organisational capacity.

We are saying, then, that the most important elements in organisational life, those which largely determine the functioning of the organisation, are of a nature which make them more or less impervious to conventional approaches to capacity building. Consider this from two angles.

First, from the point of view of the organisation itself. If you interview organisations which suffer from a lack of capacity, you will find that they complain readily about lack of resources, lack of skills, inappropriate structures, an unfavourable history or an impossible context. In other words, they place the blame for their circumstances 'out there', on others or on their situation which is beyond their control, and specifically on those visible elements which lie at the bottom of the hierarchy. But, as Stephen Covey once said, 'For those who think their problems are "out there", that thinking is the problem'. Interview organisations which have developed a certain strength, robustness, or resilience, and you will discover that they generally take responsibility for their lack of capacity, that they attribute it to their own struggles with organisational culture and value, with lack of vision, lack of leadership and management, and so on. In other words, they manifest self-understanding. Capacitated organisations will manifest both stronger invisible elements and an ability to reflect on these elements — which is itself a feature of these stronger invisible elements situated at the top of the hierarchy.

Second, from the point of view of the capacity builder. If we examine honestly the kinds of intervention that we perform, either as donors or as development practitioners, we have to recognise that most of these are concentrated on the lower end of the hierarchy. Mainly, our efforts consist in providing resources or training courses. These are sometimes accompanied by, or preceded by, 'needs assessments', or even 'audits', which themselves concentrate on the visible, more tangible, elements which have little impact if the top elements of the hierarchy are undeveloped. We also engage in advice-giving more than in facilitation; we try to get organisations to make changes which we think will be good for them, which in itself can diminish the robustness of those elements at the top, rather than strengthen them through a form of facilitation which enables organisations to come to grips with their own issues, thus developing those top elements. Finally, and more recently, we have begun to help organisations with 'strategic planning'. This in itself would be a step in the right direction, were we to include the conceptual construction of the organisation's world, as well as forays into organisational culture, in the process. Unfortunately many strategic-planning exercises consist of piecemeal attempts (that is, unrelated to other elements) which comprise the setting of goals and objectives, the 'material aspects' of planning, leaving the organisation pretty much as incapacitated as before, with a 'plan of action' but without the ability to innovate, reflect on, and adapt the plan as circumstances and time progress. (These latter abilities are what really constitute capacity, but — at the risk of repetition — they are 'invisible').

In other words, organisational life ranges from the visible, more tangible aspects to those which are less visible, more intangible. It is these latter aspects which by and large determine organisational functioning, yet it is on the former aspects that so-called capacity-building interventions tend to focus. To anyone who works intensively with organisations, this assertion should appear obvious, even 'common sense', or at the very least clearly observable. Why then do we not shift the focus of our interventions?

The answer is as obvious as the dilemma itself: because we do not see — have not been trained or conditioned to see — things in this way. Because it presents a radical challenge to our customary ways of seeing the world. Because our conventional packages and products, our short-term *ad hoc* responses and interventions, are what we have, are what we use, and we will resist the move away from them for as long as possible. Because we take comfort in what we can provide, rather than in what may be really necessary. Because these kinds of intervention are sanctioned by donors. Because organisations have learned to ask for them. Because they are tangible and quantifiable. Because they can be delivered.

Because their delivery and assessment can be easily managed and monitored. Because our fieldworkers can be (relatively easily) trained to deliver them. Because they are hard-edged, unambiguous, and certain. Because they do not embroil us in the hazy shifting sands, in the uncertain worlds of fog and mirages which characterise the reality of organisational change processes. Because they do not challenge our certainties with the hazardous obstacles of organisational contradiction. Because they do not fundamentally challenge us.

Organisational change processes are contradictory, ambiguous, and obtuse. They are long-term and not easily observed. Most of all, they are unpredictable. Therefore, while they can be influenced, they lie forever beyond our control. The world of practice in the realm of the intangibles at the top of the organisational hierarchy of complexity is a world which is itself fraught with complexity. It demands constant self-reflection, reflection on practice, if practice is to be improved. It demands the exercise of facilitation skills which are labelled 'soft' but which are the most difficult, demanding, and challenging skills to master: skills of observation and listening, the ability to ask the right question, the holding of ambiguity, uncertainty, and contradiction, the ability to draw enthusiasm out of exhaustion and cynicism, overcoming resistance to change, empathy, and the tenacity to work over long periods with little direct product to show for it – to name but a few. In other words, it demands developmental skills; and, although we talk a lot about the development of capacity, we tend to concentrate on the delivery of 'product'. In short, we do not practise what the situation demands; rather, we produce what can most easily be delivered.

The paradigm shift that is demanded by the above argument is more than radical: it should shatter our complacency and throw the entire edifice of current development practice into doubt. Yet the ability to work with intangibles is only the first of the two paradigm shifts which loom across the boundaries of our practice. The second goes something like this.

Second paradigm shift: from static model to developmental reading

While it may be true that organisations can be seen as systems of interlocking elements, arranged in a hierarchy of complexity from those which are less tangible to those which are more so, this perspective is not always real. It is not always the case that capacity-building interventions should begin with the intangible before they move on to the more visible. The reality is far more complex than any one theory or model can contain. It all depends on where a particular organisation is at a particular time, and on what kind of organisation it is.

A small, new NGO has a different level of impact and 'sophistication' from a large NGO which is established and effective. The larger NGO has more need of 'sophisticated organisational conditions', because development and growth in capacity implies greater sophistication of organisational processes, functions, and structures. While the new NGO will need clarity of vision, it may not yet have the problems which often accompany organisational vision-building activities within the older NGO. The needs of individual staff members in terms of skills — and therefore training courses — will differ at different stages of the organisation's life, as will material-resource constraints and assets. Similarly, with respect to structure, organisations will have different needs at different stages of their lives. At times, an increasingly complex structure will be called for; at other times, 'destructuring' will be required.

Or, for example, with regard to community-based organisations (CBOs), these can grow to become highly sophisticated organisations, but generally in southern Africa at present they are far less developed and sophisticated, in organisation terms, than their NGO counterparts. And within the organisational form of the CBO itself, a wide range of different capacities and competencies exists. There are communities which lack any organisational representation at all. There are embryonic CBOs, consisting of little more than a (theoretically) rotating committee, without a thought-through strategy, resources, or clarity of roles and functions. Then there is the CBO with employees, differentiated strategies, and office space and equipment.

All of these different stages of organisational development, from no organisation through organisation building through organisational differentiation to highly sophisticated national NGOs with mega-budgets, (theoretically) represent increasing capacity. And each of the elements of organisational life mentioned above recur — with their different intervention demands — at different stages in the capacity-building game.

A CBO might be struggling with the transition in 'attitude' from resistance to responsibility, while an NGO is dealing with attitudinal issues which it refers to as organisational culture – issues of meaning, principle, and motivation. An NGO in its early phases may function healthily with a flat, informal structure; later, in order to maintain the same level of health, a more hierarchical structure may be called for. A CBO may have achieved greater organisational clarity through clarifying its constitutional or membership structures, only to discover that it degenerates into chaos and conflict when it begins to employ staff without clarifying the relationship between its operational structure (staff) and its constitutional structure.

The point is that, although there is a basic order in which competency in the elements is attained, and in which organisational capacity building occurs, needs change with respect to all these elements as the organisation develops. Even more importantly, although intervention or work done on any one of these elements will not prove effective unless sufficient work has been done on the preceding elements in the hierarchy — for example, training will not 'take' when organisational vision, culture, and structure are unresolved, and it does not help to secure resources when the organisation is not equipped to carry out its tasks — even so, these elements are interdependent, and one may have to work on a number of levels simultaneously in certain situations in order to be effective. And even more importantly — and perhaps paradoxically — while the concept of a hierarchy provides us with a guide, there are many times when one has to work on lower elements in the hierarchy in order to have an effect on higher elements. For example, there are times when the acquisition of an appropriate structure will have a beneficial effect on organisational culture where work on that culture alone has proved ineffective. Such organisational examples abound throughout the hierarchy.

What this means, in essence, is that although one may have an explanatory and sensible model of what constitutes organisational health, competence, and capacity, there are two aspects of organisational reality which confound simplistic attempts to impose this model on specific situations. The first is that, while every organisation may share similar features, nevertheless each is unique, both in itself and in terms of its stage of development, and this uniqueness demands unique, singular, and specifically different responses. Second, while the model may adequately describe the elements of organisational capacity and even the order of their acquisition, it cannot predict or determine organisational change processes, which are complex, ambiguous, and often contradictory. And organisational change, rather than a static model describing organisational elements, is the essence of capacity building.

In other words, being equipped with a perspective on how organisations function, while it is a prerequisite for effective capacity building, is no substitute for direct observation of particular organisational realities in which one is wishing to intervene. One needs the intelligence, acuity, mobility, and penetrating perception to be able to 'read' the particular nature of a specific situation if one hopes to be effective in organisational capacity building. It is all too easy to presume, to make judgements, to impose one's understanding, to compare one organisational situation with another. It is all too easy to base one's interventions on a theoretical model rather than on an accurate assessment of the situation at hand. It is all too easy to design general capacity-building interventions in the office, rather than make specific and individual interventions based on observations in the field. It is all too easy to design general capacity-building interventions for mass delivery, rather than individually specific and nuanced interventions. Once again, general capacity-building interventions, programmes, courses, mass-based delivery vehicles: all these are easy to manage, easy to quantify, to raise money for, to fund, to control. But they are all inadequate.

There are too few NGOs, too few donors, too few development practitioners, who take the time to read specific situations in order to design appropriate and necessarily transitory interventions based on an intelligent reading. (They are necessarily transitory, because the organisation being worked on will develop beyond a particular intervention as a result of the effectiveness of that intervention.) The radical nature of the paradigm shift we are suggesting here is that development practitioners are normally trained to deliver interventions — or packages or programmes — rather than to read the developmental phase at which a particular organisation may be and then to devise a response appropriate to that organisation at that particular time and to nothing else. The ability to read a developmental situation requires a background theory — which few practitioners employ — but it also requires an understanding of development; the ability to observe closely without judgement; sensitivity; empathy; an ability to penetrate to the essence of a situation, to separate the wheat from the chaff, so to speak; the ability to create an atmosphere of trust out of which an organisation may yield up the secrets that it will normally hold back (even from itself) in defensive reaction; the ability really to hear and listen and see; the ability to resist the short sharp expert response which is usually more gratifying to the practitioner than to the organisation;

and then, out of an accurate reading, to bring (or arrange for) the appropriate response, one which may not even be within the ambit of the NGO's normal services.

This is a paradigm shift, a radically different approach, a far cry from the normal delivery mechanisms of NGOs, donors, and governments who hope to build capacity. It embraces the real meaning of 'people-centred development', to which we pay lip-service in terms of policy but hardly ever think through to its consequences in terms of practice. Perhaps such a paradigm shift deserves the coining of a new cliché: 'organisation-centred capacity building'. Yet it is precisely such phrases which confuse the issue: we are specifically saying that an adequate response to capacity building, albeit a complex one which turns all of our most cherished attitudes into disarray, is one which concentrates on the actual practice of the development practitioner, rather than on policy statements or well-worded programmes or well-designed courses.

Some consequences

What are the skills which we normally think of as associated with development practice and capacity building? Whatever they are in specific detail, the generic sense of these skills is captured by the one phrase, the one concept, which always arises when talking about these issues — namely, 'train the trainers'. This is our conventional response when confronted with the demand for capacity-building skills. A wealth of implied meaning underlies this phrase. That what we require for capacity building is trainers. That these trainers can be trained — which implies that they are to 'deliver' specific and fixed 'products' (perhaps courses or programmes). And generally, training implies that the trainee is to learn the skills which are to be 'imparted' by the trainer; also that replication at an exponential rate is both desirable and attainable.

This is one response. The other is to concentrate on the setting up of structures or policies which create an environment through which capacity may be built. We know what is needed, and we must thus set the conditions in place that will allow its realisation.

Both of the above responses are valid and important, but they are not always appropriate, and we may undermine their effectiveness by the very strength of our focus on them. Besides, their danger lies in the fact that they are clearly a response which we can master relatively easily, and therefore they may ensnare us in the seduction of their appeal to our abilities, rather than challenge us by the relevance of their application.

They are conventional responses, and their very conventionality should make us suspicious, because the success of our capacity-building efforts to date has been minimal.

The more radical response is to consider ourselves 'artists of the invisible', continually having to deal with ambiguity and paradox, uncertainty in the turbulence of change, new and unique situations coming to us from out of a future of which we have had as yet little experience. This more radical response would imply that we need to develop a resourcefulness out of which we can respond, rather than being trained in past solutions, in fixed mindsets, and trained behaviours which replicate particular patterns and understandings, instead of freeing us to respond uniquely to unique situations.

From the perspective of this paradigm shift there are new abilities which we as development practitioners need to develop — note, *abilities which we need to develop*, not skills in which we need to be trained. Some of these abilities may include the following:

- The ability to find the right question which may enable an organisation to take the next step on its path of development, and to hold a question so that it functions as a stimulus to exploration, rather than demanding an immediate solution, and to help organisations to do the same.
- The ability to hold the tension generated by ambiguity and uncertainty, rather than seek immediate resolution.
- The ability to observe accurately and objectively, to listen deeply, so that invisible realities of the organisation become manifest.
- The ability to use metaphor and imagination to overcome the resistance to change, to enable an organisation to see itself afresh, and to stimulate creativity.
- The ability to help others to overcome cynicism and despair and to kindle enthusiasm.
- Integrity, and the ability to generate the trust that will allow the organisation and its members to really 'speak' and reveal themselves.
- The ability to reflect honestly on one's own interventions, and to enable others to do the same.
- The ability to 'feel' into the 'essence' of a situation.
- The ability to empathise (not sympathise), so that both compassion and confrontation can be used with integrity in helping an organisation to become unstuck.
- The ability to conceptualise, and thus to analyse strategy with intelligence.

The list can go on, but such lists carry in themselves the dangers of new answers which become set routines and received methodologies. The true import of the paradigm shifts described in this paper is that we must remain awake, full of interest and wonder and awe, open and vulnerable, if we hope to find the resilience to respond to the diverse array of situations which challenge us as capacity builders. Above all, answers dampen our edge. It is living with questions that maintains the charge of our attention, and more than anything else we are called on to pay attention.

So, to conclude on a very open note, we include some questions which emerge for us if the perspective presented above is recognised as valid.

- With respect to government-sponsored, nationwide development initiatives which need to 'deliver' in the short term (and similar initiatives in the non-government sector): what needs to be in place so that they can really contribute to local-level capacity building?

- What are the implications for the way in which funding for capacity-building interventions is currently provided, and what needs to change in funding practice?

- What are the implications in respect of the current vogue for outcomes-based project planning, logical framework strategic documents, and 'business planning'?

- And what then are the implications for development management and leadership, monitoring and evaluation mechanisms, and the concept of the discrete 'development' project itself?

- Can the tendering process, with its rigid frames of reference, have any place in developmental interventions? Can it be adapted?

- Which kinds of organisations— with respect to both organisational type and organisational functioning — are capable of effectively deploying capacity-building practitioners?

- Who, of the organisations we know at present, is taking responsibility for developmental capacity-building interventions as described above? Who and where are the capacity builders?

- Who is, who could be, who should be performing developmental capacity building? And how would organisational conditions have to shift to allow them to perform effectively?

Acknowledgement

This paper was initially prepared for the December 1996 NGO Week held in Johannesburg, and was distributed in South Africa by Olive in its MULBERRY (Mostly Unread Literature Bearing Extraordinarily Rich and Relevant Yields) Series, Number 1, 1997.

References

Oliver, Di (1996) 'Capacity Building', unpublished MA thesis, University of Natal, Durban

CDRA (1995) *Annual Report 1994/95: Capacity Building: Myth or Reality?*, Woodstock: CDR

Gendering the millennium: globalising women

Haleh Afshar

Introduction

As the twentieth century came to a close in the West, the Muslims were three-quarters of the way into their fourteenth solar and in the first decade of their fifteenth lunar century. The ancient Persians would have been three-quarters of the way through their second millennium, and the ancient Chinese and Egyptians well into their third. Thus, as the differing conceptions of time move on in different places, it is worth looking at the vast distances that divide women across the globe, even as they are coming ever closer together in the global workforce.

The West is of course mesmerised by the proximity of the global village and the expanding links through the airways and networks that make communication a matter of an instant and help to create an almost unified world vision. But that vision is one that is firmly rooted in the West, and dominated by the Anglophones and their values. It has less and less time and space for those who fall outside its embrace. Hence, paradoxically, the ability to communicate may well have opened more avenues for misunderstandings, over-simplifications, and stereotypical conceptions of 'others'. Yet global communication could have created the global vision which would have shown the way forward for feminised employment. There were reasons to hope for the emergence of solidarity among industrial workers; the experiences of women working in the factories of transnational corporations mirrored the fragmented labour processes that had dominated the work patterns of the industrialised countries. But the relocation of some production processes to the home (Mitter 1986), and of other industrial processes to the Free Trade Zones

(FTZs), created divides and competition rather than unity. Yet it would have been easy to see that, even for those who have been integrated into the global market, the twenty-first century does not seem to be laden with hope and peace. There is a continuous erosion of rights and entitlements at the margins of the global economy; and an ever-widening gap between the rich and the poor that has not been helped by the relentless penetration of capitalism all over the world. The failure of modernisation and subsequently of globalisation has in turn helped to create a backlash and a return towards imaginary pasts that are extremely problematic – not least for women, who are both an important sector of workers in the global economy and also number significantly among the supporters of those who are returning to alternative views of the world, faith, and eternity (Afshar and Barrientos 1999).

To understand the ideological as well as the economic gap, and the reaction to its impact, we must move away from the blanket assumption that by the end of the twentieth century the world was no more than a global village with a considerable degree of homogeneity and integration. What requires analysis is not so much the premise, but the method of assessment, which uses the same tools and the same calculations in the hope of obtaining similar results. Many Third World feminists have long argued that it would be preferable to consider the specificities of situations (Afshar 1985). What I wish to address, however, is the interactions between the global and the local, and the divisions and counter-actions that have arisen directly as a reaction against the globalisation of cultures, values, moralities, and economies. Islamism in general and Iranian Islamification in particular are located very much at this juncture. Despite rising prosperity, undeniable economic growth, and rapid modernisation in the 1960s and 1970s, there has since been what may be called a 'backlash' in much of the Muslim world. This was seen by its participants as a 'return' to their roots and a 'rejection' of global capitalism and consumerism. This rejection has had the unequivocal support of a number of intellectual women who, in the knowledge of what feminism had to offer, chose the Islamic alternative (Afshar 1998; Karam 1998).

Globalisation

Globalisation is occurring in a complex world that has undergone rapid changes over the past decades. The entire concept of production has moved away from the 'just in case' model to the 'just in time' one

(Mitter 1986), with women regarded as a flexible, mobile, and cheap resource, increasingly pulled into production lines that stretch from the smallest agricultural producers to the largest of world factories – all producing for a global market. The various analyses of this process reflect the difficulties of coming to terms with its multidimensional nature and of containing it within the formal boundaries of theory and grand narratives. From a development perspective, much of the analysis of globalisation has been built on the overarching influence of the expansion of transnational corporations (TNCs) and the new international division of labour.

From an economic perspective, globalisation needs to be seen in the context of structural adjustment and stabilisation, which, through the policy of conditionality adopted by the IMF and the World Bank, have affected most developing countries over the past decade. These policies forced many countries into an economic and political straightjacket that would integrate them into the global process. The effect of these policies on women has been profound. As the consequences of structural adjustment have become institutionalised in the global development process, the coping strategies developed by women in times of crisis have now become embedded in their daily lives. These measures are far from simple, and the analysis must separate out the layers that make up the contradictory ways in which globalisation has affected women at different levels and in different countries.

Discussions of the advance of globalisation have on the whole concentrated on the industrial dimension, and the inability of capitalism to 'develop' equally. The main focus has tended to be on the specific localities where TNCs have operated, and on the specific effects of industrialisation and the increase of industrial employment for certain groups of women in developing countries. But the all-embracing tendencies within the process of globalisation must not be accepted without analysing its effects on non-industrial employment and economic activity, as well as on different political ideologies in different countries. Some analyses of global commodity chains have moved beyond industry as the main focus, and feminist writers have begun disaggregating the specificities of women's experiences (Afshar and Barrientos 1999). Globalisation has also been analysed from the political, spatial, and physical standpoint of uneven development. One view is to see it as a necklace connecting centres of consumer affluence to localities of production that are strung around the world, acting as links in the global chain (Amin 1997). This approach also takes a global view of the process of uneven development; a process in which the winners and losers are now distributed across the world, where the gap between the rich and the poor is widening, and the gendered wage gap is yet to close. Thus globalisation links 'world managers' to those whom they manage and permits instant contact and immediate response to market needs (Frobel et al. 1980). It also creates both telecommunicative and electronic interactions that keep a permanently open window through which the élites may observe one another. The proliferation of satellite and cable communications also provides the masses with the voyeuristic opportunity to watch the rich at play on the large and small screen. The only benefits that result for the poor are more colourful dreams and aspirations, and moments of oblivion to ease their long days of work.

Revivalism

But the global peep-show has not resulted in universal enchantment with the West and its values. In many ways, the globalisation of work and poverty and the failure of paid employment to liberate women have accelerated disillusionment with industrialisation and modernisation, and helped to create a backlash against the West and its values. This is particularly evident in the Middle East. Women have been among the high-profile supporters of what has been called 'fundamentalism'; a word that was coined to explain a Christian phenomenon and which does not translate into Arabic or Persian. For Muslims, the movement is understood to be a radical revivalist phenomenon, returning to the sources to regain a better understanding of morality and probity, and to secure a return to a more human way of life.

There are large numbers of women who feel that Islam is inherently pro-women. They claim that much of what Islamic teaching is about is similar, though preferable, to what feminists have been asking for and not getting for more than a century, the world over.

It is such women who in countries like Iran, Egypt, and Turkey actively support Islamification (Afshar 1998; Gole 1996; Karam 1998). These are not ignorant or 'backward' so-called 'traditionalists'. Often they are intelligent, Western-educated intellectuals who have thought the problems through and have come to the conclusion that Islam may deliver what feminism has not, despite appearances to the contrary (Franks, forthcoming). They have engaged critically with Western feminist analyses of women and their positions within society and the family and they may reject some of the solutions offered by white, middle-class, Western women. They argue that a different and preferable form of liberation can be found by returning to the sources of Islam. In the post-modern deconstructing phase of feminisms, at the threshold of the next Christian millennium, it is possible to look more closely at the arguments that these women present and without the blinkers of prejudice, whether male or Western or both. This is not an easy task when all too often women from both the East and the West tend to think of each other in the prejudiced, oversimplified terms popularised by the mass media.

Islamist women began expressing their concern about what they saw as the failure of Western feminism, which, after all the years of continuous struggle, has offered women the opportunity to be more like men. While academia ponders on the problems of masculinity, the workplace in much of the West continues to a large extent to work 'man-hours' and employ 'manpower' to 'man' the desks and the factories. But the labour market is no panacea. To succeed, women must be better than men, work longer hours, and be wedded to their jobs. Even then they cannot go far (Rahnavard, n.d.). Most women get drafted into badly paid, part-time, dead-end jobs. After all, they should think themselves lucky to get any pay at all for doing the same jobs that they do at home for nothing. The assumption is that their first priority is and should be their unpaid domestic work. In any case, sooner or later even those women who do succeed hit the glass ceiling. Taking this simplistic perspective, Islamist women argue that feminists fail as quasi-men and also fail as women. Much of this failure is because most women, world wide, choose to become mothers at some point, and most employers and governments brand them as mothers forever.

Islamist women have taken a position that can now be contextualised within the wider post-modern feminist analysis. They contend that the quest for equality has failed because it has not recognised the differences that exist between men and women, and the differences that exist between women of different classes, creeds, and cultures. They prefer the Islamic alternative that recognises that women are sometimes young, married, and mothers – and often old, freed of domesticity, and potential participants in the public domain (Afkhami 1995; Afshar 1994 and 1998; Ahmed 1992; Karam 1998). They argue that in their struggles to extract equal rights from men, feminists have fallen into the trap of becoming failed men.

Muslims, it is contended, need no such struggle, since the laws of Islam as stated in the Koran are God-given. Women are recognised as different and valued as such. They have non-negotiable rights to be paid as wives and mothers and to be respected as women. Since the inception of the faith, marriage in Islam has been a contractual agreement between consenting partners. No marriage can be consummated without the payment of an agreed fee, *mehrieh*, to the bride. What is more, marriage does not have to be a life-sentence and an eternal prison. It is a contract that provides a way out for those who find it difficult, by making divorce legitimate. Of course, men do better when it comes to divorce. They have the unilateral right to initiate divorce. After all, even Islam is a patriarchal faith. Nevertheless, once marriage becomes a matter of formal contract, then women can stipulate conditions that make divorce far from easy. And it is not only élite women who can safeguard their marriages through the contract. Many years ago, when I was working in an Iranian village, a sad old peasant came to me for advice. He had married a difficult wife and was desperate to divorce her. But to do so he had to repay her *mehrieh*. Like many Iranian women, she had agreed the consummation sum but had deferred the payment until such time that the husband wished to divorce her. His difficulty was that she had stipulated that he should pay her a pillowcase full of flies' wings. The old man had been killing flies for nearly 40 years and was yet to fill the pillow!

A Muslim husband is also duty-bound to keep his wife in the style to which she is accustomed. Although 'kept', Muslim women do not lose their identity on marriage, nor have they ever lost their independent economic rights and entitlements. They have never become legal chattel and have always retained what is theirs. Although they inherit half as much as their brothers, Islamist women argue that what is theirs is theirs alone and that they are also entitled to have half of what is the man's.

Muslim women have for 14 centuries been legally entitled to inherit as daughters and as sisters. In addition, Muslims do not regard motherhood as an unpaid and de-skilling job. Muslim mothers must be 'maintained' and paid for suckling their babies. These are God-given rights that date back 1400 years. So while feminists in the West were fighting for wages for housework, which they are yet to receive, Iranian women instituted parliamentary legislation to ensure that they retain what is theirs: the *ojratolmessle* (Afshar 1998).

Even the much-derided polygamy is not always as terrible as might have been thought (Dennis 1991). The arrival of a second wife who assumes a domestic role may enable a first wife to concentrate on her own commercial activities.

It is, therefore, hardly surprising that by the start of the twenty-first century Islamist women are returning to their roots, re-discovering Islam and demanding their rights. They are disillusioned with the undifferentiated quest for equality. They present a different form of feminism: one that is rooted in a critique of the priorities selected by mainstream Western struggles for women's liberation. They argue that the road to success for women in the West is through their bodies. When something does not sell, when a drink, a car, even a credit card is to be foisted on to the unsuspecting public, the advertisers drape a half-naked woman around it and parade her across the screens, the walls, and the lamp-posts. Women have become part and parcel of the advertising process. But it is only certain women, the ones with the longest legs, the slimmest hips, the sexiest bodies, who can make the grade. Meanwhile, ordinary women the world over compare themselves with these stunning examples and 'fail'. So the liberation process has created an almost universal hunger for the beauty myth. Women are forever dieting, forever painting their faces, forever changing their hair colour, the colour of their clothes, the shapes of their eyebrows. Nor is there any space for them to grow old gracefully. The pursuit of youth and beauty creates generation after generation of anorexic, disillusioned women who punish themselves for not being beautiful enough.

Islamist women believe that there could be an alternative: women could choose to cover themselves. They argue that the veil, which is not an Islamic requirement, can help them become human beings rather than objects. They wear the veil to claim the gaze and to become the ones who observe the world. In a world where men set the fashions and standards, and where men take the photographs and make the films, the only way to subvert the process is to don the veil and become minds rather than bodies.

Of course, Islamification is far more attractive in theory than it is in practice. Women choose Islam because they feel that it liberates them, allows them to have proper life-cycles, and to be rewarded for what they do. Undoubtedly, there is such a thing as Islamist feminism (Afshar 1998; Karam 1998), but it must engage with Islamist patriarchies. All too often, Muslim men in governments fail to oblige. As soon as they come to power, they cover the women up and opt for polygamy (Afshar 1982); neither of which is, strictly speaking, a divinely sanctioned practice. Islamist women argue that the God of Islam was never misogynist, and that the laws of Islam cannot be changed by the wishes of the men. So when Islamist governments come to power, the long journey to gain Islamic rights for Islamist feminists begins.

Islamist feminism in Iran

The case of Iranian women over the past 20 years is a clear example of what the process can mean. Although women were at the forefront of the revolutionary movement, they were the first to be eliminated from all positions of power after the revolution. The preamble to the post-revolutionary Constitution clearly stated that men and women were not equal. The new government 'freed' women of the objectification imposed on them by Western-style liberalisation – by shutting them up in their homes. They were given the 'critical duty' of motherhood, and placed firmly in the bosom of the family. They became guardians of the family, which was declared to be the fundamental basis of the Islamic Republic (Article 10).

Having domesticated them by law, the theocracy began an enforced exclusion of women from the public domain. In March 1979, one month after his return to Iran, Khomeini sacked all female judges and ordered the compulsory veiling of all women. In May that year, co-education was banned. In June, married women were barred from attending school, and the government began closing down workplace nurseries. In July, seaside resorts were sexually segregated, and women were flogged in public for transgression of the new rules. Morality codes were imposed, and for the first time women were executed on charges of prostitution and moral degradation. By October, the government was dismantling the checks placed on men by revising personal laws; men regained the unreciprocated right to polygamy, to unilateral divorce at will, and the right to prevent their wives from entering into paid employment. The official age of marriage for women was reduced from 18 to 13 years, and men regained the automatic custody of their children after divorce.

Universities were closed for years to cleanse them of corrupt Western ideologies. When they were re-opened, women were excluded from most faculties. They were to be herded into appropriate feminine subjects, such as literature – but not art, which meant standing about in the dangerous outdoors and looking too closely at undesirable objects!

The way forward looked dark indeed. But it is at such times that Islamist women are glad to have inalienable rights given to them by the God of Islam. In Islam there are no intermediaries between people and their God. The religious establishment is respected for its knowledge, but is ascribed no sanctity. Thus women can, and do, legitimately set about discovering the laws of God for themselves, without the help (or rather the hindrance) of male theologians and their teachings. No human being can legislate against God's wishes, and so for the past 20 years Islamist Iranian women have strenuously worked to prove that what men have been imposing in the name of Islam is not what God has decreed.

They have accepted the veil and thus become the public face of Islamification. But they have successfully used their own interpretations of the Koranic laws to regain access to almost all university faculties. They did so by demonstrating that Islam demands of all Muslims to be educated to the best of their ability. They have regained much ground in the judiciary and have made divorce and polygamy subject to rulings by the Family Courts. The reduced age of marriage is now being contested as a misunderstanding of what true Islamic teachings are about.

The successful battle for Islamic rights by women has had unexpected outcomes. Since they are the standard-bearers of the faith and the public face of Islamism in Iran, women demand their Islamic rights absolutely legitimately in the name of the faith and the revolution. It is hard to brand them as subversive oppositional groups. The élite Islamist women have emerged from the very core of the revolution; they are often closely related to leading theologians, and their arguments are always firmly rooted in the Koranic teachings. They are fighting for Islam. Nevertheless, what they are doing is opening up a path towards much greater participation by civil society in Islamic politics. They have created a legitimate form of opposition to draconian measures that cannot be easily denied by the theocracy. The need to gain internal legitimacy and establish an international credibility, particularly in the eyes of the Islamic Middle Eastern countries, has made the State gradually more responsive to women's demands.

Women have managed to demonstrate their centrality in Iranian politics. They are determined to extract a price for becoming the emblem of Islamification. They want to dictate the meaning of the Islam that their veiled presence has upheld: it is something to aspire to and something that accommodates their needs. They have refused to be brow-beaten by the more misogynistic of the religious leaders and have insisted that the revolution should pay them their due for both supporting it from the beginning and for becoming an exemplar to the rest of the Islamic world. Iranian women have constructed a multifaceted Islam which is increasingly delivering what elsewhere could have been called feminist demands. Elite Islamist women have set up new standards in the light of the lives of the women of Islam at the inception of the faith: standards that the State has had to meet in order to live up to its own slogans and avowals of fairness and revolutionary concerns.

In the absence of organised political parties, Iranian women, both secular and religious, have found common cause and have acted as an important political force in the more recent elections. They have bridged the large gap that divides the believers from the non-believers, by fighting together for the cause of women. The road has been long and hard. But they remain indomitable. Despite Khomeini's opposition to female suffrage in the 1960s, after the revolution he and the post-revolutionary State recognised the valuable contributions that women had made to the cause and rewarded them by lowering the age of suffrage to 16 years. Women have used this right wisely. From the very beginning, the Islamic parliament, Majlis, has always had a few female representatives. In the 1990s, however, the women's vote gained momentum, and the women Representatives, who eventually increased to more than a dozen, managed to push through a series of laws that at least firmed up the ground and in some cases opened new opportunities for women. Throughout, the arguments for women's liberation have been couched in the language of Islam, and every demand has been backed by the relevant textual religious evidence. They have created a new, dynamic Islam, specifically suited to their needs. They have accepted that they are different from men, but have contested fiercely that in no way can that difference be interpreted as women's inferiority to men. Their arguments have been both scholarly and politically astute, and they have obliged many of the leading male theologians and politicians to reconsider their views and their politics. It is no longer acceptable publicly to denounce women as inferior. As the presidential elections of 1997 clearly demonstrated, those, like the contender Nateq Nuri, who ignored women or denied their rights, lost out. Against the expectations of the theoreticians and the political architects of the revolution, Iranian women are now at the centre of the political stage. President Ayatollah Seyed Mohammad Khatami recognised this reality and in his inaugural speech, in August 1997, declared his commitment to furthering the cause of women in Iran. Eventually he gave a vice-presidential post to a woman, the first to have reached such heights since the revolution.

The struggle has been long and hard and the religious establishment has done its best to deny women's rights. But there have been some remarkable supporters among the Islamic scholars, such as Hojatoleslam Seyed Mohsen Saeedzadeh. One of the best revolutionary scholars, he teaches in the holy city of Qum. But the religious establishment, unable to silence women, has resorted to arresting Saeedzadeh. At the time of writing, he was under arrest awaiting trial by the religious courts!

So although Islamist women in Iran have managed to extract much from their government, they, in common with most women around the world, have not succeeded in breaking down the patriarchal power structure that rules over them. Even the laws of the God of Islam, who must be obeyed by all Muslims, have all too often been interpreted by men against the interests of women.

Challenges for feminists, questions for development agencies

Nevertheless, Iranian women's relative success in their own country has posed some difficult questions for some feminists and developmentalists who wish to be advocate for and facilitate – rather than impose – aid. It is relatively difficult to contextualise these changes within the mainstream intellectual and economic frameworks. It could be argued that in the domain of politics the need to legitimise universal positions in terms of particular conditions has enabled women to re-construct the Islamic discourse radically and to carve out not only a place, but actually a central position, within both the theory and practice of Islamic politics in Iran. This specific trajectory, however, does not lend itself easily to mainstream analytical forms and, like much of the more recent fragmented feminist experiences, must be located firmly within its own historical and geographical context. For development agencies who have a commitment to empowerment and respect for diversity (Afshar 1998; Rowlands 1997), it becomes essential to move away from centralised uniform positions to differentiated ones that are formed according to the exigencies of time and place and the perceived needs of different peoples (Afshar 1985).

Thus, although globalisation has linked the world economically and has facilitated easier intellectual exchanges among the international intelligentsia, the gaps between cultures, histories, and millennia have not been bridged. But despite the wide disparities, what allows a degree of optimism is the ability of many women worldwide to recognise and accept their differences, while retaining their solidarity in the struggle against patriarchy – and maybe, even, masculinities.

References

Afkhami, M. (ed.) (1995) *Faith and Freedom*, London: I.B. Tauris

Afshar, Haleh (1982) 'Khomeini's teachings and their implications for women' in Azar Tabari and Nahid Yeganeh (eds.) *The Shadow of Islam*, London: Zed Books

Afshar, Haleh (ed.) (1985) *Women, Work and Ideology in the Third World*, London: Tavistock

Afshar, Haleh (1994) *Why Fundamentalism? Iranian Women and their Support for Islam*, Department of Politics Working Paper No. 2, York: University of York

Afshar, Haleh (1998) *Islam and Feminisms: An Iranian Case Study*, Basingstoke: Macmillan

Afshar, Haleh and Stephanie Barrientos (eds.) (1999) *Women, Globalisation and Fragmentation in the Developing World*, Basingstoke: Macmillan

Ahmed, Leila (1992) *Women and Gender in Islam*, London: Yale University Press

Amin, Samir (1997) *Capitalism in the Age of Globalisation*, London: Zed Books

Dennis, Carolyne (1991) 'Constructing a "career" under conditions of crisis and structural adjustment: the survival strategies of Nigerian women' in Haleh Afshar (ed.) *Women, Development and Survival in the Third World*, Harlow: Longman

Franks, Myfanwy (forthcoming) *Women and Revivalism*, Basingstoke: Macmillan

Frobel, F., J. Heinrichs and O. Kreye (1980) *The New International Division of Labour*, Cambridge: Cambridge University Press

Gole, Nilufer (1996) *The Forbidden Modern: Civilisation and Veiling*, Ann Arbor: University of Michigan Press

Mitter, Swasti (1986) *Common Fate, Common Bond: Women in the Global Economy*, London: Pluto Press

Karam, Azza. M. (1998) *Women, Islamisms and the State: Contemporary Feminisms in Egypt*, Basingstoke: Macmillan

Rahnavard, Zahra (no date) *Toloueh Zaneh Mosalman*, Tehran: Mahboubeh Publication

Rowlands, Jo (1997) *Questioning Empowerment*, Oxford: Oxfam

Gender in development: a long haul – but we're getting there!

Josefina Stubbs

The women's and feminist movements have revolutionised the concept of what constitutes the public and private, and have brought to the understanding and business of politics the need to recognise individuality and to see diversity as something legitimate. These are fundamental contributions to building democracy. While we cannot ignore the downsides of aid, the political and financial support provided by the international development co-operation agencies has been important in helping to consolidate and 'globalise' feminist agendas within civil society, within governments, and within these agencies themselves.

With a wealth of achievements but also of frustrations, the women's movements, women's NGOs, and international development co-operation agencies all suffer the painful paradoxes that have accompanied the advances that have already been made, as well as the challenges brought by the new economic, political, and social realities now being experienced in both the South and North. These stumbling-blocks are not insurmountable. However, they do demand a clear-sighted analysis of our supposed victories and a measured review of the mistakes made along the way. The situation calls for a new generation of women who, on the basis of their own needs and contexts and within their domestic and work spheres, can articulate appropriate strategies and take a fresh approach to the continuing struggle for equality and equity between men and women.

In the following paragraphs I will talk about my experience as a feminist woman working for an international development co-operation agency. I will try to identify the successes as well as the setbacks and the stumbling-blocks that have impeded us from making a greater advance in gender equity and improving women's quality of life. I also analyse the paradoxes that are peculiar to international co-operation agencies as they incorporate a gender perspective in their strategies and development programmes. My information, reflections, and experience essentially relate to Latin America and the Caribbean. Aware as I am of the cultural and historical differences that give specific forms to women's resistance in other parts of the world, I in no way assume that women who do not share my own background should necessarily identify with or feel represented by these reflections.

Feminism, or the world seen from the inside looking out

The feminist movements of the last three decades have revolutionised the concept and practice of politics. Women have sought to create a new social subject, whose stimulus for political action, both collective and individual, is defined by the prohibitions, exclusions, and violence that they experience. Taking this reality as their jumping-off point, feminists have drawn on their inexhaustible energy for change to question the State, governments, and the political economy of the generally repressive régimes that were in power throughout Latin America and the Caribbean. There has been no social, political, public, or private space where women have not raised their voices against discrimination and exclusion, and for equality. During the 1980s and 1990s, countless women's organisations sprang up. And, from within their own, autonomous, forums, they began to demand that their rights be fully recognised, both in the public and private domain, 'in the streets and at home'.

The late 1990s were marked by a profound diversity of social identities, and also by the diversification of the forms and rationales around which women are continuing the struggle for meaningful change. They were also marked by a breakdown in the ways in which the women's movement and its demands had been structured in the past, particularly in the NGO sector. As Virginia Vargas puts it, 'one can go on talking about feminism, but this is no longer in the singular but in the plural, and is expressed through myriad forms and in myriad spheres. Feminist ideas have experienced a diffuse but increasing and consistent expansion in their scope of influence' (Vargas 1999: 1). This reality, which at one and the same time overturns the idea of a single, centralised, and hegemonic movement, incorporates an extraordinary richness of potential strategic alliances within the women's movement and between the women's movement and the rest of society, something that may well bring about significant changes in both the public and private lives of women and their wider contexts.

Despite the difficulties and tensions that this very diversity meant for the feminist movement of the 1990s, women have once more put on the table the importance of these differences and the need to recognise these, not only for women but also for society as a whole, stressing that each individual should be recognised, and respected, as unique (Melucci 1989). Without a doubt, this represents an enormous contribution that women have made to establishing a new definition of democracy that goes beyond the formalities of electoral systems, which are dominated by very same political parties in which many women were active (and indeed some still are) but from which many women have distanced themselves, following bitter battles to establish space for their ideas.

Women's social action and its entry into the public domain have taken many forms. One of them, perhaps the overriding one, was the establishment of women's NGOs. In the following section we will consider the advances and dilemmas that this way of structuring their organisation has meant for women and for taking forward the agenda of gender equity.

Women's NGOs

At key moments, all social movements need some form of structure in order to lend public visibility to their battles. NGOs served to provide openings for the expression of women's demands and facilitated the task of getting the feminist agenda and its ideals out to women from the poorer social sectors and later to officialdom, through a variety of means.

This way of doing things was made possible through the increase in private and bilateral international aid, in some cases initially intended to cushion the worsening poverty levels throughout Latin America that had resulted from economic structural adjustment programmes. This was accompanied by the corruption and lack of transparency that characterised most governments in the region, and by the corresponding lack of trust in the capacity of officialdom to fulfil the aims and objectives that the development co-operation agencies were proposing. The fragmentation of the left-wing parties and the efforts made by many social and political activists to get closer to ordinary people through popular education created the necessary conditions for the development of new openings and institutional formulas for political action.

The NGO model also allowed access to the material resources that facilitated the grassroots development of the women's movement. In a context where it was difficult simply to survive, the women's movement could never have built itself up on the basis of militancy and voluntary action alone (Figueiras 1995).

Thus, women's NGOs were operating in a situation which required them to engage in permanent negotiation – sometimes even hard struggle – with the aid agencies to secure funding for their activities. At the same time, the NGOs were trying to work with women from very different walks of life and from a diverse range of women's groups, all within a hostile context of *machismo* and patriarchy. Within the creative tension fostered by this kind of triangle – the international co-operation agencies, the women's NGOs, and women's groups on the ground – the latter two were able to establish themselves, consolidate, and expand.

In order to acquire social and political legitimacy and to be able to function in hostile public domains, women's NGOs had to temper their demands with moderation. As their legitimacy grew, they appeared to be a building-block of the NGO model. I share the view of some feminists that the work of women's NGOs was increasingly concentrated on addressing basic needs, focused on key themes, specific sectors, and concrete objectives; and that their impact was aimed at small groups whose relationship with the wider civil society was often somewhat limited. These behaviour patterns are in turn the logical outcome of the funding relationships between women's organisations and development agencies (Figueiras 1995), something to which I shall return below.

By the early 1990s, and more so by the middle of the decade, the outer limits defining the women's NGOs became almost like ramparts holding back their own development. They were caught in the conflict between the need to have an acceptable, open, and transparent institutional purpose, and to be simultaneously accountable to many stakeholders, on the one hand; and, on the other, having to function as a movement with the capacity to create horizontal alliances among (by now very diverse) groups of women. The result was that many NGOs descended into deep institutional crises. On top of this, many development co-operation agencies began to shift their funding policies, and rapid changes were taking place in the global economic and political order. Only those women's NGOs that managed successfully to handle the dual demands of being part of a movement – and so seeking to consolidate more democratic institutional practices – while also readjusting to the external context have been able to keep going.

The discussion about the institutionalisation of the women's movement is one of the most critical dilemmas facing the feminist movement. I agree with authors like Virginia Vargas (1999) that the fundamental problem is not the institutionalisation *per se*, but rather the lack of discussion and reflection on themes such as power relations, hegemony, and the difficulties that women's NGOs were encountering as they tried to build more horizontal alliances with other women's sectors, with civil society in general, and even with the State.

Successes and dilemmas

The women's movement has been active at various levels. First, at the symbolic level, in having succeeded in getting the idea of gender equity and the right to equality into the collective and individual consciousness. Second, and in more practical and tangible terms, we can see the material and visible changes in women's daily experiences (responsible motherhood, freer sexuality, inclusion in the labour market) and in macro-economic issues.

The work of women's NGOs has been tremendously successful in integrating the concept of equality, and of gender equity; as well as in pushing for it to be incorporated in the discourse of institutions that rule and reproduce society. However, there are natural frictions between this symbolic level and its translation into concrete actions and policies, which are in turn reflected in increased economic, social, and political well-being for women, above all the poorest.

Notwithstanding numerous difficulties, NGOs have been pushing forward the frontiers of the *status quo* in terms of issues such as violence, abortion, reproductive health, reproductive and domestic work, among others. Whatever the advances, however, the statistics show that women remain the poorest of the poor: and that, despite symbolic progress, with women in many countries having reached higher average education levels than those of men, this is not reflected in greater employment opportunities for women, or in equal pay for men and women doing comparable work.

This situation suggests that one of the challenges of the women's movements is to improve our understanding of how the economy and labour market work. The economic changes that are occurring as a result of the processes of globalisation, and the speed with which they are proceeding, are posing a threat to the openings for women's participation that had already been won. That said, there are also new opportunities of which we are as yet unable to take advantage and which could benefit women and promote equality between men and women.

These challenges compel us to redefine the role and ways of working of women's NGOs, and to look afresh at the new threats and opportunities that are arising from changes in the social, political, and economic context, not least since these changes will have a fundamental influence upon social organisations and institutions.

It is worth mentioning the acceptance on the part of governments, multilateral agencies, and some of the financial institutions (such as the World Bank) of the need to advance equity and equality of opportunity between women and men. Despite their limitations, these advances are of major political importance. In a globalised world, which is increasingly governed by multilateral structures that will have an incalculable impact on the political and economic life of every country, the concern for women in these organisations is of utmost relevance.

Similarly, though we might find it difficult to accept, these agencies succeeded in putting pressure on national governments, some of which were hostile to policies to promote equity. The governments that signed up to the agreements resulting from the conferences of Beijing (1995) and Cairo (1994), and the standards introduced by the Convention to End All Discrimination Against Women (CEDAW, formulated in 1979) defined general guidelines to measure the advances of national and international policies and action on violence and reproductive health among others. The implementation of these agreements will be successful as long as governments have the means to facilitate it. However, this also demands a capacity on the part of women and women's movements to make alliances and to link their actions with sectors beyond the movement itself. It will be essential not only for women's groups but also for civil-society organisations with which women are forming strategic alliances to develop the capacity to monitor the implementation of policies that are geared to promoting gender equity.

The paths we have already trodden, the progress that has been made, and challenges we now face, also oblige the development co-operation agencies to reflect on their structures and work practices – the subject of the next section.

Private development co-operation agencies

Stemming from their role in eradicating the causes of poverty, international development co-operation agencies have played and continue to play a crucial role in supporting the advance of women's protests and proposals for building more equitable and just societies for both sexes. However, these agencies have to face up to serious weaknesses.

First, there is a lack of coherent analysis and clear thinking in relation to the perspective of gender equity within the framework of development work. The debate on the incorporation of women in development began in the 1970s, reaching a watershed in 1975 with the UN Decade for Women. To some extent, this shaped the agendas that would define how women should be integrated into the ambit of development. The Women's Decade and the work that ensued put the issue on the table at the international level and encouraged the Decade's concerns to be taken up by various bodies and development co-operation agencies. From this point on, we see the issue of women in development (WID) being incorporated into agencies' efforts to strengthen social development – so it was not a spontaneous, organic, internal process, but the agencies' response to external events. The integration of 'women's issues' found agency staff devoid of the required conceptual tools, strategies, and methods to underpin their work on gender, women, and development.

Faced with these limitations, specialised departments and gender units sprang up within many co-operation agencies. The agencies then began to develop meaningful categories of analysis, to review certain practices, and to define general and thematic policies for work with women and/or with a gender perspective. For instance, in Oxfam GB, an institution-wide gender policy was adopted that embraced not only the funding of programmes and projects, but also the agency's overall work. Other co-operation agencies also made important advances in this direction.

To a great extent, the definition of an institutional policy on gender, which had grown out of extensive internal consultation, as well as consultation with key counterparts and with external sectors, raised the expectation that the integration of the analysis and practice of gender-sensitive work would follow on automatically. It was assumed that the issue was legitimised, and that its implementation would therefore be incorporated across the board within everything the agency proposed or did.

It seems as if the recognition of gender as a cross-cutting dimension in fact became a kind of veil that masked the real gender-related issues and so precluded an analysis of power relations and essentially thwarted the genuine integration of a gender perspective into our programmes. For me, the biggest lesson of all is that so-called 'mainstreaming' does not happen automatically. For this to happen, we must be prepared to overturn the existing theoretical frameworks and create new paradigms for our own work – for development and planning are profoundly political processes and not purely technical or technocratic ones.

Second, as a result of what I have described above, private development co-operation agencies have not made progress in reforming their working practices or revising the administrative procedures that basically dominate the institution's internal dynamics. The project, until very recently, was the quintessential administrative unit for anything to be funded, also serving as the means to demonstrate progress and impact. It remains the unit of work *par excellence*. Obviously, this has led to working methods that are based on discrete sets of activities; methods which by their very nature preclude a more holistic vision of the interconnectedness between any concrete action and the strategic changes which are taking place at the macro level.

Third, there is the weakness in any agency's own identity in negotiating with women's organisations from a clear institutional standpoint. Naturally, agency representatives and many of their Southern NGO counterparts share the same opinions on the ultimate objectives of social change. But, in the context of the women's NGOs, this gave rise to tensions and contradictions between supporting the strategies of the women's movement as such, and finding a way to advance the mutual interests of the women's NGOs and the aid agencies.

I agree with the criticisms that many women have made (Figueiras 1995) about the way in which women's agendas and the style of working of many of their organisations echo the form and work priorities of the funding agencies. In the process of negotiation that took place between the international agencies and the local women's NGOs, the latter essentially assimilated the working practices, priorities, and strategies favoured by former.

Over recent years, the development co-operation agencies have undergone major changes in their focus and ways of working. These relate mainly to the move away from the project as the unit of planning to programmes which are based on wider strategic analyses and geared to effect changes at different levels. Different ways of working are leading to programmes that have a more global perspective, are better integrated, and in which the need for changes at both the micro and macro levels is seen as being necessary to bring about real social change. There is an understanding of the importance of policies as well as direct beneficiary-led action in addressing the underlying causes of poverty. In addition, development co-operation agencies are feeling the pressure from their own donors and other stakeholders to account systematically for the results and impact of the programmes and projects that they are funding.

In spite of what has already been achieved, there are still many challenges and problems to overcome. We need to make progress in refining the frameworks and strategies, as well as methods for putting them into practice. These conceptual frameworks and strategies need to respond to what is going on in the economic and political context within which programme and projects are being implemented. At the same time, important internal changes need to be revived and catalysed within the agencies themselves.

New opportunities for a new role

We can afford no further delay in updating the conceptual framework and methodological tools used by development co-operation agencies in relation to the work on gender and development. The changes that are resulting from the re-organisation of the world economy should be seen as an opportunity for a new analysis that takes account of the changing social, economic, and political circumstances within which the countries and sectors supported by these agencies are having to function.

Without wanting to suggest that the agencies revert to their old ways of responding to their weak spots on gender issues, it is vital that they take on staff who are specialised in gender, women, and development, while at the same time putting more effort into a debate which is trying to pull together what has been learnt, in order to develop new and updated ways of working. These efforts are needed both within the agencies themselves and in relation to their dealings with women's groups.

We need also to 'systematise' the accumulated experience about the women's regional and international networks which have made it possible to build new development models, new forms of South–South and South–North relationships, and establish inter-institutional links to take forward policy reforms and legal frameworks. In view of their experience and contact with organisations across a range of different countries at any one time, development co-operation agencies have encouraged and supported the creation of national and international women's networks. These have served as spaces for discussion, for the sharing of experiences, and for forging agreements on action agendas which were to have an impact far beyond the national frontiers of any of the individuals or organisations who participated in them.

The Among Women Network (*Red Entre Mujeres*), encouraged and supported by the Dutch agency Novib, and the efforts devoted to building the network of Caribbean women fostered in its early days by Oxfam GB and Oxfam America are just two interesting and innovative examples. Many other networks have been created throughout Latin America continent and between *latinas* and women from other continents. For example, DAWN (Development Alternatives with Women for a New Era) brings together strong Third World feminists whose clear analysis has demonstrated the close relationship between the subordination of women and the global economy, structural adjustment programmes, the deterioration of services, environmental degradation, and violence against women, to name but a few (Antrobus 1997). Their proposals on the need for paradigms whose methods and strategies were capable of including women in development – beyond their simplistic involvement in marginal income-generating projects – reverberated around the world, because they turned upside-down the principles of the market economy, ways of understanding the environment, the concept of North and South, and the predominant ways of thinking about women and development (Mies and Shiva 1993).

Similarly, international co-operation agencies can play an important role in fostering mutually beneficial alliances between sectors with somewhat different characteristics. One such example was the role that Oxfam GB played in the review of how the codes of conduct adopted by the transnational jeans company Levi Strauss and Co. were being observed in the Dominican Republic. Here, Oxfam GB helped to bring the private sector and local NGOs closer together, with a view to revising the quality standards of employees' (male and female) working environment. Through this, improvements were obtained which directly benefited the company's workers – not only in the Dominican Republic but also in all the countries where the company has production plants.

In conclusion, I believe that the globalisation process offers development co-operation agencies the opportunity to go beyond simply project funding and to become strategic allies of those Southern organisations which seek to influence international policies towards equity and equality of opportunity, and against poverty. I am convinced that our experience has shown us the importance of addressing economic and social policies and their impact on the poorest. Similarly, going beyond their simple funding role, international co-operation agencies are now called upon to support and offer strategic accompaniment to those local initiatives that can in turn transform themselves into new points of reference in defending new ways of 'doing' development.

Acknowledgement

Translated by Frances Rubin and Deborah Eade. Original Spanish version available from the Editor on request.

References

Antrobus, Peggy (1997) 'Women and planning: the need for an alternative analysis', in Elsa Leo-Rhynie et al (eds.): *Gender*, Oxford: James Currey

Figueiras, Carmen L. (1995) 'Feminismo en Républica Dominicana', *Género y Sociedad* 3(2): 41-90

Melucci, Alberto (1989) *Nomads of the Present*, London: Hutchinson Radius

Mies, Maria and Vandana Shiva (1993) *Ecofeminism*, London: Zed Books

Vargas, Virginia (1999) 'De multiples formas y en multiples espacios', *fempress*, special number

Impact assessment: seeing the wood *and* the trees

Chris Roche

'*Not everything that counts can be counted. And not everything that can be counted counts.*' (Albert Einstein)

This paper summarises the results of a joint action-research project undertaken by a number of international and local NGOs, based on four continents and initiated by Oxfam GB and Novib from the Netherlands The full report of this work and the case studies are available elsewhere.[1] Stan Thekaekara's contribution, included in this volume, was one of these case studies. The purpose of this research project was to gain a more direct understanding of impact assessment than could be obtained from the voluminous literature on the subject, and to test out a variety of approaches in a range of contexts with varied types of organisation.

The paper begins by situating the discussion of impact assessment in the broader context of a growing critique of international NGOs (INGOs), before going on to describe some of the historical antecedents of various approaches to impact assessment and to explain how this was defined for the purposes of the research project. Before a consideration of the research findings, one of the key issues that impact assessment processes need to address – power and participation – is discussed. The paper ends by exploring some of the broader policy issues that emerge from the findings, notably in relation to the organisational context; poverty and gender impacts; the links between resource allocation and impact assessment; and how impact assessment, in combination with other changes, might help international NGOs not only to achieve more, but also to be more accountable.

Why impact assessment?

Despite the barrage of statistics and analysis that have appeared in recent UNDP and World Bank reports which show a marked improvement in a number of indicators of human well-being, the scale of world poverty remains a scandal which shames us all. In many parts of the world, inequality, insecurity, and conflict are growing at alarming rates. Although official aid has had its critics for many years, as we ended the old millennium a growing number of challenges to NGOs echoed in our ears (de Waal 1996; Sogge 1996; Smillie 1995). Taken together, these describe a vicious circle which entraps the NGO sector – particularly in the North – and which the sector itself has helped to create. This circle has five main elements:

- increasing pressure to show results and impact;
- increased competition between NGOs;
- the growing need for public profile and press coverage in order to raise funds and to facilitate advocacy work;
- poor institutional learning and weak accountability mechanisms, both to those whom NGOs seek to support, and to those who provide the funds to them;
- the almost total absence of professional norms and standards.[2]

In a climate of increased competition, individual NGOs, and the sector as a whole, have therefore tended to exaggerate the case for support, just as their opponents tend to exaggerate the case against. This has two potential and enduring dangers, which have been pointed out for some time (Cassen 1986; Riddell 1987). First, the support for development cooperation must be based on the public's belief in its effectiveness. The moral case for such support depends upon its achieving the objectives for which it is given. However, a reluctance to admit that the effectiveness of much that is done is unpredictable and difficult to assess makes not just NGOs, but international cooperation programmes in general, vulnerable to public scrutiny and polemic attack.

Second, the case for cooperation must not create the belief that aid flows constitute the sole, or even principal, means available to the donors and governments of improving the welfare of people living in poverty. It is often the case that other policy and practice changes, in areas such as macro-economic stability, improved terms of trade, or debt relief, may be more beneficial, or at least be preconditions for the positive impact of aid (UNDP 1999).

The case for cooperation can be sustained in the long run only by more effective assessment and demonstration of its impact, by not concealing the mistakes and uncertainties that are inherent in this type of work, and by an honest assessment of the comparative effectiveness of development cooperation versus other policy and practice changes.

Historical overview of impact assessment

Initial approaches to impact assessment date from the 1950s and were essentially about predicting, before the start, the likely environmental, social, and economic impacts of a given project – and approving, adjusting, or rejecting the project as a result. Environmental Impact Assessment (EIA), Social Impact Assessment (SIA), Cost–Benefit Analysis (CBA), and Social Cost-Benefit Analysis (SCBA) were some of the key methods used to do this (see Howes 1992). In recent years, there have been several efforts to integrate social and environmental impact assessments into more coherent forms (for example, Barrow 1997). Impact analysis, on the other hand, was basically confined to an assessment of impact several years after the project was finished.

The next generation of planning in official agencies saw the introduction of Logical Framework Analysis (LFA or 'logframe') which, along with its variants, is today the most common planning framework used by bilateral and multilateral agencies. From the early 1980s, many methods of enquiry emerged which sought to make people and communities subjects and active participants in development, rather than objects of it. Rapid Rural Appraisal (RRA), Participatory Rural Appraisal (PRA) – now often termed Participatory Learning and Action (PLA) – Participatory Action Research (PAR), and other methods all blossomed during this period (see Chambers 1997). At the same time, approaches to the evaluation of social development (Marsden and Oakley 1991) and 'Fourth Generation' ideas about evaluation (Guba and Lincoln 1989) have built on historical and anthropological theories and see evaluation as the negotiation of differing opinions and perspectives. This latter approach, in combination with participatory methods, seeks to understand the opinions of different interest groups by including the contributions of those whose voices are normally excluded. In recent years, national-level planning and development strategies have also started to include Participatory Poverty Assessments (PPAs), which seek to incorporate local perspectives and opinions generated through participatory research methods within national frameworks (Norton and Stephens 1995).

These various approaches have been described as being situated in either a 'modernisation' paradigm or a 'participation' paradigm (Howes 1992), where the former refers to an approach largely premised on promoting economic and infrastructural development as a means for 'developing' nations to catch up with the 'First' World. By contrast, the participation approach starts from the belief that poverty is primarily caused by injustice and inequality, and that overcoming poverty is not possible without the full participation of people. In this paradigm, outsiders have to relinquish control and act as catalysts for locally owned processes of empowerment and development. A limited participation approach also exists, in Howes' view, representing a sort of compromise between these two poles, and which was most apparent in the move within multilateral agencies to embrace participation and participatory approaches, while retaining a strong planning tradition and emphasis on economic development.

What do we mean by impact assessment?

The working definition of impact initially adopted by Oxfam GB and Novib was *'sustained changes in people's lives brought about by a particular intervention'*. Impact thus referred not to the immediate outputs or effects of a project or programme, but to the lasting and sustained changes that these brought about. Impact assessment therefore was defined as an evaluation of how, and to what extent, those changes had occurred. This required an understanding of the perspectives of all the stakeholders involved, as well as the social, economic, and political context in which the development intervention takes place.

However, following the first stage of the research, it became clear that, particularly in areas experiencing rapid and unpredictable change, such as conflict zones or emergency situations, the emphasis on 'sustained' or 'lasting' change was a problem. In such cases it was obvious that, for example, the provision of clean water could, literally, save someone's life; and that this could only be described as a significant impact, if not a lasting one. The modified definition of impact therefore became *'significant or lasting changes in people's lives, brought about by a given action or series of actions'*. In other words, programmes can make an important difference to people's lives, even if that change is not sustained over time.

The consultant recruited to review the existing literature, and to undertake some initial discussions with counterpart organisations of

Oxfam GB and Novib, also proposed that, given the complexity of the task, there should be two different levels of impact assessment: a narrow level, in relation to the original objectives of the project, and a broader level, which would involve the study of overall changes, positive or negative, intended or not, caused by a project. All the case studies, while recognising the importance of assessing performance against objectives, opted for a broader definition, along the lines given above. What therefore emerged was the following:

> *Impact assessment is the systematic analysis of the lasting or significant changes – positive or negative, intended or not – in people's lives, brought about by a given action or series of actions.*

It further became clear that although impact assessment is about systematic analysis, it is also centrally about *judgements* of what change is considered 'significant' for whom, and by whom; views which will often differ according to class, gender, age, etc. These judgements are also dependent on the context within which they are made. This led us to the important point that change is brought about *by a combination* of the activities of a given project or programme and the ongoing dynamics of the context in which these activities occur.

For the purposes of impact assessment, these issues are important, because they remind us that development and change are not ever solely the product of a managed process undertaken by development agencies and NGOs through projects and programmes. Rather, they are the result of broader and historical processes that are the outcome of many social, political, and environmental factors, including power struggles between interest groups. Understanding these processes is important if the changes brought about by a given project or programme are to be properly situated in their broader context.

Power and participation

If impact is defined as 'significant' or 'lasting' change, the key questions then become not only what has changed, whether it is significant, and the degree to which it can be attributed to a given set of actions, but, equally, *who decides?*

Despite the efforts made in the case studies, in many situations some groups, notably women and children, were consistently excluded from 'participatory' exercises. It was also clear that in some emergency situations, there may also be real logistical and political limits to participation. The case studies also revealed that even among the group of participating NGOs, there were several differing interpretations of the term 'participation', as well as different criteria for assessing its quality or depth. Given the growing importance that is being attached to participation, not just among NGOs but also in bilateral and multilateral agencies, the absence of clear agreements and standards for assessing the quality of participation seems particularly problematic.

While the scientific tradition sets out clear criteria for judging the quality of research, based on notions of internal and external validity, reliability, and objectivity, as yet there is no such broad agreement as to what the criteria for assessing the quality of participatory research might be. Some attempts to do this have been made, for example by Jules Pretty and others, building on the work of Guba and Lincoln. Pretty has adapted the criteria used to assess the quality of conventional research in order to find equivalent, but alternative, criteria for participatory processes of inquiry. These are based on the criteria of credibility, transferability, dependability, and confirmability (Pretty 1994; Guba and Lincoln 1989). The findings from the case studies suggest that, in cases where impact assessment is primarily initiated by external agencies, these criteria will also need to include the following factors:

- a process or time-schedule that is mutually acceptable to people (and particularly women) in communities and to the researchers or assessors;
- efficient use of existing sources of information, so as not to waste people's time in collecting data that are already available;
- the development and evolution of methods based on a mutual analysis of their strengths and weaknesses;
- the extent to which the information that is gathered actually has an impact i.e. actually produces change in practices or policies of the project or organisation being assessed.

The important difference between the scientific tradition and qualitative approaches is the degree to which the observer or the researcher is believed capable of remaining independent of what s/he is observing or measuring. In the scientific method this is generally deemed essential, and therefore a lot of effort goes into designing measurement tools, experiments, and methods of analysis which attempt to ensure this. In more participatory and qualitative research, on the other hand, it is believed that the researchers or observers are necessarily a part of what they observe, and that their own attitudes, beliefs, and behaviours will determine, at least in part, the information gathered. Emphasis is therefore put on the quality and depth of engagement and particularly on cross-checking findings from several perspectives ('triangulation').

These differences are often couched in terms of a fight between views of 'objectivity' and 'subjectivity'. In fact, the issue may be more usefully debated in terms of how to avoid bias in any given method of assessment, rather than posing the dilemma in terms of the two stark oppositional poles. If we pose the question in this way, we can ask whether the prolonged process of participant observation adopted in the Matson study (described by Thekaekara in this volume) may have been biased to emphasise the views of particular groups within the community. Or whether a large household survey based on random sampling undertaken in the study by BRAC (Bangladesh Rural Advancement Committee) reduced bias by ensuring a representative sample of village organisations was selected for study (see Husain 1998). In other words, the context of the study and the type of activity being assessed will determine the approach adopted and the mix of methods and tools employed. The various tools and methods within that mix will be subject to differing criteria or standards, i.e. a questionnaire survey which seeks quantitative information from a representative sample of a given population would have different quality criteria from a series of focus-group discussions exploring how changes in attitudes to gender relations had been brought about. However, the study as a whole, as well as the individual methods adopted, should be assessed by the degree to which the views and perceptions of staff, external assessors, and various groups of local people and other stakeholders were, or were not, taken into account.

Findings related to impact assessment

In the end, how significant or lasting a change is, and how attributable it is to a given action, is a *matter of judgement*. This will depend particularly on the context and, of course, on who decides what is significant. It will also mean recognising that change is the outcome of multiple and complex processes as well as the struggles, ideas, and actions of differing and unequal interest groups. This suggests that simple models of cause and effect, linking project inputs to outputs and impact, although important, will usually be inadequate for assessing the impact of what

NGOs do. Rather, models are required that embrace the wider context of influences and change processes that surrounds projects and programmes, and the wide variety of the resulting impacts.

The contingent and uncertain nature of change, as well as the possibility of discontinuous or catastrophic change, puts a premium on impact monitoring, learning, and adaptation. The one thing that we can be certain about is that the unexpected will happen, and that we cannot plan for every eventuality. Any action that we take might produce dramatic and significant change that was not predicted. This puts the onus on those who intervene in processes of change to monitor the impact of what they do, on a regular basis, and adapt as a result. It is simply not good enough to say that impact cannot be measured until after a project has finished, when significant, and negative, change can occur very early in the lifetime of a project or programme. Impact assessment therefore has to be able to cope with turbulent and non-linear change as well as more gradual and linear change (Roche 1994).

Approaches to impact assessment

Broadly, three different approaches were used in the case studies. The first is mainly 'project-out' and involves clarifying and specifying project objectives and indicators and then assessing the degree to which they have been met. In some cases, this involved a careful ranking of outputs, outcomes, and impacts, with a limited number of indicators being verified at each level of the 'impact chain'. In some studies, 'control groups' or individuals outside the project areas were compared with those within project areas.

The second approach focused on the projects being assessed, but looked more broadly at the potential changes that may have occurred as a result. Typically, this involved asking various stakeholders to identify the most important changes brought about by a given project, and how they happened. In some cases, this involved using a broad checklist of potential areas or dimensions of change.

Finally, some studies adopted a more 'context-in' approach, looking first and foremost at overall changes in people's lives and then seeking to explore with them the importance of those changes and the sources of change, including the project in question. Stan Thekaekara's paper in this volume describes one of these case studies. This approach seeks to situate changes brought about by a particular project within the context of other changes.

It would seem that a combination of these approaches would be ideal, but possibly not always feasible. The tendency for impact-assessment exercises in general to focus too much on 'project-out' approaches can lead to results which exaggerate the importance of projects and interventions and diminish the role of other variables – not least people's own ingenuity and agency.

On change, objectives, and indicators

Whichever approach to assessing impact was adopted, there were common areas, or dimensions of change, that were seen as significant and recurred across the case studies. These included changes in the following:

- income, expenditure, and assets, including access to land and credit;
- health, education, literacy, and other skills and knowledge;
- infrastructure, including particularly access to water and sanitation facilities;
- food security and production;
- social relations, social capital, unity, and changed community norms;
- for women in particular: ownership and control of assets; mobility; access to income-generation activities; child-care facilities; freedom to express their views; power in household decision making; household division of labour; ability to control violence;
- peace and security, law and order, declining levels of sexual violence, human-rights abuses, and destruction of lives and property;
- ability to cope with crises;
- self-confidence, self-esteem, independence, potential, and capacity to make claims and demands;
- overall quality of life.

This suggests that, although there may be important differences between people's indicators for identifying significant change in their lives, there is perhaps a common core of dimensions, or areas, of change which are important to people, and which is not location-specific. Clearly, however, the priorities that different groups of men and women, old and young, rich and poor, assign to those changes will vary both within and between regions or locations, and over time. In addition, as the Pakistan study (Alkire and Narajo 1998) suggests, there are also important matters concerning people's aesthetic, cultural, religious, or spiritual lives that are touched both positively and negatively by projects and programmes, which tend to get ignored. This may mean that, for impact-assessment purposes, the search for *common* or *generic* indicators is perhaps much less important than understanding what *areas of change* are prioritised by different groups of people, and how these domains relate to each other in different contexts. In this sense, indicators become more a means of exemplifying why and how change within a particular area has occurred, and not just a means to verify a project's progress against predetermined objectives.

On tools and methods

Although many tools and methods were used in the studies, perhaps the most important conclusion about them is that the selection of a judicious mix, and sequence, of tools and methods is heavily dependent on being clear about the purpose and focus of the assessment, and designing that assessment process in a way that is appropriate to the context, the intervention in question, and the organisations involved. The ability to develop appropriate method mixes and sequences, and the ability to adapt and innovate as the study progresses, seem to be as important as the knowledge and skills required for individual methods.

Similarly, none of the tools and methods used singly solves the problem of determining attribution, and even taken together they cannot prove it. However, combining the findings produced by different methods, if properly cross-checked, can provide a body of evidence that can be agreed, disputed, or amended, which can in turn enable a reasoned and plausible judgement to be made. As Roger Riddell has argued:

> In short, it is unnecessary to concentrate time, effort and resources on project or programme evaluation if firm conclusions can be drawn without using sophisticated techniques. Similarly if judgements made about qualitative aspects of projects are not substantially challenged by the relevant 'actors' or groups ... then purist worries about objectively assessing these factors become largely irrelevant. (Riddell 1990)

Social relations are a critical determinant of well-being or poverty. Addressing gender-related inequalities is seen not only as a prerequisite to 'achieving sustainable development and alleviating poverty', but a social-justice objective in its own right. It is well known that differences in gender, class, ethnicity, religion, ability/disability, and age are all important elements which mean that communities do not have single identities, goals, or ambitions. Given these insights, and given the points already made about power and participation, processes of impact assessment need to reflect carefully on not only what needs to be assessed and how this is done, but on who is involved and what unit or level of analysis is most appropriate. It is true that, in the past few years, increasing attention has been paid to gender issues in the design, implementation, and evaluation of development projects. Several frameworks have been developed in order to assist better gender analysis in this area, notably: Practical and Strategic Needs, the Harvard Framework, the Capacities and Vulnerabilities Framework, and the Social Relations Framework (see March et al. 1999 for detailed discussion of the advantages and disadvantages of these). However, there is still a need to operationalise these frameworks in more practical ways, and in ways which can genuinely involve women and men more systematically.

Broader policy implications

The problems of attribution and aggregation

All organisations, whether they are community-based groups, local NGOs, or international agencies, need to make sense of what they are doing. They also generally want to know what difference they are making. This produces two key problems for any organisation: how to synthesise or summarise what they are doing: the aggregation problem; and how they discover the degree to which any changes they observe were brought about by their actions: the attribution problem. These issues are further complicated if the organisation has to communicate to many other people, both internally and externally, about its achievements.

In addition, impact assessment requires looking at the deep-rooted impact on those structures that embody relations of authority, power, and control and determine the degree to which individuals and groups can exercise choice. Development agencies, including large NGOs, are not immune from the problems confronting other bureaucracies in terms of complacency, hierarchy, inertia, and poor information flow. These can lead to loops of self-deception if feedback from activities is distorted, or manipulated, as individuals seek to protect themselves.

Much of the good practice that has emerged from this research and other recent work focuses on ensuring that impact-assessment processes are kept simple, relevant, and useful. But it also underlines the need to align organisational incentives, rewards, and systems so that they are compatible with a real organisational desire to learn, and to adapt in the light of that learning. This requires a commitment from senior mangers to the following measures:

- ensure coherence with other systems;
- maintain the external and 'front-line' focus of the organisation's work; and
- provide the accountability framework in which 'bottom-up' quality-control measures are properly represented and balanced along with those of other stakeholder interests.

It is vital to provide the right incentives for this basic level of information collection to be done properly – and there is no better incentive than self-interest. If impact-assessment work and subsequent improvements in quality are to happen, then this means ensuring that resources are made available and that such work is not seen as an 'add-on' or luxury, but rather as an integral part of everyone's work. This means also creating the demands and incentives for it to become central, and for these demands to be articulated in a way that conforms with organisational policies and practices. For example, reporting on the lack of gender-disaggregated data coming from projects, Goyder et al. (1998:49) state that '[o]verall the problem is not so much the lack of gender awareness by field staff and researchers, but the lack of sufficient perceived demand by higher levels within agencies like ActionAid for gender differentiated results. If this demand had been in place it could have acted as a counter influence to the pressures felt by staff to aggregate and summarise research results from multiple meetings in multiple villages.'

Many of the problems that relate to impact assessment suggest, therefore, not only the need to develop new methods that can help to deal with the problem of attribution and aggregation, but also the need to develop different organisational cultures and relationships.

Poverty and gender issues

There is limited, if tantalising, evidence which suggests that, when asked, poorer households rank collective services (health, education, water), often provided by the State, higher than NGO projects, particularly those projects that provide individualised services such as credit or agricultural extension. By contrast, better-off households rank NGO projects higher. This, if confirmed more broadly, would clearly have important implications regarding the complementarity of NGO–State roles and, indeed, the importance of NGOs not only in helping to stimulate demand, by strengthening community organisations, but also by facilitating the supply, through lobbying for adequate funding and through support for State service provision.

As far as women's status is concerned, the majority of case studies reported improvements in material well-being, household relations, and self-image. However, some noted that this was accompanied by further increases in workload, little change in control over assets within the home, and no change to deep-seated gender norms in issues such as dowry payments, for instance. As an OECD/DAC study on NGOs also notes 'what is clearly proving most difficult is to introduce processes which have a more positive and systemic impact on the status of women' (Riddell 1997).

There is also some evidence to suggest that where poorer groups and women have started to demand, and in some cases achieve, a level of systemic change, this often requires more support from intermediaries and external agencies, albeit of a nature that is different from a traditional project relationship. This has important implications for the notions of hand-over, independence, and autonomy which litter the literature on NGO organisational development. The construction of more complicated webs of relationships and support networks which are vertical (e.g. regional, national, international) as well as horizontal and can provide more flexible and rapid response seems more appropriate than one-off project relationships. If systemic change is to be achieved, this will mean bringing pressure to bear at several levels simultaneously and being able to shift the debate to those organisations, regions, or capitals where the best chance of promoting change exists.

Resource allocation

The current importance ascribed to assessing impact, as opposed to inputs and outputs, is welcome in that it stresses the importance of understanding how a positive and significant difference can be made to people's lives. However, although past performance is a guide to future performance, it is not the only one. The relationship between projects, the organisations that run and support them, and the context in which they are situated is complex and produces a wide range of possible impacts. The same inputs at different times or in different places will produce different results. These results will in turn be different for different groups of men, women, and children.

This suggests first that an understanding of context, local power relations, poverty, and social dynamics is a necessary precondition to achieve impact. Second, the ability to listen to and learn from local people and organisations and to adapt support in the light of this learning is critical in ensuring that any past impact is likely to be sustained in the future. This in turn is dependent on organisations having a congruence between their incentives, systems, and culture that permits learning and adaptation, as well as an ability to balance the interests of various stakeholders. Fourth, the ability to innovate and take risks is also likely to be necessary, particularly if the poorest are to be included in development efforts rather than excluded from them. Investing in projects with 'safe returns' and guaranteed future impact is likely to mean sticking with the status quo.

Finally, the ability to work with others and to use and communicate the findings of impact-assessment exercises or other learning is going to be increasingly important in order to promote broader systemic change. If impact is to be increased, then this too will become a more important aspect than it has been in the past.

In short, the results of impact-assessment exercises are insufficient on their own to make sensible decisions about resource allocation to projects or organisations. Other criteria – notably, understanding of context; the ability to listen, learn, adapt, and innovate; management capacity; and the ability to work with others and to communicate learning – are also critical.

The future of NGOs: towards a virtuous circle?

This circle, like the vicious circle, also has five mutually reinforcing elements:

- increased recognition of the need to develop institutional learning and impact-assessment processes;
- the development of strategic alliances with other NGOs and other sectors, including State structures;
- a deeper engagement in processes and programmes in the NGOs' own countries of origin;
- the development of new forms of accountability; and
- the further development of professional norms and standards within and across agencies.

In order for the circle to achieve enough momentum, a number of things have to happen at the same time. The evidence from the case studies indicates that this will not only involve the development and sharing of new tools and methods of impact assessment, but also the enhancement of broader institutional learning strategies. However, for this to make a difference, the current competition for resources, personnel, and ideas between NGOs and other actors, notably the State, has to be reworked into more creative and strategic alliances. This, from an impact-assessment perspective, means less emphasis on selfishly seeking to attribute change to an individual project or organisation, and more emphasis on how agencies can combine to produce significant change for people living in poverty. This, in turn, will often mean sacrificing an individual agency's profile for the greater good. If impact assessment is to mean anything, it is about becoming more open and transparent about what is, and what is not, possible; and about what could be achieved in the future. This is not likely to happen if it simply becomes a means of blowing the organisational trumpet even harder.

One of the ways in which some of the organisations in the case studies are beginning to transform themselves is by putting down stronger and deeper roots in their own societies. For some, this has always been part of who they were; for others, including Oxfam GB and Novib, this means engaging even more in the UK and in the Netherlands respectively. It means helping to make the connections between poverty and exclusion 'at home' and elsewhere, and being committed to illustrating how the stories of change from Africa, Asia, Latin America, and Eastern Europe are not simply about the need for further compassion and money, but are also inspiring, insightful, and creative. As these roots are put down, accountability patterns will shift too. This is important if we wish to see a future based on notions of interdependence and mutuality, rather than dependence and handouts.

Change in these elements of the circle could combine to produce a situation that could be described as follows:

- There is a more realistic portrayal of what NGOs alone can achieve, and therefore a greater degree of modesty and humility, as well as a recognition of the importance of working with others – something that will help to decrease the gap between rhetoric and reality.

- There is an increased realisation that the potential to solve problems 'at home' and 'out there' comes from bringing to bear multiple perspectives that are based on a more effective and honest sharing of experience and ideas. It is interesting to note in this context that some recent research shows that the degree of a donor country's commitment to social justice at home is positively correlated to its commitment to social justice not only in its aid programme but in all its international relations (Olsen 1996).

- Increased trust is built on shared values and a respect for difference. In the face of globalising tendencies, one of the challenges facing the NGO community North, South, East, and West is how to overcome the danger of fragmentation and irrelevance. Alliances need to lead to more than liberal coexistence, where we agree to disagree, as this leads to isolation and fragmentation. The ultimate aim must be to create groupings in which organisations that *do* share realities based on common understanding and analysis, as well as common involvement in struggles for justice and equity, can move forward together.

- New notions of 'partnership' and change are created, based on clear and agreed standards of performance. The reaction to approaches to development that assume the acceptability of universal blueprints is to argue for the importance of context and diversity, considering processes, and understanding difference. While this is understandable, some would argue that it has led to an undermining of the notions of universal standards and rights. If everything is different and relative, then it is difficult to imagine universally applicable standards which suggest some absolute hierarchy of values (Duffield 1996).

Fifty years after the Universal Declaration of Human Rights was ratified, and with a current resurgence of rights-based approaches to international relations, the challenge for NGOs in general, and for impact-assessment processes in particular, remains to tell the stories of how individual men, women, and children, and their communities struggle to defend their universal rights in the face of overwhelming odds, and how they can be better supported in doing so.

Notes

1 See Roche (1999). The case studies cover four African countries (Ghana, Kenya, Zimbabwe, and Uganda), three South Asian countries (Pakistan, Bangladesh, and India), one Latin American country (El Salvador), and the United Kingdom. They represent a mix of prospective work, mid-term assessments of on-going work, and retrospective reviews.

2 Recent attempts to develop standards for humanitarian work undertaken by the Sphere Project (The Sphere Project 2000), and proposals for an Ombudsman, are the exceptions.

References

Alkire, S. and H. Narajo (1998) 'Oxfam versus Poverty: Assessing Impact in Pakistan', paper prepared for the Impact Assessment Workshop in Stanton, UK 23-26 November 1998.

Barrow, C. (1997) *Environmental and Social Impact Assessment*, London: Arnold

Cassen, R. and associates (1986) *Does Aid Work?* Oxford: Oxford University Press

Chambers, R. (1997) *Whose Reality Counts? Putting the First Last*, London: IT Publications.

Duffield, M. (1996) 'The symphony of the damned', *Disasters* 20 (3):173-93

Goyder, H., R. Davies, and W. Wilkinson (1998) *Participatory Impact Assessment*, London: ActionAid

Guba, E. and Y. Lincoln (1989) *Fourth Generation Evaluation*, London: Sage

Howes, M. (1992) 'Linking paradigms and practice: key issues in the appraisal, monitoring and evaluation of British NGO projects' *Journal of International Development* 4(4): 375-96

Husain, A. M. M. (ed.) (1998), *Poverty Alleviation and Empowerment: The Second Impact Assessment Study of BRAC's Rural Development Programme*, Dhaka: BRAC

March, C., I. Smyth, and M. Mukhopadhyay (1999) *A Guide to Gender-Analysis Frameworks*, Oxford: Oxfam

Marsden, D. and P. Oakley (eds.) (1991) *Evaluating Social Development Projects*, Oxford: Oxfam

Norton, A. and T. Stephens (1995) 'Participation in Poverty Assessments', Environment Department Papers Participation Series 20, Washington: The World Bank

Olsen, G. (1996) 'Public opinion, international civil society and North-South policy since the Cold War' in O. Stokke: *Foreign Aid Towards the Year 2000: Experiences and Challenges,* London: Frank Cass

Pretty, J. (1994) 'Alternative systems of inquiry for a sustainable agriculture', *IDS Bulletin* 25(2): 37-48

Riddell, R. (1987) *Foreign Aid Reconsidered,* Baltimore: Johns Hopkins University Press

Riddell, R. (1990) *Judging Success: Evaluating NGO Approaches to Alleviating Poverty in Developing Countries*, ODI working paper 37, London: DFID

Riddell, R. et al. (1997) 'Searching for Impact and Methods: NGO Evaluation Synthesis Study', prepared on behalf of the Expert Group on Evaluation of the Organisation for Economic Cooperation and Development, Paris: OECD

Roche, C. (1994) 'Operationality in turbulence', *Development in Practice* 4(3): 160-72.

Roche, C. (1999) *Impact Assessment for Development Agencies: Learning to Value Change*, Oxford: Oxfam

Smillie, I. (1995) *The Alms Bazaar: Altruism Under Fire – Non-profit Organizations and International Development*, London: IT Publications

Sogge, D. (ed.) (1996) *Compassion and Calculation: The Business of Private Foreign Aid*, London: Pluto Press

Sphere Project (2000) *The Sphere Handbook: Humanitarian Charter and Minimum Standards in Disaster Response*, Geneva: The Sphere Project

UNDP (1999) *Human Development Report 1999*, Oxford: Oxford University Press

de Waal, A. (1996) 'Bad aid', *Prospect*, October 1996

Does Matson matter? Assessing the impact of a UK neighbourhood project

Stan Thekaekara

Introduction

In 1994, Mari Marcel Thekaekara and I spent some time with the Charities Advisory Trust and the Directory of Social Change to look at community work in the UK, against the background of our experience with tribal communities in India. Our report, *Across the Geographical Divide*, captured the interest of Oxfam GB, which was seeking to bring its experience of the South to bear on its UK Poverty Programme. As it happens, Oxfam and Novib were also researching impact assessment (see Chris Roche's paper in this volume). This coincided with a request to Oxfam to support the Matson Neighbourhood Project (MNP), one of whose founding directors was about to leave after eight years.

This all led to my two-month visit to Matson, a large Council-built residential estate on the edge of the city of Gloucester. While seeking to share experiences between the South and North, I aimed also to look at how what could be learned from Matson might contribute to Oxfam's research on impact assessment.

Methodology

The impact assessment was to concentrate on two things: what changes have taken place (impact)? And what brought about these changes (attribution)? The Project's own slogan – *Helping to make Matson matter* – provided an apt focus: Does Matson matter? If so, why? We decided to address these questions by the following means.

- *Talking to a cross-section of people*: This involved both formal interviews and casual conversations. When numbers were crunched, it was found that 28 'formal interviews' had been conducted, of which 14 each were with men and women – the exact balance was purely coincidental! It had not been possible to interview residents who did not use the Project's services, or staff from the statutory services. I did not keep an exact record of all the 'casual interviews' – book and pen not always being at hand or appropriate at the time. Attending various meetings provided the opportunity for conversations with 'officials', such as city and county Councillors, the local MP, social-service managers, housing officers, and the like. There were also innumerable conversations with staff, board members, and the residents who dropped in at the Project. A major way to get a feel of life in Matson was through the children. Through giving a talk on India at a local school, which I coupled with a few magic tricks, I made some good friends. Walking about the estate and hanging around the community shop, I invariably bumped into these children and got talking about India, Matson, and magic – not necessarily in that order! A questionnaire was circulated to staff, and feedback from this, and from wider discussions with the staff and board members, is incorporated here.

- *Being a part of whatever was happening*: This involved spending time at the various sites, occasionally staffing the reception area, answering the telephone (a great way to get an idea of the relationship between the Project and the residents: the fact that most of them were not only on first-name terms with the staff but were always clear about who could sort out a problem was a good indicator).

- *Sitting in on meetings*: There were various kinds of meetings: the Board and its sub-committees, review meetings of staff, meetings of City and County Council bodies, meetings of Tenants' Associations and the Tenants' Federation, meetings with other Neighbourhood Projects, meetings of the Matson Forum, and meetings of the Neighbourhood Project Network.

- *Going through available documentation*: I had free access to all the files, correspondence, minutes, records, statistics, and press clippings. *Matson News*, the MNP's community newspaper, was a fascinating chronicle of growth and change. Juxtaposed with the Annual Reports, this gave a real feeling of how things had developed over the years.

So, what follows is based on reading, listening, observing, and talking about the Matson community and the MNP with people who were involved in one way or another – the stakeholders, to use a favourite Oxfam expression, or 'participatory action research' in development-speak – and from just 'hanging around', being a part of everything that was happening.

Matson: a neighbourhood community or just another Council estate?

Matson is a Council estate on the periphery of Gloucester, with the M5 motorway as one border and an artificial ski slope and country club on the hill behind. Depending on whom you ask, you get different information about Matson. The Council will tell you that it is Gloucester's largest estate, with approximately 1500 properties, and is part of the Matson electoral ward, which has 9000 residents. Matson to them seems to be just another statistic, a problem to be managed. You ask outsiders, and their response is immediate: 'You don't want to go there'. Probe a little deeper, and they will tell you that it's not safe, it's ridden with crime, it's run-down, vandalised, and seedy: all the conventional assumptions about a Council estate. Ask 'Have you been there?', and the answer is an indignant 'Of course not!'. Talk to researchers and people who live by statistics, and they will tell you that parts of Matson have the highest indicators of economic and social stress in Gloucester, that one-third of the households are run by single parents, that 17 per cent of the households have unmet caring needs, that fewer than half the households own a car, and that more than 30 per cent of them have at least one person with serious long-term illness.

Talk to the 'Matsonites' – the residents and the people who work in Matson – and a different image appears. They tell you that it's a good place to live and to work. Many of them could have moved to other Council estates but have chosen to stay. And those working in Matson are glad to work here.

So to understand Matson, we must look at its history. Various people and a lot of literature supplied a wealth of information, but one man, George Smith, who was among the first to settle in Matson in the 1950s, chronicled its history thus:

> In 1945 I was in my mid-thirties. A lot of us had come out of the war to find there was an acute shortage of housing. We had to live in

single rooms, even though we had families of our own, in rooms with our parents. I myself lived for seven years with my parents.

In 1950 the government started building houses – Council estates. Matson was one of them. All of us who moved into Matson were more or less the same age, with young families. My wife did not want to come up here, but in a very short while we were a community. There were a lot of children around, everyone knew each other, and there was a strong community spirit. She loved it in no time.

All of us were employed – there were a lot of engineering works close by that provided employment … I worked at the Gloucester Wagon Works. I used to cycle into work and back, like a lot of the others. Right through the sixties and seventies, life here was good. But in the late seventies and early eighties, things started to go wrong. You don't notice it at first. Workers' unions seemed to be a bad word, and there seemed to be an effort to destroy the unions. Businesses started closing down. I retired in 1981, and two years later the Gloucester Wagon Works closed and over 1500 people were left without jobs and most of them were from Matson … This was when the deterioration started. People started moving out, and the community began to break up. More and more properties began to fall vacant, especially the flats.

On top of the unemployment, we felt that we were being used as a dumping ground by the Council. They started moving people out of bed and breakfast into the vacant properties. These were mainly people and families who already had a lot of problems. Many of them were single, with no family support at all. And it seemed as if they were being pushed here out of sight. They were put here and forgotten. Over a period of time, crime evolved into being common-place. I don't want to be judgmental, but I am sure for many people plain survival was an issue. This was not something that was particular to Matson or even Gloucester. It was happening all over the country.

I don't want to be political, but it was a Tory-dominated Council and they clearly made us feel we were something they didn't want to know about. Things came to a head when the Council came up with the proposal to sell all the Council estates to a private association – the North Housing. We were unhappy with this. We had not been consulted and we definitely did not want the houses sold off.

This was a turning point. The Tenants' Associations decided to do something about it. We got a lot of support from the Gloucester Law Centre … Matson took the lead, and all the other Council estates joined in … We protested. We started bringing back our sense of community. I did not enjoy why we had to do it, but I enjoyed doing it.

We won. The Council decided not to sell off the houses. This gave us a lot of confidence that if we can get together we can get results. But after the campaign the enthusiasm started wearing off. Once the housing business was sorted out, the Tenants' Associations' job seemed to be done, though it wasn't. So a group of us started thinking about the community … I don't remember how exactly the idea for the Neighbourhood Project came up … Six of us started in the disused community centre. At first it was difficult to get people involved. But then all the three churches in Matson got involved. We had no idea what exactly to do, but took Mark Gale on as the Project Director. And slowly we began to grow. People began to take notice. A little bit of the community spirit started coming back. This is what we are fighting for even now. Can we really bring it back? I think so – because without a sense of community, nothing works.

We have been successful to a degree. Lots more needs to be done – it is an on-going thing. Crime has definitely come down. The Project can't claim full credit, but it has definitely contributed. It has given people something to work for – a name to live by. It has supplied people with options. My major concern at the moment is that the only people who seem to be talking about the community are from my age group. It is difficult to get young people involved. Probably because of their other problems, especially unemployment. It's a question of trying to survive. All of us older people are now on the sidelines, because we've been through it. They are the future.

The world has become a difficult place. The concerns are at a higher level, and the lower levels are forgotten. I believe different levels in society are inevitable, but we need tolerance and compassion. I can tolerate the rich if they don't stand on your head and push you down. We need a compassionate society. People need opportunities. But I am optimistic. Yes, things are definitely getting better. Not as fast as we would like it to. But we are on the up and up.

This account of Matson's downhill slide was clearly seen as part of something that was happening all over the UK. What is of interest, however, is what made the people of Matson control the slide. Many factors contributed to this, and the MNP very obviously occupies the pride of place.

The Matson Neighbourhood Project

The history of the Matson Neighbourhood Project is inextricably linked to the history of two campaigning organisations – the Gloucester Law Centre and the Gloucester Tenants' Federation – plus factors such as the nationwide response to the government White Paper on Locality Planning.

The Gloucester Law Centre was set up in the mid-1980s 'to provide much-needed free legal advice on welfare benefits, housing and employment matters'. One of its important roles was providing support to various Tenants' Associations dotted around the city. In 1987, the Centre stumbled on news of a secret move by the Council to sell off its 6500-odd houses to a private Newcastle-based company, North Housing. The Centre's staff were quick to inform the Tenants' Associations – their clients. In June 1988, Association representatives formed the Gloucester Tenants' Federation and launched what was to be a long and bitter campaign against the sell-off.

The Law Centre soon faced the threat of total closure, with the City Council citing its support for the Tenants' Federation 'political' campaign as outside its remit. A protracted battle culminated in victory for both the Centre and the Federation, demonstrating what communities could achieve if organised and united. The campaigns laid the foundation for people taking more positive action to determine what happened to their lives and their neighbourhood. Many of the individuals involved were also central to setting up the Matson Neighbourhood Project.

The Project began quietly in 1990 in a derelict church-owned building which had once been a youth club. Matson, by all accounts, was sliding downhill faster than skiers on the artificial ski slope behind it. With a majority of people on social-security benefits, the most important need was for an Advice Centre. And so the Project opened its doors with an Advice Centre and it has not looked back since. Today it offers a wide range of services, including advice and representation, special-needs services, jobs, training and education, and community and economic development. For instance, in 1996-97 there were more than 3000 enquiries, plus 1000 home visits, and an extra £250,000 was drawn into the local economy through new benefit claims; 65 residents who were recovering from mental ill health and five with learning disabilities attended a drop-in centre, and 100 people attended in response to medical referrals. Unemployment fell by 38 per cent, with the creation of 200 training and education places and 120 job placements. In addition, there were parents' support groups, lunch clubs for pensioners, a clothes-recycling service, and so on, all run from various reclaimed sites. The annual budget for 1997-98 was approximately £240,000; it came primarily from local-authority contracts and grants, charitable trusts, and businesses.

While these activities are not so very unique, what sets them apart is the process by which they were started. I shall not, therefore, describe the Centre's activities in detail, concentrating rather on the process and its impact. In terms of staffing, something that characterises the Project is that board members are not appointed. Instead, the MNP was set up as a limited company, with membership open to all residents to join an elected board, most of the member of which are residents. There are 26 paid staff (18 of them part-time) and 14 regular volunteers. Half of these people are residents. Staff are divided into four units, each of which is co-ordinated by a team leader, which allows everyone very easy access to anybody at any level.

Assessing impact

For years, projects all over the world have been engaged in the business of poverty alleviation or eradication. Most of the more successful ones have monitored and evaluated their work quite closely, but not many have assessed the *impact* of their work. While monitoring and evaluation normally track a project's tasks, activities, or programmes, impact assessment looks at their *effect*. Are they really making a difference? Are they effecting a change? Even successful programmes and activities do not always have the desired impact and they may even have an unforeseen or unintended impact on the community. It is hoped that by understanding the impact of their work, projects will become more effective.

Before assessing the impact of the MNP, we need to consider the impact of poverty itself. The corollary of its slogan would be that at some point Matson *did not* matter. Why? Was it just because of poverty? Surely not, for there are so many other communities in the UK and elsewhere where the poverty is much worse. If we look at the problem solely from an economic point of view, we get into all kinds of arguments about relative poverty and whether it is even necessary to work in a place like Matson – especially when there is a shortage of resources. But if we look at what poverty does to people and communities from a social and political perspective, we find that the impact or effect of poverty remains the same, irrespective of its degree.

Poverty is not just about a shortage or a lack of money. Nor just about meeting basic needs. No doubt these are the glaring symptoms of poverty. But if we see poverty purely in its economic context, we run the risk of overlooking what it does to people and communities. For instance, when I look at Matson or even the much worse-off parts of the UK, I cannot for a moment compare their situation with that of the communities with whom I work in India. The physical environment of those who are considered poor in the UK would actually compare well with our middle class. However, when we look at the social, psychological, and political *impact* on those living in poverty, we will find that there is not much difference between what happens to people in the UK and anywhere else in the world. The UK Coalition Against Poverty says that '[p]overty is about exclusion. Exclusion from society, and exclusion from decision making at every level.' It has to do with the feeling of powerlessness and the resulting sense of fear and entrapment, with loss of hope, discrimination, and the denial of human rights. A sense that nobody cares. And it is obvious that all these feelings were present in Matson. To use a phrase I often heard: '*They* don't want to know'. This neatly sums up what it is all about. 'They' – the powers that be – did not care about Matson, Matson did not matter to 'them'. Although it may not be an explicit objective, I imagine that the underlying purpose of the MNP and all its work would be to make Matson matter not only to the residents, but also to 'them'.

So, in trying to assess its impact, I have asked myself: does Matson (now) matter? What has been the role of the Project in making it matter? Thus, my favourite questions were: *What are the changes that have taken place in Matson? Has the quality of life improved or not over the years?* And of course the inevitable: *What do you think caused it?*

Does Matson matter? And has anything changed?

It was almost universally acknowledged that change – for the better – had taken place.

Refurbishments to the houses

This was almost always the first response from people when asked about the changes. While there was dissatisfaction about the fact that only a few properties along the main road had been improved, people agreed that this had given a 'lift' to the estate. Those who lived in older properties now at least had some hope. Someone described this as a 'not yet' feeling, instead of the 'never' feeling that existed before. Once houses were done up, they tended to be looked after. There is no denying the impact that an improvement in the living environment has on self-esteem: '*Started this garden only after they did the houses up. Everything was too grey and dirty before that. And it wasn't no use – some of the kids would be sure to destroy it. Now I'm looking for the snowdrops*', said an elderly woman tending her garden during an unusually warm February.

Crime and vandalism

'*If you could have seen the place ...*' said one resident. The sentence was eloquently left unfinished. Now, the condition of the pillar boxes, telephone kiosks, and bus shelters was in itself testimony that the level of vandalism at Matson was nothing, compared with that of other Council estates. The local headmaster graphically described the state of the school premises when he arrived 20 years ago: fences pulled down, walls defaced with graffiti, litter all around. Robinswood School today is a far cry from that.

One woman says that she would be much less afraid of walking around Matson at night than in many other neighbourhoods. The librarian commented: '*We had a lot of trouble with vandalism and even had a security guard. But for the last five years the library has not been vandalised – no more graffiti.*' (She was quick to touch wood after saying that.)

Getting rid of the blatant drug dealing was seen by many as a major triumph against crime. While it was difficult to pinpoint how exactly this was done, there had been close co-operation between the community and the police. People had had enough, and rather than turn a blind eye they began to report problems if they suspected that drug dealing was going on. Police were quick to act, and that spurred more people to report things. But nearly everyone added that this did not mean that there was no crime and vandalism or drugs. There was still plenty around, but nowhere near what it used to be. As one woman said: '... *it's not like before – when the vans would be here with dark windows and loud music. Everybody knew what was going on. But you don't see them any more.*

If they turned up, I'm sure somebody would be quick to report it.'
Project documents recorded a 24 per cent drop in domestic burglaries
between 1994 and 1996. The attempt to obtain figures from the Council
regarding crime rates and other statistics is another story in itself. Suffice
it to say at this point that they were not successful.

More significant still was the change in attitude towards crime.
I witnessed a phone call to report that some children had vandalised a
bus shelter: the MNP was the first port of call, and not the police. Even
more interesting was the staff person's reply: she had recognised the kids
from the description and said simply, *'Leave it with me. I'll be seeing
them tonight'*. And then added to me, *'It's half term, school's out, and the
Redwell Centre* (a local youth centre) *is closed. They're not bad kids,
just bored kids. We can sort them out.'* This quiet confidence in being able
to deal immediately with what is normally seen as a major social problem
– vandalism by teenagers – was an impressive indicator of how people
had taken control over the neighbourhood. So it is not just that crime has
come down: people no longer feel helpless about it; they are concerned,
and willing to voice and act on their concern.

More services on the 'patch'

This was another favourite. People were quick to point out how there was
a time when 'there was nothing here – not a thing', and you had to go into
town for everything. Under a 1993 front-page banner headline 'UNDER
SIEGE' in the local newspaper was a description of the terrible decline
in Matson. A 'Matson Factfile' box said: 'In recent weeks a co-op store,
chip shop and hairdresser have closed. There is a threat to nursery classes
at the local infants' school.' In 1998, just five years later, a resident told
me, *'It's all here, you don't have to go to town. There's a post office,
a grocery, cake shop, two chemist stores, shops, doctor's surgery and
all the other things the Project has. We even have a local housing office.'*
One woman at a sheltered-housing project for the elderly was in no doubt
that having the surgery and the chemist in Matson greatly helped most of
the residents, who would otherwise have to take a bus into town to see a
doctor or get a prescription filled out – a near-impossible task for many.
That the chemist would come by and deliver the medicines made all
the difference.

Wanting to stay in Matson

There was a time when no one wanted to stay in Matson, and many of the houses were empty. This is not so now. The fact that there are some 30 houses vacant, I was told, has nothing to do with people not wanting accommodation, but with the way in which houses are allotted by the Council. I was told there was a waiting list for these houses, surely another area where figures from the Council would corroborate – or disprove – people's views.

A better image

Something that angers most residents is the way in which others perceive them. According to the UK Coalition Against Poverty:

> Poverty is not a word people like to be associated with. There are too many myths about the poor – that they are lazy and unfit, or helpless and pitiful. The stereotypes are all negative. Poverty is maintained in part through the myths and stereotypes which blame and shame people in poverty ... Over-blaming crushes people's spirit and confidence.

But this seems to be changing. Many people talked about the fact that the image of Matson had got a 'lift', both among the residents and outside. The 1993 article in the local newspaper had described Matson as 'besieged – by poverty, unemployment and deprivation'. In February 1998, an MP stood up in parliament and referred to Matson as a 'model'.

The positive press coverage about Matson has not been lost on the residents. Because a lot of problems stem from preconceived ideas, myths, and attitudes, challenging these prejudices is often one of the early steps in a long process of change. The improved self-image has given people confidence that they can change things and influence decision makers. This confidence in dealing with the external world has translated into a reduction in apathy. For example, a call to protest against proposed cuts in grants to community projects in early 1997 saw two coachloads of angry residents gather at the City Council offices. 'Hands off our services' was clearly the message.

Strong sense of community

Underlying all these changes is a predominant sense of community. George Smith felt that this spirit was actually much stronger when

Matson was a thriving community of young families, with plenty of children and a lot of activity. But as the industries started closing down, many started moving away, leaving houses vacant: a convenient dumping ground for the Council. However, beginning with the campaign against selling the houses, the sense of community returned. *'But you can't take it for granted - you've got to work on it'*, he said.

It is not only the residents who experience this sense of community. A lot of the professionals and other service providers who work in Matson spoke of it almost enviously. Many of them talked about what I call the 'smile factor'. Run a 'smile test': smile at strangers and see how many smile back. I was never disappointed. I am willing to admit, though, that my magic tricks at the school may have had something to do with it!

But not everyone was enthusiastic. While conceding that 'some' change had taken place, a few indicated that they would prefer to leave. I tried to come to terms with this divide. At first I thought it was to do with the 'old' and the 'new' residents. But some old residents also did not feel so good about Matson, while some of the new ones did. A closer look seemed to indicate that it had more to do with their involvement with the community and its problems. Among those who were involved in the initial campaign, there seems to be a feeling of *'we did it'*: a sense of ownership over the process that turned Matson around, that gave it 'more outlook', as one resident put it.

What made Matson matter?

Attribution

This is an aspect of any impact assessment or evaluation where feathers tend to get ruffled. Everyone would like to claim credit and have their role recognised as being pivotal in the causes that effected change. My experience in Matson confirmed this. For the community, attribution was not so much of an issue. While everybody was quick to point out the changes that had taken place, people were very slow to commit themselves when asked what had brought these about. Various actors and contributory factors were identified, but everybody found it difficult to attribute the causes to any one of them. For example, the refurbishment of houses: some attributed it directly to the Council who pumped the money in, some to the better image and increased bargaining power that Matson now had with the Council, and some to the MNP, while others said that it was due to the Tenants' Associations. Perhaps the truth lies in all of these, because each clearly did have a role to play.

Local people were clear that various players contributed to the changes that have come about. That each of them played different roles, served different purposes, and met different needs was plainly accepted. Thus, it was not an issue of competition for plaudits, but a recognition of the intrinsically complementary nature of working towards change.

The roles of various actors

A range of actors was identified as having contributed significantly.

The City Council and County Council

The community perception of the role of the City Council and County Council and other statutory agencies has been ambivalent. From being seen as a heartless landlord in the late 1980s, the City Council regained some favour, primarily because of the refurbishments. That it provides substantial support to the MNP and other services is also a factor. Nonetheless, the Council represents 'power' and 'resource wealth', and that does not sit well with people who are by and large powerless and resource-dependent. But at the time of the assessment visit, relations between the community and the Council were reasonably good.

Part of this appeared to derive from the Council's acceptance of the importance of the voluntary sector and Neighbourhood Projects in general. This seems to have been reflected in the budget provisions. For example, Council staff seem more than willing to co-operate with the voluntary sector, not least because they seem to recognise that it fills up the gaping holes within the system. But there is no indication that the statutory agencies see the voluntary sector and communities as creative forces with whom they can work to bring about a sustainable social system. They tend to see the voluntary sector at best as allies to get a job done, and at worst as thorns in their side that they even have to pay for! Communities are 'customers' and 'clients' who must be satisfied – and if the voluntary sector can help, so be it. Any role for the community beyond that seems to be outside the scope and grasp of the system. All the stereotypical negative images of people in poverty are often enshrined in official attitudes and responses to the community.

A case in point: the acute shortage of foster carers came up for discussion at Matson. The Project quickly took on three part-time workers, who managed to recruit 32 possible carers. Training schedules were negotiated to match the availability of these workers. But on the crucial day when the trainers were to have an introductory meeting with the would-be carers, none of the carefully negotiated schedules had been given a second thought. The trainers had only 'one window' available, and that was for five consecutive full days! They had presumed that people living in Council estates must be poor, that poor people must be unemployed, and that unemployed people must be free to attend all-day courses for five days. Credit must go to the staff of the Project and from social services that they re-negotiated a compromise, although they lost some of the potential carers.

The Tenants' Associations

The Tenants' Associations are powerful representatives of the community in all their dealings with the Council, and they are recognised as partners in the management of Council properties. They have won a legitimate place within the system: an inside ring seat. The potential to play a vital role in protecting the interests of the tenants is inherent in this hard-won position. But so is the danger of co-option. A lot rests with the leaders to ensure that they do not end up representing the Council to the tenants, rather than the other way round.

The churches

While one does not sense that the people of Matson are especially religious, one can nonetheless feel the tremendous respect that the people have for the three churches in Matson, especially for their work with young people, and their unstinted support to all the community initiatives.

The other service providers

The number of service providers in Matson is one of the major sources of pride and comfort to the community. People who are especially vulnerable appreciate these services most, and their very presence makes the entire estate appear relatively vibrant and active. All the shops are open and full. Schools are well attended, and the doctor's surgery and the chemist are kept more than busy. That people see the increased provision of services as a measure of progress is in itself an indication of the importance of their role within the community.

The funders

While people were aware that charitable trusts and big businesses provided financial support to community initiatives, there did not seem to be sufficient interaction between them to warrant strong opinions one way or the other. The importance of financial and sometimes technical support to the Project cannot be diminished. However, donors and projects often make the critical mistake of believing that poverty is caused by a lack of resources or the improper management of these resources. The critical ingredient required for change is overlooked: a community organised and willing to tackle the systemic and structural causes of poverty. As Nadine Gordimer has said, 'The new century is not going to be new at all if we offer only charity, that palliative to satisfy the conscience and keep the same old system of haves and have-nots quietly contained.'

Funders tend to see themselves as supporting projects rather than enabling a process of change, so funding is piecemeal, insecure, and completely focused on specific measurable outputs: the number of children attending an after-school project, or the number of elderly people using the day-care centre, or the number of people who have walked through the doors of the project. This has obvious impacts on any project. First, it obliges it to spend a lot of time chasing funding, and invariably this makes great demands on project managers. The time spent on fundraising by the MNP Director in the two months that I was there was simply astounding, and frustrating for him and the staff. Indeed, more than half of the senior managers' time was taken up with this, and more if one included the time spent on retaining funders. Second, the insecurity of short-term funding does not allow a project the scope for long-term planning, although change is not just about achieving immediate targets.

Finally, even the best projects often fall into the trap of counting heads and so lose their ability to see what is happening around them: to be proactive in their plans and strategies, by being sensitive to local needs, to be able to see threats and opportunities with equal alacrity, and to see not just the trees, but also the woods. This last factor is a direct result of how donors, projects, and often communities themselves evaluate impact.

The Project

Various programmes and activities of the MNP were identified as being either directly responsible for or contributing to the changes that have taken place. There were no major differences between the perceptions of the staff and those of the community, beyond a question of emphasis. Most people saw the Project as having been a catalyst, and this was regarded as its greatest strength. Hence in the next section we consider the strengths and weaknesses of the Project in fulfilling this role.

Strengths of the Matson Neighbourhood Project

The Project had listened before acting. In general, project activities tend to stem from the individual skills of the initiators, and often also from predetermined responses to predetermined needs. Not so common is what has happened at Matson, where the activities are designed in response to needs identified by the community. A lot of effort went into trying to find out what were the community's unmet needs.

The Project's role has been to identify the resources – human and material – to meet these needs. For example, when large numbers of people were found to have unmet health-care needs, primarily due to a lack of mobility, the Project's inability to provide for this itself did not deter staff from looking for a solution – and that was to go back to the community, get a list of the doctors who were most consulted, and then contact those doctors and see which of them could be convinced to set up surgeries in Matson. The result: a doctor's surgery 'on the patch', a highly treasured service.

The Project *put the community first* and so became one of its focal points, something that everyone could turn to. There was a strong feeling among the residents that there was nothing that was outside the realm of the MNP, if it concerned or mattered to them. This determines the kind of relationship that the Project has with the community. The relationship goes beyond that of a provider and customer: it is one of two equal partners whose fortunes are inextricably woven together. In the words of the Deputy Director of the MMP:

> *We've built up some really firm friendships.* It would be so easy to take up everyone's problems and solve them, but what we're really about is empowering people to do that themselves. Having said that, though, we have to accept that there are people who will never cope, and that's where we come in. *I hope we meet people as friends, not as clients.* If someone's threatened with eviction, they know there are people around who will support them. (emphasis mine)

This approach ensured that, no matter what it does, the Project will tend automatically to involve the community - almost as a reflex response. How different from those projects where managers have to remind themselves to 'consult' the community.

This also results in a respect for and sensitivity to the problems and realities faced by local people, which again determines the way in which the MNP interacts with the community. To take two examples: in a supposedly high-crime area I was surprised to find that the Project's One Stop Shop does not pull down heavy steel shutters at night, in spite of valuable computers and other things within. Instead, a fragile wall of glass forms the shop front, completely covered with decorations in the form of job advertisements, painstakingly stuck on every day by the workers and volunteers. When I asked them about running such a risk, their reply was: '*All the kids hang out here at night. They hardly come by during the day. If we want them to see the jobs, then night it is.*' What they did not say is how people react to this kind of concern that is coupled with trust.

When people spoke of the achievements of the Project, it was with a sense of pride. This speaks highly of *community ownership* and is clearly a direct result of the strong focus on community. The community is not incidental – not just 'the beneficiaries', 'the clients', 'the customers', 'the end-users': they *are* the Project — an integral part of its structure and its functioning. This is reflected both in the way in which the Project implements its programmes and activities, and how it is structured. The high number of residents who are involved as volunteers, staff, and board members physically places the community at its core. When asked whether people would fight to keep the Project if it were threatened, the answer I got was: '*Well, we've always done it, haven't we? We fought to keep the houses, we fought to keep the chemist, we fought to keep the library – sure we'll fight to keep the Project.*'

Another strength was that the Project had helped to *raise the profile of Matson*. The way in which it has drawn funding into the area and got a lot of people interested was seen as directly contributing to changing the image of Matson, both within the community and outside. The Project has also *supported other service providers*, like the school or the library, to make them more effective; and it has played a *catalytic role* in bringing the various services together and keeping them on the patch. The MNP took the lead in creating a forum where all the various development actors and service providers in Matson could exchange notes. This included representatives from statutory services, such as school representatives, police officers, housing officers, etc., who meet once a month and share their experiences – the Matson Forum. If someone faces a problem in a particular area, someone else offers to help. For example, if someone is worried about a bunch of kids regularly hanging around at night, the youth worker immediately offers to look into it. The Matson Forum is an example of the synergetic effect (I understood its meaning only when I saw the Forum at work) created through the initiative of the Project.

The MNP is clearly seen as representing the community, both as individuals and collectively. For example, when someone needs to sort out a rent problem, he or she invariably first turns to the Project and is often accompanied by a staff member to the housing office. Similarly, if someone is applying for a job. 'Hand holding', one person called it. In so doing, the Project has placed the collective Matson community and the concept of Neighbourhood Projects on the official agenda. The role played by the Project in providing support and guidance to set up similar initiatives was seen as a matter of pride – almost a justification in itself for its existence. Indeed, all the Neighbourhood Projects of the county have formed themselves into a Network of Neighbourhood Projects.

An important strength has been the *leadership*: not just at the level of a charismatic director, but also at lower levels. In today's era of 'professionalism' in the voluntary sector, this kind of leadership has been criticised. There has been a tendency to believe that managerial skills can replace leadership skills. But it is not an either/or issue. The dynamics of social change are complex, and the different dimensions require different skills and abilities.

Recently, however, economic development has come to exert an overriding influence on the objectives, programmes, and activities of the voluntary sector. As a result, change is viewed as a management exercise: management of resources, both human and material, with inputs and outputs all being measured so that we can 'quantify' the change. Considering that fairly large capital resources are at stake, this is understandable. However, its influence seems to have been so overbearing that it has overshadowed, if not excluded, the social and political dimensions of the change process. The language of the market dominates, and charismatic leaders are re-classified as 'social entrepreneurs'.

Weaknesses and threats to the Matson Neighbourhood Project

It was not very easy to find critics of the Project, but a few objections did emerge. First, while everybody at the MNP is aware of the immediate goals and overall objectives of their teams, there does not seem to be a clear definition of the strategic objectives. Thus, while the various teams work closely together, there does not appear to be any strategic reason why they should stay together as one organisation. What unites them seems to be funding, the management board, and to some extent strong leadership. There is the danger that more successful units could drift to become independent. While there may be nothing wrong in this in itself, it might lead to the community's losing control. The history of this Project bears this out, for the community did lose ownership of one of the few economically successful projects (furniture recycling).

An in-depth analysis and understanding of the root causes of poverty would greatly contribute to evolving a more strategic role. While the MNP has had a huge impact on the changes that have taken place in Matson, it has not affected the local economy to the degree where we can safely assume that this change is irreversible. Matson still occupies the same place in the economic structure: very close to the bottom, with most people living on social-security benefits. This is not to detract from the success of getting people back into work. But they are still looking outside Matson for work. And we must recognise that part of the success is related to the improvement in the overall external economy.

No strategic moves are being made to create work in Matson, to make it a vibrant economy. On the other hand, perhaps without realising it and without intending to, the Project has contributed to the economy by bringing in a lot more jobs into the area. But is this sustainable, and is it enough? The Matson Project is almost completely dependent on external aid. At present its success attracts funding. But in my own experience, this very success will sooner or later turn away funders, because most like to look for 'the really needy'. If funds were cut or were to dwindle significantly, a lot of the changes could be reversed.

Lessons learned

It was with some trepidation that I embarked on this impact assessment, especially when confronted with all the literature on the subject. But since the terms of reference were completely open-ended – the

Project and I could evolve the methodology as we went along – the task was not as intimidating as it could have been. In fact, it was exciting and refreshing, because rather than trying to fit the Project into a pre-determined framework or methodology, so much was learned from just 'being around'. There was a sense of discovery, as much of the learning was the result of chance encounters. Too often in our concern for results — 'outputs' — the path is so well charted beforehand that there is hardly the space or opportunity for these encounters. It takes courage on all sides to be so open-ended – which is possible only if all those involved trust each other. And that was perhaps one of the most significant elements of the whole exercise: trust. This shaped and determined the direction taken by the exercise, and also produced some very interesting insights on the whole issue of impact assessment itself.

Holistic assessment

Often assessments occur at the behest of a donor. This is because the (unstated) purpose of most assessments is to provide evidence to a donor agency, and they in turn to their respective donors, that the money has been well spent. In a project that has multiple donors – as most projects do – one can imagine what happens. Such an approach is not only going to result in a fragmented and lopsided view of the change process, but it is also likely to result in confusion and competition on the issue of attribution. Such competition can affect the various teams within a given project. For example, if we were to assess the work of the One Stop Shop in order to convince the NatWest Bank, the donor, of its wonderful achievements, there is always the danger of overlooking the contribution of the Advice Team which possibly played a significant part in motivating people to look for jobs. It all leads to a lot of friction within the organisation, because the more obvious and visible activities tend to get the credit.

This fragmented and negative approach to assessment is even more evident in the way that the statutory services work, as each service finds it impossible to look beyond the tops of its filing cabinets. For example, a reduction in crime was claimed as one of the primary changes that had taken place. The police can claim that this is because of their excellent service. Some residents think that it has more to do with the refurbishment of the houses and the sense of community created by the MNP. The Youth Worker from the Baptist Church, or from Social Services, may also have contributed. In a desperate bid to justify their existence, this competition between services may result in services pitting themselves against each other. If one talks to the people themselves, one realises that the truth is that all these services, perhaps along with other factors like a general improvement in the economy have, *together*, contributed to the reduction in crime.

This does not detract from the need to monitor or evaluate the functioning of each service or sector. But let us not confuse monitoring and evaluation with impact assessment, or efficiency with effectiveness. Donors above all need to understand this: that the pounds and pennies can be counted and accounted for, but to stop there does not give us an understanding of the impact of the intervention. At the same time, to try to understand impact only through one particular intervention does not give us the whole picture either. To assess impact, we have to take a holistic approach that presupposes a complementarity between the various actors involved.

The community as the starting point

In a more traditional approach, predetermined impact-indicators are the usual starting point. In a carefully planned and well-managed project, one would expect that these indicators had been defined from the outset by the project itself. In the absence of such specified indicators, an impact-assessment team would draw up indicators with project personnel and then set about measuring impact against the chosen indicators. One way or the other, the starting point is invariably a clearly defined set of impact indicators. (Never mind all the midnight oil burned in differentiating between output and outcome and impact indicators, let alone the debate about the need for universal indicators!)

So it is pretty inevitable that any review or assessment will tend to focus on predetermined targets and quantifiable indicators against which they can be measured. In so doing, the role of the community becomes minimal as project records, survey data, figures, calculators, and computers occupy centre stage. Review teams of 'experts' are set up, and in the optimum scenario the community is 'consulted' to corroborate their findings.

However, if change is seen essentially as a political process, which must have implications for the economic life and other aspects of the community, then the starting point of assessing change has to be the community itself. How do they perceive themselves and their lives? With the Matson Neighbourhood Project, the absence of predefined indicators, coupled with an open-ended approach, allowed us to evolve a methodology in which the community was the starting point. The fact that the MNP had such a strong focus on community — not just as end-users of the services but as the protagonists in the entire development drama – left us with no doubt that the methodology for the case study would have to be community-focused, in keeping with the approach and entire culture of the Project. A community's change process is not just a management exercise: it is a part of their daily struggle, and for most poor communities it is very often the purpose of their lives. They *experience* the impact of any intervention on a daily basis, whether or not they articulate it. To quote Nadine Gordimer once more: 'How do victims themselves perceive their poverty? They live it; they know it best, beyond all outside concepts.'

NGOs need to recognise this and not presume that they are the beginning and the end of a change process. The starting point of an assessment should be to provide the forums in which (or the means by which) the community's experiences and perceptions can be articulated. Statistics can then be the add-ons to corroborate and cross-check primary evidence. A difference between community perception and figures should lead us to re-question the community's perception as well as the validity of the figures. Which brings us to another lesson learned.

The role of numbers

One cannot deny that it is important to track specific interventions, to monitor and build up a base of figures, all of which will form an essential part of any review or assessment exercise. The issue is not whether or not figures are needed, but rather the role that they play. Will they be the focal point on which the assessment is based, or will they be used instead to underscore, corroborate, or challenge the perceptions and experiences of the community, the project staff, and all the other actors involved in the change process? It is very rare to find the perceptions of the community occupying the pride of place in any review or assessment. At best they are appended to underscore a point made by a table of figures – whereas in fact it should be the other way around.

Obviously, in this impact assessment we opted for numbers to be used in this way – confident that, since we had the co-operation of the Head of Planning of the Gloucestershire County Council, obtaining the figures would be easy. The reality was somewhat different. In spite of recruiting a person who would collect the figures, we did not succeed in getting data that would be at all meaningful to this exercise. Not that it was impossible, but it could not be done in the time available and it would have required more effort than we were able to put in. For example, there were at least two sets of figures that we thought would have a direct bearing in terms of corroborating people's perceptions of two of the major changes that had taken place. One concerned crime, and the other related to whether people wanted to stay in Matson. If we could have obtained the statistics related to crime over the last few years, it should have been possible to see whether there had actually been a drop in the incidence of crime to the extent perceived by the community. However, when we attempted to collect these figures, apart from the red tape encountered, we were given to understand that they were not recorded in a way that could be easily extracted for a comparative study of the incidence of crime over the years, which makes one wonder what anyone does with all the figures in the first place. Hoping to correlate these figures with other events and happenings on the estate, like the refurbishment of the houses, and to analyse possible factors that could contribute to the reduction of crime, was obviously hoping for too much.

If this was too much, we thought that at least an analysis of the second set of figures, namely the turnaround in the occupancy of the properties, would give us an idea of whether the statistics corroborated the local perception that now more people wanted to stay on the estate. But we found at the Housing Office that the methodology for collecting the figures had been changed so often that no meaningful comparative study could be done. Perhaps if we had put in a lot more effort to extract these figures, we may have succeeded – but at what cost?

The point I wish to make, however, is that, lacking a holistic approach, each department had gone about collecting the figures in its own way. There was no indication that any of these figures had been analysed, either within the department or in conjunction with other departments, to understand what worked and what did not. The bottom line was clearly the pounds and the pennies : if the sums of money tallied, that was all that seemed to matter. At the end of the day, none of the figures would help us to understand either the change that had taken place or the causes for this change.

A more holistic approach to social services would not only affect the kinds of figures collected by each of the departments but would also affect the use to which these figures would be put, and would perhaps contribute to more effective planning, leading in turn to more sustainable and lasting change. To take another example: health and disability link-workers across the different Neighbourhood Projects all identified breathing difficulties as being the most common physical ailment. This was borne out by the pharmacist, who clearly indicated that damp could be one of the contributing factors. Comparing the incidence of breathing problems among people living in refurbished houses and those in the older and damper houses would give us a clearer picture of cause and effect – leading to a better allocation of resources. Such an approach, however, presupposes a certain element of trust on the part of all the players – something that is difficult to foster in the highly competitive scramble for resources.

Conclusion

What did we learn from this experience? The feedback from the staff, board members, and members of the community was that the exercise helped everyone to stop and take a critical look at what was happening and that it may well shape future plans. What did it take? Just someone to create the opportunity for a lot of people to articulate what they feel, what they know, what they have experienced. Simply, it meant listening to the community.

Nobody viewed the exercise as if there was going to be an expert from the outside doing an impact assessment of a project about which he had known nothing a couple of months before. All of those involved had seen it more as a process of listening to what everybody had to say and pulling this all together, with the hope that it would trigger off some critical thinking about the role and impact of the Project.

Of the elements that contributed to make this listening effective, the most critical was the fact that the key people involved in the Project themselves wanted to go through such an exercise. This created such an atmosphere of trust that even I was surprised how willing everyone was to allow me to be privy to some of the Project's innermost deliberations. There was no meeting that I was not invited to attend, and there was not the slightest hint of defensiveness. I can only ascribe this to the facts that, first, the MNP firmly believes in itself; second, there is genuine willingness and openness to learn and improve; and third, that this is because the Project is community-driven.

As managers of large resources and large organisations, NGOs all over the world have been caught up in evolving complex 'scientific' methods to enable them to be accountable to their donors. How much have these methods contributed to being accountable to the community? Unless we recognise the social and political dimensions of change and development, we will continue groping for elusive assurance that we are on the right track.

At the end of the visit there was not the slightest shadow of doubt in my mind that Matson *did* matter. And that, among a host of other factors, the Matson Neighbourhood Project has played a critical and vital role. And if you were to ask me how I know this, I must tell you very simply 'because the community told me so!'

Acknowledgements

This exercise had such an 'impact' on me that it is only fair that I devote a little space to 'attribution'. To thank Oxfam and the MNP is to thank no one in particular, so let me mention a few names: Audrey Bronstein and Chris Roche of Oxfam, Mark Gale of the MNP, Alison Cathles of Gloucestershire County Council, the board Members of MNP, especially Andy Jarrett and the Revd. Stephen, as well as Martin Simon, Amanda Williams, and the innumerable members of Matson, who were so open and friendly.

Annotated bibliography

Development in Practice *seeks to challenge conventional assumptions about development and to stimulate new approaches to the task of bringing about social and economic justice for all. We aim to bring practice and analysis together, in the belief that neither can be effective without the other.*

Based on the tenth-anniversary issue of the journal, this Reader illustrates some of the debates in which development NGOs are actively involved, seen both from inside the sector and by concerned activists, scholars, and aid-watchers. These debates range from engagement with external realities, whether the impact of macro-economic policies and the role of the corporate sector, or the complexities of working in situations of armed conflict, to concerns about internal organisational matters such as management culture or how to evaluate the impact of advocacy. For the most part, the contributions from NGO staff are grounded in practice, rather than engaging with intellectual theory. This suggests that, while they may be value-driven, today's international NGOs are guided more by pragmatism than by ideology. The exception proves the rule that, as action-oriented organisations, NGOs tend to steer clear of academic debate, and are not —and perhaps cannot afford to be — unduly concerned with radical critiques of the development paradigm within which they operate.

In compiling this Annotated Bibliography, we have therefore sought mainly to situate some of the issues addressed in the Reader within a wider context, rather than exploring more theoretical directions. (The bibliographies in earlier Readers have generally sought to do this – see the entry below.)

Unlike other titles in the series, this Reader is not strictly thematic, in the sense of being concerned with a discrete topic. So, in keeping with its celebratory nature, we have included works written or suggested by contributors, as well as information about some of the organisations with which they are connected. And, since this Reader was compiled in collaboration with Oxfam International, we have also highlighted some of the organisation's recent publications. While this brief bibliography is unashamedly idiosyncratic, we trust that it will serve to encourage further thought and reading, and to stimulate debate. It was compiled by Deborah Eade and Nicola Frost, Editor and Reviews Editor respectively of Development in Practice.

Books

Haleh Afshar and Stephanie Barrientos (eds.): *Women, Globalization and Fragmentation in the Developing World*, Basingstoke: Macmillan, 1999.
Insecurity and feminisation of the international labour market have affected women in differing ways. Many households are now headed by women as men migrate farther afield in search of work, and their burdens are further increased by the withdrawal of the State from welfare services. However, flexible employment opportunities have helped to empower some women. Contributors examine women's varied experiences of globalisation and challenge Western orthodoxies on matters such as Islam, and women-headed households, as well as illustrating the shared concerns of women at either end of the global food chain.

Samir Amin: *Spectres of Capitalism: A Critique of Current Intellectual Fashions*, New York: Monthly Review Press, 1998.
The author criticises the belief in a global capitalist triumph by focusing on the aspirations of the destitute millions of the post-Cold War era. He examines the changing notion of crisis in capitalism, misconceptions about the free market, culture in revolutions, the decline of 'the law of value', the philosophical roots of post-modernism, the impact of telecommunications on ideology, and the myth of 'pure economics'. See also *Capitalism in the Age of Globalization: The Management of Contemporary Society* (1997).

Mary B Anderson and Peter J Woodrow, *Rising from the Ashes: Development Strategies in Times of Disaster*, London: Lynne Rienner, 1989 (new edn 1998).
Building on many case studies, the authors demonstrate that relief programmes are never neutral in their impact on development, and that the nature of development contains within it the seeds of how catastrophes will affect differing social groups. The resulting Capacities and Vulnerabilities Analysis (CVA) is a practical framework to track the dynamic relationship between differing people's needs, vulnerabilities,

and capacities. *Do No Harm: How Aid Can Support Peace – or War* (1999), also by Mary B Anderson and based on the Local Capacities for Peace Project, provides a framework to analyse how international aid interacts with 'dividers' and 'connectors' in any given conflict-affected setting, and so help to feed (or reduce) intergroup tensions or to weaken (or strengthen) intergroup connections.

Helge Ole Bergesen and Leiv Lunde, *Dinosaurs or Dynamos? The United Nations and the World Bank at the Turn of the Century*, London: Earthscan, 1999.
The authors explore what can be expected of the UN and the World Bank in terms of their stated aims regarding world development. Opening with historical overviews of the two bodies, the authors go on to compare them today. They call for a scaling down of the inflated claims made by and on behalf of these institutions and they argue that their roles should be reconceived in more practical terms.

Robert Chambers: *Whose Reality Counts?Putting the First Last*, London, IT Publications, 1997.
A leading proponent of participatory approaches to development, Chambers argues here as elsewhere that unequal power relations between development professionals or agencies and their Third World 'partners' distort thinking and practice, and have a damaging effect on both parties. More than the tools and techniques with which PRA is associated, Chambers calls for development professionals to change their attitudes and behaviour.

Neera Chandhoke: *State and Civil Society: Explorations in Political Theory*, New Delhi: Sage India, 1995.
A theoretical survey of the history of civil society in Western political thought, this title includes a useful bibliography. It highlights some of the limitations of the standard theoretical constructions for how we think about civil society, for example the classification of household politics as a private rather than public concern. It also underlines the paradoxical belief that a free civil society can hold accountable the very State that constitutes it.

Emma Crewe and Elizabeth Harrison: *Whose Development? An Ethnography of Aid*, London and New York: Zed Books, 1998.
Drawing on their respective experiences of working in an international NGO and a multilateral development agency, the authors analyse the diverse and often subtle impacts of power relations all along the aid chain, in terms of discourse, gender, ethnicity, and class. While not advocating a post-development position, the authors illustrate the impossibility of pure or disinterested development interventions.

Deborah Eade (ed): *Development in Practice Readers*, Oxford: Oxfam.
Each book in this series of thematic compilations from *Development in Practice* contains an original introductory essay on the chosen theme and an annotated bibliography. The bibliographies can be viewed at <www.developmentinpractice.org>.

Of particular relevance to debates on development paradigms that are only touched upon in the present volume are *Development and Patronage, Development and Rights*, and *Development, NGOs, and Civil Society*, all of which are also available in Spanish. *Development and Social Action* includes many references to NGO advocacy and campaigning work.

Michael Edwards: *Future Positive*, London: Earthscan, 1999.
The author examines the international aid system – its purpose and effectiveness, and the role of international institutions in its administration. Edwards posits a future of collective action based on 'critical friendship', in which NGOs and civil society ('an active global citizenry') lead the drive for change. He is co-editor (with David Hulme) of: *NGOs, States and Donors: Too Close for Comfort?*, Macmillan, 1997; *NGOs — Performance and Accountability: Beyond the Magic Bullet*, London: Earthscan, 1996; and *Making a Difference: NGOs and Development in a Changing World*, London: Earthscan, 1992.

John Elkington: *Cannibals with Forks: The triple bottom line of 21st century business*, Oxford: Capstone, 1997.
The author argues that markets and corporations are increasingly sensitive not only to the financial bottom-line, but also to the need to ensure that business is both environmentally sustainable and socially responsible. While many observers question the sincerity of their commitment to the triple bottom-line, Elkington holds that enlightened self-interest could – if companies were held publicly accountable for the impact of their behaviour – eventually lead to changes in practice, much as businesses in the nineteenth century found that the political cost of the slave trade was eventually at odds with their own interests.

Paul Feyerabend: *Against Method*, London: Verso, 1993 (3rd edn, including introduction to Chinese edition).
Widely hailed as offering an essential critique of scientific reductionism, the author argues that when scientific issues of public concern are discussed, intellectuals are frequently wrong — and/or wrong-headed — while 'ignorant' lay-people often prove to be right.

Nancy Folbre: *Who Pays for the Kids: Gender and the Structures of Constraint*, London: Routledge, 1994.
The author focuses on how and why people form overlapping groups that influence and limit what they want, how they behave, and what they get. She scrutinises feminist theory and political economy, and collective action and patriarchal power. A section on how structures of constraint have shaped histories of social reproduction in Europe, the USA, Latin America, and the Caribbean illustrates the relationship between various forms of patriarchal power and the expansion of wage employment.

John W. Foster, Anita Anand, Jing de la Rosa, et al.: *Whose World is it Anyway? Civil Society, the United Nations and the Multilateral Future*, Ottawa: The United Nations Association in Canada, 1999 (also available in French).
This compilation looks at the various forms of engagement by civil-society organisations (NGOs and social movements) with the UN system, most particularly through the series of conferences and 'Plus Five' reviews of the 1990s, and examines how the rules of the game are changing as other institutional actors emerge, and as transnational networks become a political force on the world stage.

Jonathan A. Fox and L. David Brown (eds.): *The Struggle for Accountability: The World Bank, NGOs and Grassroots Movements*, Cambridge MA: MIT Press, 1998.
This book analyses reforms within the World Bank that led to the adoption of more rigorous environmental and social policies, and asks how the Bank has responded to external critique and how far NGO advocacy campaigns represent the people most directly affected by Bank projects. The Bank is shown to be more publicly accountable as the result of protest and external scrutiny, and their empowering effect on 'inside'reformers. NGO networks are also becoming more accountable to their 'partner' organisations, partly because of stronger grassroots movements, and partly in response to the Bank's demand that they demonstrate their legitimacy.

Johan Galtung: *Choose Peace: A Dialogue Between Johan Galtung and Daisaku Ikeda*, London: Pluto Press, 1995.
In this volume, the founder of the International Peace Research Institute (IPRI) in Oslo is in discussion with the Buddhist scholar and NGO leader, Daisaku Ikeda, on issues such as nationalism, nuclear arms proliferation, religious fundamentalism, Western domination, the death penalty, and the role of the UN in peace-keeping. Galtung is a leading proponent of peace studies as an academic discipline. His many other works include *Human Rights in Another Key*, and *Peace by Peaceful Means: Peace and Conflict, Development and Civilization*.

Susan George: *The Lugano Report: On Preserving Capitalism in the Twenty-first Century*, London: Pluto Press, 1999.
Written by a hypothetical team of 'policy intellectuals', convened by world leaders to consider the future of the global economy, this 'report' demonstrates the inherent instability of the existing capitalist system and identifies a set of uncompromising recommendations on the measures that would logically need to be taken for the rich to remain on top. Susan George then examines these morally repugnant recommendations and offers an alternative vision of the future. Associate Director of the Transnational Institute in Amsterdam, she is the author of several classic texts, including *How the Other Half Dies* and *The Debt Boomerang*.

Anthony Giddens and Will Hutton (eds.): *On the Edge*, London: Jonathan Cape, 2000.
Contributors, who include Manuel Castells, Richard Sennett, Vandana Shiva, George Soros, and Paul Volcher, chart the contours of contemporary capitalism,

analyse the role of business in the new context of innovation and competitiveness, and discuss the impact of globalisation on the nature of the capitalist venture. Giddens' many works include *The Third Way and Its Critics*, and *Runaway World: How Globalisation is Changing Our Lives*. Hutton is author of *The State We Are In*.

Eric Hobsbawm: *On the Edge of the New Century*, London: Little, Brown, & Co., 2000. In interview with Antonio Polito, Hobsbawm discusses topics such as US hegemony and the decline of the Western Empire, the global economy, culture and the 'global village', the disappearance of any sharp distinction between a state of war and a state of peace, and the depoliticisation of politics. This book and his earlier work, *The Age of Extremes*, offer a concise account of the thinking of one of the foremost historians of the twentieth century.

Cecile Jackson and Ruth Pearson (eds.): *Feminist Visions of Development: Gender Analysis and Policy*, London: Routledge, 1998.
Contributions from feminist scholars and development practitioners chart the route from the socialist feminism of the 1970s, to the more global issues of the late 1990s, including the environment, civil society, and macro-economic policy, while education, industrialisation, and population policy also remain high on the gender and development agenda.

Allan Kaplan: *The Development of Capacity*, Geneva: UN NGLS, 1999.
The author challenges development practitioners to rethink the 'development project' paradigm, and the values and assumptions that this entails. Any new model must be flexible enough to accommodate the wide range of development organisations, and the uncertainties of organisational change. Kaplan advocates a holistic understanding of the factors governing organisational capacity, rather than the rigid, technical approach adopted by many Northern donors and aid agencies. See also *The Development Practitioners' Handbook*, Pluto Press, 1999.

Inge Kaul, Isabelle Grunberg and Marc A. Stern (eds.): *Global Public Goods: International Cooperation in the Twenty-first Century*, 1999, Oxford: OUP.
Taking the concept of natural public goods into the international arena, this book identifies an under-supply of global public goods as the key to understanding the crises affecting the modern world, achieving financial stability, and reducing environmental pollution. Drawing on development and aid literature, and on economic theory, the contributors argue that, while there is little incentive to governments to pursue promotion of global public goods, participation in such activities remains largely limited to governments, despite an increasingly diverse civil society.

Norman Uphoff, Milton Esman, and Anirudh Krishna: *Reasons for Success: Learning from Instructive Experiences in Rural Development*, West Hartford, CT: Kumarian, 1998.

The authors draw on an earlier work, *Reasons for Hope*, in outlining their concern that development economists are increasingly neglecting rural development. Drawing on case-study material, they argue that an improvement in rural living standards depends less on money alone, and more on ideas, leadership, and appropriate methods of work.

Margaret E Keck and Kathryn Sikkink (eds.): *Activists Beyond Borders: Advocacy Networks in International Politics*, Ithaca, NY: Cornell University Press, 1998.

Contributors explore the emergence of networks which coalesce and operate across national frontiers, constituting a type of pressure group whose importance was until recently overlooked by political analysts.

Rajni Kothari: *Human Consciousness and the Amnesia of Development*, London and New Jersey: Zed Books, 1993.

Arguing that poverty is not primarily a matter of economics, but a particular state of social, political, psychological, and existential being that defines the human condition at any given point, the author examines the institutions and processes that create and maintain exclusion and immiseration. He calls not for utopian theoretical solutions, but for 'ethical intervention' by ordinary people in order to rechart the course of history.

Mary Ann Liddell and Marsha Ann Dickson: *Social Responsibility in the Global Market: Fair Trade of Cultural Products*, London: Sage, 1999.

The authors review the successes and failures of seven Alternative Trading Organisations (ATOs) in examining how, in practice, it is possible to reconcile the consumer's social concerns with the producer's financial interests. They offer a model to show how to develop an effective fair-trade system within an increasingly global market.

Marshall McLuhan: *Understanding Media*, Cambridge, MA: MIT Press, 1994.

Reprinted to mark the thirtieth anniversary of this 1960s classic on the then-emerging phenomenon of mass media, with an introduction by Lewis Lapham that reviews McLuhan's work in the light of the technological, political, and social changes that have since taken place. McLuhan's influence is alive today, as phrases like 'the global village' and 'the medium is the message' are part of the common lexicon. A major biography was written by Neil Postman, himself a leading critic of the uncritical adoption of technology without regard for its ideological meaning.

Maria Mies: *Patriarchy and Accumulation on a World Scale: Women in the International Division of Labour* (2nd edn), London: Zed Books, 1999.

A classic text in which the author argues that feminist analysis must transcend the divisions created by a capitalist patriarchal system between Northern and Southern women. Mies explores the women's movement worldwide, the history of colonialist processes, and the relationship between women's liberation and national liberation struggles. She calls for a feminist perspective that transcends the international system of gender roles and the gendered division of labour, and for a society where the liberation of some is not based on the exploitation of others.

Brian K. Murphy: *Transforming Ourselves, Transforming the World: An Open Conspiracy for Social Change*, London: Zed Books, 1999.
The author presents a personal vision of the way in which modern society immobilises individuals, fragmenting our existence, while also imposing uniformity and stifling creativity. The 'open conspiracy' of the title – with a focus on education, learning, growth, risk taking, and activism – is, Murphy argues, the best way to enact a radical humanist approach to social change and freedom from domination.

Carolyn Nordstrom: *A Different Kind of War Story (Ethnography of Political Violence series)*, Philadelphia, PA: University of Pennsylvania Press, 1997.
Describing some of the many 'civil society' activies in which people in Mozambique were engaged even in the midst of war, the author notes that, without a working system of governance, people did not become mean and brutish, but re-created their own order and systems for caring. However, the formal systems of governance – that is, the fighting forces – were brutish in the extreme. This points to lessons for how best to support civilian activity in times of war. Nordstrom's other titles include *The Paths to Domination, Resistance, and Terror*, and *Fieldwork Under Fire: Contemporary Studies of Violence and Survival*.

Robert O'Brien, Anne Marie Goetz, Jan Aart Scholte, and Marc Williams: *Contesting Global Governance: Multilateral Economic Institutions and Global Social Movements*, Cambridge: CUP, 2000.
In the face of growing popular opposition to the policies of the multilateral economic institutions, the authors suggest that a contest over global governance is the legacy of the twentieth century. They analyse the response of the IMF, World Bank, and WTO to pressure from social movements, and trace the shifting strategies of elements of civil society in their struggle to influence these institutions. The book demonstrates the growing complexity of contemporary multilateralism, which, it is argued, is applicable beyond the three institutions under scrutiny.

Sol Piciotto and Ruth Mayne (eds.): *Regulating International Business: Beyond Liberalization*, Basingstoke, UK: Macmillan and Oxfam, 2000.
A compilation of papers written as part of the debate stimulated by the proposed Multilateral Agreement on Investment (MAI), negotiations on which were suspended by the OECD in 1998. A controversial proposal, the MAI gave rise to an unprecedented level of international mobilisation, focused on transnational companies and the WTO, and against neo-liberal economic policies more generally. This book seeks to

broaden the agenda in order to address concerns about poverty and sustainable development which should be dealt with in a multilateral framework for investment.

Fenella Porter, Ines Smyth, and Caroline Sweetman (eds.): *Gender Works: Oxfam Experience in Policy and Practice*, Oxford: Oxfam, 1999.
Gender equity can be promoted only when the working culture and the underlying values of a given organisation take this concern as a point of departure, rather than as an afterthought. However, organisations are made up of individuals, who bring their own values and attitudes to their work. This volume reflects debates about gender and organisational culture, especially in the NGO sector. Contributors reflect on their diverse experience of Oxfam's application of its formal commitment to promoting gender equity.

Aseem Prakash and Jeffrey A Hart (eds.): *Coping With Globalization*, London: Routledge, 2000.
In the third in a series of volumes on advances in international political economy, contributors consider the conceptual issues raised by the asymmetrical policy and trade environment, in order to review the coping strategies of governments and businesses in the face of major changes. The companion text, *Responding to Globalization*, focuses on the political, ideological, and economic factors behind responses to globalisation, while *Globalization and Governance* examines the effects of globalisation on governance and the State, and includes a literature overview.

Majid Rahnema with Victoria Bawtree (eds.): *The Post-Development Reader*, London: Zed Books, 1997.
This original and challenging compilation brings together many incisive readings on the dominant development paradigm and on contemporary development practice, particularly from outstanding Southern thinkers such as Arturo Escobar, Gustavo Esteva, Eduardo Galeano, Ivan Illich, Ashis Nandy, and Hassan Zaoual. Its extensive bibliography suggests many other areas that development professionals would do well to explore.

Chris Roche: *Impact Assessment for Development Agencies: Learning to Value Change*, Oxford: Oxfam with Novib, 1999.
The author shows how and why impact assessment needs to be integrated into all stages of development programmes, from planning to evaluation. His basic premise is that it should refer not to the immediate outputs or effects of a project or programme, but to any lasting or significant changes that it brought about. From a theoretical overview, he moves on to discuss specific tools and methods, illustrating their application in development, emergency relief, and advocacy work. The book includes a number of case studies by Oxfam GB and Novib staff and by organisations supported by them.

Amartya Sen: *Development as Freedom*, Oxford: OUP, 1999.

In this comprehensive critique of neo-liberal orthodoxies, Sen argues that human freedoms 'are not only the primary ends of development, they are also among its principal means'. Economic growth cannot be an end in itself, nor will the gains ever 'trickle down' far enough to create a more equal society. Rather, the eradication of poverty requires the removal of tyranny and repression, and the expansion of economic opportunities that are underpinned by effective public services. A leading contributor to the UNDP *Human Development Report*, and with a consistent focus on rights and freedoms, Sen is the author of a number of highly influential works in the fields of ethics, development, and political economy.

David Sogge with Kees Biekart and John Saxby (eds.): *Compassion and Calculation: The Business of Foreign Aid*, London: Pluto, with Transnational Institute, 1996.

Large NGOs, or private aid agencies, continue to enjoy enormous public confidence, while also drawing increasing proportions of their income from government sources. The mechanisms for financial accountability are, however, far more developed than those designed to ensure political legitimacy. Contributors suggest that the NGO bubble will inevitably burst, and call on NGOs to be more honest and more courageous in deciding where their future lies.

Sphere Project: *Humanitarian Charter and Minimum Standards in Disaster Response*, Geneva: Sphere (distributed by Oxfam GB), 2000.

Based on the Humanitarian Charter, which sets out the central legally based principles governing the provision of humanitarian aid, this book defines what people affected by disasters have a right to expect from aid agencies. This field-tested manual is a tool for improving the effectiveness and accountability of humanitarian assistance. It includes sections that present minimum standards for provision of water and sanitation, food aid and other nutritional inputs, shelter, and health services. Also available in French, Portuguese, Russian, and Spanish.

UNDP: *Human Development Report 2000*, New York and Oxford: OUP, 2000.

The *HDR* was launched in 1990 as a counterweight to the influential *World Development Report* of the World Bank (see below). It focuses on the social and ethical dimensions of development, casting the enhancement of human well-being as both the end and the means to its attainment. Specifically, the *HDR* presents an alternative set of yardsticks to challenge the conventional measures of economic growth, such as gross national product and gross domestic product. Its statistics repeatedly demonstrate that economic growth alone cannot bring about equitable distribution, and that equity (between women and men, for instance) is not resource-dependent: many poor countries have a better record on gender equity than do far wealthier ones. The 2000 report focuses on human rights to development, and so breaks with the Cold War division of rights into political and civil versus social, economic, and cultural. It thus sets out the framework for a new discourse on rights-based development.

UNRISD: *Visible Hands: Taking Responsibility for Social Development*, Geneva: UNRISD, 2000.

The 1995 Social Summit, for which UNRISD produced *States of Disarray: The Social Effects of Globalization*, was followed by the Copenhagen Plus Five Summit in July 2000. This sequel report shows that few of the commitments made by UN member-states have been backed with action or resources. Neo-liberal globalisation has continued apace, albeit with greater public awareness of its harmful impacts. Technocratic decision making is undermining the accountability of State institutions and has forged a separation between economic and social policy. Corporate social responsibility has proved largely rhetorical, and a vocal but aid-dependent NGO sector is no substitute for a vibrant civil society. The hope is that rights-based development agendas can seize the public imagination, as the international finance and trade organisations at last begin to question their own assumptions. Much of the detailed original research on which *Visible Hands* is based is available in UNRISD's Occasional Papers series. Web: <www.unrisd.org>

Peter Uvin: *Aiding Violence: The Development Enterprise in Rwanda*, West Harford CT: Kumarian, 1998.

Exploring the connections between international development aid and the 1994 genocide in Rwanda, the author situates the role of aid within a network of other factors, including the complex ethnic history of Rwanda. Uvin notes how ethnic tension can obscure broader political and economic issues, and asks why the ethnic hatred that was provoked by the ruling élite for political ends was taken up so readily by ordinary people. The potential symbiosis between aid and the ruling classes revealed here is also relevant in other national contexts.

Alison Van Rooy (ed.): *Civil Society and the Aid Industry*, London: Earthscan, in association with The North–South Institute, 1999.

Among official agencies and NGOs, civil society has become what Van Rooy calls 'an analytical hatstand'. Uncritical and normative assumptions are made about what it is, how it functions, and how it can be supported by external agencies in furtherance of their own declared agendas of democratisation, good governance, and popular participation; but the lack of theoretical clarity in the context of over-hastily disbursed funds can make for interventions that are profoundly damaging in the long term. Critical case studies by scholar-activists from Hungary, Kenya, Peru, and Sri Lanka are framed by excellent opening and concluding chapters by Van Rooy.

World Bank: *World Development Report 2000/2001: Attacking Poverty*, OUP and World Bank, Oxford, 2000.

As did the 1980 and 1990 reports, this report seeks to set out a contemporary definition of poverty and to outline the Bank's broad approach to poverty eradication for the coming decade. Noting that almost half the world's population lives on less than US$2 per day, the Bank argues that major reductions in poverty can be achieved through promoting equitable economic growth, making State institutions more accountable to all in society, and enhancing the security of those who are most vulnerable. The Development Gateway is an independent non-profit foundation set up by the Bank as an Internet portal to information, knowledge, and dialogue about sustainable development and poverty reduction. Web: www.worldbank.org/gateway/

Journals

Alternatives: A Journal for Social Transformation and Humane Governance: published quarterly by Lynne Rienner. ISSN: 0304-3754. Editors: Saul H. Mendovitz, D. L. Sheth, and Yoshikazu Sakamoto.
An alternative to conventional international journals about politics, providing a forum for feminist, post-colonial and post-modern scholarship in international relations. Contributors consider emerging new forms of world politics, challenge the ethnocentrism of much modern social and political analysis, and emphasise the possibilities of a humane global polity.

Alternatives Sud: published three times a year by L'Harmattan on behalf of Centre Tricontinental Louvain-La Neuve; also in book form. Editor: François Houtart.
A journal dedicated to disseminating alternative political and economic analysis emanating from Africa, Latin America, and the Asia-Pacific region, and to redressing the imbalance between Northern and Southern scholarship. Recent themes have included liberation theologies, democracy and the market, and the construction of poverty.

Democratization: published quarterly by Frank Cass, ISSN: 1351-0347. Editors: Peter Burnell and Peter Calvert.
Dedicated to gaining a better understanding of the evolution of democratic institutions and practices, both within and across national and cultural borders, the journal makes special reference to developing countries and post-communist societies, and aims to be of interest to policy makers and journalists as well as academics. See especially Jenny Pearce, 'Civil society, the market and democracy in Latin America' 4(2), 1997.

Development: published quarterly by Sage on behalf of the Society for International Development. ISSN: 1011-6370. Editor: Wendy Harcourt.
A thematic journal to foster dialogue between activists and intellectuals committed to the search for alternative paths towards a sustainable and just world, with a particular focus on promoting local–global links. Relevant special issues include 'Globalization: Opening up spaces for civic engagement' 40(2) 1997, 'Globalization: New institutions, new partnerships, new lives' 40(3) 1997, and 'Commitments and Challenges: Reviewing social development' 43(2) 2000.

Development and Change: published five times a year by Blackwell on behalf of the Institute of Social Studies. ISSN: 0012-155X. Editors: Ben White, Ashwani Saith, and Martin Doornbos.
An interdisciplinary journal devoted to the critical analysis and discussion of the complete spectrum of current development issues, it publishes articles from all the social sciences and all intellectual persuasions. Special thematic and guest-edited issues are published regularly.

Development Dialogue: published twice-yearly by the Dag Hammarskjöld Foundation, ISSN:0345-2328. Editors: Sven Hamrell and Olle Nordberg.
A thematic and often guest-edited journal of international co-operation which, in the mid-1970s, became a vehicle for the school of thought known as 'Another Development' and associated with Marc Nerfin of the International Foundation for Development Alternatives (IFDA) and Manfred Max-Neef.

Development in Practice: published five times a year by Carfax, Taylor & Francis on behalf of Oxfam GB. ISSN: 0961-4524. Editor: Deborah Eade. Available online.
A multi-disciplinary journal of practice-based analysis and research concerning the social dimensions of development and humanitarianism. Serving development professionals worldwide, it seeks to challenge current assumptions, stimulate new thinking, and shape future ways of working. Special thematic and guest-edited issues are published regularly. Web: <www.developmentinpractice.org>

Feminist Economics: published three times a year by Routledge, Taylor & Francis on behalf of the International Association for Feminist Economics. ISSN: 1354-5701. Editor: Diana Strassmann. Available online.
A scholarly journal on the role of gender in the economy to promote a rethinking of theory and policy from a feminist perspective, explore the construction and legitimation of economic knowledge, and stimulate dialogue and debate among diverse scholars worldwide.

Gender and Development: published three times a year by Oxfam GB. ISSN: 1355-2074. Editor: Caroline Sweetman.
Focusing on international gender and development issues, this theme-based journal aims to debate best practice and new ideas, and to make the links between theoretical and practical work in this field. Each issue is published by Oxfam in book form in the Focus on Gender series. Recent titles include *Gender and Lifecycles* (2000), *Gender in the 21st Century* (2000), *Women, Land, and Agriculture* (1999), and *Violence Against Women* (1998).

Journal of Environment and Development: A Review of International Policy: published quarterly by Sage. ISSN: 1070-4965. Editor: Gordon F. MacDonald.
Seeking to further research and debate on the nexus of environment and development issues at every level, the journal provides a forum that bridges the parallel policy

debates among policy makers, lawyers, academics, business people, and NGO activists worldwide.

Journal of Human Development: published twice yearly by Carfax, Taylor & Francis on behalf of UNDP. ISSN: 1464-9888. Editors: Sakiko Fakuda-Parr, Richard Jolly, and Khadija Haq.

Since human development, popularised by UNDP, is becoming a 'school of thought', the journal acts as a conduit for its members and critics, by publishing original work on the concept, measurement, and/or practice of human development at global, national, and local levels.

Journal of Humanitarian Assistance: (electronic only) published at the University of Bradford School of Peace Studies: <www.jha.ac>. ISSN: 1360-0222. Editors: Jim Whitman, Chris Alden, and David Pocock.

Seeking to facilitate communication among diverse practitioners and analysts within the community of humanitarian actors, this electronic journal offers free access to more than 3000 documents covering all aspects of humanitarian assistance including law, politics, the military, logistics, and the work of national and international organisations.

Millennium: Journal of International Studies: published three times a year by the Millennium Publishing Group, London School of Economics, ISSN: 0305-8298. Editors: Pavlos Hatzopoulos and Fabio Petito.

Covers topics such as international relations, democracy, and poverty and humanitarianism in a global political and economic context. See 1996 Special Issue, 'Poverty in World Politics: Whose Global Era?'

Nonprofits and Voluntary Sector Quarterly: published quarterly by Sage, ISSN: 0899-7640. Editor: Steve Rathgeb Smith.

A research-based journal focusing on voluntarism, citizen participation, philanthropy, civil society, and non-profit organisations. See especially Vol. 28 Supplemental, 1999: 'Globalization and Northern NGOs: The Challenge of Relief and Development in a Changing Context'.

Race & Class – A Journal for Black and Third World Liberation: published quarterly by Sage on behalf of The Institute of Race Relations, ISSN: 0306-3968. Editors: A Sivanandan and Hazel Waters.

A multidisciplinary journal on contemporary forms of racism and imperialism, covering issues ranging from culture and identity, to globalisation, debt, human trafficking, and the information revolution.

Voluntas: published quarterly by Plenum Publishing Corporation for the International Society for Third-Sector Research, ISSN: 0957-8765. Editor: Jeremy Kendall.

An interdisciplinary forum for empirical and theoretical analysis and debate about issues of relevance to the non-profit sector, the journal aims to present cutting-edge academic debate in a widely accessible form.

Organisations

Bretton Woods Project: Established in 1995 by a network of 30 UK-based NGOs, the Project circulates information, undertakes research, and monitors and advocates for change in the Bretton Woods institutions. Issues addressed include structural adjustment programmes, conditionality, and controversial large projects. Its bulletin, *Bretton Woods Update*, is available in print, e-mail, and web versions. *New Leaf or Fig Leaf? The Challenge of the New Washington Consensus* (2000), by Brendan Martin, was co-published with Public Services International (PSI). Web: <www.brettonwoodsproject.org>

CIVICUS (World Alliance for Citizen Participation): An international alliance of organisations dedicated to strengthening citizen action and civil society worldwide, CIVICUS believes that a healthy society depends upon an equitable relationship among its citizens, their associations and foundations, business, and government. Publications include Rajesh Tandon and Miguel Darcy de Oliveira (co-ordinators) (1994) *CITIZENS: Strengthening Global Civil Society*; and Leslie M. Fox and S. Bruce Schearer (eds.) (1997) *Sustaining Civil Society: Strategies for Resource Mobilisation.* Web: <www.civicus.org>

Corporate Watch: Part of the Transnational Resource and Action Center (TRAC) based in San Francisco, Corporate Watch provides news, analysis, research, tools, and resources to monitor and respond to corporate activity around the globe, with a focus on corporate accountability, human rights, and social and environmental justice. Web: <www.corpwatch.org>

ELDIS: Includes descriptions and links to more than 3000 organisations and more than 6000 full-text online documents, covering development and environmental issues. Web: <www.eldis.org>

FoodFirst International Network (FIAN): An international human-rights organisation working in the field of economic human rights, as codified in international law. Its magazine, *Hungry for What is Right*, is available in French and Spanish. *Food and Freedom* by Rolf Kunnermann is a textbook for human-rights education. Web: <www.fian.org>

International Development Research Centre (IDRC): A public corporation created by the Canadian government, IDRC seeks to help organisations in developing countries to find research-based solutions to social, economic, and environmental problems. IDRC publishes extensively in English, French, and Spanish. Recent titles include *Transnational Social Policies: The New Development Challenges of Globalization; Altered States: Globalization, Sovereignty, and Governance*; and *Cultivating Peace: Conflict and Collaboration in Natural Resource Management*. Its comprehensive website houses a vast documentation centre. Web: <www.idrc.org.ca>

Interhemispheric Resource Center (IRC): A research and resource centre that publishes widely (in English and Spanish) on US foreign and economic policy and seeks to advance reform agendas for the benefit of ordinary citizens in the Americas. It hosts the Border Information and Outreach Service (BIOS), which tracks the negative impact of NAFTA, the first regional trading area to include both Northern and Southern partners. Web: <www.irc-online.org>

Jubilee 2000: The best-known international anti-debt movement, with national chapters in more than 65 countries, advocating a debt-free start to the millennium. Web: <www.jubileee2000uk.org>

The North–South Institute: Though focusing much of its work on Canadian foreign policy, NSI's research supports global efforts to strengthen international development co-operation, improve governance, enhance gender and social equity in globalising markets, and prevent ethnic conflict and other forms of conflict. Its research is shared through publications, seminars, and conferences. The Institute collaborates closely with IDRC (see above) and with the International Institute for Sustainable Development (IISD) in Canada. Web: www.nsi-ins.ca

Oxfam GB: A member of the Oxfam International (OI) alliance, Oxfam GB is one of the largest international aid agencies in the UK. It publishes extensively on development and humanitarian issues, both alone and in conjunction with others. Publications range from educational materials for schools to specialist works for development professionals. Best-selling backlist titles not listed in separate entries include *The Oxfam Gender Training Manual* (1995) (also available in Portuguese and Spanish), *The Oxfam Handbook of Development and Relief* (1995), *The Oxfam Poverty Report* (1995), *The Trade Trap* (1996, 2nd edn), *Capacity Building: An Approach to People-Centred Development* (1997), and *Microfinance and Poverty Reduction* (1997). Full catalogue listing on <www.oxfam.org.uk>

Rural Advancement Foundation International (RAFI): An international NGO dedicated to the conservation and sustainable improvement of agricultural biodiversity, and to the socially responsible development of technologies for the benefit of rural societies. Publications and resources are in English, French, and Spanish. Web: <www.rafi.org>

Society for Participatory Research in Asia (PRIA) promotes people-centred development initiatives within the perspectives of participatory research. It seeks to strengthen popular knowledge, demystify domininant concepts, and work for the empowerment of the poor. It publishes extensively in English and Hindi on subjects such as advocacy, capacity building, and participation and governance. Web: <www.pria.org>

UN Non-governmental Liaison Service (NGLS) works with NGOs and their networks worldwide, both in facilitating their access to and providing information about the UN system, and acting as a communication channel for the UN agencies to the NGO sector. It publishes regular bulletins (in English and in French), such as *Go-Between*, and several occasional publications and series. Most publications are available free of charge.

Addresses of publishers and other organisations

Blackwell Publishers
108 Cowley Road, Oxford OX4 1JF, UK. Fax: +44(0)1865 791 347

Bretton Woods Project
PO Box 100, London SE1 7RT, UK. Fax: + 44(0)20 7620 0719

CIVICUS 919 18th Street, NW Third Floor, Washington DC 20006, USA. Fax +1(202) 331 8774

Cambridge University Press
The Edinburgh Building, Shaftesbury Road, Cambridge CB2 2RU, UK. Fax: +44(0)1223 31505

Jonathan Cape 20 Vauxhall Bridge Road, London SW1V 2SA, UK.

Capstone Publishing Oxford Centre for Innovation, Mill Street, Oxford OX2 0JX, UK.Fax: +44(0)20 8599 0984

Frank Cass Newbury House, 900 East Avenue, Newbury Park, Ilford, Essex IG2 7HH, UK. Fax: +44(0)20 8599 0984

Cornell University Press
512E State Street, PO Box 250, Ithaca NY 14851, USA.Fax: +1(607)277 2397

Corporate Watch PO Box 29344, San Francisco CA 94129, USA.

Dag Hammarskjöld Foundation
Övre Slottsgaren 2, 75220 Uppsala, Sweden.

Earthscan Publications
120 Pentonville Road, Lodnon N1 9JN, UK. Fax: +44(0)20 7278 01142

ELDIS Institute of Development Studies, University of Sussex, Falmer, Brighton BN1 9RE, UK. Fax:: +44(0) 1273 621202

FIAN PO Box 102243, D-69012 Heidelberg, Germany.

L'Harmattan 5-7 rue de l'Ecole Polytechnique, 75005 Paris, France.

L'Harmattan Inc, 55, rue Saint Jacques, Montréal (Qc), Canada H2Y 1K9.

Intermediate Technology Publications
103-105 Southampton Row, London WC1B 4HH, UK. Fax: +44 (0)20 7436 2013

IDRC 250 Albert Street, PO Box 8500, Ottawa, Ontario K1G 3H9, Canada.

IRC PO Box 4506, Alburquerque, New Mexico 87196, USA.

Journal of Humanitarian Affairs
Department of Peace Studies,
Bradford University, Bradford BD7
1DP, UK.

Jubilee 2000 Rivington Street,
London EC2A 3DT, UK.
Fax: +44(0)207 739 2300

Kumarian Press 14 Oakwood Avenue,
West Hartford CT 06119 2127, USA.

Little, Brown Publishers
Brettenham House, Lancaster Place,
London WC2E 7EN, UK.
Fax: +44(0)20 7911 8100

Macmillan Press Houndsmills,
Basingstoke, RG21 6XS, UK.
Fax: +44 (0) 1256 330 688

Millennium Publishing Group
London School of Economics,
Houghton Street, London WC2A 2AE,
UK.

MIT Press Five Cambridge Centre,
Cambridge MA 02142, USA.

Monthly Review Press 122 West 41st
Street, New York NY 10036, USA.
Fax: +1(212)268 6349

North–South Institute
55 Murray Street, Suite 200, Ottawa,
Ontario K1N 5M3, Canada.
Fax: (613) 241 7435

NGLS Palais des Nations, CH-1211,
Geneva 10, Switzerland.
Fax: +41 22 917 00 49

Novib Mauritskade 9, 2514 HD
The Hague, Netherlands.
Fax: +31(70)361 4461

Oxford University Press
Walton Street, Oxford OX2 6DT,
UK.Fax: +44(0)1865 55664

Plenum Publishing 101 Back Church
Lane, London E1 1LU, UK.
Fax: +44(0)20 7264 1919

Pluto Press 345 Archway Road,
London N6 5AA, UK.
Fax: +44(0)20 8348 9133

PRIA 42 Tughlakabad Institutional
Area, New Delhi - 110 062, India.
Fax: 011-6080183

RAFI 110 Osbourne Street, Winnipeg
MB R3L 1Y5, Canada.

Lynne Rienner Publishers
1800 30th Street, Suite 314, Boulder
CO80301, USA.
Fax: +1(303) 444 0824

Routledge 11 New Fetter Lane,
London EC4P 4EE, UK.
Fax: +44(0)20 7842 2302

Sage Publications 6 Bonhill Street,
London EC2A 4PU, UK.
Fax: +44(0)20 7374 8741

Sage India M32 Greater Kailash
Market I, New Delhi 110 048, India.
Fax: +91(11)647 2426.

**United Nations Association in
Canada** Suite 900, 130 Slater Street,
Ottawa, ON K1P 6E2, Canada.
Fax: (613) 563-2455

UNRISD Palais des Nations, 1211
Geneva 10, Switzerland.
Fax: +41(22)017 0650

University of Pennsylvania Press
820 North University Drive, USB1
Suite C, University Park, PA 16802,
Philadelphia, USA.

Verso 6 Meard Street, London W1V
3HR, UK. Fax: +44(0)20 7734 0059

Zed Books 7 Cynthia Street, London
N1 9JF, UK. Fax: +44(0)20 7833 3960

Other titles in the *Development in Practice Readers* series:

Development, NGOs, and Civil Society
Edited by Deborah Eade and introduced by Jenny Pearce
2000 | 0 85598 444 2 | 196pp pbk
Spanish translation on-line

Development and Management: Experiences in Value-based Conflict
Introduced by Tina Wallace and co-edited by Deborah Eade, Tom Hewitt, and Hazel Johnson (in association with The Open University)
2000 | 0 85598 429 5 | 320pp pbk

Development with Women
Edited by Deborah Eade and introduced by Dorienne Rowan-Campbell
1999 | 0 85598 419 8 | 196pp pbk

Development and Social Action
Edited by Deborah Eade and introduced by Miloon Kothari
1999 | 0 85598 415 5 | 196pp pbk
Spanish translation forthcoming 2001

Development and Rights
Edited by Deborah Eade and introduced by Firoze Manji
1998 | 0 85598 406 6 | 190pp pbk
Spanish translation (*Desarrollo y Derechos Humanos*) published by Intermón, Spain

Development and Patronage
Edited by Deborah Eade and introduced by Melakou Tegegn
1997 | 0 85598 376 0 | 112pp pbk
Spanish translation (*Desarrollo y Poder*) published by Intermón, Spain

Development for Health
Edited by Deborah Eade and introduced by Eleanor Hill
1997 | 0 85598 368 X | 112pp pbk

Development in States of War
Edited by Deborah Eade and introduced by Stephen Commins
1996 | 0 85598 344 2 | 112pp pbk
Also in Spanish (*Desarrollo en Estados de Guerra*), published in association with the Centro de Investigación para la Paz and Intermón, Spain
1998 | 84 922434 | 112pp pbk | £8.95 | $15.00

Development and Social Diversity
Edited by Deborah Eade and introduced by Mary B. Anderson
1996 | 0 85598 343 4 | 112pp pbk
Also in Spanish (*Desarrollo y Diversidad Social*), published in association with the Centro de Investigación para la Paz and Intermón, Spain
1998 | 84 922434 49 | 112pp pbk

For information about these and other Oxfam publications, consult the Oxfam Publishing website:
http://www.oxfam.org.uk/publications.html, or contact Oxfam Publishing,
274 Banbury Road, Oxford OX2 7DZ, UK;
tel. +44 (0)1865 311 311;
fax +44 (0)1865 312 600;
email publish@oxfam.org.uk.

For excerpts from each title listed above, visit the journal's website:
www.developmentinpractice.org